SCHOOL FOODSERVICE

Second Edition

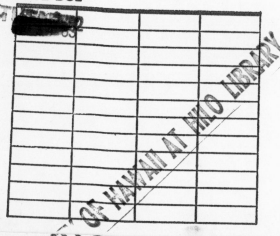

SCHOOL FOODSERVICE

Second Edition

Dorothy VanEgmond–Pannell, B.S., M.A.

Director, School Foodservices,
Fairfax County Public Schools,
Virginia

AVI PUBLISHING COMPANY, INC.
WESTPORT, CONNECTICUT

Cover photograph courtesy of U.S. Department of Agriculture

Library of Congress Cataloging in Publication Data

VanEgmond-Pannell, Dorothy.
    School foodservice.

    Includes index.
    1. School lunchrooms, cafeterias, etc.   I. Title.
TX945.V315   1981   642'.5   81-4623
ISBN 0-87055-378-X   AACR2

Printed in the United States of America by
The Saybrook Press, Inc.

Preface to Second Edition

This edition has been updated and new material has been added to make it of greater value to people studying and working in the school foodservice industry, at a time when there are so many changes facing them.

With the growth of school foodservice there has been an increased interest for learning more about the field. School feeding is a challenging and changing field requiring better qualified people today, resulting in a need for more people to be trained. This book was written as a basic source of information for the overall operation of school foodservices. Much of the book is devoted to organization and management as it applies to school foodservice.

Many good publications and much information are available, particularly from the U.S. Department of Agriculture. This book endeavors to bring together much of this information for the convenience of the students in correspondence courses, in vocational training courses, and in the colleges and universities, and for all who want an understanding of school foodservice.

Many people have contributed to this book. I wish especially to thank the staff at the Food and Nutrition Information Center of the National Agricultural Library in Beltsville, Maryland, and to the many people at the U.S. Department of Agriculture who furnished information and materials, and for the opportunity to be a part of the Nutrition and Technical Services staff on an Intragovernmental Personnel Agreement contract during 1979−80.

My thanks to my colleagues and employer in Fairfax County Public Schools, where I have been afforded a great opportunity. My thanks to Randy Altenberg of Los Angeles School District for help with the personnel chapter and to Lyle Root of School Foodservice, Baltimore (Md.) County Public Schools.

My special thanks to my family, especially my husband, for their help, encouragement, and patience.

Dot VanEgmond-Pannell

November 1980

Contents

Overview and History of School Foodservice

School foodservice is the world's largest foodservice business. The National School Lunch Program alone boasted a business under its regulations in 1980 that added up to serving 5 billion nutritious meals annually to an average of 27.4 million students daily. There has been a tremendous growth since 1946 when an average of 4.5 million children ate their lunches at school at a year's cost of $231 million. The growth of school foodservice started with the National School Lunch Act in 1946. School foodservice has grown and been expanded to include breakfast, snacks, a la carte, and in some cases, a dinner meal to the elderly as well as children.

All public and nonprofit private elementary and secondary schools and any public or non-profit child care institution which maintains children in residence and operated principally for the care of children are eligible to participate in the National School Lunch Program. Many private schools participate in the program; however, some public and private schools have chosen to operate without Federal controls and funds. The number of schools participating has increased in the last 7 yr from only 75% in 1972 to 90% in 1979. The number of children served free or reduced price lunches doubled between 1973 and 1979.

The growth can be contributed to funding which was legislated as a result of the attention that was brought to hunger in the United States in the late 1960s by Senator George McGovern's Committee on Nutrition and Human Needs; the White House Conference on Food, Nutrition, and Health; and such books as *Their Daily Bread* and *Hunger U.S.A.* Groups such as the United League of Women, American School Foodservice Association, Children's Foundation, American Dietetic Association, private industry, and individuals including Senators Hubert Humphrey (Minn.) and Allen Ellender (La.), Congressman Carl Perkins (Ky.), Dr. John Perryman, Dr. Jean Mayer, and Miss Josephine Martin, have had much influence on this progress.

Twenty yr ago many schools found themselves feeding free lunches out of funds from the paying student. There is no such thing as a free lunch. Someone has to pay for it. If the paying student paid 25¢ in 1963, one can imagine how difficult it was to pay the cost of preparing 2 lunches (one being free) out of that 25¢ with perhaps a Federal cash reimbursement of 4¢ and commodities valued at another 6¢. It was a matter of pure survival on the part of the school lunch programs. Making students work for their lunches, scrutinizing free lunch applications, and serving a different lunch to the free-lunchers all sound inhumane, but the lack of funds caused this to exist in some parts of the country.

Foodservice administrators in 1970 had hope of universal feeding but were fearing revenue sharing by 1978. Congressman Carl Perkins (Ky.) first introduced in March 1971 a bill to establish a universal foodservice and nutrition education program for children. Bills are no longer introduced yearly in the House of Representatives and the Senate for a program to provide lunch to all children free of charge. How much would universal feeding cost the Federal government? Estimates are outdated by the time they are compiled.

Federal funds currently pay about 56% of the total cost of the school lunch program. State and local governments put in roughly 18% and the remaining 26% comes from student payments. The cost of preparing a lunch has had a steady increase yearly (Table 1.1) until the Spring of 1973 and 1979 when prices of food sky rocketed. Some estimate that the cost per lunch may be averaging over $4.00 by the end of the fiscal 1985.

School foodservices have become more sophisticated and in turn have become more attractive to businessmen in all phases of the food industry as Federal regulations have permitted participation. Operating a school foodservice that serves 20,000 lunches and 2,000 breakfasts daily takes a qualified business person with a strong background in management, nutrition and foods, and much patience to interpret the detailed Federal rules and regulations that will govern his operation. Preparing and serving a nutritionally balanced lunch that has cost $1.25 for food, labor, and other operating costs, of which 15¢ of the income is in the form of USDA-donated foods, takes good management and in some cases much ingenuity. The dedication of the school foodservice workers, primarily mothers, has been responsible for the growth and endurance of a sound nutritional program in past years. It is an exciting, challenging business with student customers who keep management on its toes. The worker who might have the attitude "that's all you get; take it and don't be so

TABLE 1.1. AVERAGE COST PER LUNCH AND SOURCE OF INCOME

Year	Contributions (c)		Student's Payment (c)	Total (c)
	Federal	State and Local		
1968	13.5	13.7	30.9	58.1
1969	14.1	14.1	30.9	59.1
1970	15.9	15.3	31.0	62.2
1971	21.1	15.4	28.3[1]	64.8
1972	27.2	15.5	26.5	69.2
1973	30.2	17.3	28.0	75.5
1974	35.2	20.0	29.5	84.7
1975	42.0	20.9	32.2	95.1
1976	43.4	22.3	31.4	99.1
1977	49.9	22.6	30.4	102.9
1978	56.7	NA[2]	NA[2]	NA[2]
1979	61.5	NA	NA	NA
1980	70.8	NA	NA	NA

Source: Based on Fiscal Year 1947−1971 Report and Yearly Fact Sheets, Food and Nutr. Serv., U.S. Dept. Agr., Washington, D.C.

[1] Payment decrease is based on average and is less due to the 6% increase in lunches served free or reduced to the child between 1970 and 1971 and another 6% increase in lunches served free or reduced to the child between 1971 and 1972.

[2] States were not required to furnish this information to U.S. Dept. of Agr. after 1977.

choosy," has been replaced with finesse and a desire to please even the fussiest customer.

So much has happened in the last ten years in school foodservice that perhaps one should start there. However, a brief—but more complete—history follows. Many publications that trace the history and background developments of school feeding are available. The handiest is the publication edited by Gordon W. Gunderson, *The National School Lunch Program: Background and Development* (1971), on which I have relied heavily in relating this history.

SCHOOL FEEDING FROM 1853 TO 1939

The Children's Aid Society of New York was, in 1953, one of the first recorded programs for serving meals to students. Philadelphia, Milwaukee, Boston, and other cities were serving lunches at some of their schools as early as 1853. Two books, *Poverty* (Hunter 1904) and *The Bitter Cry of the Children* (Spargo 1906), brought to public attention the hunger and malnutrition that was in existence. Hunter estimated that at least ten million persons were living in poverty in 1904. He observed that poverty's misery falls most heavily upon the children. Hunter also estimated that in New York City alone from 60,000 to 70,000 of the children "often arrived at school hungry and unfitted to do well the work required." Spargo gave case after case of deplorable poverty in New York City. He pointed out that the land where these people fondly dreamed their

Utopia might be realized had been instead, as Fourier prophesied, "poverty through plethora." What Spargo (1906) said might well apply to the 1960s:

The poverty problem is today the supreme challenge to our national conscience and instincts of self-preservation, and its saddest and most alarming feature is the suffering and doom it imposes upon the children.

Volunteer Groups

The groups feeding children at lunch in the early 1900s had been primarily volunteer groups. Shortly after these publications, school lunches were served in many more schools all over the country. In 1921 Chicago claimed it had "the most intensive school lunch system in America." All its high schools and 60 elementary schools were serving lunch as a responsibility of the Chicago Board of Education. The Chicago Board of Education had started this as early as 1910. The school feeding program then did not resemble the dining rooms or the nutritious menus of today. The lunchroom in 1913 in Lower Merion, Penn., was described by Cronan (1962) as "under the main stairway. The everyday menu consisted of soup, sandwiches, beans and ice cream."

By 1918, lunch of some type was being provided in schools in approximately one-quarter of the larger cities. It could hardly be compared to today's "Type A" lunch and most often was a cold lunch. A health officer in Pinellas County (Fla.) who knew that milk is valuable to children, started by placing a large white cow on the playground as an advertisement for his milk program. He was so pleased with the results that a bowl of hot soup was added to go with the milk.

Depression

The years of the depression were important to the expansion of school lunch, and it started the legislation that put the lunch program on firmer grounds with funds made available. The first Federal funds came from the Reconstruction Finance Corporation in 1932 and 1933. This paid labor costs for preparing school lunches in several towns in the southwestern part of Missouri. By 1934 the funding had expanded to 39 States under the Civil Work Administration and the Federal Emergency Relief Administration. In the 1930s there was high unemployment and little money for buying food, so the congress found it necessary to give Federal assistance to support the agriculture, provide employment, and furnish lunches for children at school and to aid the general economy. The 74th Congress passed a bill August 24, 1935, that gave 30% of the receipts from duties collected under the custom laws during each calendar year to be used to purchase surplus foods for use in school lunch programs and for needy families (Fig. 1.1).

The Works Progress Administration was created in 1935, and women in needy areas were assigned jobs in the school lunch program. This resulted in the school lunch programs being relatively organized and supervised by each State. Some type of standardization of menus and recipes and procedures resulted. This grew and in 1941 the program was operating in all States, the District of Columbia, and Puerto Rico. Some 23,000 schools were serving an average of nearly 2 million lunches daily and employing over 64,000 persons (Fig. 1.2).

GROWTH FROM 1941 TO 1960

The school lunch program had grown so that 78,841 schools in 1942 were serving some type of lunch to over 5 million children. The Federal funds that year were used to purchase $21 million of food for the schools. According to Gunderson (1971), the food was available to a school if the school administration signed an agreement with the State distributing agency agreeing:

(1) That the commodities would be used for preparation of school lunches on the school premises.

Courtesy of U.S. Dept. Agr.

FIG. 1.1. THE LUNCH OFTEN CONSISTED OF SOUP AND MILK

Courtesy of U.S. Dept. Agr.

FIG. 1.2. MENUS WERE EXPANDED TO INCLUDE SANDWICH, SOUP, MILK, AND FRUIT

(2) That the commodities would not be sold or exchanged.
(3) That the food purchases would not be discontinued or curtailed because of the receipt of surplus foods.
(4) That the program would not be operated for profit.
(5) That the children who could not pay for their meals would not be segregated or discriminated against and would not be identified to their peers.
(6) That proper warehousing would be provided and proper accounting would be rendered for all foods received.

The foods came directly from the farms to the schools. It meant a lot of perishables at one time. A superintendent in North Carolina remembered receiving a train carload of cabbage which arrived on Tuesday before the Thanksgiving holidays. The weather was warm and by the following week the classroom used to store the cabbage was reeking of the odor of rotten cabbage.

As a result of many innovations, the improvement in children's nutrition was noticed by educators and parents (Fig. 1.3). By 1943 the program reached 92,916 schools serving 6 million children and employed many people. The effects of World War II were felt by every part of the economy and especially by school lunch. The program decreased to only

Courtesy of School Lunch Journal

FIG. 1.3. IN 1942 CHILDREN COULD BUY MILK BY THE BOTTLE AT A REDUCED COST AT SETTLEMENT HOUSE IN NEW YORK CITY'S LOWER EAST SIDE

34,064 schools, hardly a third. Federal assistance was cut and commodities were no longer available. WPA workers were not available for school lunch, but were now employed to produce the supplies needed for the war. However, Congress had amended Section 32 of the Agricultural Act of 1935 to make money available for maintaiing the school lunch and special milk program in the form of cash for 1944. The lunch program had become so much a part of the child's school day that it was not destroyed but temporarily halted.

By 1946 the program had surpassed the size it had been prior to World War II. However, the uncertainty of the program caused school administrators to be cautious in starting the program for fear that funds would be cut off.

NATIONAL SCHOOL LUNCH ACT OF 1946

The end of World War II did much to spur the school lunch program on. General Hershey in a statement about the malnutrition among the armed forces and about the national security being in jeopardy did much to bring the importance of good nutritious food to the attention of the legislature. Jobs were needed again. Agriculture was flourishing. Money previously spent on war was available. In June 1946, President Harry S. Truman signed into law Public Law 396, the National School Lunch Act, as legislated by the 79th Congress (Fig. 1.4). The law is published in its entirety in Appendix I. Some sections are pertinent.

The philosophy and purposes behind the law are stated in Section 2 of Public Law 396:

SECTION 2. It is hereby declared to be the policy of Congress, as a measure of national security to safeguard the health and well-being of the Nation's children and to encourage the domestic consumption of nutritious agricultural commodities and other food, by assisting the States, through grants-in-aid and other means, in providing an adquate supply of foods and other facilities for the establishment, maintenance, operation, and expansion of nonprofit school-lunch programs.

Surplus Foods

The second objective of the law certainly was an important factor in its passage—to provide markets for agricultural production and a larger share of the national income to farmers. The school lunch program provided a ready and desirable outlet for disposing of surplus crop products. The State education agency and the schools in the State agreed that those schools participating in the National School Lunch Program must:

(1) Serve lunches which meet minimum nutritional requirements prescribed by the Secretary of Agriculture.
(2) Serve meals without cost or at a reduced cost to children who were determined by local school authorities to be unable to pay the full cost of the lunch.
(3) Make no discrimination against any child because of his inability to pay the full price of the lunch.
(4) Operate on a nonprofit basis.
(5) Utilize foods declared by the Secretary as being in abundance.
(6) Utilize free commodities as donated by the Secretary.
(7) Maintain records of receipts and expenditures and submit this report to the State agency as required.

FIG. 1.4. THE NATIONAL SCHOOL LUNCH ACT WAS SIGNED INTO LAW ON JUNE 4, 1946, BY PRESIDENT HARRY S. TRUMAN (SEATED)

Witnesses were (left to right): Rep. Clarence Cannon (Missouri); Clinton Anderson, Secretary of Agriculture; Rep. Malcolm Tarver (Georgia); Sen. Richard Russell (Georgia); Sen. Allen Ellender (Louisiana); Rep. Clifford Hope (Kansas); Sen. George Aiken (Vermont); Rep. Ron Flanagan (West Virginia); Nathan Koenig, Assistant to the Secretary of Agriculture; Paul Stark, Director of the Food Distribution Division, USDA; Robert Shields, Administrator, Product and Marketing Administration, USDA; and N. E. Dodd, Undersecretary of Agriculture.

Type A Lunch

The minimum nutritional requirements were defined in 1946 by the Secretary as three types of lunches—Type A, Type B, and Type C. Type A lunch was defined as containing:

(1) ½ pt of fluid whole milk.
(2) Protein-rich food consisting of one of the following or a combination: 2 oz (edible portion as served) of lean meat, poultry, or fish; or 2 oz of cheese; or 1 egg; or ½ cup of cooked dry beans or peas; or 4 Tbsp of peanut butter.
(3) ¾ cup serving consisting of two or more vegetables or fruits, or both.
(4) 1 portion or serving of bread, cornbread, biscuits, rolls, muffins, etc., made of whole-grain or enriched meal or flour.
(5) 2 tsp of butter or fortified margarine.[1]

---

[1] Later reduced to 1 tsp of butter or fortified margarine, later eliminated, and milk requirement was relaxed to include chocolate milk, skim milk, and buttermilk as well as whole milk and changed again to more stringent requirements.

Type B lunches were smaller quantities of those in the Type A pattern and were served primarily in those schools with inadequate cooking facilities. Type C lunches consisted only of ½ pt of fluid whole milk served as a beverage. The cash reimbursements were established by the Secretary of Agriculture and were a maximum of 9¢ for a Type A lunch, 6¢ for a Type B lunch and 2¢ for a Type C lunch. Each State was to receive money on the basis of school lunch participation in the State and the per capita income of the State. The Federal funds were to be matched within the State. From 1947 through 1950 the Federal funds were to be matched dollar for dollar, and then progressively the State was to take a greater share of the financing. The child's payment for lunch was included in the State's matching funds and contributed the greatest part of the matching funds. When the per capita income of a State was less than the average per capita income in the United States the matching funds were reduced. In addition to the cash reimbursement, commodity donations were provided by Section 416 of the Agricultural Act of 1949 and Section 32 of the Agricultural Act of 1935 (Fig. 1.5).

The National School Lunch Act has been amended numerous times since its passage into law in 1946 (Appendix I). Appendix II and III contain the Child Nutrition Act of 1966 and the National School Lunch Act, respectively, as amended. Some 16 or more laws directly or indirectly

Courtesy of Prince George's County (Md.) Public Schools

FIG. 1.5. BY 1960 COMPLETE LUNCHES WERE BEING SERVED WITH THE AID OF FEDERAL FUNDS AND COMMODITY DONATIONS IN OVER 45% OF THE SCHOOLS

affected the feeding programs in the schools, as well as several agencies other than the USDA. The regulations were stiff and in many instances States were unable to utilize all the money allotted under the laws not because of lack of need, but because of the restrictions placed on it.

POVERTY REDISCOVERED: THE 1960s

Focus was placed upon poverty again in the middle 1960s, bringing new legislation and new interest in nutrition. The Economic Opportunity Act of 1964 established programs which fed the pre-school age children in Head Start programs. Also, the Elementary and Secondary Education Act of 1965 provided for funds (under Title I) to be used for the school foodservices in deprived areas.

Concern for the nutritional status of the United States was caused after the reports of the Household Food Consumption Survey of 1965–66 showed a definite decrease in the nutritional intake over the last 10 yr. The Child Nutrition Act of 1966 provided funds to initiate new programs. Included under this act was the continuation of the Special Milk Program, which had previously been designated as Type C by the Secretary under the National School Lunch Act and later under PL 85-478. The Child Nutrition Act also provided for a pilot breakfast program, for funds to purchase school foodservice equipment in low-income areas, and for State administrative expenses. The USDA was designated as the one agency of authority over the program.

The nonfood assistance program assists States through grant-in-aid and other means to supply schools that draw from areas in which poor economic conditions exist and the equipment for storage, preparation, transportation, and serving of food was needed. The State or local funds pay a quarter of the cost of the equipment.

In 1968 several groups brought national attention to poverty with the stories they told. The Committee on School Lunch Participation published *Their Daily Bread* in which they reported their findings of poverty to the House Committee Hearing. They pointed at poverty as one of the main reasons for unrest in America. Discrimination against children who were receiving free and reduced-price lunches was brought to light. That same year the Citizens Board of Inquiry into Hunger and Malnutrition in the United States focused on poverty in their book, *Hunger USA*. They were critical of the school lunch program as it was being administered. The agricultural policies were blamed for restricting and limiting the growth of the program. The Committee declared that 280 counties in the United States needed emergency assistance due to hunger. CBS television's documentary "Hunger in America" brought the hunger that existed in America to the attention of the average American, and the response was immediate.

Professional organizations passed resolutions supporting the policy that all students should have lunch at school. Committees were created by Congress to study the hunger and malnutrition. *Let Them Eat Promises* (Kotz 1969) described the politics involved in the Federal programs thus far established for feeding the hungry. Churches and volunteer groups in many cities found a cause to work for, and lunches were being served in schools that had never had a foodservice.

Funding for Free Lunches

The concern for hunger stimulated the passage of legislation in 1968 which authorized funds for foodservices for some of the summer programs, and it extended the breakfast program. The President of the United States sent a message to Congress in May 1969 urging legislation that would eliminate hunger and malnutrition. It was not until fiscal 1969 that the free lunch program was actually funded. Prior to this, the formula for apportionment of Federal funds to the States had only increased the funding slightly where the largest number of free lunches were. The higher reimbursement rates still did not provide adequate funds until 1969 when money was allocated to provide free and reduced price meals in addition to what was allocated for the regular child foodservice programs. The funds were a boost to the needy children (Table 1.2). The President's White House Conference on Food, Nutrition, and Health of 1969 brought many experts in food and nutrition together to discuss the needs. The Conference recommended that the school lunch program be expanded to provide free lunch (and breakfast when needed) to all children through the secondary school years.

Even though funding was available, many school districts were cautious in entering the program. Also, many of the school buildings which had been built in the inner city did not have proper facilities. It took time for remodeling if funds were made available on the local level. Industry was now involved and new ideas of how to feed students a meal even if kitchen facilities were not available resulted in heat-and-serve type lunches, engineered foods, Vit-A-lunches, and other new feeding concepts being tried as solutions to the problem.

In the seventies funds were made available for equipment, and schools designated as "specially needy" were entitled to extra federal funds. Children from families with income at or less than 125 percent of the poverty level were eligible to receive free meals, and those at an income less than 195 percent of the poverty level were eligible to receive reduced-priced meals. A few schools had such high percentages of free meals that it was more economical to operate a "universally" free program, paying for those who did not qualify for free out of local funds.

UNIVERSALITY AND THE 1970s

The beginning of the 1970s looked very bright for school feeding with important new pieces of legislation enacted and the introduction of the Universal Food Service and Nutrition Education Program for children by Carl Perkins (Ky.) in the House of Representatives and by Hubert Humphrey (Minn.) in the Senate.

In 1970 the National School Lunch Act and the Child Nutrition Act clarified the responsibilities related to providing free and reduced price meals, revised the program's matching payment requirements, strengthened the nutrition training and education benefits of the program, and provided for special assistance to the States on the basis of family income. Discrimination against children receiving free and reduced price meals was declared unlawful. The 14th Amendment to the United States Constitution was used to bring law suits against school districts in a least nine States having no lunches at school. The Children's Foundation became active in looking out for the welfare of children. The USDA has its own monitoring agency in the form of the Office of Inspector General (OIG) in coordination with Office of General Counsel and the Department of Justice—to detect illegal practices—through audit of 1% of the programs. Their objectives are to determine if free and reduced priced lunches are being served to all needy children, protecting their anonymity, and to see that there are controls of receipts and of disbursement of funds.

In August 1979 auditors from the Office of the Inspector General reviewed 2,842 lunches at 22 school districts and found 70% did not meet the minimum meal requirements. Earlier that year 171 of 488 meals sampled in one school district did not meet minimum meal requirements. The problems pointed up two broad problems: inadequate, vague requirements and guidance, and ineffective or complete lack of monitoring.

The seventies were years of much legislation, amending and reamending the school lunch and breakfast programs. The most stabilizing action was the escalating clause which assured that funding would increase in accordance with the food-away-from-home-index. This was a short lived stabilizer. In 1980 this escalator clause barely escaped Congress' budget cuts and was suspended for one year. The funding had grown from $100 million in 1946 to more than $2.7 billion in 1980.

The number of schools participating in the National School Lunch Program increased steadily, with the largest increase between 1970 and 1971. The number of free and reduced priced lunches doubled (Table 1.3). In 1979 it was estimated that 85% of those in need of free lunches were receiving them. The legislations in 1970 and 1971 (PL 91-248, PL 92-32, and PL 92-153) were forceful in that they contained the funding necessary to put them into action. Thousands of inner-city schools were

TABLE 1.2. CONTRIBUTIONS TO NATIONAL SCHOOL LUNCH PROGRAM AND VALUE OF USDA COMMODITIES—FISCAL YEARS 1947–1980

| | Federal Contributions ($) | | | | | |
| | Cash | | | Donated Commodities[1] | | |
Fiscal Year	Section 4	Section 11	Section 32	Sec. 32 & 416	Section 6	Total
1947	62,338,155	—	—	2,312,479	5,735,269	70,385,903
1948	54,000,000	—	—	19,340,561	13,438,329	86,778,890
1949	58,875,000	—	—	21,550,031	14,474,763	94,899,794
1950	64,565,000	—	—	38,504,934	16,684,026	119,753,960
1951	68,275,000	—	—	34,836,455	15,089,210	118,200,665
1952	66,320,000	—	—	16,582,743	15,590,016	98,492,759
1953	67,185,000	—	—	51,724,476	14,744,071	133,653,547
1954	67,266,000	—	—	94,217,791	14,826,278	176,310,069
1955	69,142,000	—	—	70,305,837	12,830,253	152,278,090
1956	67,145,648	—	—	99,946,204	14,802,020	181,893,872
1957	83,915,000	—	—	131,972,002	14,659,931	230,546,933
1958	83,830,000	—	—	75,961,833	14,802,256	174,594,089
1959	93,890,000	—	—	66,821,691	42,669,843	203,381,534
1960	93,814,400	—	—	70,915,823	61,108,847	225,839,070
1961	93,746,304	—	—	71,623,432	61,080,734	226,450,470
1962	98,760,000	—	—	113,026,690	69,074,090	280,860,780
1963	108,600,000	—	—	120,970,681	58,875,807	288,446,488
1964	120,810,000	—	—	135,660,411	59,270,071	315,740,482
1965	130,435,000	—	—	212,949,375	59,458,642	402,843,017
1966	139,090,000	2,000,000	—	116,849,780	58,006,289	315,946,069
1967	147,685,000	2,000,000	—	130,418,911	57,938,924	338,042,835
1968	154,947,000	4,807,199	—	220,455,672	55,520,976	435,730,847
1969	162,041,000	10,000,000	31,754,686	207,790,939	64,165,362	475,751,987
1970	168,034,775	44,603,745	87,619,690	200,758,518	64,434,166	565,450,894
1971	224,710,499	202,798,419	104,682,578	214,877,594	64,306,096	811,375,186
1972	225,700,000	237,000,000	276,100,000	312,100,000[2]	—	1,050,900,000
1973	225,700,000	236,800,000	419,700,000	328,500,000	—	1,210,700,000
1974	409,000,000	255,600,000	420,000,000	316,100,000	—	1,401,400,000
1975	463,400,000	825,600,000	—	416,700,000	—	1,705,700,000
1976	516,000,000	963,400,000	—	414,100,000	—	1,893,500,000
1977	564,800,000	1,013,200,000	—	542,200,000	—	2,120,200,000
1978	618,800,000	1,206,300,000	—	608,500,000	—	2,433,600,000
1979	688,300,000	1,321,500,000	—	683,700,000	—	2,693,500,000
1980	762,000,000	1,567,000,000	—	773,000,000	—	3,102,000,000

Source: U.S. Dept. of Agr., Food and Nutrition Service.
[1] Value is cost to Federal government.
[2] Section 32, 416, & 6 are shown in one figure starting with 1972.

able to convert rooms into kitchens and buy the equipment needed for preparing and serving the food from the funds made available.

Also, in 1972 the quantity of USDA-donated foods distributed were far less than expected, with only a little over half of the funds appropriated spent, because of the high cost and limited amounts of available surpluses. The purpose of USDA-donated foods was to help relieve the market of surpluses and to support the prices. By 1972 the purpose of

State & Local Contributions ($)				Value of Food ($)		
Children's Payments	State & Local Govern- ments	Other	Total	Total	Local Purchase	% Local (of Total)
112,540,000	20,616,000	17,532,000	150,688,000	136,696,026	128,648,278	94.1
138,282,000	29,052,000	22,674,000	190,008,000	175,592,098	142,813,208	81.3
158,553,000	35,418,000	23,887,000	217,858,000	204,267,052	168,242,258	82.4
177,336,000	39,000,000	31,553,000	247,889,000	236,341,759	181,152,799	76.6
207,213,000	46,477,000	32,627,000	286,317,000	263,436,309	213,510,644	81.0
242,370,000	54,418,000	38,457,000	335,245,000	281,714,016	249,541,257	88.6
275,926,000	57,162,000	46,380,000	379,468,000	331,257,279	264,788,732	79.9
303,276,000	62,962,000	51,782,000	418,020,000	387,380,392	278,336,323	71.9
336,362,000	68,991,000	53,908,000	459,261,000	407,148,099	324,012,009	79.6
377,212,000	65,427,000	72,335,000	514,974,000	482,139,449	367,391,225	76.2
418,151,000	71,671,000	83,651,000	573,473,000	587,453,989	440,822,056	75.2
453,227,000	83,623,000	98,018,000	634,868,000	559,926,193	469,162,104	83.8
505,083,000	90,478,000	113,203,000	708,764,000	618,535,992	509,044,458	82.3
555,707,000	92,608,000	127,522,000	775,837,000	671,513,132	539,488,462	80.3
594,840,000	94,943,000	134,898,000	824,681,000	714,585,141	581,880,975	81.4
642,374,000	93,920,000	151,519,000	887,813,000	780,895,494	598,794,714	76.7
694,030,000	97,076,000	156,377,000	947,483,000	825,978,443	646,131,955	78.2
741,856,000	103,260,000	166,323,000	1,011,439,000	884,948,482	690,018,000	78.0
797,572,000	113,682,000	178,700,000	1,089,954,000	979,351,017	706,943,000	72.2
852,773,000	122,004,000	210,380,000	1,185,157,000	986,447,833	811,591,764	82.3
925,018,113	146,527,947	253,965,941	1,325,512,001	1,061,876,791	873,518,956	82.3
995,756,029	161,972,891	278,551,294	1,436,280,214	1,143,999,085	808,022,437	75.9
1,041,241,376	154,979,002	320,276,653	1,516,497,031	1,232,247,012	880,200,711	77.9
1,104,959,419	185,056,427	361,594,582	1,651,610,428	1,276,296,310	1,011,103,626	79.2
1,090,209,734	216,377,796	376,943,927	1,683,531,457	1,411,696,309	1,132,512,619	80.2
1,080,400,000	616,000,000	1,050,900,000	2,747,300,000	1,562,800,000	1,250,700,000	80.0
1,123,700,000	692,700,000	1,210,700,000	3,027,100,000	1,666,100,000	1,408,400,000	84.5
1,174,000,000	797,000,000	1,401,000,000	3,372,400,000	1,931,300,000	1,615,200,000	83.6
1,308,500,000	848,800,000	1,705,700,000	3,863,000,000	2,239,300,000	1,827,700,000	81.6
1,310,000,000	930,000,000	1,893,500,000	4,133,500,000	2,264,100,000	1,850,000,000	81.7
1,290,000,000	960,000,000	2,120,200,000	4,370,200,000	2,392,200,000	1,850,000,000	77.3
NA[3]	NA[3]	2,433,600,000	2,433,600,000	NA[3]	NA[3]	
NA	NA	2,693,500,000	2,693,500,000	NA	NA	
NA	NA	3,102,000,000	3,102,000,000	NA	NA	

[3] Since 1977 states have not been required to furnish this information to U.S. Dept. of Agr.

USDA-donated foods was questionable. The unspent funds were appropriated in cash to the school districts in the spring of 1973 (PL 93-13).

Competition

New challenges were placed on the administrators of the National School Lunch Program who had no experience at competition. First food-

TABLE 1.3. NATIONAL SCHOOL LUNCH PROGRAM PARTICIPATION IN ELEMEN-
TARY AND SECONDARY SCHOOLS, NUMBER OF LUNCHES, AND COST PER
LUNCH—FISCAL YEARS 1947–1980

Fiscal Year	No. Schools			No. Children		
	Total of US[2]	Participat- ing in N.S. L.P.[3]	Rate of Partici- pation (%)	Total Enrollment[2]	Participat- ing in N.S. L.P.[3]	Rate of Partici- pation (%)
1947	188,077	44,537	23.7	26,606,077	6,596,633	24.8
1948	188,077	44,542	23.7	26,606,077	6,594,952	24.8
1949	168,985	47,803	28.3	26,982,687	7,631,764	28.3
1950	168,985	54,157	32.0	27,525,345	8,596,765	31.2
1951	164,091	54,436	33.2	28,065,023	9,471,704	33.7
1952	164,091	55,663	33.9	29,059,023	10,220,720	35.2
1953	154,900	56,851	36.7	29,690,331	10,740,018	36.2
1954	154,900	56,337	36.4	30,998,048	11,117,567	35.9
1955	149,562	58,458	39.1	34,029,035	12,030,970	35.4
1956	149,562	56,140	37.5	35,636,445	11,552,663	32.4
1957	141,004	57,261	40.6	36,656,246	11,683,736	31.9
1958	141,004	59,929	42.5	38,364,195	12,601,228	32.8
1959	137,836	61,033	44.3	39,480,239	13,294,368	33.7
1960	137,836	62,325	45.2	40,664,042	14,078,149	34.6
1961	128,757	63,961	49.7	42,204,978	14,751,546	35.0
1962	128,757	64,447	50.1	43,415,735	15,552,706	35.8
1963	125,703	66,715	53.1	45,194,438	16,400,458	36.3
1964	125,703	68,526	54.5	46,935,514	17,547,843	37.4
1965	122,101	70,132	57.4	48,151,723	18,666,270	38.8
1966	122,101	70,597	57.8	49,676,224	19,781,064	39.8
1967	116,666	72,944	62.5	50,509,016	20,237,423	40.1
1968	116,666	71,983	61.7	51,245,895	20,614,410	40.2
1969	116,307	74,861	64.4	51,733,867	22,078,808	42.7
1970	116,307	75,593	65.0	52,100,765	23,127,222	44.4
1971	113,626	79,924	70.3	51,982,123	24,639,663	47.4
1972	98,502	83,333	84.6	52,000,000	24,900,000	56.6
1973	101,386	86,381	85.2	51,400,000	25,200,000	57.5
1974	101,365	87,579	86.4	51,400,000	25,000,000	56.3
1975	101,508	88,921	87.6	51,000,000	25,300,000	56.6
1976	100,141	89,426	89.3	50,500,000	25,900,000	57.4
1977	101,654	91,285	89.8	50,100,000	26,700,000	59.3
1978	100,973	93,097	92.2	48,900,000	27,100,000	60.1
1979	102,533	94,535	92.2	48,600,000	27,400,000	60.2
1980	101,421	94,554	92.3	48,000,000	27,000,000	60.3

[1] Data for Type C lunches are included for FY 1947 through FY 1959, except for cost per lunch which is computed on Type A lunches only for all years.
[2] Includes District of Columbia, Puerto Rico and Virgin Islands; Alaska as a territory prior to Statehood in FY 1959; Hawaii as a territory prior to Statehood in FY 1960; Guam beginning in FY 1957; American Samoa beginning in FY 1963. Number of schools and

No. Lunches[1]				Cost per Lunch (¢)			
Average Served Daily[3]	Total	Free or Reduced	Rate of Free or Reduced (%)	Contributions Federal	State & Local	Children's Payments	Total
6,016,129	910,926,717	109,352,390	12.0	9.3	5.6	15.5	30.4
6,014,596	972,008,521	123,306,846	12.7	11.5	7.2	18.3	37.0
6,960,169	1,119,094,198	165,454,817	14.8	10.9	7.2	18.1	36.2
7,840,250	1,275,923,146	212,193,369	16.6	12.1	7.4	17.7	37.2
8,638,194	1,393,145,667	177,654,075	12.8	10.7	7.5	18.7	36.9
9,321,297	1,489,890,214	169,621,882	11.4	8.3	8.2	20.4	36.9
9,794,896	1,583,638,073	167,378,873	10.6	10.6	8.5	21.7	40.8
10,139,221	1,661,403,101	173,340,769	10.4	12.9	8.5	21.8	43.2
10,972,245	1,806,586,577	189,878,731	10.5	10.0	8.3	22.1	40.4
10,536,029	1,726,598,923	181,005,485	10.5	11.2	8.6	23.4	43.2
10,655,567	1,771,179,627	186,014,151	10.5	13.0	8.8	23.7	45.5
11,492,320	1,882,570,199	202,881,028	10.8	9.3	9.7	24.2	43.2
12,124,464	2,008,685,185	211,822,563	10.5	10.2	10.2	25.3	45.7
12,839,272	2,142,312,115	217,192,652	10.1	10.5	10.3	25.9	46.7
13,453,410	2,264,989,097	228,059,654	10.1	10.0	10.1	26.3	46.4
14,184,068	2,415,269,937	240,135,558	9.9	11.6	10.2	26.6	48.4
14,957,218	2,552,744,662	245,731,540	9.6	11.3	9.9	27.2	48.4
16,003,633	2,696,471,800	266,076,086	9.9	11.7	10.0	27.5	49.2
17,023,638	2,892,260,684	285,839,648	9.9	13.9	10.1	27.6	51.6
18,040,330	3,093,120,784	336,017,462	10.9	10.2	10.7	27.6	48.5
18,456,530	3,147,004,666	384,814,451	12.2	10.7	12.7	29.4	52.8
18,800,342	3,217,886,186	417,078,904	13.0	13.5	13.7	30.9	58.1
20,135,873	3,368,155,438	507,705,712	15.1	14.1	14.1	30.9	59.1
20,887,870	3,565,092,824	738,541,361	20.7	15.9	15.3	31.0	62.2
22,260,092	3,848,301,437	1,005,691,831	26.1	21.1	15.4	28.3	64.8
22,900,000	3,972,100,000	1,285,300,000	32.4	26.5	15.5	27.2	69.2
23,200,000	4,008,800,000	1,402,400,000	35.0	30.2	17.3	28.0	75.5
23,000,000	3,981,600,000	1,478,100,000	37.1	35.2	20.0	29.5	84.7
23,200,000	4,063,000,000	1,637,900,000	40.3	42.0	20.9	32.2	95.1
23,432,000	4,170,900,000	1,766,800,000	42.4	47.4	25.2	30.1	102.7
23,870,000	4,249,000,000	1,906,100,000	44.9	49.9	22.6	30.4	102.9
24,109,000	4,291,500,000	1,907,700,000	44.5	56.7	NA[4]	NA	NA
24,594,000	4,377,800,000	1,911,500,000	43.7	61.5	NA	NA	NA
24,522,000	4,365,000,000	1,958,900,000	43.2	70.8	NA	NA	NA

total enrollment source: U.S. Department of Health, Education, and Welfare. Total schools in U.S. are compiled biennially. Private schools are partially estimated in all years.
[3] Peak month nationally. Children participating in N.S.L.P. includes an adjustment for absenteeism based on information supplied by Office of Education on attendance rates.

service management companies were made eligible for commodities and cash reimbursement in school programs. Foodservice companies had been in a few schools over 25 yr, but previously had not been eligible for Federal funds since they were profit making. The next challenge came as a surprise to many in school foodservice when the passage of PL 92-433 (1972) opened schools to competitive food operations as stated in Section 7.

Such regulations shall not prohibit the sales of competitive foods in food service facilities or areas during the time of service of food under this Act or the National School Lunch Act if the proceeds from the sales of such foods will inure to the benefit of the schools or of organizations of students approved by the schools.

School administrators, school foodservice leaders, parents, and Congressmen spoke out against the amendment. Perryman (1972) called it "the most permissive legislation in the 26-year history of school food service." Senator Edward Kennedy (1972) voiced his concerns about the "pressures which may now be placed on our local school officials to permit the sale of food items that will directly compete with the school lunch and breakfast programs." Senator Edward Brooke (1972) wrote "I realize the valuable role that the present school lunch program plays in insuring that students be afforded diets that are high in nutritional value, . . . The results of Section 7 could be both nutritionally and financially harmful to students, parents, and foodservice programs through the country." The American Medical Association also supported the school lunch program's nutritious foods and disapproved the availability of confections and soft drinks on school premises. In the Spring 1973 new bills were before Congress to rescind the opening of the doors to competitive foods followed by years of public comments and hearings on what foods should and what foods should not be made available for sale, and when. Finally in 1980 the "competitive foods" regulations were issued (discussed later in this chapter).

Residential Child Care Services

In 1975 the National School Lunch Act was amended to extend the definition of a "school" to include any public or nonprofit private child care institution which maintains children in residence; operates principally for the care of children; and if private, is licensed to provide residential child care services under the appropriate licensing code by the State or local level of government. Therefore children in homes for the mentally retarded, emotionally disturbed, and physically handicapped are eligible to participate in the National School Lunch Program, extending the ages from infancy to age 21.

The economy had tremenduous impacts on the programs, with the cost of each lunch increasing by 70 percent between 1970 and 1977. The Fair Labor Standards Amendments of 1977 called for $2.65 per hour minimum wage with $2.90 in 1979, $3.10 in 1980 and $3.35 in 1981. Union strikes closed foodservices temporarily in several large cities. During that period school enrollment fell by about 3 million students, however, participation grew 3 million for a 54 percent participation. The number free lunches increased from 21 percent in 1970 to 43 percent in 1980.

Plate Waste and Studies

School foodservices became highly visible during the seventies, making headline news across the country on television, as well as leading newspapers, regarding plate waste. Plate waste was found high among elementary children and particularly in schools serving frozen preplated meals. This visibility has started bringing about many changes: (1) offering of choices and more variety, (2) improvement in food quality, (3) new meal patterns, which allow for portions to be varied according to the age of the child, and (4) attitudes changed among those in the school foodservice business, whereas the child is now thought of more as a customer.

The plate waste publicity also marked the start of USDA studies to be done under contract by outside firms. The studies became so numerous and big money that it takes a large staff at USDA to monitor them. Congress continues to ask for more studies, taking a large chunk of Federal dollar each year, and too often the studies are not used.

USDA-DONATED FOODS

Foods are purchased by the USDA with funds made available under Section 6 of the National School Lunch Act, Section 32 of Public Law 320, and Section 416 of the Agricultural Act of 1949. Approximately 20 percent of the food used in preparing a lunch in USDA-donated foods.

These foods may or may not be processed. Fresh fruits are even shipped across the United States. These foods are packaged and delivered to a receiving point inside the State. The school districts are responsible for picking up commodities at a designated pick-up area and distributing to the individual schools.

As high labor costs and a lack of skilled labor changed traditional food preparation, more school districts started using prepared items or convenience foods, such as bakery bread, hamburger patties, and turkey rolls. Many school districts have found that fresh cranberries, whole turkeys, hard-wheat flour, non-fat dry milk, shortening, and rolled wheat were commodities that were sometimes a problem to utilize. One solution to this problem has been the processing of commodities into foods ready for use or more acceptable for use in the schools.

As far back as 1958 a few school districts had donated foods processed or repackaged by industry into a different end-product. Since 1969, when written instructions were issued by the Food Distribution Program, USDA, many more school districts started having the commodities processed. Prior to 1969 the contracts for processing donated foods had to go through USDA, but the changes meant now that the State's distributing agent for donated foods would approve the contracts. In some cases the donated foods are shipped directly to the factory for processing for which the school district pays the cost. By 1979 thirty-eight states had processing contracts with about 425 companies. Flour is the single largest item converted under these contracts.

Though the local school district usually agreed that the quality of the USDA-donated foods is excellent, there are problems with little advanced notice of when foods will be received. Lack of storage facilities particularly for frozen foods, lack of skilled labor, high labor costs, food likes and dislikes of the locale, and not being able to plan ahead are a few of the problems facing the school foodservice administrator. Many began to question whether there were surpluses to remove in the late 1960s and if help to the farmer kept the economy stable.

During the 1978–79 school year eight school districts were on a one-year pilot and received all cash from USDA's budget for their lunch programs in place of donated foods. The study confirmed that schools could get more out of the money and serve lunches that cost less if they had cash and no commodities. While USDA was still calculating data, the National Frozen Food Association issued a report prepared by Kansas State University of the pilot projects reporting a potential annual savings of $162 million.

During the Spring of 1980 the "voucher system" or "letter of credit" was promoted by the National Frozen Food Association and many foodservice directors. Under this arrangement schools would receive a "letter of credit" for a given quantity and grade of a particular commodity. Congressmen listened with interest but details had not been thought out and the time was not right. Foreseen problems of getting quick reaction when a particular food needed to be removed from the market, bookkeeping, and assuring fair prices would be charged, needed to be worked out. Pilot programs will allow that to be done.

Starting in the 1980 school year States are required to set up advisory councils to let USDA know what kinds of donated foods their schools can use. The councils will meet at least once a year to discuss which commodities school like best, as well as new products they want.

VARIED MEAL PATTERNS REPLACE TYPE A

The Type A Pattern had lasted thirty-five years with only three changes. Nutritionist proclaimed that the pattern was out-of-date and was not keeping pace with today's eating practices and life styles. Frequent criticisms were that the Type A Pattern was not responsive to the protein contributions of food components of both meat and milk and that the pattern did not take into consideration the different age children's needs. In 1977 the proposed changes in the meal pattern and other regulations were published in the Federal Register for comments. After field test and public comment the Department of Agriculture published the regulations in two steps. The interim regulations issued in August 1979 included:

(1) the expansion of bread alternates to include rice and pasta;
(2) the requirement that schools offer unflavored lowfat, skim, or buttermilk;
(3) the requirement that schools devise a program of student involvement;
(4) the requirement that schools devise a program of parent involvement; and
(5) the recommendation that schools which do not offer a choice of meat/meat alternate each day serve no one meat alternate or form of meat more than three times per week; and other menu planning recommendations included keeping fat, sugar, and salt at a moderate level; and emphasized three previous menu planning recommendations to include several foods for iron each day, vitamin A foods at least twice a week, and vitamin C foods several times weekly.

On May 16, 1980, the final regulations were released, dropping the "Type A" name and simply calling the new patterns "School Lunch Meal Patterns." These regulations called for:

(1) varying portion sizes for children of various ages;
(2) allowing schools to serve lunch to children age 1 to 5 years at two service periods;
(3) increasing the required quantities of two meat alternates—eggs and dry beans/peas—to be nutritionally equivalent to meat and the other meat alternates; and
(4) changing the bread requirement to specify the number of servings required by week and to increase the total number of servings required.

The new School Lunch Meal Patterns (see Ch. 5) offer much flexibility, as discussed in detail in the *Menu Planning Guide for School Food Service* (U.S. Dept. Agr., 1980).

BREAKFAST PROGRAM

The Federally-supported School Breakfast Program was created on a pilot basis by Congress in 1966 (PL 89-642) when $7.5 million was spent. The program was established with first consideration to be given to schools in poor areas and where children had to travel long distances to reach school. The 1968 Congress seemingly removed the program from the pilot status but it was not declared permanent by Congress until 1975. In 1972 the program was expanded, making all schools wishing to apply eligible (PL 92-153). The funds are primarily from Section 4 of the Child Nutrition Act and Section 32 of the Agricultural Adjustment Act of 1935. It is apportioned to all States according to participation and the economic need of the State.

From 752 schools on a pilot basis in 1967 where 80,232 breakfasts were served, it grew to 30,971 schools serving 3.4 million by 1979. As of January 1980, breakfast was being served to 3.5 million children daily. The program grew in spite of temporary freezes on new programs in 1969 and in spite of a number of problems, such as (1) lack of guidelines and regulations for operating the program; (2) inadequate funding; (3) uncertainty of future of program and permanency; (4) detailed reports and records required for funding; (5) convincing those who question the value of breakfast program; (6) scheduling of breakfast.

A report entitled *If We Had Ham, We Could Have Ham and Eggs* (Food Res. and Action Center 1972) cited the problems that the pilot program faced with cost and convincing the administrators of a need for a breakfast program. Some resistance occurred because administrators felt that the parents were responsible for the breakfast and not the school. Testimonials from school nurses, principals, and teachers all over the country praised the breakfast program. Many related the positive effect of increased classroom performance, improved behavior, and increased attendance. Testimonies at the Senate Hearings as recorded in the Congressional Record indicated ". . . improved attendance records, improved behavior, and alertness throughout the morning, less drowsiness due to hunger and of course improved performance and marks as a result of this program." The Food Research and Action Center and Dwyer, Elias, and Warren (1973) studies pointed out the important part the breakfast program could play in eradicating hunger in this nation. In 1979 Congress instructed USDA to institute an outreach breakfast promoting activity, and extended the breakfast program to public and private residential child care institutions.

The Breakfast Program has much research to back its value. Nutritionists have often declared breakfast as the most important meal of the day. The nutrients missed by skipping a meal, particularly breakfast, are not usually regained, leaving the day's consumption below the Recommended Dietary Allowances. The Iowa Breakfast Studies indicated that children who were hungry could not perform to their full potential in the classroom and had trouble concentrating and paying attention. Research done by the University of Maryland has shown more frequent adequacy of Vitamin C in the diets of children participating in the school breakfast program.

Breakfast Meal Requirements

Nutritionally the breakfast pattern was set by the Secretary of Agriculture as a minumum of:

½ pt of fluid milk
½ cup of fruit or vegetable or fruit juice or vegetable juice
1 slice of whole grain or enriched bread or an equivalent serving of biscuits, muffins, rolls, etc., or ¾ cup or 1 ounce, whichever is less of wholegrain, enriched, or fortified cereal
A meat or meat alternate is recommended as often as practicable

Many nutritionists and school foodservice administrators feel that the minimum breakfast in USDA regulations is inadequate nutritionally, because a meat or meat alternate should be a requirement, not a recommendation of USDA. Therefore, some States have added these as a requirement in administering the program locally where reimbursement rates allowed the costs. The lack of funds for paying labor during the pilot stages of the program also encouraged the use of high-carbohydrate breakfasts that required little or no preparation. Schools without facilities served the "engineered cake" which met the vitamin requirements through fortification and took the place of fruit and cereal in the breakfast. This practice could encourage poor food habits, it was argued. With the funding made more adequate and permanent after 1975, the breakfast programs has served more nutritionally adequate breakfasts; however, the cuts by Congress in 1980 eliminated the USDA-donated foods for breakfast and studies were showing the cost of breakfast exceeding the income.

Schools can qualify for extra Federal funds if they are designated as "specially needy." To qualify the school must serve 40 percent or more of their lunches free or at a reduced price, or be required by their state to serve breakfast. For example, Texas has mandated breakfast in all schools with 10% or more students eligible for free or reduced-priced breakfast, thus they are considered "specially needy."

SPECIAL MILK PROGRAM

Federal subsidy for special milk had been in uncertain positions many times since its first appropriated funds were authorized in 1954. In 1966 it was put under the Child Nutrition Act and funds were appropriated until June 1970. With free lunches being funded and growing rapidly, the President and Congress were asking if special milk funds were needed. Many expressed their concerns about the program continuing as it was funded hesitantly year by year through 1974. The special milk program subsidized the milk purchased by children in excess of the number of half pints served as a part of the lunch and breakfast. For example, if the school purchased milk for $0.071 per half pint in 1972 the child might pay $0.04 and the Federal subsidy would be $0.04.

The program is available for "nonprofit schools of high school grade and under and nonprofit nursery schools, childcare centers, settlement houses, summer camps, and similar nonprofit institutions devoted to the care and training of children." The consumption of milk from 1946 to 1947 was 228 million half pints, whereas from 1969 to 1970 it had grown to 2.7 billion half pints, to 1.9 billion half pints in 1980. However, there was a decrease between 1978 and 1979 as over two thousand schools dropped the program. The yearly change in regulations and the accountability necessary has caused school districts to drop the program. Additionally, many foodservice directors feel that the milk program takes from the lunch program and even adds to the plate waste. The program has been nearly lost several times, but the milk proponents prevail.

ASSESSMENT, IMPROVEMENT AND MONITORING SYSTEM

The Assessment, Improvement, and Monitoring System (AIMS) is a system directing state agencies in their review and audit of local school food services. Interim rules of this new approach for assuring the Federal regulations are being carried out were issued in September 1980 and were effective January 1981. School districts are checked on the following five performance standards:

(1) Applications for free and reduced-price meals—to determine if correctly approved or denied;
(2) The numbers of free and reduced-price meals claimed for reimbursement—to determine if the number of children claimed are correctly

and currently approved applications by category times days of service;

(3) System for counting and recording reimbursable meals—to determine if it yields correct claims;

(4) Meals claimed must contain the required food components (see School Lunch and Breakfast meal patterns);

(5) Meals claims for Federal reimbursement—to determine if cost are allowable and are documented by acceptable and reviewable records.

The reviews are required by the state agency once every four years or if audits are done, then every two years. A state agency will review at a minimum on the first four standards listed above with a follow up when errors are found. Sanctions may be taken after the first review if state agency thinks it is warranted. Sanctions are required on standards 2, 3, and 4 on the second (follow up) review, when corrections have not been made. Emphasis under this system is on corrective action.

If a state agency uses the audit method, they must assess a claim against districts anytime a violation is uncovered.

STUDENT AND PARENT INVOLVEMENT

As of August 1979 Federal regulations require that school food authorities (school districts) promote activities that involve children and parents in their foodservice programs. These activities, such as menu planning, promoting the program, enhancing the eating environment, have brought many positive changes.

COMPETITIVE FOODS

Competitive foods regulations were issued in 1980 after a couple of years of commenting and legal battles led by candy and cola manufacturers. The guidelines did not resemble the initial approach, but rather limits only the sale of a few foods. The four categories of foods are soda water, water ices, chewing gum, certain candies, including hard candies, such as jellies, gums, marshmallow candies, fondants, licorice, and spun candies. The foods have only to contain 5 percent or more of the Recommended Daily Allowance for one of the eight basic nutrient per 100 kilo calories or per serving. Those eight basic nutrients are: protein, vitamin A, ascorbic acid, niacin, riboflavin, thiamin, calcium, and iron.

National School Lunch Week

An annual observance of school lunch was established by Congress (PL 87-780) when it set "the seven-day period beginning on the second Sunday of October in each year is hereby designated as National School Lunch Week, and the President is requested to issue annually a proclamation calling on the people of the United States to observe such a week with appropriate ceremonies and activities."

FACING THE EIGHTIES

The eighties will be the most revolutionary of the centuries for institutional foods, especially school foodservice. Food and labor costs are increasing faster than can be dealt with. Energy costs will cause conserva-

FIG. 1.6. DURING THE '80'S, VARIETY IN CHOICES OF FOOD HAS ADDED MUCH TO SCHOOL LUNCH PROGRAMS

tion to spread and will place more demands on the equipment manufacturers to provide energy efficient equipment. Use of computers in the kitchen, as well as in the manager's office, will provide unlimited possibilities.

School foodservice will continue to be a political football, facing reoccurring Federal cuts, last minute funding approvals, and threats of more cuts and audits. The continual changes in regulations, the need for more training and guidance materials, the political influence on the guidance materials, and more complicated accountability will make the manger's job harder. A letter-of-credit replacing USDA-donated foods and the relocating of child nutrition programs in the Department of Education are potential events. The "bloc grant" that was feared in the seventies may be a relief from regulations, audits, and detailed accountability in the eighties.

The future of school foodservice is an ever-changing program, depending entirely on the legislation passed next. Lobbyists, from apple growers to carbonated drink vendors, from the American Dietetic Association to the National Restaurant Association, will plead yearly for changing or maintaining the directions of school foodservices. School foodservice has become as much a part of a school day as English and will stay in one form or another. For so many years it was slow to change, and now it has the flexibility to change, for progress.

BIBLIOGRAPHY

AM. MED. ASSOC. COUNCIL ON FOODS and NUTR. 1972. A council statement; confections and soft drinks in schools. School Foodservice J. *26*, No. 10, 26.

ANON. 1971. In the beginning . . . more beginning. School Lunch J. *25*, No. 6, 18–30.

BARD, B. 1968. The School Lunchroom: Time of Trial. John Wiley & Sons, New York.

BRIGGS, H.L., and CONSTANCE C. HART. 1931. From basket lunches to cafeterias—a story of progress. Nation's Schools *8*, 51–55.

BROOKE, E. 1972. Letter to the editor. School Foodservice J. *26*, No. 10, 24.

CITIZEN'S BOARD OF INQUIRY INTO HUNGER AND MALNUTRITION OF THE U.S. 1968. Hunger, U.S.A. Beacon Press, Boston.

CRONAN, MARION. 1962. The School Lunch. Chas. A. Bennett Co., Peoria, Ill.

DEPT. OF INTERIOR. 1921. Bureau of Education Bull. *37*, Washington, D.C.

DWYER, J.T., M.F. ELIAS, and J.H. WARREN. 1973. Effects of an Experimental Breakfast Program on Behavior in the Late Morning. Master's Thesis, Harvard School of Public Health, Cambridge, Mass.

FAIRFAX, JEAN. 1968. Their Daily Bread. Committee on School Lunch Participation. McNelley-Rudd Printing Service, Atlanta, Ga.

FOOD AND NUTR. SERV. 1970. Chronological Legislative History of Child Nutrition Programs. U.S. Dept. Agr., Washington, D.C.

FOOD RES. AND ACTION CENTER. 1972. If We Had Ham, We Could Have Ham and Eggs . . . If We Had Eggs: A Study of the National School Breakfast Program. Gazette Press, Yonkers, N.Y.

FORD, WILLARD STANLEY. 1926. Some Administrative Problems of the High School Cafeteria. Columbia University, N.Y.

GUNDERSON, G.W. 1971. The National School Lunch Program: Background and Development. FNS 63. U.S. Dept. Agr., U.S. Govt. Printing Office, Washington, D.C.

HUNTER, R. 1904. Poverty. (Reprinted 1965. Poverty: Social Conscience in the Progressive Era.) Harper & Row, New York.

KENNEDY, E. 1972. Letter to the editor. School Foodservice J. *26*, No. 10, 24.

KOTZ, N. 1969. Let Them Eat Promises: The Politics of Hunger in America. Prentice-Hall, Englewood Cliffs, N.J.

PERRYMAN, J. 1972. Log of the executive director. School Foodservice J. *26*, No. 10, 18.

POLLITT, ERNESTO, MITCHELL GOISOVITZ, and MARITA GARGIULO. 1978. Educational Benefits of the United States School Feeding Program: A Critical Review of the Literature. AJPH, 68, No. 5, 477–481.

READ, M.S. 1973. Malnutrition, Hunger, and Behavior. J. Am. Dietet. Assoc. 63, 379–385.

SANDSTROM, M.M. 1959. School lunches. Yearbook of Agriculture. U.S. Dept. Agr., U.S. Govt. Printing Office. Washington, D.C.

SPARGO, J. 1906. The Bitter Cry of the Children. Macmillan, New York.

TUTTLE, D., et al. 1962. Iowa Breakfast Studies, University of Iowa. Cereal Institute, Chicago.

U.S. DEPT. AGR. 1980. Factors Influencing School and Student Participation in the School Breakfast Program, 1977–78. U.S. Govt. Printing Office, Washington, D.C.

U.S. PUBLIC LAW 396, 79TH CONGRESS. 1946. 60 Stat. 231 (June 4).

U.S. PUBLIC LAW 87-780, 87TH CONGRESS. 1962. 76 Stat. 779 (Oct. 9).

U.S. PUBLIC LAW 89-642, 89TH CONGRESS. 1966. 80 Stat. 885–890 (Oct. 11).

U.S. PUBLIC LAW 90-302, 90TH CONGRESS. 1968. 82 Stat. 117 (May 8).

U.S. PUBLIC LAW 91-248, 91ST CONGRESS. 1970. 84 Stat. 207 (May 14).

U.S. PUBLIC LAW 92-32, 92ND CONGRESS. 1971. 85 Stat. 85 (June 30).

U.S. PUBLIC LAW 92-153, 92ND CONGRESS. 1971. (Nov. 5).

U.S. PUBLIC LAW 92-433, 92ND CONGRESS. 1972. 86 Stat. 724 (Sept. 26).

U.S. PUBLIC LAW 93-13, 93RD CONGRESS. 1973. (April 6).

U.S. PUBLIC LAW 93-150, 93RD CONGRESS. 1973. (November 7).

U.S. PUBLIC LAW 94-105, 94TH CONGRESS. 1975. (October 7).

U.S. PUBLIC LAW 95-166, 95TH CONGRESS. 1977. (November 10).

U.S. PUBLIC LAW 95-627, 95TH CONGRESS. 1978. (November 10).

WHITE HOUSE CONFERENCE ON FOOD, NUTRITION AND HEALTH. 1970. Final Report. U.S. Govt. Printing Office, Washington, D.C.

2

Organization Management

With school foodservices growing from a "soup kitchen" to a business organization, it has been necessary for the operation to become more and more organized. School foodservices are now competing for business within the school in many parts of the country and have had to become more accountable and very cost-conscious. A successful operation must operate on sound business principles—well organized and well managed. This is particularly true in the food industry, whether a large chain operation or a small sandwich bar. Each year one half of the new commercial restaurants that open fail, and another 25% fail by the end of the third year. The food industry is a business of fragile intangibles. The basic principles of management are the same for restaurants, hospitals, residence halls, and school foodservices. The larger the foodservice operation, the more complex the organization becomes. School foodservice operations range from small individual schools serving less than a 100 to large centralized city and county units as large as 250–600 schools serving 100,000–500,000 meals per day.

PURPOSE OF ORGANIZATION

The purpose of an organization dealing with manpower is, according to West *et al.* (1977), "to accomplish with the efforts of people some basic purpose or objective with the greatest efficiency, maximum economy, and minumum effort, and to provide for the personal development of the people working in the organization."

For an organization to function effectively and to grow, it must utilize all resources—people, materials, and facilities—to their fullest. The most important of the resources is people. To be effective, an organization must provide for the people to be utilized to their fullest capabilities. To accomplish this the organization must operate under some general principles:

(1) Clear line of authority must be established and understood by the employees.
(2) Objectives and goals are set and used as a measurement of success.
(3) Responsibilities are clearly identified for each member of the organization.
(4) Leadership is effective.
(5) There are materials and equipment to work with.

One of the very basic questions to be asked about the organization may be "who decides there is one?" The board of education in school foodservice is the overall governing body which enters into an agreement with the State education agency to carry out the Federal and State rules and regulations. The agreement is made in order to receive Federal and State cash reimbursement and USDA commodities. The sample organization chart shows how a State's line of authority may be established (Fig. 2.1). Foodservice is located within the state department of education in all States; however, that is about all the different states have in common. The audits in the late 1970s clearly established the lack of training and directions in the very basic area of meeting meal pattern requirements.

An organizational chart, if well prepared, can show: the person who holds the job, responsibilities of the job, whom he is responsible to and who is responsible to him, and the relationship of departments and services. Persons with the greatest authority are shown at the top of the chart with those with the least authority at the bottom. The line of authority is best shown and understood when displayed in an organization chart form such as the examples given (Figs. 2.2, 2.3, 2.4). It is important that each person know to whom he is responsible and who is responsible to him. A clear line of authority should go with this responsibility. For a school foodservice to function effectively within a centralized unit or in individual units the *foodservice* needs to be an established part of the school system. If the board of education which establishes the policy puts the responsibility for management and sale of all food and beverages under the school foodservice division, theirs will be a more successful program. The advantages of centralization are lost if the authority and responsibility of school feeding are not centralized. Sometimes foodservice management fails in school foodservice because of all the different factions operating foodservice. The foodservice administration is merely a consultant when the authority becomes divided. It cannot be held responsible for the successes or failures if the *authority* for carrying out the policies, rules, and regulations have not been given with the *responsibility.*

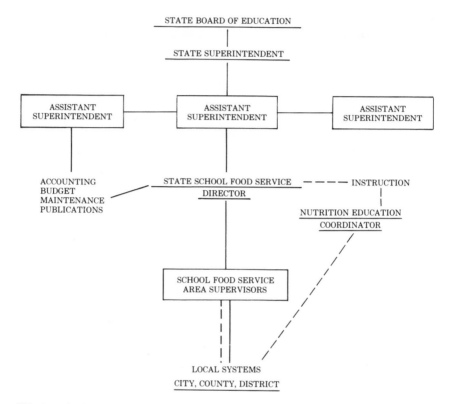

FIG. 2.1. ORGANIZATIONAL CHART—STATE

OBJECTIVES OF MANAGEMENT

Management is responsible for planning, directing, and controlling the foodservice in a sound financial manner and serving good, nutritious food as a part of the educational system. Management should (1) set the standards; (2) develop the objectives and goals; (3) make the policies; (4) do the planning and organizing; (5) communicate with the workers, the public, the parents, the school administration, and the board of education; (6) control quality of food; (7) control costs; (8) carry out the objectives and goals; (9) supervise and direct; (10) evaluate; (11) teach and encourage the growth of the foodservice workers; and (12) look out for the foodservice's welfare.

Standards are needed as a point of reference—as a means of evaluating. How can the cook know if he is doing a good job? How does the manager know if he is managing well? How does the director know if the foodservice is doing a good job? There are several measurements of

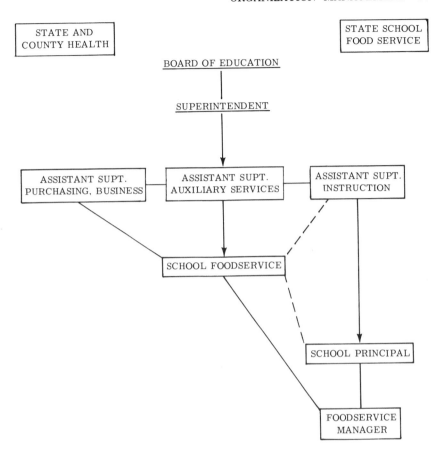

FIG. 2.2. ORGANIZATIONAL CHART—LOCAL SYSTEM

success of the school foodservice: comments from customers; percentage of participation (number served is some indication of customer satisfaction); cost per meal; number of meals produced per labor-hour; good morale among employees; and more income than expenditures. These can be tools of measurement if there is a reference point. Standards must be set by which to evaluate. The director can look at each of the school foodservice units and evaluate on the basis of objectives, goals, and standards. The objectives and goals may differ from one school system to another. The National School Lunch Program was founded as stated in the original bill "as a measure of national security to safeguard the health and well-being of the nation's children and to encourage the domestic consumption of nutritious agricultural commodities and other food . . . ." Unless the program operates on a financially sound basis it may cease to have the opportunity "to safeguard the health and well-being of the

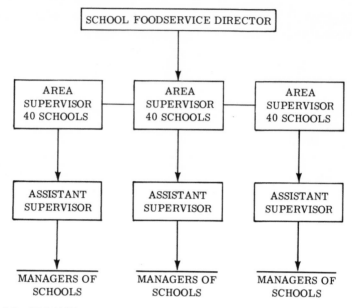

FIG. 2.3. ORGANIZATIONAL CHART—LOCAL SYSTEM FOODSERVICE (120 SCHOOLS)

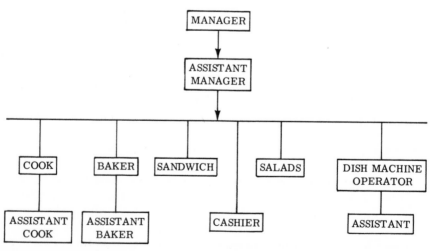

FIG. 2.4. ORGANIZATIONAL CHART—LARGE SECONDARY SCHOOL (SINGLE UNIT) WITH A LA CARTE

nation's children." Five important objectives of the administration should be:

(1) Operate the program on a sound financial basis within the budget.
(2) Serve good quality, nutritious food to all students.
(3) Teach good food habits.
(4) Meet the needs of the students in a satisfying way.
(5) Give employees an opportunity for personal development.

The objectives, goals, and standards should be set by the people involved—the school foodservice staff, the students, and the board of education. All three segments may have different aims or measurements of success. The dietitian-oriented food director may be mostly concerned about serving nutritious food, whereas the student may not like the food served or may be tired of it and want changes, more choices, or different foods. The board of education may be most concerned if the foodservice has a deficit. The objectives for foodservice have to be a realistic combination of the three.

JOB ANALYSIS AND DESCRIPTION

Once the basic plan of an organizational chart has been established, the line of authority is set; then it is important to analyze each job. The job and the responsibilities are to be described and the specifications made for carrying them out. A job analysis is a look at the whole job, what the duties of the job are, qualifications required, job promotions possible, physical conditions, and salary and fringe benefits. It is used by management in preparing the job description and specifications.

An Outline for Analyzing a Job

    I. Title
       A. Code number
       B. Job definition
    II. Duties
       A. Regular or daily duties
       B. Periodic duties (weekly, monthly, etc.)
       C. Occasional duties
    III. Minimum Starting Requirements for Position
       A. Education
          1. Read, write, and speak English
          2. Elementary school—8 grades
          3. 1−2 yr high school
          4. 3−4 yr high school
          5. High school and some special training
          6. Partial college, 1−2 yr

B. Special Training
1. Pre-job training necessary
2. On-the-job training needed
3. Additional training recommended for advancement
C. Experience
1. Minimum required to enter occupation
2. Related experience in other occupations
3. Experience desirable to enter occupation
D. Personal Qualifications
1. Age range
2. Sex
3. Physical size and strength desired
4. Skills essential to performance on the job
5. Social and personal qualities, necessary for success in the particular job
E. Other
1. Certificate, such as health
2. License
3. Union membership
4. Civil service examination
5. Minimum score on standardized test
IV. Ways of Entering
A. Public and special employment services
B. Apprenticeship
C. Other methods
V. Equipment and Materials Used
A. Kinds of equipment and materials used
B. Safety risks
C. Equipment and uniform to be supplied by the worker
VI. Responsibility of the Worker
A. Supervising work of others
B. Independent judgment required
VII. Conditions of Work
A. Hours
1. Regular hours
2. Overtime and frequency
3. Vacations with or without pay
4. Regulations
a. Local, State, Federal
b. Union
B. Regularity of employment
C. Physical demands: amount of time spent standing, walking, sitting, lifting, etc.

D. Physical conditions of surroundings: heat, air conditioning, noise
E. Contact with others: alone, few others, many others
VIII. Advancement
   A. Lines of promotion
   B. Opportunity for advancement
   C. Related Occupations
     1. Occupations to which the job may lead
     2. Occupations from which one may transfer
IX. Earnings
   A. Basis for pay
     1. Amount of payment determined by hour, piecework, day, week, or month
     2. Frequency of payment, e.g., week, month
   B. Average pay for a beginner
   C. Average pay for a highly skilled worker
   D. Benefits
     1. Pensions
     2. Social Security
     3. Unemployment insurance
     4. Sick leave
     5. Workmen's compensation
   E. Rewards and satisfactions in addition to monetary rewards

JOB DESCRIPTION

A job description is a general description of the job and is used by management and the employees for the two to have a mutual understanding of what the job entails. An example follows:

JOB DESCRIPTION
JOB TITLE: Foodservice Assistant
GRADE STEP: II
JOB DEFINITION: Prepare the main dish and vegetables.
GENERAL DUTIES:
Responsible for the preparation of the main dish and cooked vegetables. Is to prepare food for the serving line and keep all foods on the serving line at lunchtime. Responsible for the cleaning and maintaining of the small equipment, washing of pots and pans when needed. Will help with the general preparation and serving of food and the cleaning.

REQUIREMENTS:

Must be able to read and write English, to do simple arithmetic, be able to follow oral and written direction. Must have the capacity to grasp and adjust to new and changing situations. Manual dexterity and ability to work under pressure are desirable. Must be neat in appearance and is required to wear a uniform type clothing, hairnet or cap-type covering on hair, comfortable shoes. Health certificate is required.

TOOLS AND EQUIPMENT:

Scales for weighing ingredients and portion control, mixer, ovens, ranges, steam cookers, steam-jacketed kettle, fryer, food chopper, meat slicer, vertical-cutter-mixer.

WORKING CONDITIONS:

Work an average of 35 hours per week, Monday through Friday with school holidays. Ten months a year. Kitchen is well lighted, ventilated, and comfortable. Much standing on feet required and some lifting.

SUPERVISION:

Responsible to the School Foodservice Manager. Gives supervision in large operations to an assistant cook.

PERSONAL REQUIREMENTS:

High school education or equivalency test. At least one year experience in foodservice preparation. Male or female.

JOB SPECIFICATION

A job specification is a combination of the analysis and description. The job specification is used primarily by personnel in interviewing and selecting the person for a specific position. It is important for the prospective employee to know what a job entails, clothes to wear, hours to work, and what will be expected of him before accepting the position. For example:

JOB SPECIFICATION

JOB TITLE: Foodservice Assistant   GRADE/STEP: II
DEPARTMENT: Foodservice
SUPERVISED BY: Foodservice Manager
JOB SUMMARY: Prepares main dish and vegetables
EDUCATION: High school education or equivalency test. Must be able to speak, read, and understand English. A test score of 50 or above required on "Knowledge Test."
EXPERIENCE: 1 year previous experience in foodservice.
HEALTH REQUIREMENT: Recent health certificate.

PERSONAL: Male or female, neat, clean, wears uniform.
REFERENCE: Personal, 2 previous employees.
HOURS: 7:30 to 2:30 p.m., Monday through Friday. School holidays, 30-minute lunch breaks.
WAGE CODE: II-a   FRINGE BENEFITS:
                    Insurance, Health
                    Lunch
                    Retirement
                    Personal Leave Days
                    Sick Leave Days
POSSIBLE PROMOTIONS: To assistant foodservice manager or cook-manager.

State Administrative Staff

There are no official guidelines set for the administrative staffs on the State, county, or city levels. The responsibilities, authority, and salary of the State director and staff differ significantly from one State to another. State directors have realized this and asked time and again for job descriptions to be made by one of the governing agents as models. This is an area in which surveys, studies, and recommendations are needed. In the broad sense of the word the State director and staff are responsible for:

(1) Providing leadership in the State.
(2) Interpreting legislation, policies, rules, and regulations of the Federal agency.
(3) Instructing, informing, and teaching school foodservice workers within the State.
(4) Representing the State school foodservices.
(5) Provide accounting systems for reporting to the Federal agency.
(6) Claiming, collecting, and distributing Federal funds to the schools in the State.
(7) Administering and evaluating the school foodservice programs.

The State staff's responsibilities and the way they are carried out within the States vary as much as: the divisions under which they function within the State, the number on the staff, and the qualifications of that staff.

CENTRALIZED ADMINISTRATION

More and more school foodservices are operating yearly under a centralized organization. Counties, cities, and districts may organize under a board of education and have a group of schools under the control of one administration. When foodservice administration is centralized, a director or supervisor of foodservices is usually appointed to work under the general direction of the superintendent of schools or school business administrator. This person is responsible for working with the school managers in the units. The degree of control this central administration has over the school foodservices may vary from a flexible one with only the financial aspects being centralized to a very rigid control. Centralized planning may include planning menus, purchasing on bid, warehousing, fiscal control, and personnel. Many advantages can result from centralization of the administration. In consolidating the resources more qualified leadership can be afforded, more purchasing power obtained, better organization and management possible, and all resulting in significant savings.

Local Director and Supervisor

The administrative staff on the local level may or may not have official guidelines, depending on the State. Many recommendations have been made in speeches by leaders and by task force groups in committee meeting reports, but little has been published. Task force groups, and leaders, such as Josephine Martin, have recommended that "a foodservice specialist is needed for each 20 foodservice programs; this formula allows the specialist to devote a minumum of 4 hours individualized help per month to each program." This specialist is most frequently called a "supervisor." Supervisor is defined by Spriegal et al. (1957) as: ". . . any person who is responsible (1) for the conduct of others in the achievement of a particular task; (2) for the maintenance of quality standards; (3) for the protection and care of materials; and (4) for services to be rendered to those under his control."

Other school systems call the head administrator a *director*. The director of a county or city school foodservice, according to the American School Foodservice Certification Committee, is "one who plans, organizes, directs, administers the food service program in a school system according to policies established by the Board of Education." In smaller systems the director and supervisor may be one and the same. Ordinarily a director is employed when the system becomes complex and consists of more than 30 programs. Regardless of the size of the system, a director should have as a minimum qualification a Master's degree in foodservice administration or a related field with a strong background in business. The larger the system and responsibility the more experience, leadership, and education may be desired. As a part of an educational program it is desirable that the director of this service be not only a business person but an educator.

The *supervisor* is under the director, if there is one, in the line of authority. A supervisor is responsible for evaluating the programs, aiding, and generally directing the individual foodservice units. He or she works directly with the school foodservice units. The minimum qualifications for a supervisor should be a baccalaureate degree in foods. The larger the system and the more supervisors there are in the system the more specialized they may be. For example, in Dade County Schools (Fla.) the director is assisted by four specialized people: business coordinator, supervisor of planning and production, supervisor of personnel and development training, and eight area foodservice coordinators (Fig. 2.5).

An *assistant to the supervisor* is a term used for the position just below the supervisor but of the supervisory category. The assistant to the supervisor is responsible to the supervisor and/or director for evaluating, supervising, training, aiding, and carrying out the policies, and objectives of the foodservice. The greatest part of this person's time is spent in the school foodservices. A minimum of a baccalaureate degree or a high school education and at least five or more years experience as a successful, outstanding manager of a school foodservice should be required. A college degree is most desirable for an assistant supervisor, but a person with good training and experience in actual management can work very effectively with managers and workers in the schools.

Supervision is needed for effective administration of a program. A supervisor or an assistant supervisor for every twenty schools is a realistic span of control.

As shown in Table 2.1, the amount of time that can be spent in the schools is one of the important factors. The director will have less time than any of the other positions due to the administrative demands on him. A minimum of 20% of the director's time should be spent in school foodservices. The assistant to the supervisor should be in the schools 75% of the time; whereas the supervisor, due to special assignments, may be limited to 50% of the time in actual supervision.

The line of authority is usually as shown in Fig. 2.6. The reason the principal is put into the line of authority over the manager is that the manager of the foodservices should be considered a member of the school's staff and under the principal's responsibility and authority. The manager will receive directions from both, with the school foodservice supervisor working with the principal.

Good sound leadership from the director and supervisors is necessary for progress and success of the program. Some of the characteristics of a good administrative leader are:

(1) Stimulates leadership within the group.
(2) Builds morale.

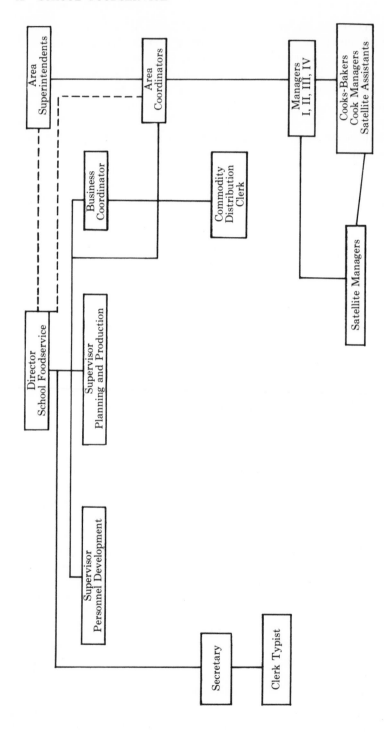

Courtesy of Dade County (Fla.) Public Schools, School Foodservice

FIG. 2.5. THIS IS A GOOD EXAMPLE OF A WELL–STRUCTURED–SCHOOL FOODSERVICE WITH 8 AREA COORDINATORS FOR 168 MANAGERS

(3) Develops cooperation.
(4) Disciplines when needed.
(5) Has knowledge and understanding of human nature.
(6) Delegates responsibility and authority.
(7) Has the ability to make decisions.
(8) Instructs properly those under him.

The attitude of the director and the leaders has a significant influence on the people he supervises and their accomplishments. Workers respect a leader who informs his staff of policies, of what is expected of him, maintains set standards, and disciplines those who do not abide by those standards. The leader should maintain good working conditions, represent and fight for his workers to management, have a good attitude and boost morale, and have good public relations. It is desirable for a leader to encourage workers to think, to give suggestions, and then give recognition to those who deserve it. A leader should: make decisions carefully and stand by the decision, accept the responsibility for his workers, and impartially promote workers when merited. More and better work is obtained by praising an employee at the right time than by criticizing him. Employees must want to do the job if their efforts are to produce good results.

There are basically three types of management: (1) Authoritarian—one who gives orders, dictator; (2) Laissez-faire—one who gives free-rein; (3) Democratic—one who leads through cooperative means. The democratic type management produces more creativity, ingenuity, and involvement. When a group of employees acts as "one" and shares ideas with everyone aware of the goals, then the group can feel satisfaction for the service of good food. Good work should be recognized, and poor work deserves constructive criticism. Employees deserve to be trained, given guidance, and have a clear understanding of what is expected of them. The job description, followed by work schedules, can give the guidance and understanding of what is expected of them.

TABLE 2.1. ADMINISTRATIVE STAFFING GUIDE FOR SCHOOL FOOD-SERVICE

No. School Foodservice	Director	Supervisor or Specialist	Assistant to Supervisor
1−15		1	
16−30		1	1
31−40		1	1
41−60	1	1	2
61−80	1	1	3
81−100	1	2	4
101−125	1	2	5
126−150	1	2	6
151−175	1	3	7
176−200	1	4	9
201−225	1	4	10

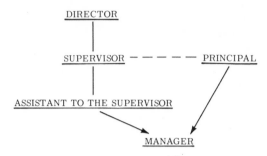

FIG. 2.6.   SCHOOL ADMINISTRATIVE LINE OF AUTHORITY

The management of school foodservice needs more qualified people to fill its positions. In 1972 the American School Foodservice Association conducted a survey which indicated that of the 16,530 school districts in the United States that were participating in the National School Lunch Program, only 1461 school districts had educationally qualified supervisors, that is, supervisors with degrees in the foodservice field.

School Foodservice Manager

A manager has the responsibility for the administration of the unit school working under the authority of the school's principal and system's school foodservice director. The duties of the manager differ considerably in the decentralized system where the manager may be responsible for all the planning, purchasing, and staffing as well as her other responsibilites. The duties and responsibilities of a manager in a centralized system will include:

(1) Carrying out the rules and regulations of the Federal, State, and local board of education.
(2) Preparation and serving of food that meets the nutritional needs of the students. To prepare the food in a safe and sanitary way. To prepare appetizing and attractive food in the correct quantities and of high quality. Prepare food by standarized recipes and procedures and serve in standardized portions.
(3) Management of personnel in a way to help prevent grievances and undesirable situations. To promote teamwork and efficient production. Provide on-the-job training and means of growth for employees. Provide a safe and pleasant atmosphere in which to work. Plan and assign work of the employees by means of outlining duties and work scheduling.

(4) Purchasing food and supplies in the quality and quantity needed. Checking, receiving, and storing food and other items properly.
(5) Promoting good public relations with the students, faculty, and parents. Assist in offering nutrition education to the students.
(6) Maintaining a sanitary foodservice. Responsible to see that employees have had health examinations and are healthy. To promote high standards of sanitation and comply with the local and State health regulations and codes of sanitation.
(7) Controlling the financial management within the budget. Preparing and maintaining accurate and adequate records of the income and expenditures, and the number of meals served.
(8) Evaluating the operation and correcting deficiencies.

To carry out all of these responsibilities, a manager must have training and experience. The manager must be able to perform all the jobs in the foodservice, have a knowledge of nutrition and menu planning, food cost control, personnel management and must know and understand the importance of good sanitation. The manager must have a knowledge of the general care and operation of all the equipment in the kitchen. The booklet *School Food Service Workers Other than the Director and Supervisor* (Am. School Food Serv. Assoc. and Assoc. Business Officials, n.d.) lists the desired qualifications for a manager as:

(1) Graduation from high school.
(2) A knowledge of nutritional requirements for children and youth.
(3) A knowledge of basic factors for menu planning based on the nutritional requirement of the Type A lunch pattern and other types of school foodservice. Other food factors to be included are contrasts in flavor, texture, temperature, color, and shape or form and attractive servings.
(4) Knowledge of menu planning work sheets.
(5) A knowledge of purchasing procedures.
(6) Personal cleanliness.
(7) Sanitary practices in food preparation.
(8) Responsibility for training programs for accident prevention and use of safety precautions.
(9) Experience in use of standardized recipes and methods of quantity food preparation which retain nutritive values.
(10) Keeping accurate records of food cost control, recipe costing, menu costing, inventories, participation records, labor cost control, and profit and loss.
(11) Organization and management of a school foodservice program, which includes in-service training program on personnel relations,

work schedules, and policies relating to the school foodservice program.

(12) The ability to work with others in a pleasant and cooperative manner.

To obtain a person with these qualifications, school foodservice nearly always has to train their own people or work closely with the local community college, vocational or technical training center, and universities for this purpose. The basic knowledge may be obtained through courses, but experience as an assistant to a manager is desirable to become acquainted with the responsibilities.

BIBLIOGRAPHY

AM. SCHOOL FOOD SERV. ASSOC., and ASSOC. BUSINESS OFFICIALS. 1965. The School Food Service Director. Bull. *3*, Joint Am. School Food Serv. Assoc., Denver, Colo.

AM. SCHOOL FOOD SERV. ASSOC., and ASSOC. BUSINESS OFFICIALS. (n.d.) School Food Service Workers Other than the Director and Supervisor. Am. School Food Serv. Assoc., Denver, Colo.

ANON. 1972. State directors cost out school meals. School Foodservice J. *26*, No. 7, 22.

BELASCO, JAMES A., DAVID R. HAMPTON, and KARL F. PRICE. 1975. Management Today. John Wiley & Sons, Inc., N.Y.

CLOYD, FRANCES. 1972. Guide to Foodservice Management, Institutions Volume Feeding Magazine, Chicago, Ill.

COLEMAN, JOAN. 1970. Instructor's guide: management of food service. Fla. Dept. Educ., Tallahassee.

DONNELLY, JAMES H., Jr., JAMES L. GIBSON, and JOHN M. IVANCE-VICH. 1975. Fundamentals of Management, 2nd Edition. Business Publication, Dallas.

DRUCKER, PETER F. 1974. Management. Harper & Row Publ., N.Y.

ESHBACH, CHARLES E., Editor. 1976. Food Service Management. Cahners Books, Boston, Mass.

JUN, JONG S. and EILLISM N. DYOTM. 1973. Tomorrow's Organizations: Challenges and Strategies. Scott, Foresman and Company, Glenview, Ill.

HANNI, R. B. 1968. Development of evaluative procedure for assessing operational-efficiency of school food service. Ph.D. Dissertation, Ball State Univ., Muncie, Ind.

KAHRL, W. L. 1973. Planning and Operating A Successful Food Service Operation. Chain Store Age Books, N.Y.

MALI, PAUL. 1972. Managing by Objectives. John Wiley & Sons, Inc., N.Y.

NICHOLSON, R. H. 1966. Centralization trends in school lunch systems. Proceeding from Association of School Business Officials. The Association, Evanston, Ill.

SISK, HENRY L. 1974. Management and Organization, 3rd Edition. Southwestern Publishing Co., Cincinnati, Ohio.

STOKES, JOHN W. 1973. How to Manage a Restaurant or Institutional Food Service, 2nd Edition. Wm. C. Brown Co., Dubuque, Iowa.

U.S. SENATE, 92ND CONGRESS. 1971. Hearing Before the Committee of Agriculture and Forestry. U.S. Govt. Printing Office, Washington, D.C.

WEST, BESSIE, LEVELLE WOOD, VIRGINIA HARGER, and GRACE SHUGART. 1977. Food Service in Institutions, 6th Edition. John Wiley & Sons, N.Y.

ZABKA, J. R. 1971. Personnel Management and Human Relations. ITT Educational Services, N.Y.

3

Personnel Management

Managing people is one of the most challenging of all the jobs of an administrator or supervisor. The people in an operation—their attitudes, abilities, desires, and interests—influence the success or failure of the operation. Management sets the standards but must work through people in carrying them out. *Personnel management* can be defined simply as the directing of people in carrying out the jobs to be done.

Why do people want to work at a certain place? Money may come to mind. However, surveys have shown that money is low on the list of reasons for wanting to work at a certain job. Five of the main reasons employees list for being happy with a job are (1) security; (2) feeling of belonging; (3) good supervision; (4) opportunity for promotion; (5) job satisfaction—interesting, challenging, and feeling of accomplishment. The turnover rate for school foodservice is relatively low at 11% nationwide when compared with another foodservice, such as fast foods industry with 165%.

"How much labor is enough?" is a difficult question to answer. Some foodservices may be staffed with twice the labor hours that are really needed to carry out the job and still complain "we need more help." Low productivity and unplanned work may be the main reasons for the situation. To staff a foodservice properly may mean that more than a staffing guideline is needed. It usually requires a combination of several of the following: time and motion studies, work schedules planned, finding more efficient ways of carrying out the job, purchasing labor-saving equipment, rearrangement of equipment, and changes in menus and serving periods.

STAFFING

No magic formula can be used for staffing all foodservices. The employees needed and the labor hours will differ for numerous reasons from one operation to another. Management has to set and enforce reasonable restrictions as to the number of labor hours. However, a follow-through with training and making changes will be necessary for high productivity to result.

Factors Influencing Amount of Labor Needed

Some of the factors that should be considered in determining the number of employees needed and the number of labor hours needed are:

Foodservice System Used.—Labor needs will be different for on-site preparation, satellite, etc.

Number of Meals to be Served.—The smaller operations (serving under 200 meals) will have a higher labor cost percentage than the larger operation serving 400 or more meals. The larger the operation, the higher productivity there should be and proportionately fewer labor hours.

Menus.—The no-choice lunch menu will take less labor hours than a choice menu. A la carte service and preparation will require additional labor hours. Breakfast menus usually require less preparation, therefore fewer labor hours.

Type Food Used.—Pre-prepared food or partially pre-prepared food is a factor. A hamburger menu can mean purchasing ground beef in bulk, hamburger patties frozen, or precooked hamburger patties. The greater degree of preparedness costs more, but should require less labor. When a commercial bakery bakes breads and other baked goods for the foodservice, the food cost goes up and the labor costs must go down. It should not require the same number of labor hours if the baking is done by the commercial bakery. Preplated frozen dinners, frozen entrees, preportioned foods, precooked foods, and other forms of preparedness will have an effect on labor needs. Consequently, labor hours have to be decreased as convenience items are used more. The greatest pitfall in using the convenience items, which usually cost more but require less labor in preparation, is that the management does not cut the labor. Therefore, the cost of food goes up and the labor cost stays the same and a deficit results.

Number and Length of Lunch Periods.—Most staffing formulas are based on three 30-min lunch periods. When the lunch periods are 45 to 60 min or are increased to 4 or 5 lunch periods, additional labor hours are usually required. The increased labor hours will be needed to give adequate time for preparation before lunch and adequate time after lunch for clean-up and pre-preparation.

Kind and Arrangement of Equipment.—Labor-saving equipment can make for higher productivity and labor economy. The conveyor dishwasher in a foodservice serving 350 to 400 meals will wash the dishes in less time and the operator's time is better utilized than if a door-type dishwasher is used. The arrangement of the equipment in an efficient manner can ensure more productivity. A spacious, spread-out kitchen will mean additional labor hours needed and a lot of wasted steps for the employees. The more compact kitchen with efficiently arranged equipment will save in cost of building and later in labor cost.

Number of Serving Lines.—One serving line will require from one to three people serving the food, depending on the menu, and a cashier. Two lines may require twice the number of people to cover the stations at serving time. In order to have the number of people needed at serving time, some employees may work two or four hours only when needed.

Experience and Training of Employees.—The training and years experience of the employees will have an influence on productivity. However, perhaps "training" of employees rather than "experience" is more important because the employee's prior experience may have involved inefficient work methods.

Supervision.—The ability of the manager to assign duties and train the employees will determine staff needed.

Using Disposables or Washing Dishes.—When all disposables are used, the labor hours needed should be approximately one-half labor hour less per 100 lunches than would be needed if dishes are washed. If the amount of labor cannot be reduced proportionately as the cost of disposables increase, an unbalanced budget may result.

The guidelines published by many of the States' school foodservices shown an average of 13 to 16 meals per man-hour. West, Wood, Harger, and Shugart (1977) recommend 12 to 14 lunches per man-hour. Wynn (1973) in Broward County (Fla.) has found that the positive approach of "how many meals can we produce with a certain number of labor hours?" has obtained very high productivity. The county averages 16 meals per labor hour and has set 12 meals per labor hour as their minimum goal in schools using a dish machine and 13 meals per labor hour in schools using disposables. Training has increased their productivity, also.

With wages and fringe benefits costs having increased threefold in the last 10 yr, it is essential to increase productivity with the use of some convenience food items and labor-saving equipment. The following formula for staffing has worked successfully in hundreds of school foodservices (Table 3.1). It is proposed here for a self-contained unit, where the

TABLE 3.1. STAFFING GUIDELINES

No. Lunches Served[1]	Meals Per Labor Hr	Total Hrs
Up to 100	9½	9−11
101−150	10	10−15
151−200	11	15−17
201−250	12	17−20
251−300	13	20−22
301−350	14	22−25
351−400	14	25−29
401−450	14	29−32
451−500	14	32−35
501−550	15	35−36
551−600	15	36−40
601−700	16	40−43
701−800	16	43−50
801+	18	50+

[1]This staffing formula does not include hours for breakfast, a la carte, or dinner.

menu choice is limited, some labor-saving devices are available, dish-washing is done, some baking of bread is done on the premises while some is purchased.

Distribution of Labor Hours

The distribution of the labor hours throughout the work day with sufficient number of people at serving time means that the labor hours will be assigned according to need. A combination of part-time and full-time workers is usually the most efficient way of using labor hours. One-meal-a-day school foodservices do not need cooks and bakers for 8 hr. It may be necessary for the manager of a large school foodservice to work 8 hr per day, but seldom is any other employee needed for more than 6 hr. The productivity of foodservice workers is greater for the first 6 hr and declines after that. Also, school foodservices in most of the country draw their labor force from "housewife-mothers" who make excellent workers, but who may want a job that will enable them to be home when their children get home from school. Those female employees who are totally self-supporting will want and probably need more hours. Students have been successfully used in many school districts at serving time. With increased energy cost many of the adult working force will not come to work for 2 hr. High school students can work, if class schedule permits, 1 or 2 hr and be paid accordingly, as in Las Vegas, Nev.

Breaking down the labor hours and distributing them wisely over the work day will require some experimenting and adjusting of employee time of arriving for work and leaving. Wynn (1973) has worked out high productivity on the assumption that in an elementary school "no one except the manager needs to arrive more than 3 hr before serving time."

In distributing the hours, the number of employees needed at serving time should be decided first. For example: in a school cafeteria serving 300 lunches per day, at serving time 2 employees are needed to serve, one cashier, dish machine operator, and 1 person backing up the line—4 to 5 people. According to the staffing guide above, this size operation would be entitled to 20−22 hr of labor (see also Table 3.2).

An operation that serves 600 lunches would be staffed with 36 to 40 labor hours according to the staffing guide. If the school had two serving lines with three lunch periods (11:30, 12:00, and 12:30), the distribution of hours could be as shown in Table 3.3. The 6 hr assigned to the cook is needed in this size operation. It is questionable whether the 3½ hr before serving time is needed; however, with the serving periods starting at 11:30, it is suggested that the employees eat their lunch before serving.

TABLE 3.2. STAFFING GUIDE FOR SCHOOL CAFETERIA SERVING 300 STUDENTS

Position	Hr
Manager-cashier	6½
Cook (backup line)	6[1]
Baker (serve on line)	5[1]
Dishmachine operator and serve on line	3½
	21

[1]Fifteen minutes for break is included in this time. The employees eat lunch on their own time.

TABLE 3.3. STAFFING GUIDE FOR SCHOOL CAFETERIA SERVING 600

Position	Arrival/Departure	Total Hr	At Serving Time
Manager	7:30−3:00	6½[1]	Supervision
Cook	8:00−2:30	6[1]	Cashier line I
Assistant Cook	8:30−2:30	5½[1]	Serving line II
Baker	8:30−2:30	5½[1]	Serving line II
Salad, etc.	9:00−2:00	4½[1]	Serving line I
Desserts	9:30−2:30	4½[1]	Serving line I
Dishroom	11:00−2:30	3½[1]	Backup line
Cashier	11:15−1:15	2	Cashier line II
		38	

[1]Fifteen minutes for break is included in this time. The employees eat on their own time (thirty minutes allowed).

School foodservices should be conscious of how much time is spent in preparation and cleanup. The more skilled employees should be utilized in preparation, using the less skilled employees for cleanup. Figure 3.1 shows how Wynn (1973) distributed the labor hours in an elementary school and was able to produce 15 to 15½ meals per labor hour.

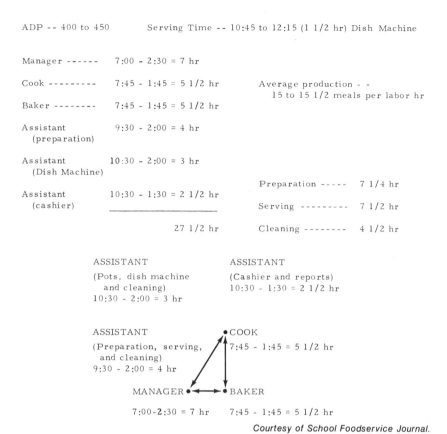

ADP -- 400 to 450   Serving Time -- 10:45 to 12:15 (1 1/2 hr) Dish Machine

Manager ------   7:00 - 2:30 = 7 hr

Cook ---------   7:45 - 1:45 = 5 1/2 hr   Average production - -
                                                        15 to 15 1/2 meals per labor hr
Baker --------   7:45 - 1:45 = 5 1/2 hr

Assistant   9:30 - 2:00 = 4 hr
 (preparation)

Assistant   10:30 - 2:00 = 3 hr
 (Dish Machine)
                                                        Preparation -----   7 1/4 hr
Assistant   10:30 - 1:30 = 2 1/2 hr
 (cashier)   _____   Serving ---------   7 1/2 hr

                                       27 1/2 hr   Cleaning --------   4 1/2 hr

                ASSISTANT   ASSISTANT
                (Pots, dish machine   (Cashier and reports)
                 and cleaning)   10:30 - 1:30 = 2 1/2 hr
                10:30 - 2:00 = 3 hr

                ASSISTANT   ●COOK
                (Preparation, serving, 7:45 - 1:45 = 5 1/2 hr
                 and cleaning)
                9:30 - 2:00 = 4 hr
                        MANAGER ●◄─────►● BAKER

                7:00-2:30 = 7 hr   7:45 - 1:45 = 5 1/2 hr

Courtesy of School Foodservice Journal.

FIG. 3.1. DISTRIBUTION OF LABOR HOURS IN AN ELEMENTARY SCHOOL

Foodservices serving under 200 meals with no additional income from a la carte will run labor cost taking up over 35% of the income. In most cases they should be satellited or co-managed. The larger the operation the greater the productivity should be. Centralized preparation kitchen will have higher productivity as the volume increases and the labor-saving equipment is made available, as illustrated in Los Angeles (CA) and Corpus Christi (TX), where centralized preparation is taken a step further. The food is pre-plated in the central kitchen eliminating the need for as many labor hours in the kitchen where the food is to be served.

LABOR COST

The labor cost in a foodservice where food is being prepared on-site and served with use of limited convenience foods and few disposables should average between 30 and 35% of the income. As pointed out previously, the more convenience foods and disposables used, the lower the percentage of income that can be spent on labor. The staffing formula and the labor cost must be correlated. How much will it cost to staff according to the formula in Table 3.1? It will depend on the wages and fringe benefits paid. In order to determine if the staffing formula is within the labor cost that can be afforded, multiply the anticipated income by 30% to obtain the dollars available. Take the average wages per hour and multiply by the number of labor hours (from the staffing formula). Does this figure compare with the 30 to 35% of the anticipated income? See the following example.

STAFFING FORMULA AND THE PERCENTAGE
OF LABOR COST COMPARISON

Anticipated Income Per Day:
Elementary School Serving 300 lunches, charging 60¢ per lunch

250 pd. lunches @ $0.60 .... $150.00		
50 free lunches @ $0.80 Federal .	40.00	
50 free lunches @ $0.10 State ...	5.00	
300 lunches @ $0.19 Federal	57.00	
Value of USDA Donated Food @		
$0.15 per child lunch (300)	45.00	
10 adult lunches @ $1.25	12.50	
	‾‾‾‾‾	
Anticipated Income per day	$309.50	$309.50
Labor cost at 30−35%	× .30	× .35
	‾‾‾‾‾	‾‾‾‾‾
Available for labor	$ 92.85	$108.33

If staffed with 21 labor hr and the average wages are $3.85 plus 25% fringe benefits, labor cost would be:

$3.85 $80.85
× 21   × .25
‾‾‾‾‾   ‾‾‾‾‾
$80.85 $20.21 (fringe benefits)
+ 20.21
‾‾‾‾‾
$101.06 Labor Cost

A LA CARTE STAFFING

Many of the secondary schools and some elementary schools sell food separately or in addition to the regular meals. Staffing for a la carte preparation and serving varies depending on the amount of service offered and preparation to be done. If the foods being sold a la carte are prepared on premises, including the baking, the labor needs will be greater and the labor cost higher. The food cost will be lower than it will be if prepared items are bought and sold. Two different methods may be used to arrive at a staffing. Using a labor cost of 20 to 35% of the income is workable in some situations. Use 20% of the income for labor cost when the food is all prepared items and requires no preparation, only recording and selling. Thirty percent labor cost can be used when some preparation is required and the percentage will increase as the food cost decreases and the amount of labor needed increases. For example:

$220 a la carte income (sale for the day)
$220 × 0.30 (30%) = $66.00 can be spent on labor

To determine how many hours can be used, divide the $66.00 by the average wages and fringe benefits paid:

$66.00 ÷ $4.20 per hr = 15.7 hr

A school serving 300 Type A lunches plus $220 a la carte would be staffed with:

21 hr
15
---
36 hr

Another method to use is to convert all food sales (in addition to regular lunches) to the equivalent of work as preparing the lunches (Table 3.4). This means that the staffing is done on the basis of meals per labor hour as previously discussed (Table 3.1). The formula of $1.25 equal to 1 meal is based on the time needed in preparing and serving a la carte foods of $1.25 sales. The $1.25 sales take approximately the same amount of time to prepare and serve as one lunch. This formula should be worked out to fit the individual situation. If the a la carte or other food sales are purchased prepared items, then the labor needs will be less. The above formula is with some preparation being done in the kitchen, such as, making salads, hot sandwiches, soup, and mixing juices. If the menu is extensive with many choices, additional labor will be needed.

TABLE 3.4. CONVERT ALL FOOD SALES TO MEALS

$ 1.25	1 lunch
25.00	20 lunches
50.00	40 lunches
75.00	60 lunches
100.00	80 lunches
110.00	88 lunches

BREAKFAST STAFFING

The amount of labor needed will depend on number served and how much preparation is necessary (Table 3.5). With the "engineered cake" and ½ pt of milk menu hardly any labor is needed. Volunteer labor should certainly be used. Labor cost can be kept at a minimum by preparing foods which can be prepared with the lunch the day before. By dovetailing the preparation and cleanup with that of the lunch, the labor needs will be less. Using disposables versus dishwashing may be to an advantage if the labor is needed for only a short time and is unavailable for that short a time.

With a relatively simple breakfast such as the Federal guidelines would provide (½ pt milk, ½ cup fruit or vegetable or fruit juice or vegetable juice, and serving of cereal or bread with protein-rich foods when budget will allow) the staffing that seems to work is based on 20 to 30 meals per labor hour.

TABLE 3.5. BREAKFAST STAFFING

No. Breakfasts	No. Labor Hr	No. Persons Assigned	Hr Breakdown Per Person
Up to 20	1	1	1
30	1½	1	1
40	2	2	1½
			½
50	2½	2	1
			1½
75	3	2	1½
			1½
100	4	3	1½
			1½
			1
125	5	3	2
			2
			1
150	5−6	3	2
			2
			1−2

Scheduling of Work

With careful planning and preparation, ½ to ¾ hr should be adequate for preparing most breakfasts for serving. Serving usually takes less than 15 min with cleanup requiring ½ to 1½ hr. An example of the scheduling of time is below:

Menu

Orange Juice ½ cup
Scrambled Egg 1
Cinnamon Toast 1 slice
Milk   ½ pt

No. Serving: 50
Employees: 1½ hr employee (7:30 to 9:00) In charge of breakfast
           1 hr employee (7:45 to 8:45)   Assistant

Time	Person in Charge of Breakfast	Assistant
7:30	Turn oven on Pour juice in disposable cups	
7:45	Prepare scrambled eggs	Prepare cinnamon toast
8:00	Set up line	Set up line
8:10	Serve breakfast	Serve breakfast
8:25	Cleanup	Cleanup Portion jelly for tomorrow
8:45	Prepare records and reports	

The a la carte sale of juice, sweet rolls, cereal, milk, and other items on the menu, particularly in the secondary schools, can add to the income. Usually the labor hours assigned for breakfast are added to a part-time employee's hours; for example, a 4-hr employee may be assigned one additional hour for breakfast and become a 5-hr employee. Many foodservices are able to add the preparing, serving, and cleaning up for the breakfast without increasing labor hours. If the foodservice is operating at a deficit or over-staffed, this should certainly be considered. Also, this is a way of increasing productivity and encouraging better use of employees' time. Time and motion economy, pre-preparation, dovetailing (combining jobs), and good planning will result in a smooth operation with high productivity.

Any foodservice with a reasonably smooth operation will adjust to the breakfast program with little or no problems with the above staffing formula.

RECRUITING

Recruiting is best done on a continuous basis. Preparing for the vacancy and being selective, rather than being forced to take less than the desired qualified person because of immediate needs, is good personnel management. It may be a problem to find labor in one area, and thus there is a greater need for recruiting. In order to recruit, job descriptions are needed (see Ch. 2) with required minimum standards for employment.

Making people interested in the job, in the organization, in foodservice, and being known as a good employer can go a long ways toward self-perpetual recruiting. Making the job titles more appealing in sound can increase the desirability of the job. "Cafeteria hostess," "dish machine operator," and "cafeteria aid or assistant," have more appeal than "kitchen helper," "dishwasher," "pot washer," and "kitchen worker." Good public relations are also important for the foodservice. A story on the foodservice, concerning the valuable service provided to a community's children, employees' accomplishments, or other publicity of this nature, carried in a local newspaper can make people interested and the job more appealing. Some effective ways of recruiting follow.

(1) Internal recruitment is good for employee morale. Whenever a position is available, it should be announced so that employees of the foodservice have a chance to ask for the advancements. The immediate supervisor should encourage good workers to advance and take a better position. Going outside to get the person when there are qualified people within will kill incentive.

(2) Employees can be a source of finding people who want a job. They can spread the news to friends, neighbors, and relatives. However, relatives of employees should not be employed in the same cafeteria.

(3) Advertising through the newspaper, trade journals, notices in windows, notices in public places, and over radio or television can get results. Many local papers and ratio stations will carry public service announcements free of charge.

(4) Recruiting at high schools, vocational schools, and colleges can be very effective. Many schools have placement offices or a school newspaper, which can be used for recruiting. In some cases, the work can be instructional in nature and count toward laboratory experiences in vocational training programs.

Personnel management should have potential managers, cooks, and bakers lined up for promotion. The position of assistant manager can be utilized to train someone for management. When a vacancy comes up, management should not desperately have to pick an untrained replacement. Training programs should consist of continual courses for people interested in management, with on-the-job-training under the direction of a good manager until a vacancy occurs. Most skilled cooks and bakers can be utilized to teach others their skills. This prepares someone to assist them, to take their place if they are sick, and have someone ready for promotion when the opening occurs. Training for promotion can often be done on an employee's own time. Adult education schools are often eager to help sponsor classes in this area. Recruiting outstanding people into the foodservice will result in a better program. Recruiting should mean looking ahead and having replacements ready.

APPLICATION AND INTERVIEW

The written application is mandatory regardless of the size of the operation. The application form should be simple and ask only questions that are pertinent, legal, and useful to the employer. Figure 3.2 shows a very simple form of application.

Applications usually ask for *references*, and checking these references can be very valuable. It can help in making a better choice when hiring. If references are not checked, an application has lost much of its value. References are often checked by telephone, in which case a few simple questions will probably be adequate, as to honesty, attendance and punctuality, length of employment with company, quality of services, and reason for leaving.

Turnover is expensive and careful hiring practices can cut down the amount of turnover. A *personal interview* with an applicant provides the applicant with a chance to see if he wants the job and would like working for this foodservice, and most importantly it gives management an opportunity to evaluate the applicant's attitudes, interest, ability, and adjustability to the other employees with whom he would work. The interview can help significantly in the selection of a qualified person. When interviewing for a head cook or baker, a test involving the interpretation of a recipe can help determine knowledge of food preparation, as well as the ability to read and write.

An interviewer should keep in mind the two purposes of the interview before employment, and they are (1) to introduce the applicant to the school foodservice, kind of work, pay scale, fringe benefits, hours, personal leave, etc.; (2) and to enable the interviewer to evaluate the applicant as to whether or not he or she is qualified to do the job, would fit into the organization, and has the appropriate attitude toward the work. The objective of the interview when choosing management for a foodservice is a little more complex. The interviewer is then interested in the

CLASSIFIED EMPLOYMENT BRANCH	DO NOT WRITE IN THIS SPACE
LOS ANGELES UNIFIED SCHOOL DISTRICT	
APPLICATION	

EXACT NAME OF JOB YOU ARE APPLYING FOR

PLEASE ANSWER EVERY QUESTION BELOW. RETURN THE APPLICATION AS SOON AS YOU HAVE COMPLETED IT. ASK FOR HELP IN COMPLETING THE APPLICATION IF YOU NEED IT. PRINT IN INK OR TYPE.   Your Social Security Number will be used for employment related identification purposes only.

DATE	YOUR STREET ADDRESS	CITY	ZIP CODE

PHONE NUMBERS State Area Code (If not 213):	HOME	BUSINESS	SOCIAL SECURITY NUMBER

EDUCATION (CIRCLE HIGHEST GRADE COMPLETED)   7   8   9   10   11   12   AA   BA-BS   MA-MS

DATE COMPLETED

What other training or education have you had which might help you on this job?
For example: Have you taken any special courses? Do you speak, read, or write a language other than English?

WORK EXPERIENCE (PAID AND UNPAID) Start with the job you have now, or your last job, if you are not working now.
Check (√) this box ☐ If you do not want us to contact your present supervisor.

1. EMPLOYER	ADDRESS	EMPLOYMENT DATES FROM: TO:

YOUR JOB TITLE AND DUTIES

YOUR SUPERVISOR'S NAME	CHECK (√) ONE:	☐ FULL-TIME ☐ PART-TIME

2. EMPLOYER	ADDRESS	EMPLOYMENT DATES FROM: TO:

YOUR JOB TITLE AND DUTIES

YOUR SUPERVISOR'S NAME	CHECK (√) ONE:	☐ FULL-TIME ☐ PART-TIME

3. EMPLOYER	ADDRESS	EMPLOYMENT DATES FROM: TO:

YOUR JOB TITLE AND DUTIES

YOUR SUPERVISOR'S NAME	CHECK (√) ONE:	☐ FULL-TIME ☐ PART-TIME

Have you ever taken a test for a job with the Los Angeles Unified School District? ☐ Yes ☐ No
If yes, was the test on a tape recorder? ☐ Yes ☐ No
If the test is given in more than one place, (√) check the place you'd rather take it.
☐ South-Central L. A.   ☐ East L. A.   ☐ Harbor Area   ☐ West L. A.   ☐ Central L. A.   ☐ San Fernando Valley   ☐ Pacoima Area

IF YOU HAVE EVER WORKED FOR THE LOS ANGELES UNIFIED SCHOOL DISTRICT, COMPLETE THE FOLLOWING:

YOUR EMPLOYEE NUMBER	PRESENT OR LAST JOB TITLE	EMPLOYMENT DATES FROM: TO:

WHERE DID YOU WORK?	YOUR NAME WHEN YOU WORKED FOR US, IF DIFFERENT

IF YOU ARE NOT NOW EMPLOYED BY THE LOS ANGELES UNIFIED SCHOOL DISTRICT STATE REASON FOR LEAVING

ALL OF THE ANSWERS ON THIS APPLICATION ARE TRUE
TO THE BEST OF MY KNOWLEDGE   (SIGNATURE) ➡

DO NOT WRITE BELOW THIS LINE

PRINT YOUR NAME HERE   LAST   FIRST   MIDDLE (MAIDEN)

Courtesy of Los Angeles Unified School District, School Foodservice.

FIG. 3.2. SAMPLE APPLICATION FOR EMPLOYMENT

ability of this person to direct others, his or her knowledge of the overall foodservice, personality, characteristics important to the job, and overall qualifications. Two or more persons interviewing an applicant, particularly for management, is suggested; then a pooled judgment is possible and usually more reliable.

Conducting an Interview

Interviews should be conducted in privacy without interruptions, in a pleasant, comfortable situation. Since the applicant may be nervous, an "ice breaking" question of mutual interest and unrelated to the job will help relax the applicant. The interviewer should be in charge of the interview. Questions are to get the person talking and most questions should require more than a yes or no answer. Some typical questions that can be used in interviewing an applicant are:

(1) Have you had any experience in cooking and serving food to large numbers of people? Do you like to cook?
(2) What do you see yourself doing five years from now?
(3) How would you describe yourself?
(4) What really motivates you to do your best?
(5) Why should I hire you? What do you think you will contribute to the program?
(6) How do you work under pressure?
(7) Why do you want to work for school foodservice?
(8) Where have you worked before? Which jobs did you like best? Which did you like least? Why? If no previous experience, you may relate back to high school, and ask, "What was your best subject"?
(9) Do you know of anything that will prevent you from being at work regularly and on time?
(10) Does our starting salary meet your current needs?
(11) What courses have you taken in high school or college pertaining to foodservice?
(12) Do you have any questions about the job?

Questions should be limited to those that are relevant and legal. The Equal Opportunity Law (Title VII of the Civil Rights Act of 1964) prohibits an employer from discriminating against job applicants because of race, color, sex, religion or national origin. Questions related to political beliefs, age, marital status, dependent status, sexual preference and handicaps which are not job restrictive should not be asked. The employer could be subject to a discrimination complaint. A conscious attempt should be made to hire, at all levels of the organization, employees who are representative of the sex and ethnic balance of the community's labor force.

The written application and the personal interview may be sufficient for a supervisory position where past experience can be checked and the educational background can be evaluated through college transcripts. Written tests are an added tool for evaluating a person's qualifications and ability for management. Such a test should question basic knowledge needed for carrying out the job. The overall qualifications the interviewer is looking for with the application, references, test and interview include:

(1) Physical—good health, not overweight, walks easily, good sight and hearing; someone who can work at the speed desired, free from infectious diseases and skin conditions. (These are all best determined through a physical examination.)

(2) Education—ability to read, write, and comprehend simple directions are essential for all positions in foodservice. The greater the responsibility, the more education desirable.

(3) Personal appearance—clean, well-groomed, cheerful, direct, alert, and interest in the work offered.

When there are a number of applicants for a position, the evaluation of the interview, the application, the references, and the test become more important. In all fairness to the applicants, these tools for evaluation should be weighed on the same scale. A rating chart may be very helpful. Assign a numerical rating to each qualification, such as: education—1 point for less than 6th grade education, 2 points for 6th to 9th grade education, 3 points for 10th to 12th grade education, 4 points for high school diploma, 5 points 1 year college, 6 points 2 yr college, 7 points 3 yr college, 8 points bachelor's degree, etc.

EMPLOYMENT

Contracts

Employees feel much more secure and more responsible when they have a signed contract. However, most school district simply notify the employees of their assignment and salary for a coming year with a specified time to notify if an employee does not plan to accept the position. Contracts in the true sense of the word are uncommon. Civil service procedures do protect the employee.

Performance Review

The first four to six months of employment may be a probationary period in which the worker is evaluated and at the end of this predetermined period, the employee is given a written evaluation. (Fig. 3.3) It is determined by this evaluation whether the employee is terminated, given an extended probationary period if in doubt, or made a permanent employee. The first evaluation or performance review is the most important; however, another evaluation should be done at the end of four to six more months and yearly thereafter. The task of rating an employee is very difficult and can be unpleasant. It is easier to give a good or excellent rating to all than it is to tell someone they are not doing a job well. Good management has to face this responsibility because the entire operation suffers if one employee is not doing his/her share or is not doing the job well. The performance rating can be very valuable and should be carefully done and written with the employee fully aware of the evaluation. The employee's signature and the evaluater's signature should appear on the evaluation.

The performance review or evaluation should be used in determining salary increases, promoting, transferring, determining lay-offs, and dismissals. Too often, length of service is the basis for promotion. The ability of the person, not his age or years of service, will determine the success of the operation.

Performance of managers and supervisors should be reviewed and evaulated too. They are appraised on entirely different standards than other employees. The manager and supervisor should be appraised on the quality of work and quantity of work they get done through others. Some means of measuring would be:

(1) Employee turnover, problems with employees, morale of employees who work under the person.
(2) Standards of sanitation—health department checks.
(3) Quality of food and service—customer satisfaction and income, percent of participation.
(4) Profit and loss of the foodservice—sound financial situation.
(5) Personal appearance, public relations.
(6) Absenteeism and tardiness.
(7) Efficiency in carrying out the rules and regulations of the system, and duties of the job.

Personnel Policies

Communication is the single most important way of preventing misunderstandings and avoiding unhappy employees. The policies of the organization should be known to the employees. A written handbook is desirable and can prevent misinformation. The handbook does not have to be an elaborate publication but it should inform the employees of the

PERFORMANCE EVALUATION FOR CAFETERIA MANAGERS
FOOD SERVICES BRANCH — LOS ANGELES UNIFIED SCHOOL DISTRICT

Last Name	First Name	Employee Number

Job Title	School or Other Work Location

Report for .... to :... Indicate dates during which employee is being evaluated.
(Date)   (Date)

If "Below Work Performance Standards" is checked, please see Paragraph 5 on the reverse side of this form.

Exceeds Work Performance Standards
Meets Work Performance Standards
Below Work Performance Standards

Comments Made by Supervisor

1. SUPERVISORY ABILITY

a. Organizing and scheduling staff work   a. ☐ ☐ ☐
b. Training and instructing staff   b. ☐ ☐ ☐
c. Dealing with staff fairly and impartially c. ☐ ☐ ☐
d. Maintaining staff adherence to rules
   and regulations   d. ☐ ☐ ☐
e. Ensuring use of standard recipes and
   menus, meal component requirements,
   and principles of good nutrition   e. ☐ ☐ ☐
f. Ensuring use of approved price and
   portion schedules   f. ☐ ☐ ☐
g. Maintaining attractive food appearance
   and merchandising   g. ☐ ☐ ☐
h. Menu planning, including student and
   community involvement   h. ☐ ☐ ☐
i. Ordering, storing and inventorying of
   food supplies   i. ☐ ☐ ☐
j. Maintaining records, reports, and monetary and ticket controls   j. ☐ ☐ ☐
k. Ensuring good housekeeping, sanitary
   and safety practices   k. ☐ ☐ ☐
l. Controlling labor and food costs   l. ☐ ☐ ☐
m. Maintaining cafeteria security   m. ☐ ☐ ☐
n. Assuring proper equipment use and
   energy conservation   n. ☐ ☐ ☐

2. WORK HABITS

a. Maintaining a good attendance and
   punctuality record   a. ☐ ☐ ☐
b. Complying with oral and written
   instructions   b. ☐ ☐ ☐
c. Keeping supervisors informed of major
   work problems   c. ☐ ☐ ☐
d. Adaptability to emergencies and new
   situations   d. ☐ ☐ ☐
e. Willingness to undertake additional
   needed training   e. ☐ ☐ ☐

3. RELATIONSHIPS WITH OTHERS

a. Other classified employees, faculty, and
   supervisors   a. ☐ ☐ ☐
b. Pupils   b. ☐ ☐ ☐
c. Parents and community representatives   c. ☐ ☐ ☐

4. OVERALL WORK PERFORMANCE

It is understood that, in signing the Performance
Evaluation Form, the employee acknowledges having
seen and discussed the report. The employee's signature does not necessarily imply agreement with the
conclusions of the supervisor. If desired, the employee
may attach a written statement.

Signature of Site Administrator   Date

Signature of Area Food Services Supervisor   Date

Signature of Employee

(OVER)

INSTRUCTIONS FOR PREPARING PERFORMANCE EVALUATION FORMS
FOR CAFETERIA MANAGERS

1. An evaluation must be completed and discussed with each permanent employee at least once a year, prior to the closing of the regular school year in June.

2. The evaluation is to be completed by the employee's immediate supervisor *and* technical supervisor. In most cases, this is the site administrator in charge of the cafeteria and the school's Area Food Services Supervisor. The evaluation can be prepared and served jointly or separately, depending upon the wishes of the site administrator.

3. The employee's evaluation is recorded by placing a check mark (**V**) in the appropriate box opposite the factor being evaluated. Evaluations are to be based on observation or knowledge, and not on unsubstantiated or undocumented charges or rumors. No evaluation may be based on derogatory materials in the employee's personnel file unless the employee has been given prior notice of and an opportunity to review and attach his or her comments to such material.

The supervisor shall:

a. Discuss the written evaluation with the employee.

b. Review with the employee the duties of his/her current job, job performance standards, and how well the employee meets those standards.

c. Sign the performance evaluation form and obtain the signature of the employee or a witness.

d. Give the employee a copy of the completed form. If the employee has left the work location, forward the employee's copy to the local Classified Personnel Office, requesting that it be mailed to the employee.

e. Send the original copy of the performance evaluation to the Classified Selection Section, Business Services Center, by school mail.

f. Retain the triplicate copy for school files.

USE OF COLUMNS AND ADDITIONAL FORMS

4. **Meets or Exceeds Work Performance Standards.** A check in either of these columns indicates that the employee's work is satisfactory or better. If the employee's work is truly exceptional and worthy of special notice and commendation, a Notice of Outstanding Work Performance (Form 80.21) should be used.

5. **Below Work Performance Standards.** If any factor is rated below work performance standards, the following must be included in the **Comments** box:

a. A statement of the problem or concern.

b. The desired improvement and suggestions on how to improve.

Continued failure of the employee to show improvement should lead to preparation of a Notice of Unsatisfactory Service (Form 5302).

6. An employee who disagrees with the evaluation should contact the Head Office of the Food Services Branch.

Courtesy of Los Angeles Unified School District, School Foodservice.

FIG. 3.3. PERFORMANCE EVALUATION FOR FOOD SERVICES MANAGERS

policies for (1) promotion, (2) termination, (3) leaves of absence, (4) pay scale, (5) overtime pay, (6) calendar with holidays, (7) pay periods, (8) personal or annual leave, (9) sick leave, (10) health benefits, (11) insurances, (12) workmen's compensation, (13) transfer policy, (14) demotions, (15) grievances, (16) dress code, (17) health certificate or tuberculosis test requirements, (18) retirement, and any other policies or benefits that the employee would be interested in.

The pay scale should be comparable to other jobs in the community requiring similar skills. The State labor laws, the minimum wage laws, and local laws will influence the pay scale. Pay increases should be worked out in steps and grades to give an incentive and to keep the morale of the employees high. Most employees want to feel they are being paid what the other person is being paid for the same job with the same or comparable qualifications. People are happier or more content with their jobs if they know what kind of raise to expect, what they have to do to obtain it, and when they can expect to obtain it.

A manager of a foodservice should be paid on the basis of how many meals served, the size of the operation, years of experience, formal education completed, number of State-approved courses complete, and performance. Some foodservice units have used the total income of the operation to determine the rate of pay a manager will receive. This should be correlated with the profit and the quality of the operation. Some school systems use the salary scales of the instructional staff for their manager's pay. Certainly if the manager has education equal to that of a teacher, the responsibility of manager warrants such a pay scale.

Personnel Records

The application, references, testing, and evaluation of the interview will all be a part of the employee's personnel record and this will grow with each performance review. Correspondence concerning the employee's work and any actions taken as to promoting, leaves of absence, etc., should become part of the record. This record should be kept for at least 10 yr after the employee has left for reference purpose. For management's convenience, an active personnel file should be made, possibly using an 8×5 in. card for pertinent information (Fig. 3.4).

Orientation of New Worker

The new employee is almost always ill-at-ease. He needs to be informed of the rules and know what is expected of him. An informative talk with the manager should let the worker know the hours of work, coffee breaks,

Name_____ S. S. Number_____

Home Address_____ Telephone No._____

_____

Date Employed_____ Position_____

Rate of Pay_____ Place Assigned_____

Raises and Changes:

Date	Salary Increase	Step/Grade Change	Place of Assignment

Leave of Absence_____ Returned_____

Termination_____ Reason _____

Comments:

FIG. 3.4. SAMPLE PERSONNEL RECORD THAT CAN BE KEPT ON 5 × 8 IN. CARDS
FOR QUICK, EASY REFERENCE ON ALL ACTIVE PERSONNEL

lunch breaks, rules and regulations, use of the time sheet, whom he is responsible to and whom he can ask questions of, location of washroom and toilet facilities, and the philosophy of the foodservice. An introduction to the fellow workers and a friendly reception from them should be expected. The new worker should be shown the kitchen, storerooms, dining room, and given a tour of the operation with explanations about the equipment. Any equipment that is dangerous and perhaps new to the employee should be explained and demonstrated and safety features pointed out. Systematic job training should begin at this point. Detailed work schedules (see Chap. 4) should be given to the worker and a step-by-step instructions of what he is to do and how. If the manager does not do the training, then the training should be planned and the employee put under the guidance of a well-trained employee.

The personnel handbook or policy manual should be explained to the new employee. A more detailed explanation and discussion of the foodservice, traditions, aims, and policies should be given the employee as the training period continues. The objective of this orientation period is to challenge his interest and encourage him in his learning.

TRAINING PROGRAMS

Management owes it to its employees to provide personal development. There are many advantages to be realized from good training programs, such as (1) Reduction in labor turnover; (2) Less absenteeism; (3) Fewer accidents; (4) Lower production costs; (5) Increase in good morale of employees; (6) Job satisfaction, less complaints and grievances; (7) Higher rate of productivity; (8) Better sanitation practices; (9) Lower food cost, less waste.

Group training saves time and the group acts as a stimulus. It is important to use well-trained teachers and not fellow workers. The group will accept a certain amount of instruction from a fellow worker but not much. An able instructor can stimulate and inspire the employee to want to learn. It is important to develop the individual as well as help him master routine skills.

The American School Food Service Association set certification standards which is operated under the School Food Service Foundation. It encourages the expansion of foodservice courses being offered. These standards are set as guides to each State for making the courses available, issuing certification and compensating the advancement. A few States have required certification programs. Since 1960, Mississippi's State Department of Education has required that all schools' managers hold a certification. Their certificates are valid for a period of 1 yr, but can be renewed for 3-yr periods by completing a Basic II Course of Study offered by the approved school lunch institute.

North Carolina's Dept. of Public Instruction has developed a series of six training courses in cooperation with the Department of Community Colleges. Instruction is presented via television with classroom instruction being provided by the community colleges and technical institutes throughout the State. The courses ar designed for 30 hr of instruction, and on completion the trainee is awarded a certificate from the institute. Pay increments are recommended to local boards of education. The State legislature passed a bill in 1971 which requires the local supervisor to attend one of the three supervisor's workshops sponsored by the State department yearly.

The State of California has made much available in the way of training their foodservice employees. Many other states offer similar training programs. Also, universities and colleges, adult education classes, and technical institutes offer school foodservice courses. An outstanding collection of materials—audio and visual aids—useful in teaching such courses is housed at the Food and Nutrition Information and Educational Materials Center, National Agriculture Library in Beltsville, Maryland.

In late 1970 Federal funds were made available to states and local districts through the Nutrition Education and Training Program (P.L. 95-166) for training of foodservice employees. The need for these funds was pointed out by the Inspector General's Office with the audits that were done in the late 1970s. The funds have made it possible for all states to offer training to their foodservice employee.

Promotions

Foodservice employees should expect opportunities for growth and reasonable chances for promotion. The possibility of promotion to a position that will pay more with more responsibility is an incentive to perform better. Therefore, fairness in promotions is essential. Merit is of prime importance in promotion; however, the length of service should be used when there is a choice between two people of equal qualifications and equal quality of performance. Midwest City-Del City School Foodservice (Okla.) promotes to a higher classification or an increased number of hours depending upon: job performance, tenure and training, willingness to work the number of hours and time of day required, and attitude toward job and ability to work with people.

PERSONNEL PROBLEMS

One person can be a very destructive force on group spirit. Management can hope by careful selection processes to select workers that will build morale and can work with others well. However, this is sometimes not the case. Experienced management is often able to observe symptoms of problems and forestall any serious difficulties with the staff. Upward and downward communication are the most important steps to keeping a smooth operation. When employees are informed and involved in decision-making, a feeling of belonging and togetherness will occur. When employees do have complaints, the manager should listen very carefully. If an argument has occurred between employees, it is usually advisable to let the employees get over their emotional upset and then gather all the facts from all individuals involved.

Personnel problems can often be prevented if there is

(1) a definite line of authority,
(2) a definite field of responsibility,
(3) work schedules,
(4) clear, concise instructions,
(5) adequate supervision
(6) good working conditions.

If a problem does arise, management should look at some ways of preventing it from happening again. Often it has happened because management has failed to discipline or correct one or more of the workers but rather "let it ride." Action should be taken, in the form of a talk with the employee about the problem, and what you expect him to do to correct it. Tardiness, frequent absences, wasting time, excessive talking, spreading rumors, gossiping, stealing, refusal to obey orders, drinking liquor or taking narcotics on the job or a hangover, and using foul language are varied actions that warrant the manager discussing the problem with an employee.

A mature manager should avoid losing his temper when handling these matters. Other pitfalls to avoid are idle threats, bluffing, using profanity, humiliating a worker in front of another, scolding a worker publicly, striking a worker, and being sarcastic, or apologetic.

Counseling

When an employee is not carrying out the duties of the job or when personnel problems are being caused by his action, it is the responsibility of the supervisor or manager to counsel the employee or discipline him in some way. Disciplining an employee may be done through: oral warning, demerits on the employee's record, a separate (isolated) job, less desirable work assignment, being sent home for the day, restricted chances for promotion, suspension or dismissal. The method used will depend on the seriousness of the situation and the policy of the operation. There are some points to remember when counseling an employee:

(1) Wait until you and the employee have had a chance to cool down if anger and excitement has been displayed.
(2) Counseling should take place in private. It is embarrassing to be reprimanded in front of other employees.
(3) If you criticize the employee for his performance, do not compare his performance with another employee's performance.
(4) Allow the employee an opportunity to tell his side of the incident or to explain why his performance has been as it has.
(5) Discuss ways of improving and changes that will need to be brought about.

A manager or supervisor owes the employee being counseled, as well as all the other employees, fair disciplinary measures. It is an important part of personnel management. Employees desire to work in a climate that encourages cooperation and high morale. One employee with an attitude of resentment, sullenness, or uncooperative behavior can destroy the morale of others and keep the whole group of employees upset. An unsigned employee survey might help an employer uncover the reasons for poor morale and personnel problems.

When counseling is necessary, an interview or talk with the employee should be the first step in solving the problem. He should be made aware of the problem and given a chance to give his side of the story. He should then be given time to improve. It may be advisable to put what action will be taken in writing.

Transfer

In a centralized school system a transfer of an employee from one unit to another may solve the problem. This is particularly true if a personality clash is the cause of the problem. Some people cannot work peacefully together. If the employee has references showing he is capable of being a good worker, the reason for his present problems should be analyzed to determine if a transfer is recommended. However, the employee should be made aware of why he is being transferred to another school and that he is being given another chance.

Demotion/Suspension

In some cases demotion of the person to a less important position may be the desired action. An employee should be warned of this possibility before the actual demotion is made. This method of discipline may be a possible solution if the employee does not take on the responsibilities of the position very well, or if he is unable to give orders to those under him satisfactorily.

Suspension or time off from the job without pay may be appropriate action for an employee with excessive absenteeism or tardiness. This may especially work well with younger employees, less mature employees.

Dismissal

Dismissal may be defined as when a person leaves a job involuntarily Studies have shown that the most frequent reasons for dismissal are inability to get along with others and unsatisfactory work. It is only natural that all people do not get along, and if there is a personality conflict, it is usually wise to make some type of change. Undesirable traits may be such that the person cannot work in a "people" oriented job and should be dismissed. It is only fair to an employee to give a warning if he is failing to perform his duties or if his attitude at work is unsatisfactory. A talk in private about this, with a chance for the employee to correct the problem, is good policy. The way an unsatisfied employee is treated, even if the other employees do not like him or think he should be kept, has an effect on the morale of the employees and may cause insecurity among them if they feel they may be dismissed without adequate warning.

For the personnel records, for future reference, and, just to be safe, the warning about unsatisfactory work and what is to be done to correct it and the time allowed for an outcome, should be in writing. The larger the system and the more employees, the more important this policy is. Dismissals are unpleasant, usually have a defensive air about them, and should be handled by a mature person.

Dismissals on the spot in the fit of anger should be avoided. If a manager has this authority he may act in an irrational way when angered. Reasons for dismissal should be written in the employee handbook. Listed below are some reasons for disciplinary action:

(1) Excessive absence and tardiness.
(2) Unsatisfactory performance and inability to perform the tasks assigned.
(3) Proven dishonesty.
(4) Conviction of a job-related crime.
(5) Insubordination, discourteous conduct, and disobedience.
(6) Drinking alcoholic beverages or taking narcotics on the job or being under the influence on the job.

 (7) Accepting gratuities from suppliers.
 (8) Violating administrative rules and regulations.
 (9) Immoral or unethical conduct that affects the work.
(10) Inability to work with others.

The dismissal should be put in a written notification form. The person should be given a final interview in which the reasons for his dismissal are reviewed. His strong points should also be brought out. If the employer feels he can recommend this person for another position he should be told this and perhaps helped in obtaining another position. He should have a chance to express himself and a right to appeal if he feels he has been treated unjustly.

Resignation

Resignation may be defined as when an employee voluntarily decides to give up his job. It is good administrative policy to require that resignations be submitted in writing when an employee decides to terminate his services. This written resignation will prevent any misunderstanding and will become a part of the employee's permanent personnel record. The person should be interviewed to find his reasons for leaving. If his reasons are related to the job, the employer should want to be aware of these reasons and correct them. Reasonable notice of resignation should be expected by the employer. "Reasonable" will depend on cause for resignation, but under ordinary circumstances a two-week notice is adequate.

UNIONS

Any foodservice is subject to becoming unionized. A Union will start a recruitment effort until it has gained the necessary membership to become recognized. As soon as management becomes aware of union activity in its organization it should prepare for the relationship with the union. When the union has sufficient members it will demand consultation or meetings with management. Each of the steps in the union establishing itself entail detailed procedures and legal requirements. Experts in the field can be of tremendous assistance and advise management on the legal aspects.

The union generally drafts a contract for management's consideration. This draft can include anything from already established practices to some outrageous non-negotiable items. Sooner or later contract negotiations come about. It is usually not advisable for the top management to be present during the actual negotiations, because once he has spoken the negotiations take on a degree of finality. Negotiations usually require some give and take by both sides to arrive at a document that both sides can live with.

The contract between the union and management is a binding agreement. The contract usually gives the union the right to protect the workers' right, help solve their problems, enforce the agreement (contract), recruit new members, and work with management. Management retains the right to manage, but with a contract, has another party looking over their shoulders. However, there can be advantages to a contract which does spell out who can do what and under what conditions. Dismissing someone who has broken the contract becomes a "business matter" and management may feel more action can be taken in this respect with the union.

Written reports and good records of actions becomes more important and essential with a union.

BIBLIOGRAPHY

BEACH, DALE S. 1975. Personnel: The Management of People at Work, 3rd Edition. Macmillan Publishing Co., N.Y.

BLACK, J.M. 1970. How to Get Results from Interviewing. McGraw-Hill Book Co., New York.

CLOYD, FRANCES. 1972. Guide to Foodservice Management. Institutions Volume Feeding Magazine, Chicago, Ill.

FLIPPO, EDWIN B. 1976. Principles of Personnel Management, 4th Edition. McGraw-Hill Co., New York.

HARRIES, JEFF O., JR. 1976. Managing People at Work. John Wiley & Sons, New York.

HUGHES, CHARLES L. 1976. Making Unions Unnecessary. Executive Enterprises Publications Co., New York.

KNOLL, ANNE POWELL. 1976. Food Service Management-A Human Relations Approach. McGraw-Hill Co., New York.

SIEGEL, JEROME. 1980. Personnel Testing Under EEO. AMACOM, American Management Assoc., New York.

SWEENEY, NEIL R. 1980. Managing People, Techniques for Food Service Operators. Lebhar-Friedman Books, New York.

U.S. DEPT. OF AGR. 1977. A Profile of School Food Service Personnel. U.S. Govt. Printing Office, Washington, D.C.

WEST, BESSIE B., LEVELLE WOOD, VIRGINA HARGER and GRACE SHUGART. 1977. Food Service in Institutions, 6th Edition. John Wiley & Sons, New York.

WYNN, JANE T. 1972. Staffing Broward County Style. School Foodservice J. 27, No. 1, 44–54.

ZABKA, J. R. 1971. Personnel Management and Human Relations. ITT Educational Service, New York.

4

Work Planning and Simplification

Organizing and planning the use of time are essential to efficiency. The purpose of personnel management should be effective utilization of human resources and personnel's time. The food industry is known to have very low productivity—40 to 45%. The employer is receiving only 40–45 percent useful labor. If the employee makes $4.00 an hour, it is really costing $8.75 for an hour of useful work. Planning the work with a conscious effort toward improved performance can increase the productivity and result in lower labor cost.

WORK SCHEDULES

Planning the work takes many forms—an understanding may exist as to what each one does and that everybody helps each other, or planning may be all verbal directions from the supervisor, or plans may be written. Written plans prevent misunderstanding and forgetting. A plan for work should be made regardless of the staff size, whether the staff consists of 2 or 22 people. A work schedule is a written assignment of jobs, assigning someone to do a specific job at a particular time until all jobs and duties are planned—daily, weekly, and monthly. Daily work schedules of the day's preparation are the heart of organizing time.

Why work schedules? The purposes are: to inform employees of the work to be done, to inform each employee of his responsibility, and to inform each employee of the sequence for each of his duties with time requirements. Some of the advantages of using work schedules are:

(1) Saves time and energy. Setting deadlines will encourage speed. If an employee is to make 50 sandwiches with no time limit, he probably will not finish as soon as the employee who is given a time limit.

(2) Makes the job easier, less effort. When an employee does know what to do next and doesn't have to constantly ask someone, he can do the job better and with less effort.

(3) Helps make a smooth, efficient operation. Efficiency is not obtained by close supervision.

(4) Helps employees develop a sense of security and pride in their work. When goals are set, the employee responsible can feel pride and accomplishment in fulfilling the goals, completing the job.

(5) Provides less possibility for a job being left incomplete or undone. It helps assure that the jobs will be done on time and that the food will be ready to serve on time. Jobs that are frequently left undone or forgotten are jobs such as putting the condiments out, cutting butter, and filling napkin and straw dispensers.

(6) Distributes responsibilities and workload more evenly. Helps prevent the possible complaint that "she doesn't do her share."

(7) Gives a manager more time to "manage" without the constant interruption of employees asking "what should I do now?"

Of course, work schedules do not assure that the quality of the food will be better or that the nutritional value will be improved, but they do help. They simply let all personnel know what jobs they are responsible for and when the work must be done.

A closely-staffed or correctly-staffed kitchen can seldom do the work without being organized and planned. Delegating duties and responsibilities are important parts of management. Work schedules should be prepared ahead.

The manager is responsible for preparing the work schedules, though the staff can help divide the duties. The assignment of work should always be done by someone who knows both the operation and the workers' abilities.

With cycle menus, work schedules can be made and reused with slight changes, saving considerable time. In a centralized school district, work schedules can be standardized to some extent and save considerable time for each manager. The manager, however, will still need to assign the person to the job.

Work schedules should include housekeeping and general cleaning. The cleaning chores that are done daily, weekly, and monthly can be standing assignments. Rotating of some of the undesirable jobs may be advisable in some cases. With cleaning jobs this works, but with jobs that require skills, rotating is obviously not recommended. Efficiency and improvement come from experience and conscious efforts to improve, whereas rotating the job tends to reduce pride and feeling of responsibility and does not afford the chance for improvement and increased efficiency. Preparation for the next day's menu should be included in the work schedule. Pre-preparation means always looking ahead, rather than working for just today—prepare, serve, and cleanup. When the menu requires little preparation, much time can be wasted unless the time is utilized in preparing for another day's menu. Work schedules should even the workload, so that the employee does not feel overworked on any particular day.

Preparing work schedules helps a manager to set the particular hours she needs a worker most. For example, a 4-hr worker may be needed for serving and cleanup more than during the morning preparation. Each person's work should be distributed evenly over the entire day or hours he works. A trained cook should be utilized with the less skilled person assisting and cleaning up. Rest periods should be distributed over the day with a short break after every 2 to 3 hr of work. A snack or lunch should be eaten before serving. The productivity from 11 o'clock on will be greater usually if the person has something to eat before he becomes too hungry. The advantages to eating lunch before serving lunch are:

(1) Food can be tasted for seasoning.
(2) Discourages nibbling, licking fingers, or eating while serving.
(3) Prevents the nervousness that sometimes results from being hungry.
(4) Less over-eating and feeling stuffed.
(5) Less likelihood of being sleepy and lacking energy in the afternoon.
(6) Shorter lunch breaks.

Perhaps the most difficult part of making written work schedules is putting a time limit on the jobs. Assigning too much work without giving sufficient time may result in the employee being under pressure and even defeated before getting started. The aim is to get the work done in an organized manner in the time that is necessary. A schedule should help the employee to look ahead and should assure that everything is ready when needed. The person assigned to a particular job should also be responsible for completing the job, whenever possible. Following through with the completion of the job will result in more pride in the work.

The following points should be considered in preparing work schedules:

(1) Assign a responsibility when possible to each person. Avoid assigning all "helping" jobs to a person.
(2) Determine when a person is needed on basis of job assignments.

(3) Distribute the work load over the hours to work.
(4) Put time limits on jobs. Avoid overloading one person and giving too little time within which to perform the tasks.
(5) Give instructions when possible on work schedules to prevent need for questions.

Types of Work Schedules

Many different types of work schedules and forms are used by various foodservices. The form shown in Fig. 4.1 is one. There are basically three types of work schedules: individual, daily unit, and organizational. Most managers do not have the time to prepare, on a daily basis, the detailed individual work schedules. Therefore this type, though very desirable, is recommended for new employees or when many changes are made in the daily procedure (Fig. 4.1).

The daily unit work schedule is recommended for most operations (Fig. 4.2). If the employees are trained and know generally their responsibilities and how to carry them out, this type of work schedule works beautifully. In a large operation where the employees are more specialized and the employee spends his time on basically the same job every day, it may not be necessary to use the individual or the daily unit work schedule. An organizational work schedule may be used with individual assignments made daily (Fig. 4.3). The organizational work schedule must be accompanied by daily assignments, or it will be of little value.

As a result of effective work-scheduling, many operations are able to cut labor cost. Also, food cost may be cut when an employee's time is utilized more effectively for making mixes, cookies, etc., rather than wasted. Effective organization means delegation of duties in such a way that manpower can be used more productively.

WORK SIMPLIFICATION

Perhaps no other industry needs work simplifications more than school foodservice. Foodservices on the institutional level have low productivity with much wasted effort and time. And yet, these people may be working too hard due to inefficient and difficult methods of performing the job. Productivity can be improved with work simplification by 25% easily and result in more being done by fewer people.

Work simplification is defined as a conscious effort to find the easiest, quickest, and simplest way to perform useful work by avoiding and eliminating wasted work. It does not mean working harder or necessarily faster but working smarter. It means eliminating the unnecessary. This may involve changing habits, equipment, materials, or arrangements.

Schedule for: Mary Dobson Hours: 8:00— 1:00

Serving time: 11:30, 12:00 Date: Monday, April 2

Position: Baker

Menu: Hamburgers on Bun
Tater Tots
Lettuce and Tomato Salad
Chocolate Cake
Milk

TIME	PREPARATION	NUMBER TO PREPARE FOR	RECIPE	DIRECTIONS
8:00	Prepare cake	250	C–28	2½ times recipe
9:00	Clean area			
9:30	Coffee break			
9:40	Make icing		C–26	2½ times recipe
10:15	Wash pots and pans			
10:30	Cut cake and ice			Cut cake 6 × 10, portion onto "ice cream square" dish
	Portion up			
11:00	Eat lunch			
11:20	Set up line with desserts			
11:30	Serve on line			
12:00	Serve on line			
12:20	Put fruit in refrigerator for tomorrow			4 cans fruit cocktail 3 cans sliced peaches 2 cans USDA pineapple tidbits
12:30	Wash dining room tables			
12:45	Clean milk cooler			

FIG. 4.1. SAMPLE INDIVIDUAL WORK SCHEDULE

MENU: Lasagne Casserole
Tossed Salad
Chilled Peach Halves
Buttered French Bread
Milk

TIME	MANAGER 7½ HR	6 HR ASSISTANT	5 HR ASSISTANT	4 HR ASSISTANT*
7:30—8:00	Make coffee or tea for teachers			
8:00—8:30	Help with lasagne sauce	Prepare lasagne		
8:30—9:00	Lunch count—Tickets		Dip up fruit and refrigerate	
9:00—9:30				
9:30—10:00	Teachers' salads		Wash vegetables for salad	
10:00—10:30	Cut bread and butter	Prepare bread crumbs for fried chicken tomorrow		Cut up vegetables for salad
10:30—11:00	Eat lunch—20 min	Eat lunch—20 min	Put out desserts	Set up line—napkins, straws dishes
11:00—11:30	11:15 Put food on steam table	Put food on steam table	Eat lunch—20 min	Mix salad for first lunch
11:30—12:00	Cashier	Serving Set up for next line	Wash pots and pans	Back up line Dishroom
12:00—12:30	Serving	Serving Set up for next line	Serving Help in dishroom	Back up line Dishroom
12:30—1:00	Serving	Serving Put away food	Cashier Help in dishroom	Back up line Dishroom
1:00—1:30	Count money—10 min break Help to clean tables	10 min break Clean tables	Cashier 10 min break	Eat lunch* (eat on own time)
1:30—2:00	Prepare reports	Cleanup	Clean steam table	Clean dishroom
2:00—2:30	Place orders			Help with kitchen cleanup
2:30—3:00	Take topping out of freezer and put in refrigerator for tomorrow			

FIG. 4.2. SAMPLE ELEMENTARY SCHOOL WORK SCHEDULE

Habits or routines play an important part in a worker's performance, and to perform in a way different than he is used to requires breaking the habit and replacing it with a new routine. It is not until the new routine becomes a habit that performance is at full efficiency. However, it may be easier at first for employees to continue the old pattern than try something new. In the home the housewife can use 5 to 10 min in preparing 2 sandwiches, and she has the time to pat the biscuits and put them onto the pan one at a time. To establish the routine of picking up a biscuit in each hand in a rhythmic way and place them on the pan will take practice and encouragement.

The increased productivity that can result from training employees in simplification can cut labor cost as much as 55%, ensure safer and better working conditions, lessen the employees' fatigue, make the quality of production better and more uniform, and result in higher wages.

MOTION AND TIME ECONOMY

The principles of motion economy as given by Barnes (1968) and by Kazarian (1969) should be utilized more for increasing productivity. Some principles of motion have been drawn from Barnes and Kazarian and examples of how they can be applied to school foodservice are given.

Motion economy can be generally divided into three categories: (1) Hand and body motions; (2) Work process or sequence; (3) Design of tools, equipment, and work place.

(1) Both hands should do useful work at the same time when possible.
Examples:
  (a) Panning rolls. Pick up a roll in each hand and put onto the pan.
  (b) Racking dishes. Pick up a plate in each hand to put into the dishwashing racks. Use both hands to take dishes out of the racks and stack.
  (c) Serving the line. Pick plate up with one hand and bring mid-way to meet the food that has been dipped or picked up by the other hand. Put the fastest person at the beginning of the serving line and set the speed for the other workers.
(2) Perform work in a rhythmic way.
Examples:
  (a) Cutting with French knife. Place French knife point on the cutting board and with left hand move the vegetable under the knife, rock the knife up and down cutting the vegetables and developing a rhythm.
  (b) Natural rhythm. Stirring, racking dishes, panning biscuits, etc., are movements that can be done effectively by the natural rhythm.

	MANAGER (7½)	COOK (6½)	ASS'T COOK (6)	BAKER (6½)	SALADS (6)	SANDWICH (6)
7:30–8:00	Organizing day	Prepare ingred. for MAIN DISH				
8:00–8:30	General supervision		Prepare vegetables	Baking breads and desserts	Prepare salads and juice	Prepare sandwich for
8:30–9:00	General supervision		or helping cook		or help ass't. cook	a la carte & help baker
9:00–9:30	General supervision					
9:30–10:00	General supervision	Special cleaning	Special cleaning Steamer and /or	Special cleaning bake oven	Special cleaning salad	Prepare dishroom
10:00–10:30	General supervision		steam jacketed kettle		refrigerator	and wash pots, pans
10:30–11:00						and small equipment
11:00–11:30	Eat lunch	Prepare food for line / Eat lunch	Prepare food for serving line	Eat lunch	In charge of set up line II	Eat lunch 20 min.
11:30–12:00		Back up lines	Serving on line or Cashier	Serving on line or Cash.	Serving on line	Help on serving line dishroom
12:00–12:30	Lunch periods	Back up lines	Serving on line or Cashier	Serving on line or Cash.	Serving on line	Help on serving line dishroom
12:30–1:00		Back up lines	Serving on line or Cashier	Serving on lin or Cash.	Serving on line	Help on serving line dishroom
1:00–1:30	Check leftovers and give instruc. / 10 min break	Put away left-overs / 10 min break	10 min break	Put away left overs / 10 min break	Cleanup line II and put food away	
1:30–2:30	Prepare bank deposit and reports	Prepare for tomorrow		Prepare for tomorrow		
2:00–2:30	Check kitchen					
2:30–3:00	Prepare orders, etc.					
3:00–3:30						

TIME	A LA CARTE SNACK BAR (5)	SNACK BAR 4	DISH MACHINE OPERATOR 4	LINE 4	LINE 3
9:00–9:30	In charge of snack bar or a la carte				
9:30–10:00				Dishing up desserts	
10:00–10:30	Prepare sandwich	Prepare fruits, cakes, etc. for snack bar. Prepare condiments (catsup, mustard)	Prepare condiments (mustard, catsup, salad dressing)	Help baker	
10:30–11:00					
11:00–11:30	Eat lunch, 20 min. set up line	Break. Set up a la carte	Break	Break	In charge of set up line 1
11:30–12:00	A la carte or snack bar	A la carte or snack bar	Dishroom	Serving on line	Serving on line
12:00–12:30		A la carte or snack bar	Dishroom	Serving on line	Serving on line
12:30–1:00		A la carte or snack bar	Dishroom	Serving on line	Serving on line
1:00–1:30	Put away food. Prepare records	Put away food. Eat lunch	Eat lunch	Eat lunch	Put away food. Eat lunch
1:30–2:00	10 min break. Prepare for tomorrow	Clean steam table or snack bar	Finish dishroom and clean up		Cleanup line 1
2:00–2:30		Refrigerate fruits etc. & prepare for tom.	Put dishes away		
2:30–3:00			fill napkin, straw dispensers		

FIG. 4.3. ORGANIZATION WORK SCHEDULE FOR SECONDARY SCHOOLS*
Staffed with 55½ hr. Special individual instructions and job assignments can be attached to the organizational chart daily.

(3) Use smooth, continuous, curved motions when possible rather than straight-line with sharp changes in direction. Productivity can be increased 25%.
Examples:
  (a) Wiping tables. When wiping tables wipe in a wide arch circular motion rather than a straight-line one.
  (b) Mopping floors. Mopping in a circular motion from side-to-side is less tiring and easier than a push-and-pull, back-and-forth motion.
  (c) Spreading sandwich fillings. When spreading sandwich fillings on the bread, a circular motion without lifting the tool is most efficient.
(4) Use the fewest, shortest, and simplest motions.
Examples, use:
  (a) Pastry Brush. Use a 2-, 3-, or 4-in. pastry brush instead of 1-in. wide brush for greasing pans, buttering bread, and putting mayonnaise on sandwiches. By using the largest size practical, the number of strokes can be reduced fourfold.
  (b) Correct measure. Use the largest measure—the cup measure instead of 16 Tbsp and the quart measure instead of 4 cups. Use the correct size spoon, ladle, or scoop to portion with. Avoid dipping twice because it takes twice the time.
  (c) Wire whip for mixing flour and water.
(5) Use the available equipment that is *best* for the job.
Examples, use:
  (a) Pastry bag. Use the pastry bag for stuffing celery, filling deviled eggs, weiners, potatoes, cream puffs and for putting decorative mayonnaise, salad dressing or whipped cream on as toppings (Fig. 4.4).
  (b) Sifting and blending. Use wire whip attachment on mixer to incorporate air and blend ingredients instead of sifting.
  (c) Dish Machine. Wash all nonelectrical equipment or parts of equipment that are small enough to fit in the dish machine. Wash all small tools, pots and pans that will fit in the dish machine.
  (d) Slicer attachment. Use slicer attachment on mixer for slicing potatoes, carrots, cucumbers, radishes, etc.
  (e) Grater attachment. Use the grater attachment for chopping carrots and cabbage for salad, for making bread crumbs, and grating cheese. Attach a plastic bag to the chute of the attachment and the grated product goes directly into the bag for easy storing.
  (f) Food slicer. Use the food slicer for slicing tomatoes (several at a time) and shredding lettuce. Make a chart of dial settings for

FIG. 4.4 PASTRY BAG CAN MAKE JOB EASIER AND TAKE HALF THE TIME

cutting French bread, ham, cheese (½-oz, 1-oz, 2-oz. portions), and other foods that are cut frequently. Place chart on wall over the machine (Fig. 4.5).

(g) Portion scoops. Use portion scoops for filling muffin pans (No. 12 or 16), for cookies (No. 40), for sandwich fillings (No. 30 or 40) and portioning Salisbury steak patties (No. 10).

(h) Automatic timers. Use timers, not memory, to keep time.

(i) Scales. It is faster and more accurate to weigh ingredients rather than to measure.

(6) Combine operations and eliminate all unnecessary parts of job. Examples:

(a) Cook in serving pans.

(b) Add dry milk to dry ingredients, then add water, eliminating reconstitution of milk.

(c) Congeal gelatin in souffle cup or dish in which to be served.

(d) Use one-bowl method of mixing cakes.

(e) Combine butter and spreads for sandwiches, combine peanut butter and jelly.

(f) Roll biscuit dough into pan and cut into squares or triangles. Approximately 9 lb of dough into an 18 × 26 in. pan cut 6 × 16 will yield 96 biscuits.

(g) Cut several stalks of celery at one time.

(h) Roll pastry for cobbler onto 18 × 26 in. sheet pan, cut 8 × 10 and bake. Thicken juice from fruit with cornstarch, sugar, and spices, add pre-cooked fruits (or canned fruits). Portion and top with pastry square. Saves time, pans, oven space, and is more attractive.

FIG. 4.5. FOOD SLICER CAN MAKE
SLICING TOMATOES EASIER AND
QUICKER

(7) Tools, materials, and supplies should be located close to the point
of use and at a definite place.
Examples:
(a) Serving tools. Store serving tools near the serving line.
(b) Spices. Store spices most frequently used by baker at the
baker's area; those used by cook at the cook's area.
(c) Attachments. Store attachments for mixer with mixer.
(d) Label. Label drawers for ease in locating tools. Label shelves
in storeroom in categories in alphabetical order and coordinate
the arrangement with the inventory sheet for ease in taking
inventory.
(e) Color coding. Use color coding of scoop handles.
(f) Duplicate. If a tool is needed frequently at more than one
location, purchase a duplicate, particularly measuring spoons,
cups, thermometers, and other small equipment.
(g) Provide home base storage places for all tools and materials
with place of storage marked.
(h) Store vegetables near sink where they will be cleaned. Store
food ready to be served near serving line.
(8) Arrange work, tools, and material in sequence.
Examples:
(a) Work Centers. Equipment should be arranged to avoid
crisscrossing.
(b) Portioning. The worker should arrange the item being
portioned and the tools in such a way that it is not necessary
to reach across or backtrack and that the work flows in
sequence (Fig. 4.6).

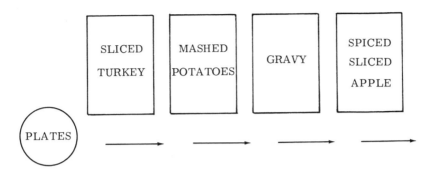

FIG. 4.6. THE LEFT HAND PICKS UP THE PLATE, RIGHT HAND DIPS, AND THE PLATE IS PASSED ON TO THE SERVER TO THE RIGHT

    (c) Numbering Directions. Directions for operating equipment or performing certain tasks can be numbered—1, 2, 3, etc.

(9) Arrange for physical comforts most conducive to work.
    Examples:
    (a) Good lighting—35 foot candles on equipment, 35–50 ft candles on work surface.
    (b) Temperature at 75 to 80°F.
    (c) Relative humidity at 50 to 60%.
    (d) Ventilation that will change air every 5 min.
    (e) Light-colored walls and ceiling without glare.
    (f) Have working surface at the correct height (35–37 in. high) for the worker.
    (g) High-back stools at work table allow worker to alternate between standing and sitting during long jobs. This will improve circulation and is less tiring than staying in one position for a long time.
    (h) Reduce noise and distractions.
    (i) Allow 10-min rest breaks after 2 hr of work.

(10) Keep tools and equipment in good working condition.

(11) Eliminate unnecessary walking and reaching, stretching, and bending.
    Examples:
    (a) Use cart to carry supplies needed from storeroom to place of work.
    (b) Put equipment on wheels so it can be brought to the place of use.
    (c) One person fills orders and delivers food from storeroom. At $4.00 per hour it is costing 32¢ for every 5 min used walking back and forth to the storeroom to get items. Take recipe or list of ingredients to the store room.

(d) Use foot pedal controls and knee lever when possible.

(e) Put materials where they can be reached without stretching. The normal work area reach is *12 to 14 in.* range and the maximum reach without stretching is from *22 to 24 in.* range. To test the normal work area, place a 25-lb. bag of salt in the normal work area and one in the maximum reach area. Lift one at a time with both hands. The one farther away seems much heavier and takes more energy to lift. Place materials in the normal work area when possible.

(12) Standardized procedures.
Examples:

(a) If the recipes need further seasoning, finishing touches, such as more salt or sugar, measure or weigh the amount needed and change the recipe to make "to taste" standardized. If it requires 10 min and not 8 min as the recipe indicates, change the recipe.

(b) Put cartons of milk in the milk cooler the same way each time. It may not be necessary to count them daily.

(13) Eliminate any body motion that is unproductive.

(14) Hands should be freed of any work that can be done by other parts of the body.

(15) Use force of gravity whenever possible.
Examples:

(a) Let product drop through a chute to get to where it is to go.

(b) Place receiving pan lower than chopping board so chopped product can fall into receiving pan.

(16) Use the simplest way of performing job.
Examples:

(a) Use uncooked noodles in assembling lasagna casserole for baking (Table 4.1).

(b) Oven-frying many foods is easier.

(c) Use hands (clean or plastic gloves) for picking up rather than tongs, scoop, other equipment when practical.

(d) Add oil to the water when cooking rice and pasta to prevent it from boiling over.

(e) Weighing all dry ingredients is faster and more accurate than measuring.

(f) Shape rolls or biscuits or cookies in long roll and cut off with dough cutter. Two rolls can be placed parallel to each other and cut at the same time with a knife.

(g) Put cold water over hard-cooked eggs immediately for ease in removing shell.

(h) Heat only enough liquid to dissolve gelatin and sugar and add cold or iced liquid for quick congealing.

   (i) Coat sides and bottom of pan gelatin is congealed in for ease in removing it from the pan.

   (j) Fasten a plastic bag to the mouth of the shredder or grater to receive shredded vegetables or grated cheese.

   (k) Put oil on stainless steel baker's table and rolling pin rather than flour when rolling out biscuits, pastry, or rolls.

   (l) Have pot sink ready with soapy hot water to soak pans. Five minutes in the steamer will loosen hard cooked on residue.

 (m) Kitchen scissors cut small amounts of parsley quickly.

  (n) Save time and oven space by placing hamburger patties three layers deep in pan. Separate each layer with a strip of aluminum foil just wide enough to cover each row of patties.

  (o) Separate egg whites and yolks by breaking them through a small funnel. The whites go through but the yolks will not.

  (p) Use large rubber scraper to remove batter from mixing bowl.

TABLE 4.1. EXAMPLE OF JOB SIMPLIFICATION BY CHANGE WHICH ELIMINATES STEPS IN A RECIPE FOR LASAGNA CASSEROLE

| | 100 Portions | | |
| | Weight | | Measures |
Ingredients	Lb	Oz	
Onions, chopped	1	2	3 cups
Oil or melted fat		4	½ cup
Tomato puree			3¼ qt
Tomato paste			2¼ qt
Water			2 gal.
Sugar		1½	3 Tbsp
Salt		2	3 Tbsp
Worcestershire sauce			1½ Tbsp
Garlic powder			1 Tbsp
Ground beef	8		
Salt		2	3 Tbsp
Pepper			1 tsp
Cheese, shredded	7	4	
Lasagna noodles (uncooked)	6		

Method

1. Cook onions in fat until onions are clear but not brown.
2. Combine onions, puree, paste, water, sugar, and seasonings.
3. Season meat with salt and pepper. Brown lightly. Drain.
4. Combine meat, 6 lb of cheese and sauce.
5. Pour about 1 qt meat-cheese sauce in each of 4 greased baking pans (about 12 × 20 × 2 in.).
6. Cover with a layer of noodles. Repeat layers of sauce, noodles and end with layer of sauce. Three layers of noodles (12) and 1 gal. sauce per pan. Sprinkle 5 oz. cheese on top of each pan.
7. Cover pans tightly with aluminum foil and bake 1 hr at 350°F (moderate oven).
8. Let stand 15 to 30 min before removing aluminum foil. Then cut into servings.

(17) Plan for tasks that can be done in slack time. All employees should be producing steadily at useful and productive tasks.

  (a) Make mixes for cakes, biscuits, and pudding in "off hours" to store for future use.

  (b) Grate cheese and store in 5-lb amounts in labeled plastic bags.

  (c) Grind bread crumbs and store in labeled plastic bags.

  (d) Prepare refrigerator cookie and store for future use (Table 4.2).

(18) Question all jobs being done.

  (a) Should different raw materials be used?

TABLE 4.2. BASIC COOKIE RECIPE (Yield: Approx. 2000 Cookies)

Ingredients	Weight Lb	Oz	Measure	Method
	2000 Portions			
Butter	8			(1) Cream butter and sugar in mixer.
Sugar, granulated	6			
Sugar, light brown	4			
Flour, all-purpose	16			(2) Combine dry ingredients.
Baking powder		12		
Salt		3		
Eggs			3 dozen	(3) Add the eggs and vanilla to the butter and sugar mixture.
Vanilla			¾ cup	(4) Gradually add the dry ingredients.
				(5) Use the variations you desire (see below).
				(6) Roll each one pound portion of dough to a 12 in. long roll (the width of wax paper).
				(7) Wrap in wax paper and chill overnight, or wrap tightly with aluminum foil, label, and freeze.
				(8) Slice on slicing machine set at 12 or thickness desired.
				(9) Baked on greased baking sheet in in 375°F oven for 7−10 min.

Variations: For making 6 kinds of cookies at one time, divide the dough into equal parts— about 6 lb in each part.
To each 6 lb. add one of the following variations:
Peanut Butter Cookies: add 3 cups peanut butter.
Vanilla Cookies: as is.
Coconut Cookies: add 2 cups coconut.
Chocolate Cookies: add 1 cup cocoa and 3 Tbsp water.
Nut Cookies: add 2 cups finely chopped nuts.
Raisin Cookies: add 2 cups raisins.
Date Cookies: add 2 cups dates.
To make all one kind of cookies, add one of the following to the entire base dough:
Peanut Butter Cookies: add 1 gal. plus 2 cups peanut butter.
Vanilla Cookies: as is.
Coconut Cookies: add 3 qt of coconut.
Chocolate Cookies: add 6 cups cocoa and 1½ cups of water.
Nut Cookies: add 3 qt nuts.
Raisin Cookies: add 3 qt raisins.
Date Cookies: add 3 qt dates.

(b) Would partially preprocessed or preprocessed products be advisable?

(c) Can the frills be afforded?

(d) Would changing forms or shapes of the finished product reduce time required?

(e) Would changing the order, sequence, make the job simpler? Example: Cut cake into portions before frosting is a simpler order of doing the job.

(f) Can labor-saving machines be used?

Sandwich Assembly

A sandwich assembly incorporates many of the economy principles just mentioned (Fig. 4.7). The tools and materials are assembled in the best sequence. The tools and materials are within maximum reach with the most movement in the normal reach range. Both hands are used to place the bread on the cutting board. A circular motion is used in putting the mayonnaise on the bread with a pastry brush. Both hands are putting the lettuce and meat on the bread and then putting the top slice of bread on.

To become more efficient at assembling sandwiches:

(1) Use both hands.

(2) Have all supplies in front of you when you start.

(3) Arrange supplies in the order to be used.

(4) If more than one person is making sandwiches, prepare an assembly line production.

(5) Leave bread in wrapper until ready to put on board to assemble.

(6) Cut bread wrapper in half and turn down each half on tray at assembly area; remove wrapper as bread is needed. (Have trash can near for dropping wrappers in.)

(7) Use spatula for spreading butter, mayonnaise, or fillings. Economize on motions—two strokes of the spatula should evenly spread to edges of bread.

(8) Corresponding slices of bread (slices next to each other in loaf) make a more uniform sandwich.

(9) Cut three to four sandwiches at one time.

SIMPLIFYING AND IMPROVING A JOB

Most jobs in the operation could probably be improved by rearranging or simplifying the way they are being done. To improve or simplify a job, it is necessary to analyze what is being done—by standing back and watching the job being performed and making notes on the movements

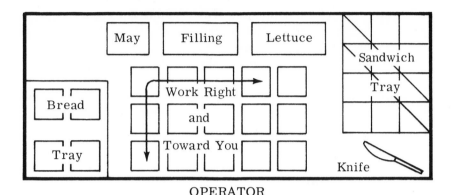

OPERATOR

FIG. 4.7. SANDWICH ASSEMBLY—SETUP OF SANDWICH AREA

made. Charting the flow of the work will point out unnecessary or awkward movements. Taking a motion picture of the job being performed can be most helpful. Then analyze by questioning: what is being done and why? Is it really necessary to do the job that way? Work out simpler and better methods. Putting them into practice may be the hardest to accomplish.

When the employees are involved in the process and their ideas become a part of it, they can make it work with greater determination. If all employees become interested and do not feel that their jobs are in danger because of greater efficiency, a group effort can get significant results. If the employees are made aware of motion economy and work simplifications, they can study their own movements and cut out unnecessary ones. In a class of foodservice workers studying work simplification several years ago in the Chapel Hill City Schools (N.C.), the class members demonstrated how they performed an operation. The others in the class offered improvements and new methods. Some of the members of the class said "it won't work" even before it was tried. However, each was asked to try the new methods during the next week. At the next weekly class, a stopwatch was used to test the new way against the old way. The group became very interested and suggested new, improved, simplified methods of performing several different jobs.

There are three main parts to any job in a foodservice: (1) getting ready, (2) doing, and (3) cleaning up. The getting-ready time should be as short as possible and not be slowed down by looking for the tools to perform with. The cleanup should go quickly. The important part of the job is the doing. Planning all parts of the job before starting to perform the job saves time. This means asking any questions or getting any explanations needed, then collecting all food and equipment needed for performing the job before starting the job.

Some school districts have increased from 12 meals per labor hour to 16 and 18 meals per labor hour and the primary factor in making it possible was training in work simplifications.

BIBLIOGRAPHY

AVERY, A.C. 1967. Work design and food service systems. J. Am. Dietet. Assoc. *51*, 148.

BARNES, R.M. 1968. Motion and Time Study: Design and Measurement of Work, 6th Edition. John Wiley & Sons, New York.

CHAPPELL, V.M., B.J. CRAIG, R.L. SWENSON, and W.C. TURNER. 1975. "Work productivity: getting the most for the time." *School Foodservice J.* 29, No. 8, 614.

COLEMAN, JOAN. 1970. Instructor's Guide: Management of Food Service, Dept. of Educ., State of Florida, Tallahassee.

JOEL, ROSS. 1977. *Managing Productivity.* Reston Publishing Co., Inc. Reston, Va.

KAZARIAN, E.A. 1969. Work Analysis and Design for Hotels, Restaurants and Institutions. AVI Publishing Co., Westport, Conn.

PEDDERSEN, RAYMOND B., ARTHUR C. AVERY, RUTH D. RICHARD, JAMES R. OSENTON, and HARRY H. POPE. 1973. *Increasing Productivity in Foodservice.* CBI, Boston, Mass.

WELCH, JOHN M. and GEORGE HOCKENBERRY. 1975. "Everything you always wanted to know about work sampling." *School Foodservice J.* 29, No. 1, 71.

WEST, BESSIE, LEVELLE WOOD, VIRGINIA HARGER and GRACE SHUGART. 1977. Food Service in Institutions, 6th Edition. John Wiley & Sons, New York.

WYNN, JANE T. 1973. Staffing broward county style. *School Foodservice J.* 27, No. 1, 44−54.

5

Nutrition

"... to safeguard the health and well-being of the Nation's children..."

Institutional foodservices, such as schools, hospitals, and college residence halls, cater to a captive audience and therefore should feel a special obligation to serve nutritious foods. School foodservices were established on the premise that they are to aid in maintaining a good nutritional status in healthy children and improving the nutritional status when the need exists. Therefore, those who plan menus for a school foodservice should have an understanding of nutritional requirements for children from the age 5 through 18. And those preparing the food must know the characteristics of vitamins and minerals in order to conserve them during preparation.

In order to eliminate hunger and malnutrition in the United States, good food habits need to be taught to students at home and through programs in nutrition education. Unless a student is taught to like nutritious foods and to understand his body's needs, he may often turn away from the well-balanced meal to snack foods. These snack foods are usually high in carbohydrates and fats. Poor eating habits, not the lack of food, are the primary reason for malnutrition in this country.

Nutrients are chemical compounds needed for good health, for building and repairing body tissues, for regulating body processes, for normal growth, and for providing energy needs. There is a great variety of foods year-round in this country to furnish all the nutrients needed. Therefore, the challenge is to get students to eat the foods containing the nutrients needed.

People require different amounts of food depending on age, sex, activity, and size. Some bodies can utilize food better than others. However, when more food is eaten than the body requires, it is stored in the form of fat.

The characteristics of well-nourished people are (1) strong bones, muscles, and teeth; (2) healthy skin and blood; (3) feeling good; (4) enough energy for everyday activities; and (5) radiant and vigorous appearance. Poor nutrition or malnutrition occurs when too little food is eaten or the wrong kinds of food are eaten. When this happens children may grow slowly or not at all, may have bowed bones and enlarged joints; may have skin dry, flaky, and rough; may have inflamed eyes, dry hair, decayed teeth, anemia, and nervous disorders, and be listless and tired.

Food, when eaten, is digested and then absorbed from the digestive tract. Nutrients in food are classified into six main groups: protein, fats, carbohydrates, minerals, vitamins, and water. No one of these nutrients act completely independently of the others. Protein, carbohydrates, and fats furnish the energy needed, which is measured by calories. A calorie is defined as the amount of heat it takes to raise the temperature of a kilogram of water 1°C.

Nutrient density is a concept that compares calories and nutrients in a food. It is particularly valuable when one is trying to cut down on calories. For example, potato chips are high in calories and low in nutrients and would be less nutrient dense than spinach. This is important to remember when planning menus for small children.

PROTEIN

Protein is in abundance in this country. It is found in meats, poultry, eggs, fish, dairy products, fruits, vegetables, and cereal products. However, protein from animals is superior to that of plants because there is a greater number of amino acids present in meats. Proteins are made up of 20 amino acid materials and many sources of protein lack some of the amino acids. However, a combination of animal and plant protein sources is very satisfactory. The functions in the body are:

(1) building and maintaining body tissues,
(2) providing energy,
(3) regulating body processes,
(4) building resistance to disease.

Protein is not stored in the body; therefore, it is essential that good sources of protein be eaten daily. Any excess protein in the body is used for energy. When extreme cases of protein deficiency exist, there may be poor muscle tone and posture, lowered resistance to disease and slow recovery from illnesses, stunted growth, and anemia.

FATS AND CARBOHYDRATES

Fats and carbohydrates are important sources of energy. Some foods high in fat are butter, margarine, oil, shortening, fat meat, cream, chocolate, nuts, and cheese. Fats provide a more concentrated source of energy than carbohydrates and protein. Fats also function in the body by carrying fat soluble vitamins and supplying essential unsaturated fatty acids. The average lunch provides 39 to 40% of its calories from fat.

Carbohydrates are simple sugars and starches. Foods which are classified as largely carbohydrates are honey, syrup, molasses, sugars, dried fruits, cereal products, and starches. It is recommended that 60−65% of the calories come from complex carbohydrates, such as grain and vegetables. Special emphases should be put on reducing fat in the diet. USDA issued in the 1979 interim meal pattern regulations a recommendation for decreasing the fats and sugars.

MINERALS

Minerals are needed in small quantities but perform very important jobs in the body. Minerals make up a large part of the body's bones and teeth. Not all the minerals present in the body are known to be essential. Calcium, iron and phosphorus are three minerals that are essential and may be deficient in a diet if foods are not carefully chosen.

Calcium

The primary source of calcium is milk and milk products. Leafy green vegetabes and fish also contribute to calcium needs. However, Vitamin D is required to be present in the body for efficient absorption of calcium. Calcium needs are greater during the growing years; however, the requirement for calcium continues through life. The functions in the body are:

(1) building bones and teeth,
(2) regulating the heart,
(3) aiding in blood coagulation,
(4) regulating nerves and muscles to react normally.

Deficiencies of calcium may cause poorly formed bones and teeth and slow bood clotting.

Iron

According to a nationwide study by the USDA of nutrients in school lunches, more lunches were deficient in iron than any other nutrient. Iron is needed for forming red blood cells and other body cells and carrying oxygen to the body tissues. Therefore, the quantity of iron needed depends upon the individual's sex and age, with females requiring more iron than males. If one lacks adequate quantities of iron, nutritional anemia may result, which is characterized by shortness of breath, dizziness, pale skin, gastric disturbances, and feeling weak.

Small amounts of iron are found in a wide variety of foods, such as lean muscle meats, liver, fish, poultry, dry beans, molasses, and dark green vegetables (except spinach). Since no one food or group of foods furnishes large quantities of iron, it is important that cereals and breads be enriched with iron. Foods rich in iron are listed in the pamphlet *Menu Planning Guide for School Food Service* (U.S. Dept. Agr. 1980) and are also shown in Table 5.1.

Phosphorus

Phosphorus is usually in adequate supply where there is iron since many of the iron-rich foods are also good sources of phosphorus. Phosphorus is fundamental in the building of bones and teeth.

Iodine

Iodine is usually in adequate supply in nongoitrous regions without particularly having to watch the diet. In some areas of the country, iodized salt will aid in supplying the small quantity of iodine needed to help the thyroid gland function properly.

VITAMINS

Vitamins are chemical compounds found in foods and are known to be essential to good health. There are over 20 vitamins believed to be important for optimal health. Letters of the alphabet have been used to differentiate the vitamins along with the chemical names to identify some. Vitamins are classified as either water soluble or fat soluble. Since preparation of food can destroy some vitamins, it is very important for those who prepare food to be made aware of how to retain the vitamins in food. This is discussed further in Chap. 8.

Vitamin A

Vitamin A is present in animal sources, such as liver, egg yolks, butter, whole milk, cheese, and cream. Also, the body can convert carotene into vitamin A. Carotene is the yellow pigment found in yellow and orange

TABLE 5.1.   IRON-RICH FOODS

Vegetables	Fruits	Breads (Enriched or Whole-Grain)	Cereals and Cereal Products (Enriched or Whole-Grain)	Miscellaneous
Asparagus	Apples (canned)	Biscuits	Bulgur	Dry beans
Beans green, lima, wax	Berries	Boston brown bread	Noodles macaroni, spaghetti	Dry peas
Dark green leafy beet greens, chard, collards, endive, escarole, kale, mustard greens, turnip greens	Dried fruits apricots, dates, figs, peaches, prunes, raisins	Cornbread	Rice	Meat especially liver and other organ meat
		Loaf	Rolled wheat and oats	Peanut butter
Other dark green broccoli, Brussels sprouts		Muffins	Molasses and syrups	Poultry
		Rolls		Shellfish
Peas green, immature and cowpeas, immature seed				Tuna
Squash				
Sweet potatoes				
Tomatoes (canned)				
Tomato juice, paste, puree				

fruits and vegetables and is present in dark green vegetables. Therefore, "dark green and deep yellow" fruits and vegetables are good sources of vitamin A, as shown in Table 5.2.

The functions of vitamin A in the body are:

(1) promoting growth,
(2) helping eyes to adjust to dim lights,
(3) maintaining a healthy lining in the digestive tract,
(4) promoting healthy skin.

Since mineral oil will reduce the absorption of carotene and vitamin A, it should not be combined with foods. Vitamin A is stored in the body and it is a fat soluble vitamin, therefore not easily destroyed in preparation. Studies of the lunches served in schools across the country have shown that the vitamin A nutritional goals are usually met. However, it is recommended that a good source of vitamin A be included in the menus every other day along wtih the daily consumption of butter, milk, and other foods which help meet the requirement. Deficiency symptoms may be retarded growth, dry eyelids, and reddened eyes, night blindness, lowered resistance to infection, and poor teeth formation.

TABLE 5.2. FOODS RICH IN VITAMIN A AND CAROTENE

Vegetables	Fruits
Good Source	
Beet greens	Apricots
Broccoli	Cantaloupe
Carrots	Mangoes
Chili peppers, red	Papayas
Chard, Swiss	Purple plums (canned)
Chicory greens	
Collards	
Cress, garden	
Dandelion greens	
Kale	
Mixed vegetables (frozen)	
Mustard greens	
Peas and carrots (frozen)	
Peppers, sweet red	
Pumpkins	
Spinach	
Squash, winter	
Sweet potatoes	
Turnip greens	
Fair Source	
Asparagus, green	Cherries, red sour
Endive, curly	Nectarines
Escarole	Peaches (except canned)
Chili peppers, green (fresh)	Prunes
Tomatoes	
Tomato juice or reconstituted paste or puree	
Vegetable juice cocktail	

B Vitamins

Thiamin (B_1), riboflavin (B_2 or G), and niacin (nicotine acid) are the best known of the 11 B vitamins.

Thiamin.—Thiamin is a water soluble vitamin which is present in plants and animal sources. However, the amounts present are relatively small. Cereal grains contribute the greatest part of thiamin in our diets and we depend on the enrichment of cereals and grain products to put thiamin back into the products after refining. Meats, poultry, fish, and some dairy products also contribute small quantities of thiamin.

The functions in the body are:

(1) promoting normal appetite and digestion,
(2) helping convert carbohydrates to energy,
(3) helping the heart, nerves, and muscles function properly.

Deficiency of thiamin will cause poor appetite and poor digestion, listlessness and fatigue, retarded growth and nervousness.

Riboflavin.—Riboflavin is a water soluble vitamin that is highly unstable. It is widely distributed in foods with liver being an excellent source. However, about 80% of the riboflavin in the diet is concentrated in milk, meat, poultry, fish, and cereal products. Egg yolks and green leafy vegetables are rich sources of riboflavin. The functions in the body are:

(1) promoting well-being and vitality,
(2) aiding in converting carbohydrates into energy,
(3) increasing resistance to infection,
(4) helping maintain good vision and healthy clear eyes,
(5) building healthy skin and mouth tissue.

A riboflavin deficiency may cause eyes to be over-sensitive to light and blurred vision. Cracks may appear in the corners of the mouth and the tongue may become inflamed.

Niacin.—Niacin is like vitamin A in that it has two forms. Tryptophan, an amino acid found in protein-rich foods, can be converted in the body to niacin. Niacin as such is present in poultry, fish, meats, enriched flours, and cereal products. Niacin is water soluble, but is much more stable than riboflavin and thiamin. The functions in the body are:

(1) helping to convert fuel foods into energy,
(2) promoting healthy skin,

(3) helping the nervous system function,

(4) aiding in digestion,

(5) preventing and curing pellagra.

Niacin deficieny will cause mental depression and nervousness, digestive disturbances, and rough inflamed skin.

Vitamin C.—Vitamin C is frequently called by the chemical name, ascorbic acid. It is the most unstable of the vitamins. Being water soluble, it can be destroyed by heat and light. Much care should be taken in preparation and serving of vitamn C rich foods. The handling of these foods is discussed in Chap. 8.

Citrus fruits and tomatoes and dark green leafy vegetables are some of the best sources of ascorbic acid. Ascorbic acid is not stored by the body; therefore a good source of this vitamin is needed daily in the diet. Some of the best sources of ascorbic acid are listed in *Menu Planning Guide for School Food Service* (U.S. Dept. Agr. 1980) and are presented in Table 5.3.

TABLE 5.3. FOODS RICH IN VITAMIN C

Vegetables	Fruits
Good Source	
Broccoli	Acerola
Brussels sprouts	Acerola juice
Cauliflower	Grapefruit
Chili peppers, red and green	Grapefruit juice
Collards	Grapefruit-orange juice
Cress, garden	Guavas
Kale	Kumquats
Kohlrabi	Mangoes
Mustard greens	Orange juice
Peppers, sweet, red and	Oranges
green	Papayas
	Strawberries
	Tangerine juice
	Tangerines
Fair Source	
Asparagus	Cantaloupe
Cabbage	Honeydew melon
Dandelion greens	Raspberries, red
Okra	Tangelo juice
Potatoes (baked, boiled or	Tangelos
steamed)	
Rutabagas	
Sauerkraut	
Spinach	
Sweet potatoes (except canned in syrup)	
Tomatoes	
Tomato juice or reconstituted paste or puree	
Turnip greens	
Turnips	

The functions of vitamin C in the body are:

(1) promoting healthy gums,
(2) helping build resistance to infection,
(3) promoting healing of wounds,
(4) helping in proper utilization of iron,
(5) helping build and maintain bones, tissues, and blood,
(6) preventing scurvy.

Many of the vitamin C rich foods are unpopular with most students. Either they are not familiar with these foods or dislike their taste. Over 90% of the vitamin C in the diet is found in fruits and vegetables, and unfortunately the largest plate waste seems to be fruits and vegetables. Nutrition education can do much to correct this. Means of motivating the students to eat fruits and vegetables are needed. Since vitamin C is not stored in the body, it is of importance to include a source of vitamin C in the menus that students *will* eat. A choice of more than one source of vitamin C will increase the possible consumption. For example, offer a choice of buttered spinach and chilled orange juice, or a choice of sweet potatoes and white potatoes. A deficiency of ascorbic acid in the body may cause weakened bones, tendency to bruise and bleed easily, swollen and painful joints. Scurvy is the disease caused in extreme cases of deficiency of ascorbic acid.

Vitamin D

Vitamin D is needed for the absorption of calcium. A severe deficiency of vitamin D may result in rickets. Milk fortified with vitamin D is the most reliable source of vitamin D in most school menus. One half-pint of fortified milk will furnish at least three-fourths of the required vitamin D, or approximately 100 I.U. Also, the sterols of the skin are changed into vitamin D through the exposure of the skin to sunlight.

DIETARY GUIDELINES FOR AMERICANS

The *"Dietary Guidelines for Americans"* were issued in February 1980 in the publication *Nutrition and Your Health* by the U.S. Department of Agriculture (USDA) and the U.S. Department of Health, Education, and Welfare. The seven dietary guidelines concentrated on decreasing consumption of fat, refined sugar, and sodium (salt), with which few nutritionists had trouble. However, the lobbyists for various industries have challenged the harm. Inspite of the political power, these guidelines have brought national attention to the consumption of fat, refined sugar, and sodium (salt). The meal requirements introduced in 1980 are designed to provide for a lower level of fat.

RECOMMENDED DAILY DIETARY ALLOWANCES

The Food and Nutrition Board in 1940 developed the Recommended Daily Dietary Allowances which list the nutrients needed and the quantities needed for men, women, children, and infants and became the dietary standard in the United States. Though first published in 1943, it has been revised eight times (Table 5.4). The nutrients recommended are based on research started before the turn of the century. The recommended allowance includes the actual requirements plus a safety factor.

Five Food Groups

The Five Food Groups, still referred to by many as the Basic Four, is a simple guide prepared by the Institute of Home Economics based on the Recommended Daily Dietary Allowances and is most useful to the average person in meeting those recommended requirements without having much knowledge of nutrition. The Basic Four Groups were reduced from the Seven Basic Food Groups and are easily rememebered as: Milk Group, Meat Group, Vegetable and Fruit Group, and Bread and Cereal Group. In 1980 the fifth group, fats and sugars was added. By using the number of servings suggested in each group one can plan an adequate menu which will supply most of the nutrients needed.

Type A Pattern

The Type A pattern was established as a part of the guidelines of the National School Lunch Act. It was like the Four Food Groups in that it was a simplified means of planning the nutritional needs. Schools participating in the National School Lunch Program used the Type A pattern in planning their menus, rather than using the Recommended Daily Dietary Allowances along with the Nutritive Value of Foods Table published by the USDA, to compute the nutrients in the meals. The Ad Hoc Committee (1969) appointed by the Secretary of Agriculture to study the school lunch program recommended, among other things, that:

Any program that can present evidence of its ability to consistently meet one-third RDA by a combination of ordinary foods differing from the Type A pattern should be authorized to do so and the resultant meals should be eligible for reimbursement from federal funds. Ethnic, economic and other consideration may make a variety of patterns desirable and should be given consideration in the formulation of program regulations.

TABLE 5.4. RECOMMENDED DIETARY ALLOWANCES REVISED 1980[a]. FOOD AND NUTRITION BOARD, NATIONAL ACADEMY OF SCIENCES-NATIONAL RESEARCH COUNCIL

Designed for the maintenance of good nutrition of practically all healthy people in the U.S.A.

Category	Age (Years)	Weight (kg)	Weight (lb)	Height (cm)	Height (in.)	Protein (g)	Fat-Soluble Vitamins			Water-Soluble Vitamins		
							Vitamin A (µg R.E.)[b]	Vitamin D (µg)[c]	Vitamin E (mg α T.E.)[d]	Vitamin C (mg)	Thiamin (mg)	Riboflavin (mg)
Infants	0.0–0.5	6	13	60	24	kg × 2.2	420	10	3	35	0.3	0.4
	0.5–1.0	9	20	71	28	kg × 2.0	400	10	4	35	0.5	0.6
Children	1–3	13	29	90	35	23	400	10	5	45	0.7	0.8
	4–6	20	44	112	44	30	500	10	6	45	0.9	1.0
	7–10	28	62	132	52	34	700	10	7	45	1.2	1.4
Males	11–14	45	99	157	62	45	1000	10	8	50	1.4	1.6
	15–18	66	145	176	69	56	1000	10	10	60	1.4	1.7
	19–22	70	154	177	70	56	1000	7.5	10	60	1.5	1.7
	23–50	70	154	178	70	56	1000	5	10	60	1.4	1.6
	51+	70	154	178	70	56	1000	5	10	60	1.2	1.4
Females	11–14	46	101	157	62	46	800	10	8	50	1.1	1.3
	15–18	55	120	163	64	46	800	10	8	60	1.1	1.3
	19–22	55	120	163	64	44	800	7.5	8	60	1.1	1.3
	23–50	55	120	163	64	44	800	5	8	60	1.0	1.2
	51+	55	120	163	64	44	800	5	8	60	1.0	1.2
Pregnant						+30	+200	+5	+2	+20	+0.4	+0.3
Lactating						+20	+400	+5	+3	+40	+0.5	+0.5

[a] The allowances are intended to provide for individual variations among most normal persons as they live in the United States under usual environmental stresses. Diets should be based on a variety of common foods in order to provide other nutrients for which human requirements have been less well defined.

[b] Retinol equivalents: 1 retinol equivalent=1 µg retinol or 6 µg β-carotene.

[c] As cholecalciferol: 10 µg cholecalciferol=400 I.U. vitamin D.

[d] α-tocopherol equivalents: 1 mg d-α-tocopherol=1 α T.E.

[e] 1 N.E. (niacin equivalent)=1 mg niacin or 60 mg dietary tryptophan.

[f] The folacin allowances refer to dietary sources as determined by *Lactobacillus casei* assay after treatment with enzymes ("conjugases") to make polyglutamyl forms of the vitamin available to the test organism.

ESTIMATED SAFE AND ADEQUATE DAILY DIETARY INTAKES OF ADDITIONAL SELECTED VITAMINS AND MINERALS[a]

Category	Age (Years)	Vitamins			Trace Elements[b]	
		Vitamin K (µg)	Biotin (mg)	Pantothenic Acid (mg)	Copper (mg)	Manganese (mg)
Infants	0–0.5	12	35	2	0.5–0.7	0.5–0.7
	0.5–1	10–20	50	3	0.7–1.0	0.7–1.0
Children and Adolescents	1–3	15–30	65	3	1.0–1.5	1.0–1.5
	4–6	20–40	85	3–4	1.5–2.0	1.5–2.0
	7–10	30–60	120	4–5	2.0–2.5	2.0–3.0
	11+	50–100	100–200	4–7	2.0–3.0	2.5–5.0
Adults		70–140	100–200	4–7	2.0–3.0	2.5–5.0

Source: from Recommended Dietary Allowances, Revised 1980. Food and Nutrition Board, National Academy of Sciences-National Research Council, Washington, D.C.

[a] Because there is less information on which to base allowances, these figures are not given in the main table of the RDA and are provided here in the form of ranges of recommended intakes.

Water-Soluble Vitamins				Minerals					
Niacin (mg N.E.) e	Vitamin B₆ (mg)	Folacin f (μg)	Vitamin B₁₂ (μg)	Calcium (mg)	Phosphorus (mg)	Magnesium (mg)	Iron (mg)	Zinc (mg)	Iodine (μg)
6	0.3	30	0.5 g	360	240	50	10	3	40
8	0.6	45	1.5	540	360	70	15	5	50
9	0.9	100	2.0	800	800	150	15	10	70
11	1.3	200	2.5	800	800	200	10	10	90
16	1.6	300	3.0	800	800	250	10	10	120
18	1.8	400	3.0	1200	1200	350	18	15	150
18	2.0	400	3.0	1200	1200	400	18	15	150
19	2.2	400	3.0	800	800	350	10	15	150
18	2.2	400	3.0	800	800	350	10	15	150
16	2.2	400	3.0	800	800	350	10	15	150
15	1.8	400	3.0	1200	1200	300	18	15	150
14	2.0	400	3.0	1200	1200	300	18	15	150
14	2.0	400	3.0	800	800	300	18	15	150
13	2.0	400	3.0	800	800	300	18	15	150
13	2.0	400	3.0	800	800	300	10	15	150
+2	+0.6	+400	+1.0	+400	+400	+150	h	+5	+25
+5	+0.5	+100	+1.0	+400	+400	+150	h	+10	+50

g The RDA for vitamin B_{12} in infants is based on average concentration of the vitamin in human milk. The allowances after weaning are based on energy intake (as recommended by the American Academy of Pediatrics) and consideration of other factors, such as intestinal absorption.

h The increased requirement during pregnancy cannot be met by the iron content of habitual American diets or by the existing iron stores of many women; therefore, the use of 30 to 60 mg supplemental iron is recommended. Iron needs during lactation are not substantially different from those of non-pregnant women, but continued supplementation of the mother for 2 to 3 months after parturition is advisable in order to replenish stores depleted by pregnancy.

Trace Elements b				Electrolytes		
Fluoride (mg)	Chromium (mg)	Selenium (mg)	Molybdenum (mg)	Sodium (mg)	Potassium (mg)	Chloride (mg)
0.1−0.5	0.01−0.04	0.01−0.04	0.03−0.06	115−350	350−925	275−700
0.2−1.0	0.02−0.06	0.03−0.06	0.04−0.08	250−750	425−1275	400−1200
0.5−1.5	0.02−0.08	0.02−0.08	0.05−0.1	325−975	550−1650	500−1500
1.0−2.5	0.03−0.12	0.03−0.12	0.06−0.15	450−1350	775−2325	700−2100
1.5−2.5	0.05−0.2	0.05−0.2	0.1−0.3	600−1800	1000−3000	925−2775
1.5−2.5	0.05−0.2	0.05−0.2	0.15−0.5	900−2700	1525−4575	1400−4200
1.5−4.0	0.05−0.2	0.05−0.2	0.15−0.5	1100−3300	1875−5625	1700−5100

b Since the toxic levels for many trace elements may be only several times usual intakes, the upper levels for the trace elements given in this table should not be habitually exceeded.

With the increased use of computers this method was more feasible. However, the Type A pattern was commonly used, since it will provide approximately one-third of the Recommended Daily Dietary Allowances for a student between the ages of 10 to 12 yr. (See Figs. 5.1, 5.2, and 5.3)

The Type A pattern was:

½ pt fluid milk as a beverage

2 oz. edible portion of lean meat, poultry or fish, 2 oz. cheese, 1 egg, ½ cup cooked dry beans or dry peas, 4 Tbsp of peanut butter, or an equivalent quantity of any combination of the above listed foods

¾ cup serving of 2 or more vegetables or fruits, or both

1 serving of whole grain or enriched bread

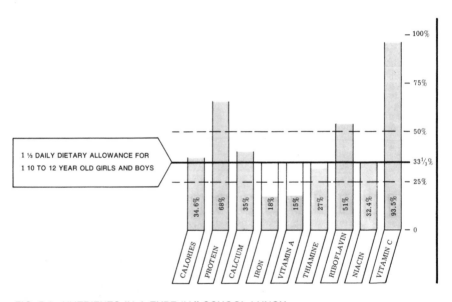

FIG. 5.1. NUTRIENTS IN A TYPE "A" SCHOOL LUNCH
When daily dietary allowances are different for girls and boys, the greater requirement is used. Menu is listed below.

MENU	SIZE SERVING
Fish Square	3.6 oz. cooked
on Bun	1
Buttered Potatoes	½ cup
Red and green	
Cole Slaw	⅓ cup
Cake with Choco-	
late Icing	1 serving
Milk	½ pt

When using the preceding pattern for planning menus, some attention had to be given to foods rich in iron, vitamins A and C to assure the nutritional goals are met.

Many nutritionist felt that the Type A lunch pattern was out of date and did not meet the needs of today's children at different ages as the life styles had changed. Nutritional analyses of actual lunches showed some B vitamins lacking in the menus and the plate waste publicity in the seventies pointed up a real need for change. Older children were complaining that the lunch did not provide enough food to meet their needs.

New Meal Patterns

In 1977 a complete change in the Type A lunch pattern was introduced into the Federal Register for comments and suggestions. The proposed

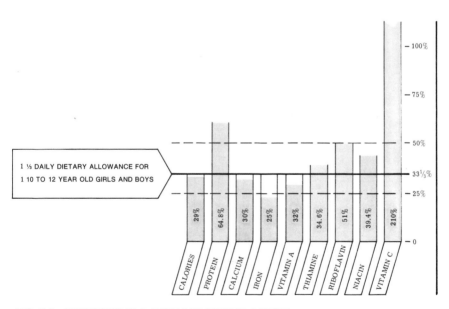

FIG. 5.2. NUTRIENTS IN A TYPE "A" SCHOOL LUNCH
When daily dietary allowances are different for girls and boys, the greater requirement is used. Menu is listed below.

MENU	SIZE SERVING
Hamburger Pattie	2 oz.
on Bun	1
French Fries	½ cup
Catsup	1 Tbsp
Sliced Tomato	1 slice
Orange Juice	½ cup
Butter Cookie	2
Milk	½ pt

changes would mean many additional requirements that were later removed from the new meal pattern. After thirty-five years of using the
Type A lunch pattern, comment periods, many studies and surveys, the
new meal patterns were released in two steps. The interim regulations
were introduced in 1979 followed by the final regulations and new meal
patterns in the Spring of 1980.

The new meal patterns dropped the name "Type A" and are simply
known as the school lunch meal patterns. They clearly state what the
minimum portion sizes are to be for five different age/grade groups. The
regulations had for many years encouraged portion size variations to
better meet the needs of children of various ages, however many state
agencies did not allow the smaller quantities to be served. Determining
how much to serve should no longer be a problem and there is much

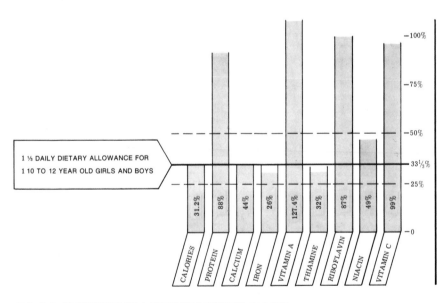

FIG. 5.3. NUTRIENTS IN A TYPE "A" SCHOOL LUNCH
When daily dietary allowances are different for girls and boys, the greater requirement is used. Menu is listed below.

MENU	SIZE SERVING
Fried Chicken	1 leg
Potato Salad	½ cup
Cooked Spinach	⅓ cup
Hot Roll	1 serving
Butter	1 tsp
Vanilla Pudding	½ cup
Milk	½ pt

flexibility. Features of the meal patterns (see Table 5.6) and the new regulations to be noted are:

(1) minimum quantities of the four lunch components, five foods, are stated for five age/grade groups;
(2) preschoolers can be served in two seatings;
(3) if one does choose to serve the larger portions of Group V, smaller portions should be made available for those who prefer less; however, minimum quantities for that age/grade must be offered;
(4) elementary children must be served all four components, five foods, at least at the minumim quantity specified in order for the meal to qualify for federal reimbursement;
(5) the bread alternates were expanded to include enriched or whole-grain rice, macaroni, noodles, and other pasta;
(4) the bread requirements of one serving a day was extended to include a minimum requirement for the week, making the weight, or amount of the bread and bread alternate important;
(6) the egg, cooked dry beans and peas and cottage cheese requirements were increased, whereas the portions more equal the protein value of other meats and meat alternates;
(7) clarifies the milk requirement by stating that unflavored or flavored whole milk may be offered as a choice but at least one of the following milks must be made available: unflavored fluid lowfat milk, unflavored skim milk, or buttermilk;
(8) choices of variety of foods should be offered children to better meet their needs, their likes and dislikes and to introduce children to new foods;
(9) recommends that iron-rich foods be offered frequently, as well as foods high in vitamins A and C;
(10) recommended that the quantity of fat, salt, and sugar be controlled; and
(11) requires that students and parents be involved in the foodservice activities.

There are many points to consider when planning menus to assure that the nutritional needs of the children are met and realistically within the other restrictions and with foods that students will eat.

The milk requirement of the meal pattern can be met by offering at least one of the following forms of fluid milk: unflavored lowfat milk, unflavored skim milk, or unflavored buttermilk. Choice of whole milk or chocolate milk is encouraged. Some nutritionists frown on using chocolate-flavored milk because of the increased carbohydrates and additional calories. However, in some schools when both plain and chocolate-flavored milk are offered the milk consumption is greater than previously. (see Fig. 5.4) Many teenage girls, along with the American Dietetic Association, were pleased when the milk guidelines were changed in 1979 to require a lowfat milk be offered. However, when the nutritive content of plain whole, chocolate-flavored whole milk, and skim milk are compared (see Table 5.5), one can see that vitamin A content of skim milk is considerably less. Since calcium requirements for a 10 to 12 year old boy and girl are 1.2 gm and the ½ pt of milk will provide only about 80% of the nutritional goals for calcium, other sources of calcium should be provided to supplement the milk.

Protein-rich foods are expensive and may consume one-third or more of the food dollar. For economy reasons a combination of meat, poultry, or fish and one of the less expensive meat alternates such as eggs, dry beans or peas, and peanut butter may be used in meeting the nutritional needs. The use of textured protein made from soybeans to meet a part of the protein requirement is a practical solution to the rising food cost and to the possible shortage of meats anticipated in 10 to 20 years from now. Since the USDA approved the use of textured protein up to 30% of the requirement, there has been a noticeable increase in the number of different brands of the product available on the market. Nutritionists question the long-range effects of the product being used in the diet.

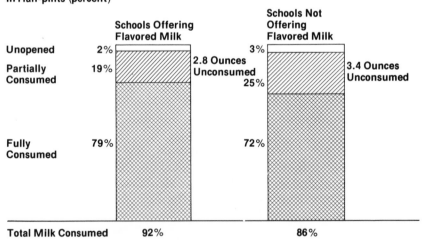

MILK CONSUMPTION
in Half-pints (percent)

FIG. 5.4. IN 1975 A USDA STUDY SHOWED 92% MILK CONSUMPTION WHEN CHOCOLATE MILK WAS SERVED

TABLE 5.5. NUTRITIONAL COMPARISON OF MILKS

1 Cup Serving (½ Pt)	Calories	Protein (Gm)	Calcium (Gm)	Iron (Mg)	Vitamin A (IU)	Thiamin (Mg)	Ribo-flavin (Mg)	Niacin (Mg)	Vitamin C (Mg)
Milk									
Whole	160	9.0	0.29	0.10	350	0.08	0.42	2.25	2.0
Skim	90	9.0	0.30	0.10	10	0.10	0.44	2.25	2.0
Chocolate whole milk	215	9.0	0.28	0.50	325	0.08	0.40	2.30	2.5
Chocolate drink skim milk	190	8.0	0.27	0.50	200	0.10	0.41	2.30	2.5

Following studies in 1968 by USDA, the butter or margarine requirement was lowered from 2 tsp to 1 tsp. In 1975 the butter requirement was eliminated.

Since the meal patterns are to meet nutritional needs of children of all ages, it is desirable to adjust the portions to meet the needs of a younger and an older child. The USDA has given definite guidelines as are shown in Table 5.6.

In 1966, 1970, 1972, and 1975 samples of lunches from different parts of the United States were analyzed for vitamins and other nutrients in nationwide studies conducted. On an average the lunches served exceeded the goal of one-third of the 1968 recommended allowances for thiamin, riboflavin, niacin, vitamin D, and vitamin B_{12} for children 10 to 12 yr of age. Riboflavin was in all cases in excess of the goal. Laboratory analyses were not made for Vitamin C. Vitamin B_6, vitamin A, vitamin D, and thiamin were most often short of the goals. Other studies have shown that the school lunches have not achieved the goal for iron. The new meal patterns should better meet the goals, particularly for the B vitamins.

NUTRITION EDUCATION

Nutrition education should go hand in hand with a school feeding program aimed at meeting the nutritional needs of its customers. Funds are now being made available for local programs in nutrition education. The Nutrition Education and Training Program was first funded by P.L. 95-177 in 1977 and much credit goes to Senator Hubert Humphrey for this. It provides funds to states to encourage effective dissemination of nutrition information to children, to provide training for foodservice workers, and for training of teachers to teach nutrition. In 1978 the states received for distribution $26 million or 50 cents per child. The cuts in 1979 and 1980 reduced this considerably.

Nutritional labeling laws have increased the interest in nutrition. The public is beginning to realize that malnutrition can and does exist in this land of plenty due to a lack of knowledge, not a lack of food. Nutrition education can provide a person with a knowledge to enable him to choose the food needed for him to build a healthy body. The goals, however, are to change food behavior and habits. Therefore, nutrition education should attempt to bring about behavioral change. It is easier to establish good food habits than to change or modify food habits already established.

As pointed out by the White House Conference on Food and Nutrition in 1969, there has been a lack of interest in nutrition education for the past 20 yr. Everyone leaving it to someone else to teach nutritional

TABLE 5.6. SCHOOL LUNCH PATTERNS FOR VARIOUS AGE/GRADE GROUPS

U.S. Department of Agriculture, National School Lunch Program

USDA recommends, but does not require, that you adjust portions by age/grade group to better meet the food and nutritional needs of children according to their ages. If you adjust portions, Groups I–IV are minimum requirements for the age/grade groups specified. If you do not adjust portions, the Group IV portions in the shaded column are the portions to serve all children.

COMPONENTS	MINIMUM QUANTITIES				RECOMMENDED QUANTITIES[2]	SPECIFIC REQUIREMENTS
	Preschool ages 1–2 (Group I)	ages 3–4 (Group II)	Grades K–3 ages 5–8 (Group III)	Grades 4–12[1] age 9 & over (Group IV)	Grades 7–12 age 12 & over (Group V)	
MEAT OR MEAT ALTERNATE A serving of one of the following or a combination to give an equivalent quantity:						• Must be served in the main dish or the main dish and one other menu item. • Textured vegetable protein products, cheese alternate products, and enriched macaroni with fortified protein may be used to meet part of the meat/meat alternate requirement. Fact sheets on each of these alternate foods give detailed instructions for use. NOTE. The amount you must serve of a single meat alternate may seem too large for the particular age group you are serving. To make the quantity of that meat alternate more reasonable, use a smaller amount to meet part of the requirement and supplement with another meat or meat alternate to meet the full requirement.
Lean meat, poultry, or fish (edible portion as served)	1 oz	1½ oz	1½ oz	2 oz	3 oz	
Cheese	1 oz	1½ oz	1½ oz	2 oz	3 oz	
Large egg(s)	1	1½	1½	2	3	
Cooked dry beans or peas	½ cup	¾ cup	¾ cup	1 cup	1½ cup	
Peanut butter	2 Tbsp	3 Tbsp	3 Tbsp	4 Tbsp	6 Tbsp	
VEGETABLE AND/OR FRUIT Two or more servings of vegetable or fruit or both to total	½ cup	½ cup	½ cup	¾ cup	¾ cup	• No more than one-half of the total requirement may be met with full-strength fruit or vegetable juice. • Cooked dry beans or peas may be used as a meat alternate or as a vegetable but not as both in the same meal.
BREAD OR BREAD ALTERNATE Servings of bread or bread alternate	5 per week	8 per week	8 per week	8 per week	10 per week	• At least ½ serving of bread or an equivalent quantity of bread alternate for Group I, and 1 serving for Groups II–V, must be served daily. • Enriched macaroni with fortified protein may be used as a meat alternate or as a bread alternate but not as both in the same meal. NOTE. *Food Buying Guide for School Food Service*, PA-1257 (1980) provides the information for the minimum weight of a serving.
A serving is: • 1 slice of whole-grain or enriched bread • A whole-grain or enriched biscuit, roll, muffin, etc. • ½ cup of cooked whole-grain or enriched rice, macaroni, noodles, whole-grain or enriched pasta products, or other cereal grains such as bulgur or corn grits • A combination of any of the above						
MILK A serving of fluid milk	¾ cup (6 fl oz)	¾ cup (6 fl oz)	½ pint (8 fl oz)	½ pint (8 fl oz)	½ pint (8 fl oz)	At least one of the following forms of milk must be offered: • Unflavored lowfat milk • Unflavored skim milk • Unflavored buttermilk NOTE. This requirement does not prohibit offering other milks, such as whole milk or flavored milk, along with one or more of the above.

Source: U.S. Dept. Agr. Food and Nutrition Service.
[1] Group IV is shaded because it is the one meal pattern which will satisfy all requirements if no portion size adjustments are made.
[2] Group V specifies recommended, not required, quantities for students 12 years and older. These students may request smaller portions, but not smaller than those specified in Group IV.

education has often meant that only those students taking home economics have been reached. From this it has been realized that nutrition education will have to become a part of the curriculum in order to assure that it is taught (Fig. 5.5). The parents need to be reached since the early impressions and attitudes toward food are often lasting ones. Television provides an excellent means for reaching the parents and the small child during the very impressionable years.

With vending machines carrying a range of tempting snack foods, commercial food services with a concern for profits, and rising costs of nutritious foods becoming factors in school feeding, nutrition education is essential. The school foodservice program should provide a model laboratory-classroom for nutrition education in the years ahead.

FIG. 5.5. SCHOOL FOODSERVICE AS A PART OF THE TOTAL EDUCATION OF STUDENTS CAN BE A MODEL LABORATORY-CLASSROOM FOR NUTRITION EDUCATION AS WELL AS MANY OTHER SUBJECTS

BIBLIOGRAPHY

AD HOC COMMITTEE. 1969. Recommendations of Ad Hoc Committee on Nutrition Standards for School Lunch and Other Child Feeding Programs. U.S. Govt. Printing Office, Washington, D.C.

AMERICAN ACADEMY OF PEDIATRICS. 1979. Pediatric Nutrition Handbook. American Academy of Pediatrics, Evanston, Ill.

BETTELHEIM, B. 1972. Why school lunch fails. School Foodservice J. *26*, No. 3, 36–39.

CALLAHAN, D.L. 1971. Focus on nutrition—you can't teach a hungry child, Part II. School Foodservice J. *26*, No. 8, 25.

DWYER, J.T., M.F. ELIAS, and J.H. WARREN. 1973. Effects of an Experimental Breakfast Program on Behavior in the Late Morning. Master's Thesis, Harvard School of Public Health, Cambridge, Mass.

FOOD AND NUTRITION BOARD. 1980. Recommended Dietary Allowances, 9th Edition. Natl. Res. Council, Natl. Acad. of Sci., Washington, D.C.

GUTHRIE, H.A. 1977. Effect of a Flavored Milk Option in A School Lunch Program. J. American Dietet. Assoc., 71, No. 1.

HILL, MARY M. 1968. Nutrition and the type A lunch. Nutrition Program News. U.S. Dept. Agr., U.S. Govt. Printing Office, Washington, D.C.

LABUZA, T.P. 1977. Food and Your Well-Being. AVI, Westport, Conn.

LEVERTON, R.M. 1965. Food Becomes You, 3rd Edition. Iowa State Univ. Press, Ames.

LOWENBERG, MIRIAM E. *et al.* 1968. Food and Man. John Wiley & Sons, New York.

McWILLIAMS, MARGARET. 1975. Nutrition for the Growing Years, 2nd Edition. John Wiley & Sons, Inc., New York.

MURPHY, ELIZABETH W., PERCILLA C. KOONS, and LOUISE PAGE. 1969. Vitamin content of type A school lunches. J. Am. Dietet. Assoc. *55*, No. 4, 378.

POLLITT, ERNESTO, MITCHELL GOSOVITZ, and MARITA GARGUILO. 1978. Educational Benefits of the United States School Feeding Program: A Critical Review of the Literature. American Journal of Public Health, 68, No. 5, 477–481.

READ, M.S. 1973. Malnutrition, Hunger, and Behavior. J. Am. Dietet. Assoc., 63.

ROBINSON, CORINNE H. 1978. Fundamentals of Normal Nutrition. Macmillan Publishing Co., New York.

U.S. DEPT. AGR. 1975. Nutritive value of American foods in common units. U.S. Govt. Printing Office, Washington, D.C.

U.S. DEPT. AGR. 1980. Menu Planning Guide for School Foodservice. U.S. Govt. Printing Office, Washington, D.C.

U.S. DEPT. AGR. & HEALTH, EDUCATION & WELFARE. 1980. Nutrition and Your Health: Dietary Guidelines for Americans. U.S. Govt. Printing Office, Washington, D.C.

U.S. DEPT. OF HEALTH, EDUC. & WELFARE. 1979. Healthy People, the Surgeon General's Report on Health Promotion and Disease Prevention Background Papers. U.S. Govt. Printing Office, Washington, D.C.

U.S. OFFICE OF TECHNOLOGY ASSESSMENT. 1978. Nutrition Research Alternatives. U.S. Govt. Printing Office, Washington, D.C.

U.S. PUBLIC LAW 396, 79TH CONGRESS. 1946. 60 Stat 231 (June 4).

WHITE, P. and N. SELVEIG. 1972. Chocolate Milk vs Whole Milk in School Lunch Programs. J. American Dietet. Assoc., 220.

WILLETT, ROSLYN. 1972. The dramatic age of nutrition. Food Management 7, No. 1, 54–67.

WILSON, E.D., K.H. FISHER, and M.E. FUQUA. 1975. Principles of Nutrition. John Wiley & Sons, New York.

6

Menu Planning

The menu is the single most controlling factor in a foodservice operation. It would be ideal if the kitchen layout were planned around the menus and the equipment purchased for the menus to be prepared; however, this is seldom the case. Certainly menus should be planned before the purchasing of food, before the labor needs are determined, and before the price of the meal to the clientele is decided. Planning menus requires a great deal of knowledge about the operation. Consequently, when planning menus the following should be considered; each of these will be discussed in turn: (1) nutritional needs; (2) food preferences; (3) compliance with Federal regulations; (4) the amount of money available; (5) equipment in the kitchen; (6) staff—the amount of labor and their skill; (7) type of service; (8) food supply and USDA-donated foods; (9) season and climate; (10) aesthetics; and (11) what choice will be available.

NUTRITIONAL NEEDS

School foodservices use the USDA meal patterns (see Table 5.6) in planning nutritional needs; however, a few school systems have tested computing the nutrients. With the increased use of computers, the Computer Assisted Nutrient Standard (CANS) system developed by USDA has become feasible. The lunch should contribute a minimum of one-third the Recommended Daily Allowances, which is discussed in more detail in Chap. 5. When using the meal patterns the *Food Buying Guide for School Food Service* (U.S. Dept. Agr. 1980) provides the yields by purchased units and is a companion to *Menu Planning Guide for School Food Service* (U.S. Dept. Agr. 1980).

The meat/meat alternate in the menu may be made up of a combination of foods. The meal requirement specifies the following:

K-3 grades Group III	4-12 grades Group IV
1½ oz meat	2 oz meat
or	or
1½ oz cheese	2 oz cheese
or	or
1½ eggs	2 eggs
or	or
¾ cup cooked dry beans/peas	1 cup cooked dry beans/peas
or	or
3 Tbsp peanut butter	4 Tbsp peanut butter

Commercially prepared combination foods, such as chicken pot pies, may be used if the amount of meat is known. Other meat alternates, such as the quantity of eggs used in baking a cake or making bread, peanut butter in cookies, or cheese in the sauce can be counted toward meeting the protein needs. For example, in the menu—spaghetti with meat and cheese sauce, tossed salad, French bread with butter, chocolate brownies, and milk—the combination contributing is:

ground beef	10 lb	(6 serving/lb)	60 2-oz servings meat
cheese	3 lb	(8 serving/lb)	24 2-oz servings meat alternate
eggs	32	(2 egg/serving)	16 2-oz servings meat alternate
			100 2-oz servings for Group IV

Using protein-fortified enriched macaroni, spaghetti, and other noodles in combination with meat, poultry, fish, or cheese to meet one-half of the minimum requirement is a way of stretching the food dollar. Also, textured vegetable proteins (soybean products) can be used to meet up to 30% of the requirement; however, most cooks have found that 15% with 85% meat is a more desirable ratio. For example:

> 6 lb dry textured vegetable protein (10% moisture and 50% protein)
> 9 lb. water
> Yields: 15 lb hydrated product
> Combined with: 85 lb meat
> Yields: 100 lb mixture

Recipes will need some alteration when using the textured vegetable protein. Therefore, FNS Notice 219 from the USDA will be very helpful in making the adjustments.

The vegetable-fruit requirement must be met with at least two sources.

Minimum quantities for students, grades K-12 are:

Group III ages 5-8 Grades K-3	Group IV ages 9 and over Grades 4-12
½ cup	¾ cup

The vegetables used in the main dish (such as, tomato products used in spaghetti) may be counted in meeting this requirement. Full-strength fruit or vegetable juice can be counted toward meeting up to one-half of the vegetable/fruit requirement. Large combination salads, however, if containing at least ¾ cup of 2 or more vegetables and/or fruits, such as a chef salad or a salad bar arrangement will meet the full requirement. The challenge is planning fruits and vegetables the students will eat.

Pies, cakes, cookies, brownies, etc., are considered additional foods for energy. But pizza crust, pasta, rice, as well as breads if made with enriched or whole grain, can be counted toward meeting the bread requirement.

Butter or fortified margarine may be used in cooking or as a spread on bread. Since 1975 there has not been a butter-margarine requirement.

The milk requirement is a serving (½ pint or 8 fl oz.) of fluid milk. At least one of the following forms of milk must be offered: unflavored lowfat milk, unflavored skim milk, and unflavored buttermilk. Other milks, either flavor or unflavored, may be offered as a choice. Milkshakes must contain ½ pint of fluid milk meeting State or local standards for fluid milk. This does vary from State to state and should be checked with the proper state agency. Assuring that ½ pint of fluid milk is present in the milkshake requires close monitoring.

Food in addition to those needed to meet the meal patterns are desirable for older children whose energy needs are greater than the meal patterns furnishes. Children 6 to 8 yr old frequently find the meal patterns provides more food than they can eat. Additional foods in those cases may be undesirable.

COMPLIANCE WITH FEDERAL REGULATIONS

The meal requirements are numerous coupled with many more recommendations. Refer to the *Menu Planning Guide for School Food Service* (U.S. Dept. Agr. 1980) for detailed discussions. Regulations do allow for certain variations in the food components of the basic meal patterns on an experimental basis and in the instance where individual children are unable to consume certain foods for medical reasons. Also, religious, economic, ethnic, and physical needs have reasons for approving variations from the basic meal requirements; however, these exceptions must be granted by the Food and Nutrition Service, USDA, Washington, D.C.

Schools are required to serve all parts of the meal pattern to students in elementary school; however, students in senior high may choose to take only those food items he/she plans to eat.The federal regulation requires that "offer versus serve" be carried out in senior high schools. It may be extended to middle and junior high schools at the discretion of local school food authorities. In "offer versus serve" school lunch programs are required to plan and offer all five food items of the school meal patterns. Students must choose at least three of the five items for their lunch to be reimbursable as a lunch. This should be kept in mind when planning go-togethers, particularly how the foods will be served.

FOOD PREFERENCES

Food preferences are instilled in people at an early age and are slow to be changed. Regional food habits should be considered in menu planning. Menus served in the New England States may include Boston baked beans and brown bread, whereas in the South the menu may include regional favorites of candied yams, black-eyed peas, and hominy grits. However, regional foods among today's students are not as popular as they once were. The universal favorites seem to be hamburgers, spaghetti with meat sauce, and sandwiches in general.

Black Americans enjoy soul foods, and these preferences are to be considered in planning the menu. In communities with a large foreign population the food preferences may be different from others in the same region. It is important that the menus be planned to reflect the regional, racial, religious, and nationality preferences of the groups to be served.

There are also fads of the time in food as in dress and should be capitalized on when planning the menus. These fads change and it takes close communication with the students to keep up with the changes. If the menus include the food that the students like, there will be greater participation, less plate waste, and better morale. Food means many different things to people, as pointed out by Rountree (1949):

Food is eaten for enjoyment, for emotional release, for social prestige, and for attention, adverse or otherwise. Food is refused because of such unconscious emotions as the pleasure of paining others and showing self-assertion.

What a person will accept and what he prefers are two different things. Some menus can be used that are acceptable, but most of the menus should be ones preferred in order to keep the students happy. It is possible to do this and still serve a nutritious meal. Certainly it is the aim of school feeding programs to teach students to like new foods or different foods, but putting them on a menu and serving them seldom does this without the aid of nutrition education. When nutrition education is being taught, much can be done with new, different combinations of foods and greater variety can be offered.

TYPE MENUS—STANDARD OR CHOICE

Standard Menus

A standard menu is a set menu meeting all the meal requirements without any choice. This type menu is commonly used in elementary schools where the administration is often concerned about the amount of time needed to serve the children. Decision-making may take too much time for the first-grade students. The advantages of using a standard menu are: (1) greater productivity and lower labor cost, (2) faster moving lines, (3) less equipment needed, (4) easier to judge quantities of food needed.

It is impossible to plan one menu that 100% of the students will like. Also, older students object to someone else deciding what they will eat. Therefore, the standard menu is more acceptable in elementary schools than in secondary schools.

Multiple-choice Menus

Choice menus take close planning and are more difficult to produce, but have several advantages: (1) the number served usually increases, (2) less plate waste, (3) fewer complaints from the students, (4) greater opportunity to meet the students' nutritional requirements.

When parts of the menus are offered for students to make some choices, it may be referred to as a multiple-choice menu. For example:

Salisbury Steak
Mashed Potatoes—Gravy
Choice: Buttered Spinach or Orange Juice
Hot Rolls and Butter
Choice: Gelatin Dessert or Brownies

Choice: Lowfat Milk or Chocolate Milk

Care must be taken in offering choices within the meal pattern, since all combinations possible must meet the nutritional needs. In the above menu, potato chips cannot be offered as a choice with mashed potatoes, because potato chips are not considered a vegetable. However, buttered spinach and orange juice can be offered as a choice. Any of the above combinations will meet the meal pattern. Another consideration in planning choice is that serving time will be increased, and with careful planning it can be kept at a minimum. For example, if the choices are tossed salad and tomato juice, each can be served in individual serving dishes, so the student can pick up his choice without having to be waited on by the foodservice worker. In the above menu, each of the choices can be made without individualized service, since only one choice item goes on the plate. One plate can be ready with spinach and another without.

Offering choices is particularly desirable when a less popular item is on the menu. This also will make it possible to increase the variety. Though it appears that the students would be happy with hamburgers every day, this is seldom the case. Studies have shown that one's desire for a food diminishes after having eaten it, and even a popular food will become less appealing after continued repeating, particularly if the person does not make the choice of repeating. Since vegetables are the lowest on the preference list with students, a choice of vegetables can lessen the plate waste and in turn meet the nutritional goals. It is common for people to complain about food. The complaints seem to be less when a choice of well-prepared food is offered. When an individual makes the decision of what he will eat, he tends to be less critical then when he does not have the option. With the multiple-choice menus, as many choices can be offered as the cafeteria staff can handle. A choice of main dishes may be offered without slowing the line if one of each choice is dished up and ready at all times to be picked up by the student. When there are two or more items to go on the plate that are choices, it will be necessary to dish the food up on request of each student. This will slow the speed of the serving line and increase the labor cost per meal served.

Multiple Menus

Multiple menus are when more than one entire menu is offered for students to choose from. This may be accomplished with two entirely different menus, such as:

Grilled Cheese Sandwich	Sliced Beef and Gravy
Tomato Soup	Whipped Potatoes
Potato Chips	Buttered Green Peas
Fresh Fruit Cup	Hot Rolls Butter
Milk	Milk

These two menus might be referred to as the "soup and sandwich" line and the "regular" lunch line. Some school foodservices have been able to

successfully serve four or more choice menus. However, this seems unnecessary. The same can be accomplished with some choices within the
menu frame. When choices are offered, additional time is needed in
preparation, which means more labor. The "soup and sandwich" or
"speed line" has been very successful in secondary schools. It is desirable
to have more than one serving line when multiple menus are offered,
though it is possible to manage them on one line. One of the menus can be
a rather routine, fixed menu with few changes. Students like the security
of knowing what to expect. The speed line might have the following
framework:

Soup of the Day: Monday—Tomato
                      Tuesday—Vegetable
                      Wednesday—Chili
                      Thursday—Tomato
                      Friday—Chicken Noodle

          (or a choice of two soups each day)

Sandwich   Hamburger
                          or
                      Fishburger
                      Peanut Butter and Jelly or Cheese
French Fries or Salad
Milk

The dessert can be sold extra. Though the above menu offers little
variety, it may make a large number of the students happy. The regular
lunch line menu can present the variety. Since this is the "sandwich"
generation, it may be capitalized on. Again, the goal is to serve a nutritional lunch that will be eaten. The nutritional value is there even if
the variety is not.

Since many teenage girls are concerned with their weight and their
calorie needs are less than the athletic teenage boy's needs, it may be
desirable to offer—as a multiple menu—a salad plate that meets the
meal lunch patterns, such as shown in Table 6.1.

TABLE 6.1. TWO DIETER'S LUNCHES

Chef salad with 2 oz. ham, cheese, or 1 egg, 1 oz ham	Grated American cheese or cottage cheese
Hot roll with butter	Peach and pear halves
Jello cubes	Lettuce leaves
Choice of Milk	Sliced bread with butter
	Choice of Milk

Salad Bars

With the popularity of self-service during the seventies in fast food operations, schools have found it simple to promote salad bars and with much success. The salad bar is being used to provide the complete lunch and as a salad with a meal. To assure that all Federal meal requirements are carried out, careful supervision may be necessary. Large combination vegetable and/or fruit salads of this type, containing at least ¾ cup of 2 or more vegetables and/or fruits, are considered as 2 or more servings and will meet the full vegetable/fruit requirement. Some points to consider when setting up a salad bar:

(1) meat and meat alternates are the most expensive part of the meal and preportioning will help assure the correct amount is served or taken;

(2) eight servings per week of bread and bread alternate may be slightly difficult to serve on the salad bar. Croutons, pasta products, and crackers add variety and help meet the bread requirement;

(3) station a cashier at the end of the salad bar where the tray can be checked to assure all components of the meal patterns are on the tray. In high schools (and junior high schools, if approved by local school district) students do not have to take all foods under "offer versus served".

Suggested Salad Bar Offerings:

Offer at least four of the following daily for a variety of colors, shapes and textures:
  Bean spouts
  Chick peas
  Cauliflower flowerettes
  Sauerkraut
  Radishes, sliced or whole
  Julienne beets
  Carrots, sliced or grated
  Tomatoes, cherry or wedges
  Green pepper rings or slices
  Cucumber slices
  Broccoli flowerettes
  Celery, chunks or chopped
  Spinach leaves
  Three-bean salad
  Green peas with onion

Offer at least three of the following daily (preportion to assure the meat/meat alternate meal requirement are met):
  Cheese, grated or cubed
  Eggs, sliced or wedged
  Cottage cheese
  Chicken, tuna or egg salad
  Julienne ham
  Julienne roast beef
  Julienne salami
  Julienne turkey
  Macaroni salad, (made with protein fortified macaroni)
  Three bean salad, (made with dry beans/peas)
  Combination of the above

Beans (green, wax or kidney)
Peanut granules, peanuts
Pickle chips, dill or sweet

Offer one of the following daily:
Peaches, diced or sliced
Pears, diced or sliced
Pineapple
Orange wedges
Apple slices or applesauce
Melon pieces
Fruit cup
Grapes
Raisins

Offer at least eight servings of
bread weekly, or two a day:
Sliced breads and rolls, enriched
or whole grain
Crackers
Soft pretzels
Croutons
Bread sticks
Muffins
Pasta products

Offer at least two salad dressings
each day.

There are many attractive pieces of equipment for salad bars, however, some schools have successfully turned a regular serving line into a salad bar.

The choices can be planned into a menu so that the preparation is not so difficult. For example, when turkey and dressing are served on the regular menu, turkey salad is on the salad plate or in a sandwich on the sandwich line. When planning choices, the amount of labor needed for preparation and serving must be considered. There are also usually more leftovers and waste when choices are offered. This can be expensive if the use of leftovers is not planned into the menu. Ease in preparation and serving of choices are possible in desserts by offering choices like chilled canned fruit and cake with a variety of icings. The chilled canned fruit takes very little time to portion up. The same cake can be used with various icings.

When offering a meat dish or any dish requiring much preparation, the other choice can be one needing little preparation, such as frozen fish squares or ground beef patties which require only the cooking.

THE AMOUNT OF MONEY AVAILABLE

In order to have a sound program, a knowledge of the amount of money that is available to be spent on food must be known. It should never be a guessing game, hoping there will be enough income at the end of the month to cover the cost. Recipe and menu costing are discussed in Chap. 10. Determining labor cost is far easier then determining food cost. Waste and price increases in food make it difficult to predetermine how much the served food will cost.

Perhaps the best start in determining the amount of money that can be spent for food, is to determine what the income is on each lunch served. In most instances this can be determined by adding together the sources of income (Table 6.2).

No formula can be applied to every situation. The cost of labor is higher in some parts of the country than others, as is the price of food. If many prepared foods are used, the food cost would be higher and the labor lower. The formula most frequently applicable for on-site preparation is 50 to 55% of the income used for food, 35 to 40% of the income used for labor, and 5 to 10% for miscellaneous, such as paper items and detergents and other indirect cost.

Using the formula of 55% of the income for food and the above sample of income, 59¢ would be available for food. The cost of the ½ pt of milk, a relatively constant price, could be subtracted first. If the milk costs 13¢, this would leave 46¢ in the above example to cover all the other foods in the menu. If the cost of the menu is greater than the amount of money available, the next day's menu can be under, so that it evens out.

TABLE 6.2. DETERMINING THE INCOME FOR SCHOOL LUNCHES

Source of Income	Sample Amt (¢)
Student's payment for lunch	.65
Federal reimbursement	.19
State reimbursement (if any)	.04½
County or city funds (if any)	.04
Donations (if any)	
Value of USDA commodities	.16½
Total income	$1.08½

EQUIPMENT IN THE KITCHEN

It would be ideal if the equipment were planned around the menu; however, in many cases the lack of equipment or the existing equipment determines what can be on the menu. If the oven space is limited, a menu which includes cake, yeast rolls, and baked potatoes may be physically impossible. The number and size mixers will determine also how many mixed items are possible on the single menu. If a deep fat fryer is not available, French fries will need to be of a type that will brown in the oven, and fried chicken will need a different type batter than when deep-fat fried. The serving utensils and dishes may also be controlling factors in menu planning.

STAFF—THE AMOUNT OF LABOR AND THEIR SKILL

If the foodservice is staffed closely, the number of foods requiring extensive preparation will need to be limited. A balance in the amount of preparation required is desirable, so that one day is not almost impossible and the next is very light. Also, overloading one employee should be avoided. For example, strawberry shortcake and yeast rolls may overload the baker if prepared the same day. Menus that require a lot of last-minute preparation should be avoided.

The skills and abilities of the personnel may limit the menus. On-the-job training can help develop the skills, but in most cases a less elaborate dish that can be prepared successfully may be the solution. Using some prepared foods, such as dehydrated potato flakes instead of fresh potatoes for mashed potatoes, pre-portioned hamburger patties instead of making the patties out of meat purchased in bulk, and cakes from mixes, can make it possible to get the variety of food desired; and in many cases a better quality results then when inexperienced or rushed personnel are preparing it. A comparison of using dehydrated potato flakes versus fresh potatoes has persuaded many foodservice directors that they cannot afford to pay the labor costs needed to prepare fresh potatoes. More and more mixes, pre-portioned items, pre-cooked foods, and bakery products are being used to reduce labor cost. A comparison should be made to determine if there is really a savings to the individual operation before increasing the use of convenience foods. Too often the labor cost is not reduced, and the cost of food increases when convenience foods are used.

TYPE OF SERVICE

When food is prepared and served from the same location, a greater variety of foods can be planned in the menus. If the food is to be taken to other locations, certain foods may have to be eliminated from the menu because the food does not transport well or there may be danger of high bacterial count. Foods that contain eggs, mayonnaise, poultry, especially when in mixed dishes, should be handled with great care and kept at a temperature below 40°F or above 150°F at all times and served at these temperatures. If it is not possible to keep hot foods at 150°F or above and keep cold foods at 40°F or colder, combination dishes with protein-rich food in them should be eliminated from the menu. Bacterial growth is discussed in detail in Chap. 9.

Though most school foodservices use cafeteria style service, some classes eat family style. When students eat in their classrooms in common areas, or other such arrangements, soups and juices may have to be

TABLE 6.3. GUIDE TO SEASON WHEN FRESH FRUITS AND VEGETABLES ARE MOST AVAILABLE

Food	Jan	Feb	Mar	Apr	May	Jun	Jul	Aug	Sept	Oct	Nov	Dec
Apples	x	x	x	x	x	—	—	—	x	x	x	x
Apricots	—	—	—	—	—	x	x	—	—	—	—	—
Asparagus	—	—	x	x	x	x	—	—	—	—	—	—
Avocados	x	x	x	x	x	x	x	x	x	x	x	x
Bananas	x	x	x	x	x	x	x	x	x	x	x	x
Blackberries	—	—	—	—	x	x	x	x	—	—	—	—
Blueberries	—	—	—	—	—	x	x	x	—	—	—	—
Broccoli	x	x	x	x	x	—	—	x	x	x	x	x
Cabbage	x	x	x	x	x	x	x	x	x	x	x	x
Cantaloupe	—	—	—	—	x	x	x	x	x	—	—	—
Carrots	x	x	x	x	x	x	x	x	x	x	x	x
Celery	x	x	x	x	x	x	x	x	x	x	x	x
Cherries	—	—	—	—	x	x	x	—	—	—	—	—
Collards	x	x	x	x	x	—	—	—	x	x	x	x
Corn	—	—	—	—	x	x	x	x	x	x	—	—
Cranberries	—	—	—	—	—	—	—	—	x	x	x	x
Cucumbers	—	—	—	x	x	x	x	x	x	x	x	—
Grapes	—	—	—	—	—	x	x	x	x	x	x	x
Honeydew	—	—	—	—	—	—	—	—	—	x	—	—
Kale	x	x	x	x	—	—	—	—	x	x	x	x
Lettuce	x	x	x	x	x	x	x	x	x	x	x	x
Mustard greens	x	x	x	—	—	—	—	—	—	x	x	x

Item												
Nectarines						x	x	x	x			
Onions, green			x	x	x	x	x	x	x	x	x	x
Oranges, all	x	x	x	x	x	x	x	x	x		x	x
Parsley	x	x	x	x	x	x	x	x	x	x	x	x
Parsnips	x	x	x	x	x	x	x			x	x	x
Peaches						x	x	x	x			
Pears	x	x	x	x	x	x	x		x	x	x	x
Peppers, sweet	x		x	x	x	x	x	x	x	x	x	x
Persian melons							x	x	x	x		
Pineapples	x	x	x	x	x	x	x			x		
Plums						x	x	x	x			
Potatoes	x	x	x	x	x	x	x	x	x	x	x	x
Radishes	x	x	x	x	x	x	x	x	x	x	x	x
Rhubarb	x	x	x	x	x	x	x		x			
Spinach	x	x	x	x	x	x	x	x	x	x	x	x
Squash	x	x	x	x	x	x	x	x	x	x	x	x
Strawberries				x	x	x	x					
Sweet potatoes	x	x	x	x	x			x	x	x	x	x
Tangerines	x	x								x	x	x
Tomatoes			x	x	x	x	x	x	x	x	x	x
Turnips-rutabagas	x	x	x	x	x	x	x	x	x	x	x	x
Watermelons						x	x	x	x			

Source: Anon. (1964).

omitted from the menu. However, all of these factors may have little effect on the menu when the employees are determined to overcome them or serve the food in spite of them.

FOOD SUPPLY AND USDA DONATED FOODS

The availability of food will limit the menus for some locations. The frequency of deliveries and storage space in the kitchen may also enter into menu planning. A small lunchroom located some distance from the city may find the availability of foods very limited.

For school foodservices participating in the National School Lunch Program there is an additional factor that has to be considered when planning the menus—USDA-donated foods. In order to get the value of the commodities issued by the USDA and keep the cost of the lunch to the students at lower prices, it is necessary to utilize the USDA-donated foods. This may be the greatest challenge of menu planning—particularly when the food is very unpopular with the students or is very difficult to prepare. For the most part, the USDA-donated foods are of top quality and, for most on-site preparations, easily used in the menus.

Donated food can be used in numerous ways and the ingenuity of the personnel can mean great savings in the food budget. Some donated foods are out of the ordinary or unfamiliar to the students. Some nutrition education may be needed to make the students familiar with the food. For example, canned purple plums and fresh cranberries are unfamiliar foods to children in some parts of the country. Also, the irregular distribution of donated foods may require sudden menu changes or flexibility in menus. The donated foods should be treated as if they were purchased from funds in the local budget—that is, utilized effectively.

SEASON AND CLIMATE

People tend to want heavier, hotter foods in cold weather; cool salads, gelatin desserts, and cold sliced meats are more appealing in the hot summer. Chili in summertime will not go over as well as when snow is on the ground.

The seasons will also affect the cost of the food purchased. Corn-on-the-cob will be very expensive in March, whereas in August and September when it is in season, the prices are less. It is helpful to have a list of foods with season most plentiful at hand when planning the menu (Table 6.3). The availability in California and Florida may not correspond with the middle States.

Holidays and special occasions should be planned into the menus. Serving foods traditionally served on holidays in the area (region) will create festivity and be appreciated by students of all ages. Starting in January, there are many holidays that lend themselves to special dishes or to decorating the common foods. Education Week, National School Lunch Week, United Nations Day, and special days in the school, such as a championship football game, French Week, etc., are occasions that give the foodservice an opportunity to participate in the school's activities.

AESTHETICS

"People eat with their eyes" is a saying that is very true. A meal can be nutritionally adequate and contain the favorite foods, but if it is not attractively served with eye appeal, it may not be eaten. When planning eye appeal into the menu, the planner will use some basic principles used by an artist in obtaining good design. The list of rules or principles seems long and perhaps too involved at first using, but after practice it becomes automatic. Variety plays an important part in eye appeal—variety in color, shapes, flavors, textures, and temperatures. To plan a menu with aesthetic appeal, the following should be considered:

Color Combinations.—A colorless menu with all white food is uninteresting and pale looking. Sliced turkey, mashed potatoes, cauliflower, and vanilla pudding makes a very unattractive plate. But sliced turkey, candied yams, green beans or broccoli, and lemon pudding with a cherry on top, make a very beautiful colorful plate and will stimulate the appetite.

Variety of Foods.—Avoid the use of the same food in more than one dish. When apple juice or applesauce is on the menu, the addition of apple pie lacks variety; whereas, cherry pie or peach pie would add the necessary variety.

Texture.—Refers to the way the food feels in the mouth—soft, crisp, smooth, hard, chewy. Variety in texture is desirable, and a good rule is to plan a soft or smooth food, crisp food, and a hard food into each menu for interest in texture. A menu of creamed chicken, mashed potatoes, rosy applesauce, and chocolate pudding would have basically the same feel in the mouth, whereas a menu of creamed chicken over toast squares, green peas, Waldorf salad, and chocolate pudding would give the variety in texture desired.

Shape.—Variety in the form in which food is presented plays a big part in eye appeal. A menu of all square shapes lacks variety in shape, for example: Fish square, hash brown potatoes, cole slaw, cornbread square, and cake square. A variety of shapes, such as a combination of diced, squares, circles, and strips, is more appealing. The use of the scoop for portion control has lent itself to "mounds." Portioning of food can make variety in shapes and the scoop should not be used for more than two items.

Flavors.—Flavors that are combined should offer variety. Highly seasoned foods should be combined with foods of mild flavor. A good example of this is of traditional go-togethers: cranberries with turkey; tartar sauce with fish squares; mint jelly with lamb; and spaghetti with tossed green salad. The basic flavors are sweet, sour, salty, and bitter. A combination of spicy foods with bland, of sweet foods and sour foods, with a balance of the flavors is desirable.

Consistency.—Consistency refers to the degree of firmness, density, the way they are held together. Foods with sauces should be combined with foods that are not runny, but rather with foods that are firm. Since children prefer firm foods, but few combination or casserole items, care should be taken in planning a menu so that if the main dish is a casserole-type dish that the vegetable is not a mixture. Plain foods add balance when combined with casserole dishes. A variety in the way the food is prepared may be helpful if listed for the menu-planner. Fried, baked, broiled, steamed, or boiled and raw forms offer variety when a combination of two or more of these methods of preparation is used.

Menu planning is one of the most challenging responsibilities for a school foodservice manager or planner. Most menus can be criticized in one way or another because it is almost impossible to accomplish all of the goals or rules of menu planning.

TOOLS FOR MENU PLANNING

In order to be successful, menus take time, concentration, reference materials, and a knowledgeable person or persons. Menu planning should be planned far enough ahead so that orders can be placed and received. It is poor management to plan the menu by the day and depending on what is on hand. Other school foodservices' menus can be used as a guide or to get ideas from, but seldom can someone else's menus completely meet the demands of another foodservice.

Reference materials that can be helpful in planning menus are the *Menu Planning Guide for School Food Service* (U.S. Dept. Agr., 1980, PA 1260), *Food Buying Guide for School Food Service* (U.S. Dept. Agr., 1980, PA 1257), recipes, past records, and list of commodities to be used and an inventory of what is on hand.

Plan menus at least two weeks in advance. Start by selecting a meat or meat alternate for each day of the menus, then select the vegetables and fruits to go with the main dish. Add the breads, butter, and milk and additional foods desired. Check the menus to see that all the previously mentioned factors in good menu planning have been met in each menu. A check list that may be helpful is shown in Fig. 6.1.

Menus should be left for a period of time and then gone back over to catch errors or problems that may have gotten by the planner when planning them. The form often used by school foodservices resembles the one used in the sample menus (Fig. 6.2).

When the menus are planned it is a good time to indicate on the menus the recipe number or source that will be used in preparing the foods on the menu and the size serving. For example:

Spaghetti with Meat Sauce	Tossed Green Salad	Apple Crisp
D-30	E-18	C-3
¾ to 1 cup serving	½ cup	⅓ cup

This information becomes more important when the planner is not the person who will be in charge of the preparation of the menus. When menus are planned by someone other than the one in charge of preparation, it is important that notes of explanation be given.

Student Committee

Good communication with students is necessary to accomplish the goals of school feeding. The adults planning menus may like scalloped tomatoes, okra gumbo, and tuna casserole, but these may be unfamiliar or unpopular foods with students. Student committees of secondary schools, consisting of a good representation of the cultural and social groups within the student population, should be made a part of the planning committee. This committee should consist of students, teachers, parents, board members, foodservice manager, and foodservice administrator in order to open the communications between the interested people. This committee can act as adviser in menu planning, testing new foods, can cutting and selecting qualities of foods to be purchased, and policy changes to be brought about.

Surveys and polls conducted by student leaders can give valuable information to menu planners. Student complaints and comments should be listened to and action taken to improve situations. Students should be thought of as the "customer."

Elementary age students enjoy menu planning. A class studying food units will be excited about planning a school menu. It is a good opportunity for making them feel a part of the planning. And it affords an opportunity for teaching nutrition and telling the school lunch story.

	YES	NO
NUTRITION:		

1. Do all menus meet meal requirements?
2. Is a Vitamin C-rich food included frequently?
3. Is a Vitamin A-rich food included twice a week?
4. Is an Iron-rich food included?

PHYSICAL ASPECTS:

5. Has an inventory of what's on hand been considered in planning?
6. Is the equipment adequate to prepare each menu?
7. Is the work load among workers balanced?
8. Do the menus fit the skills of the employees?

AESTHETICS:

9. Are the lunches planned with good color contrast?
10. Do the lunches have foods of both mild and strong or pronounced flavors?
11. Are there varieties in shape of foods?
12. Do the meals contain something crisp and something soft? Something hot? Something cold?
13. Are most of the foods and food combinations familiar to the child and liked?
14. Have holidays been considered in the preparation?

OTHERS:

15. Have ways of using USDA-donated foods been included in the lunches?
16. Are lunches planned in order that some preparation can be done the day before?
17. Have the lunches been planned in keeping with the season of the year?
18. Has excessive use of foods high in fats been avoided?
19. Is there a balance in the week between low cost and high cost meals?
20. Are the menus within the food budget?
21. Is the menu acceptable to the students?

FIG. 6.1. SAMPLE CHECKLIST FOR A WEEK'S MENUS

CYCLE MENUS

From the list to be considered when planning a menu it is easy to see that good menu planning is time consuming, and the success of the operation will probably depend on how well they are planned. Cycle menus are a set of menus carefully planned to be rotated over a certain

Lunch Pattern	MONDAY	PORTION SIZE		TUESDAY	PORTION SIZE	
		Group	Group		Group	Group
Meat and Meat Alternate						
Vegetable and Fruit						
Bread and Bread Alternate						
Milk						
Other Foods						

Lunch Pattern	WEDNESDAY	PORTION SIZE		THURSDAY	PORTION SIZE	
Meat and Meat Alternate						
Vegetable and Fruit						
Bread and Bread Alternate						
Milk						
Other Foods						

Lunch Pattern	FRIDAY	PORTION SIZE	
Meat and Meat Alternate			
Vegetable and Fruit			
Bread and Bread Alternate			
Milk			
Other Foods			

Menu Planning Worksheet

Courtesy of U.S. Dept. of Agr.

FIG. 6.2. SAMPLE MENU PLANNING WORKSHEET

period of time. The menus are used consecutively and repeated. Not only do cycle menus save time, but it becomes possible to forecast what foods are needed over an entire year with fair accuracy. This is very important information for bid buying (discussed in Chap. 7). Cycle menus also make scheduling the work easier. It becomes possible to standardize preparation and enables the personnel to become more experienced. If the cycle menus are taken a few steps further, food orders for the cycles, work schedules for the cycles, and quantities to be prepared can be planned for the cycles and then become cycle food orders, cycle work schedules, and cycle preparation information to be reused or rotated with the menus. Knowing the needs, it is possible to buy foods in larger quantities if there is an advantage to do so and if storage is available.

For school lunch programs where the students are captive customers, cycle menus have to be long enough, contain enough menus, so the cycle does not become monotonous, repetitious, and have a definite pattern, making obvious to the students when a certain dish will appear. Cycle menus can be of any length. Two- to five-week cycles, with 10 to 25 menus to be rotated, are very workable and satisfactory. Each of the five-day or week of menus is called a "set" to be numbered and charted as to the week of the year the "set" is to be served (Fig. 6.3).

A cycle of three weeks to be used over a three-month period or for a season can solve the seasonal food problems. This would mean a fall cycle, winter cycle, spring cycle and, if needed, a summer cycle. Cycles longer than six weeks lose their purpose and advantages. The number of menus in the cycle is determined by how many entrees or main dishes to be served with the repeats of popular entrees. To determine how long a cycle a school system needs, list all the main dishes to be served as illustrated in Table 6.4. Put three stars beside the most popular one, two stars by the next popular, and one star by the main dishes that warrant repeating due to abundance of food supply, USDA-donated foods or for pure economy of the food.

From this list 25 menus can be planned. The alternates are used to add variety. Ground beef is in so many of the popular foods that special attention needs to be given in planning menus in which ground beef does not appear more than three times per week, and preferably only twice.

Set I	Sept 6	Oct 11	Nov 15	Dec 27	Jan 31	Mar 6	Apr 10	May 15
Set II	Sept 13	Oct 18	Nov 22	Jan 3	Feb 7	Mar 13	Apr 17	May 22
Set III	Sept 20	Oct 25	Nov 29	Jan 10	Feb 14	Mar 20	Apr 24	May 29
Set IV	Sept 27	Nov 1	Dec 6	Jan 17	Feb 21	Mar 27	May 1	June 5
Set V	Oct 4	Nov 8	Dec 13	Jan 24	Feb 28	Apr 13	May 8	June 12

FIG. 6.3. EXAMPLE OF 5–SETS OF CYCLE MENUS CHARTED AS TO WEEK OF YEAR TO BE SERVED

TABLE 6.4. SAMPLE LIST OF MAIN DISHES

Spaghetti with meat sauce***[1]	Hamburgers***
Meat loaf with Spanish sauce	Fishburgers**
Meat balls with gravy	Hot dogs**
Lasagna	Steak Sub***
Chili con carne (alternate)[3]	Grilled cheese sandwich*[4]
Salisbury steak with gravy	Peanut butter and jelly sandwich
Pizza***	Hoagies or submarines**
Beeferoni	Barbecue on bun**
	Pizzaburger***
Roast beef and gravy (alternate)	Ham and cheese sandwich
	Sliced turkey sandwich
Tacos with refried beans	
Fried chicken**[2]	Baked ham (alternate)
Barbecued chicken	Tuna salad (alternate)
	Fried fish (alternate)
Batter fried fish	

[1]The *** indicates that this is a popular menu to be repeated in the cycle up to three times.
[2]The ** indicates this is a popular menu to be repeated in the cycle up to two times
[3](alternate) indicates this may not be as popular an item, too expensive, seasonal, or too difficult in preparation to repeat often. It can be shown as an alternate on the cycle and repeated every other time the menu comes up to be served.
[4]The * indicates this is economical or is a government commodity and is to be repeated once.

More frequent serving will cause the children to feel that only ground beef is being served. A good rule to follow in planning a week of menus is to use two beef meals, one fish or pork meal, one chicken meal, and one meat alternate in the set.

Some dishes may be wanted on the menus but are seasonal, too expensive, not popular enough, or are too hard to prepare to be repeated as often as the cycle will repeat itself. In this case, these dishes can be made alternate menus.

Cycle menus are planned as you would plan a standard week's menu, but there is one additional step—checking the adjoining menus. It is wise to lay the sets of menus out in such a fashion that they can be seen as a whole. Make sure that repeats are not too close; particularly check the Friday and the following Monday's menu and the last menu in the cycle and the first menu of the cycle.

FREQUENCY CHARTS

A frequency chart is a chart that lists the number of times foods appear on the menu. Frequency charts can indicate meats, vegetables, breads, fruits and desserts, and at a glance repeats of foods can easily be seen (Figs. 6.4 and 6.5). If a food is repeated frequently, the question should be asked "Is this a popular food?" If not, why is it being repeated? This chart is now valuable in determining the quantities of meats, of certain vegetables, etc., that will be used during the cycle or year. This information will be useful and needed in estimating quantities for bid buying and for buying in large quantities.

Item	Set I					Set II					Set III					Set IV				
	M	T	W	T	F	M	T	W	T	F	M	T	W	T	F	M	T	W	T	F
Ground Beef																				
Spaghetti																				
Meat Loaf																				
Meat Balls																				
Lasagna																				
Chili																				
Salisbury Steak																				
Tacos																				
Beeferoni																				
Hamburgers																				
Roast Beef																				
Chicken																				
Fried																				
BBQ																				
Turkey																				
Fish, batter fried																				
Fishburgers																				
Hot dogs																				
Luncheon Meat																				
Ham																				
Tuna																				
Cheese																				
Grilled																				
in other dishes																				

FIG. 6.4. SAMPLE FREQUENCY CHART OF MEAT AND MEAT ALTERNATE FOOD FOR 4-WEEK CYCLE

If the cycle menus are to be used by the planner or planners there is much that may not be explained. However, if the cycle menus are to be followed by other food managers who were not a part of the planning, as in large centralized systems where perhaps as many as 100 different school cafeterias are to use them, then much explanation is needed. Notes and memos should be made at the side or bottom of the menu sets.

Item	Set I					Set II					Set III					Set IV				
	M	T	W	T	F	M	T	W	T	F	M	T	W	T	F	M	T	W	T	F
Canned																				
Beans, Green																				
Beans, Lima																				
Beans, Kidney																				
Corn																				
Potatoes, dehydrated																				
Sauerkraut																				
Carrots																				
Peas																				
Tomatoes																				
Sweet Potatoes																				
Pork 'N Beans																				
Frozen																				
French Fries																				
Temptaters																				
Mixed Vegetables																				
Spinach																				
Collards																				
Kale																				
Fresh																				
Tossed Salad																				
Cole Slaw																				
Celery Sticks																				
Tomatoes																				

FIG. 6.5. SAMPLE FREQUENCY CHART OF VEGETABLES FOR 4-WEEK CYCLE

Recipe numbers or recipe sources should be given; if recipes are not available to all that will use the cycle, recipes should be furnished with the menus. The size servings should be indicated since the planners have worked the menus out to meet the nutritional needs of the children.

Disadvantages of the cycle menus are that they can be monotonous if the menus are not carefully planned and if the cycle is not long enough. The customer should not be able to notice a pattern. Other disadvantages may be that USDA-donated foods are often unknown to the planner at the time the menus are planned; cycle menus can be too expensive if seasonal foods are not taken into consideration; holidays and special occasions may not be included in the cycles. There are, however, some solutions to these disadvantages.

Monotony

Monotony or repetition of unpopular menus can be avoided. For example, if on a four-week cycle meat loaf or chili con carne is to be put on the menu but because of unpopularity or expense it is undesirable to repeat them every four weeks (or as frequent as the menu cycle repeats), then they can be put as a "Manager's Choice: Meat Loaf or Chili Con Carne." Then meat loaf could be served every other time the menu is repeated.

USDA Donated Foods

Cycle menus should be made flexible and general, not too specific. Changes should be made when need be, hopefully not too frequently, because the menus lose their importance as a guide. By using terms such as, green leafy vegetable rather then specifying spinach, the manager can use what is available or preferred, giving a variety of ways vegetables can be prepared. USDA-donated foods can usually be utilized soon after arrival. By putting "a variety of fruit" or "choice of fruit" the manager can utilize the commodities that are available.

Holiday Menus

Holiday menus can be attached to the cycle menus to be used on the appropriate dates. By blocking out the cycle to see when each holiday to be celebrated with special food falls, it is possible to arrange desserts to celebrate the occasion. For example, if cake is on the Valentine's Day menu or pie is on George Washington's Birthday, then the cherries can be used without having to change the entire menu.

Seasonal Foods

Notes or footnotes to the menu can indicate use of what is available. For example, sliced tomatoes can be used in season; chilled canned tomatoes or scalloped tomatoes out of season, depending on what is available. General terms may be used, such as "fruit," "corn," etc.

Leftovers

Unused leftovers are very expensive. In planning the menu it should be kept in mind that leftovers are to be used within 36 hr. The leftovers can be changed slightly and offered as a choice the next day. Some leftovers may be frozen for use the next time this food appears on the menu.

BREAKFAST MENU PLANNING

The USDA regulations specify that a Federally subsidized breakfast shall consist of a minimum of:

½ pt of fluid milk as a beverage, or on cereal or a part used for both purposes
½ cup of fruit or vegetable or fruit juice or vegetable juice
1 serving of whole grain or enriched bread, or cornbread, biscuits, rolls, muffins, etc.; or ¾ cup serving (or 1 ounce, which ever is less) of wholegrain or enriched ready-to-serve or cooked cereal

It is recommended that a meat/meat alternate (such as an egg, meat, cheese, and peanut butter) be added when practical. Most nutritionists feel that a protein-rich food should be a part of the minimum requirement or at least twice a week. Additional foods may be added to help satisfy appetites, such as: potatoes, bacon, donuts, butter or fortified margarine, jellies, jams, honey, and syrup.

The same basic guides to planning of lunch menus can be applied to planning breakfast menus. The menus should be planned 2 to 4 weeks in advance. Cycle menus consisting of 2 or 3 weeks of menus are advisable. Menus should have variety, contrast in textures and flavors. Sample menus are given in Table 6.5.

SUMMARY

Menu planning is a complicated job and controls many parts of the operation. What are the goals in planning the menus? The nutritionist would like primary emphasis on serving nutritional foods with variety and introducing new foods. However, the business-minded nutritionist is also faced with cost, labor, and customer dissatisfaction. Putting nutritious food on the menu does not accomplish the goal. Menus should be planned around what the children will eat and not what the planner likes. Unless there is a close working situation with cafeteria and teacher with new foods introduced in the classroom with the cafeteria as laboratory, a new food may end up as plate waste.

In order for a lunch to be complete and adequate for Federal reimbursement many managers force children to take a little of all the lunch—knowing that part will be plate waste. When a food is known as unpopular "but nutritious" a substitute more popular and almost equal nutritionally should be offered as a choice. Unpopular menus can affect participation—there is often a definite correlation between what the

TABLE 6.5. SAMPLE BREAKFAST MENUS

Monday	Tuesday	Wednesday	Thursday	Friday
Orange juice (½ cup)	Applesauce (½ cup)	Orange juice (½ cup)	Apple juice (½ cup)	Pineapple juice (½ cup)
School-made sweet roll (1 to 2)	Hash-browned potatoes with chopped ham	Open-face grilled cheese sandwich	Cream chipped beef on toast	Scrambled eggs Toast and jelly
½ pt milk	Toast and jelly	½ pt milk	½ pt milk	½ pt milk
	½ pt milk			
Apple juice	Orange juice	Pineapple juice	Applesauce	Orange juice
Cereal	Soft boiled egg	Cream of wheat	Link sausage	Sweet roll
Cinnamon toast	Toast and jelly	Toast and jelly	Toast and jelly	½ pt milk
½ pt milk	½ pt milk	½ pt milk	½ pt milk	
Apple juice	Orange juice	Banana	Orange juice	Applesauce
French toast	Cooked oatmeal	Cereal	Scrambled eggs	Hash browned potatoes with chopped ham
½ pt milk	Cinnamon toast	Donut	Cinnamon toast	Toast and jelly
	½ pt milk	½ pt milk	½ pt milk	½ pt milk

menu is and how many buy lunch. If there is, then how great a difference? Some schools have experienced a difference of as much as serving only 250 when an unpopular menu is served and as high as 450 when a popular menu is served. Staffing is usually done on an average (in this case an average of those two is 350). Staffs find it difficult to adjust to that much quantity difference. It is also a financial loss when the participation fluctuates so much. Menus causing low participation should be reworked or possibly discarded.

BIBLIOGRAPHY

ANON. 1964. Guide to Average Monthly Availability of 88 Fresh Fruits and Vegetables. United Fresh Fruit and Vegetable Assoc., Washington, D.C.

ANON. 1972A. In behalf of breakfast. School Foodservice J. *26*, No. 1, 31−34.

ANON. 1972B. Notebook on Soy. School Foodservice J. *26*, No. 7, 51−84.

ECKSTEIN, ELEANOR F. 1967. Menu planning by computer: the random approach. J. Am. Dietet. Assoc. *51*, 529.

ECKSTEIN, ELEANOR F. 1978. Menu Planning, 2nd Edition. AVI Publishing Co., Westport, Conn.

FOOD RES. AND ACTION CENTER. 1972. If We Had Ham, We Could Have Ham and Eggs . . . If We Had Eggs: A Study of the National School Breakfast Program. Gazette Press, Yonkers, N.Y.

HARPER, J.M., and G.R. JANSEN. 1973. Comparison of Type A and NSM Menus in the National School Lunch Program. Colorado State University, Fort Collins.

HARPER, J.M., and G.R. JANSEN. 1979. Pilot Study to Compare Type A Lunches with Alternative Subsidized Lunches among High School Students. Colorado State University, Fort Collins.

PENNINGTON, JEAN, and A. THOMPSON. 1976. Dietary Nutrient Guide. AVI Publishing Co., Westport, Conn.

SCHNAKENBERG, D.D. 1976. The Impact of Novel Military Feeding Systems on Dining Hall Attendance, Plate Waste, Food Selection and Nutrient Intake. Letterman Army Institute of Research, San Francisco, Calif.

SKEABECK, ANNE. 1974. "Why Won't Some Teenagers Eat?" *School Foodservice Journal*, 28, No. 1, 52–55.

U.S. DEPT. AGR. 1980. A Menu Planning Guide For School Food Service. U.S. Govt. Printing Office, Washington, D.C.

U.S. DEPT. AGR. 1971. Quantity recipes for type A school lunches. U.S. Govt. Printing Office, Washington, D.C.

WEST, BESSIE BROOKS, GRACE S. SHUGART, and MAXINE F. WILSON. 1978. Food for Fifty, 6th Edition. John Wiley & Sons, New York.

WEST, BESSIE, LEVELLE WOOD, VIRGINIA HARGER, and GRACE SHUGART. 1977. Food Service in Institutions, 6th Edition. John Wiley & Sons, New York.

WYMAN, JUNE R. 1972. "Teenagers and Food." *Food and Nutrition News*, February.

7

Purchasing Food

Fifty to sixty percent of the school foodservice dollar will be spent for food. Therefore, good purchasing practices can make the difference in whether there is a profit or a loss, as well as determine the quality of food purchased. Purchasing consists of more than merely ordering. "Purchasing" means that planning has gone into the ordering. Buying the *right product* in the *amounts needed* at the *time needed* within the *price that can be afforded* are, according to Lendal Kotschevar, the challenges of purchasing.

The purchaser should have a knowledge of food and have contact with the customer in order to know what is needed, as well as the best sizes, or cuts and grades, or qualities desired. In large school systems where all purchasing is done through a purchasing agent, a good line of communication between the agent and the foodservice personnel is necessary. Specifications should be written by foodservice personnel with the help of the purchasing department. It takes foodservice testing and comparing products to determine the best buy and best product for the job.

FACTORS INFLUENCING PURCHASING

The factors that influence what is to be purchased are the menu, food budget, labor cost and skill of personnel, season and availability of food, storage, number of meals, equipment available, the USDA-donated foods and Federal regulations. Each of these factors is discussed in turn.

144

Menu

The menu is the blueprint for purchasing. One should buy for the menu rather than planning the menu around what has been purchased. The menu should be planned, however, with a knowledge of what is available on the market and what can be afforded. Cycle menus make it possible to plan and purchase ahead.

Food Budget

The food budget will have considerable control over what is put on the menu and consequently what is purchased. The food budget can be divided among the components (foods) of the lunch. Thus a range is set of how much of the food dollar is to be spent for meat and meat alternates, milk, vegetables, fruits, bread, and additional food, and used to help assure that total purchases are within the budget. For example, if the income is $1.18, and if 50% of the money is budgeted for food, there will be 59¢ to use for food. The 59¢ can be further divided among the components of the lunch (Fig.7.1).

Labor

The labor available and skill of the labor should be considered when deciding if fresh or frozen, mixes, preportioned or bulk, pre-prepared or precooked products will be purchased. The cost of labor has increased so much in the last 10 yr that more and more foodservices are purchasing prepared items and convenience foods. Factories are able to produce, on assembly lines with conveyor belts and automation, food for less than can be prepared by the foodservice, particularly where productivity is low. The lack of skilled personnel has also make it necessary in many cases for foodservices to purchase prepared items, such as bakery products. When the use of convenience foods increases, the food cost will increase and a greater percentage of the dollar will be spent on food, and consequently the percentage spent for labor will have to decrease.

Season and Availability

The price and quality of the food will be affected by the season and availability of the food. Purchasing fresh bell peppers in January will cost considerably more than when they are in season. In January frozen green peppers or dehydrated green peppers could be a better buy and could be substituted for the fresh in most instances. Cantaloupe in season is the time to put them on the menu and on the purchasing list. The chart of availability and seasons of fruits and vegetables in Chap. 6 will be helpful in planning menus and purchases.

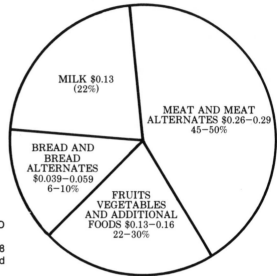

FIG. 7.1. SAMPLE FOOD
BUDGET
This sample is based on $1.18
income being available and
using 50% for food, or 59¢.

Storage

The type of storage needed and what is available should be considered
when purchasing. Storage may determine the quantities purchased and
how frequent deliveries will have to be made. Canned items must be
purchased rather than frozen, if temperatures of 0°F or below are not
available for holding frozen food until time of use. The keeping ability of
fresh fruits and vegetables determines how frequently they are purchased.

Number of Meals

Naturally the number of meals to be served will determine the quantities needed. Usually these are projected figures based on past experience. Recipes may be used in determining quantities, along with buying
guides, such as the *Food Buying Guide for School Food Service* (U.S.
Dept. Agr., 1980).

Equipment Available

The equipment, type, and amount available will also determine what
foods will be purchased. For example: If a deep-fat fryer is not available
the frozen french fries purchased should be for oven reconstitution. If a

slicer is not available, cheese and luncheon meat should be purchased pre-portioned. When sufficient oven space is not available, it may be necessary to purchase bakery bread when other oven foods are being prepared.

USDA-Donated Foods

The commodities received by the schools from the USDA will make considerable difference in what is purchased. The donated foods, which account for about 17−20 percent of the total food, have to be worked into the menus and in some cases immediately if the product is a fresh produce. To buy large quantities of canned and frozen items could be unwise unless the type and quantity of donated foods that may be received are known.

Processing Contracts.—Can the product be made with USDA-donated foods? This is only important if the product you want to purchase is made from foods you have a large supply of or can get more of. Nearly 20 percent of the total commodities are being processed. Using these foods effectively in the manufacturing of prepared foods through processing agreements, for example, contributes another four to five cents to each food dollar in the schools in the state of New York and in Fairfax County, Virginia.

Thirty-eight state agencies have processing contracts with over 425 food companies. The purchaser can contact the state agency to see which companies have agreements that are approved. As long as the USDA-donated foods are continued, the processing contracts should be utilized, particularly in any product containing grains and dairy products, such as bread, pizza, crackers, ice cream, burritos and meat/fruit turnovers. Additionally, when a USDA-donated food is in a form that you can not use, the processing contract can be very useful, or when you don't want to change the quality of the product you are using. For example, if students like the particular hamburger patty being used and it is a prepared patty, a processing agreement would allow the USDA-donated ground beef to be sent directly to the company for adding seasoning and forming into patties.

The requirement of using USDA-donated foods and having a processing agreement approved by the state agency should be written into the bid specifications. It is important to have competitive bidding in the processing.

FEDERAL REGULATIONS

The Federal regulations that effect what to purchase are many, thus this section will name only some of those unique to school foodservices.

The School Lunch Patterns and Breakfast Pattern have much control on size package, portion sizes, and ingredients that go into the product. The *Food Buying Guide for School Food Service* (1980) is an essential aid to determining yields of foods and how large the portion must be to contribute x amount to the meal requirements.

Enriched or whole grain breads, pasta products and rice are needed to be considered a bread or bread alternate. For pasta products to count as a meat alternate it must be fortified with protein.

Vegetable or fruit juice must be full-strength to count as a vegetable or fruit and it can be counted for no more than ½ of that requirement.

Unflavored fluid lowfat milk, skim milk or buttermilk must be made available at lunch as a beverage. This requirement may be extended to the other programs.

Some commercially prepared foods have been evaluated by USDA's Food and Nutrition Services to determine their contribution to the meal requirements and have a Child Nutrition (CN) label. This label assures you, the purchaser, of how much meat and meat alternate, vegetable, bread, etc. in a specific size portion. The importance of knowing exactly what is in a product and having more than a sales representative's word, came with the audits in the late 1970s when meals were shown as being deficient, or there was not way of telling. A foodservice director needs to know what is in a commercially prepared meat product, for example, such as pizza or burrito. Does it contain 1 oz or 2 oz of meat, a serving of bread, and ⅛ or ¼ cup of vegetable? The CN label is somewhat a guarantee and will become extensively used as government programs are held more accountable and more prepared foods are used. Inspectors of USDA or U.S. Department of Commerce check the products packaged under the label to assure the product does have what is stated on the label.

WHOM TO BUY FROM

For many school systems an important question is who to buy from—the broker, wholesale house, or manufacturing company. The wholesale house is the most frequent market used by school foodservices, though the markup is more than it would be from the manufacturer. The wholesaler may average a 25% markup to cover the middleman's expense and service, particularly delivery as needed. The fewer middlemen, the lower the cost.

Some school systems use centralized storage for storing supplies for several months. The goods then are distributed as needed to the individual schools by the system's trucks and drivers. The purchase cost of the goods to the system will be less when purchased in larger volume delivered to this one location than if the wholesale house were to deliver to individual schools. This can mean a 10 to 15% savings in the purchase price. The question: how much does it cost the school system to store and then to deliver from the central storage to the individual schools? In some cases, it may cost more for the school system to store and distribute, than for the wholesaler to perform this service and charge for it. The savings possible will depend on how well-organized and efficient the system's distribution methods are.

CENTRALIZED PURCHASING

Small foodservices are at a disadvantage when purchasing because of their lack of buying power and are paying about 18 percent more for food than do large school districts. Centralizing purchasing has many advantages in addition to greater buying power. Some of the advantages of centralized purchasing are:

(1) The person purchasing can become more proficient and specialized.
(2) Budget and fiscal controls are centralized.
(3) Buying power is greater with volume.
(4) Saves the managers' time, as well as the salesmen's time, who would have to call on each school.
(5) Written specifications can be developed and bid buying used. Can obtain a greater degree of standardization.
(6) Evaluation of the products received can be made frequently. More power for correcting errors and receiving credits for poor qualities delivered.

Vendors

A good business relationship with salesmen and jobbers can be very valuable to the purchaser. The salesmen and jobbers can be helpful and furnish information on new products on the market.

Kickbacks.—Trading stamps, gifts of any type, and discounts or bid prices for purchases for home use should be discouraged and refused. There are many means that salesmen and company representatives can use to win favoritism. Accepting gifts and favors puts the purchaser in a position that can stand in the way of good, sound business practices.

Delivery Charges.—Delivery charges are high. Each stop a company's truck makes costs the company. One company calculated it cost at least $25.00 per delivery stop. The purchaser should keep this in mind and should consider the cost. It will save both the purchaser and vendor money in the long run if a month's order can be delivered at one time rather than in four different trips on a weekly basis. Dividing business among too many vendors can also result in a high cost to the vendor and in turn to the purchaser as well as increase paper work with paying invoices. It is desirable to encourage competition among vendors, but the larger the volume of business with a single vendor, the better the price.

Charge Accounts.—Charge accounts at local grocery stores should never be started. Buying in quantity from "family size" packages is very costly. Running out and using the local grocery store can become a habit—a bad habit—that should be replaced with good planning. Good management practices show up very strongly in purchasing practices.

TYPES OF PURCHASING

There are three basic types of purchasing: buying on the open market, buying on informal bid, and buying on formal bid. Open-market purchasing means that the purchaser buys from whomever he wishes and that the prices may change from week to week. Open-market purchasing may be done over the telephone, or the salesman calls on the purchaser (manager) and takes the orders. Informal bids are a type of gentleman's agreement after two or three prices have been compared. Actually this method takes on many of the qualities of the formal bid except the contract signing. Formal bids are signed legal contracts between the purchaser and a vendor who agrees to supply an estimated quantity of items meeting written specifications at a certain price for a certain period of time.

Open Market

The open-market type of purchasing is used most frequently with purchasing of fresh produce and often by small establishments which do not have the buying power to go in to the informal or formal bid methods. When the open market is used, the prices should be compared with at least two or three companies and more if the time and the vendors are available. The greatest disadvantage to open-market buying is the time required in comparing prices and the problems that may result from oral commitments. However, the time spent on checking prices can result in quite a savings. The form in Fig. 7.2 is one that could be used to compare the cost of fresh produce.

Informal Bid

The informal bid is used most frequently when limited quantities of an item are needed or when there is not time to receive formal bids. Often

Date_____

PRICE QUOTATIONS ON FRESH PRODUCE

Spec. No.	Quantity	Item	CARTER'S PRODUCE	HENRY'S INC.	ELLIS BROTHERS
FP 2		Apples, 138 Delicious			
FP 3		Apples, 100's Winesaps			
FP 5		Bananas, med.			
FP 6		Cantaloupes, No. 45s			
FP 7		Grapefruit, 64s			
FP 9		Grapes, Thompson			
FP 10		Oranges, Navel, 200s			
FP 11		Oranges, Valencia, 200s			
VP 1		Cabbage, Red			
VP 2		Cabbage, Green			
VP 4		Carrots			
VP 5		Celery			
VP 7		Cucumber			
VP 9		Lettuce			
VP 10		Onions			
VP 12		Parsley			
VP 14		Radishes			
VP 16		Peppers, Bell			
VP 17		Potatoes, Idaho Russetts			
VP 18		Potatoes, Red Triumph			
VP 20		Sweet Potatoes			

Received by:_____

FIG. 7.2. SAMPLE FORM FOR PRICE COMPARISONS

the agreement is verbal though sometimes written, but it is not bound by legal contract. Since there are no legal ties, the vendor and the purchaser can break the contract.

Formal Bid

A formal bid is a signed agreement between the vendor and purchaser and is bound by legal contract. In formal bid situations the purchasing agent should submit an invitation to bid to several vendors. This requires written specifications and estimates of quantities to be purchased. The vendor who submits the lowest bid will be awarded the bid. The specifications should convey clearly what the buyer wants. This becomes more and more important with large quantity purchasing and competitive bidding.

Formula Purchasing

Formula Purchasing is a type of formal bidding where a base price is bid and a special factor price is bid. Together the two prices constitute the net price to be paid the contractor. The base price is usually based on the market quotations, in the case of meat the National Provisioner Daily "Yellow Sheet" is often used. The "Special Factor" is the amount added or subtracted from the base price as offered by the contractor. This factor remains constant during the duration of the contract. The base price goes up and down as that market quotations go up and down. Baltimore County (Md) Schools have used this method of setting the prices successfully. It usually works best when carloads of a food is being purchased to come into a central location. This method of setting the prices is expected to be used more and more as companies find they are taking too great a risk guessing what the price will be two to six months later. Better prices can often be gotten with formula purchasing since that risk is removed.

SPECIFICATIONS

Writing specifications can be defined as telling someone else what you want. Good specifications may be a simple description of the product wanted.

All specifications should contain the following:

(1) Trade or common name of the product,
(2) Quantity required in a can or package—weight, measure, number, etc.
(3) Brand name or quality designated by trade or Federal grade,

(4) Description of the product, color, size, texture, cut, style pack, etc.

(5) Unit (size) on which prices shall be quoted (6 No. 10 cans per case; 4 1-gal. jars; per lb),

(6) Sanitation standards under which product is to be packed (U.S. inspected).

Buying by Brands

Buying by brands has its pros and cons. Brand names may stand for a company's reputation for quality or standards, as a sort of advertisement. Many purchasers buy by brands, writing their specifications by brands. Well-known brands, however, can be higher than an equivalent quality under an unknown brand. Is it necessary to pay the extra price for the assurance of what one will get? It requires time and expertise to save on food cost and at the same time not lower the standard of the foodservice. Through can cuttings, trying limited quantities, experimenting, and keeping informed, it is possible to write specifications that can get the best price, assure the quality wanted, and not necessarily limit bidding to well-known brands.

Writing specifications usually starts with what you know you want, being as restrictive as necessary to insure the quality desired. It is customary to write the specs around a product and then add the phrase "or equal." For example:

Apricot, Halves, U.S. Grade B (Choice), Unpeeled, Pitted, in Heavy Syrup, Count 130—145. Packed 6/10, Wt. 70 ounces. Libby Brand or equal.

After some experience through experimenting with different brands and qualities and finding that two or three different brands will satisfy the needs, then the specifications may be written more broadly. If the products are so different that one specification cannot be written to cover both, two different specifications can be be written with one as the "alternate." This will encourage more than one bid and the lowest can be accepted. The "or equal" scares some bidders, because they don't want to run a chance of losing the bid. When a bidder bids a product as "equal" he must be prepared to prove it. When large quantities of an item are involved this may result in a court case.

Writing specifications can become very involved. A simple guide to writing specifications for a milk bid is shown in Appendix IV. Each foodservice will find from experience certain other clauses and restrictions that need to be written into their specifications. The *School Food Purchasing Guide* (Am. School Food Serv. Assoc. and the Assoc. of

School Business Officials, 1965) and *Food Purchasing Pointers for School Foodservice* (U.S. Dept. Agr., 1977) are excellent guides to writing specifications.

GENERAL CONDITIONS OF CONTRACTS

The specifications should include in the general conditions of the contract:

(1) when the products are to be delivered,
(2) frequency of deliveries,
(3) place to be delivered,
(4) condition delivered—frozen, refrigerated, etc.,
(5) how the orders are to be placed,
(6) billing procedures,
(7) payment of bills.

The frequency of deliveries will affect the bid price. If the deliveries are expected daily, weekly, or bi-weekly this will be taken into consideration in bidding. Some food items fluctuate more than others on the market, and it may be a gamble for a company to agree on a price for a period of 1 yr. Fresh produce, meats, and eggs usually fluctuate in price over the year. Therefore, bid periods for shorter periods of time than a year should be considered for many items. Also to be considered is whether the bids should expire at the same time or be staggered. Since viewing bids, testing samples, etc., are time-consuming, it is advisable to stagger the expiration date of the bids. The timetable in Table 7.1 is workable.

ORDERING FORMS

After the bids have been received, evaluated, and awarded, the successful bidder and the purchasing agent should work together in the ordering procedure. If the market order form is worked out with both parties, it can cut down on the number of records and the possibility of error. The example shown in Fig. 7.3 uses the bid number that correlate with the specifications, list the bid price, and the computerized number of the item for the convenience of the wholesale company's warehouse and billing department. If the form has several copies, the one form can act as a purchase order, requisition, invoice, delivery ticket, and bill—saving much time and decreasing the possibilities of errors. Ordering forms, inventory forms, and storage arrangement should be coordinated.

TABLE 7.1. BIDDING TIMETABLE

Commodity	Delivery	Bid Period
Dairy	Daily or every other day	Annual
Bakery products	Daily as required	Annual
Paper supplies	Monthly or bi-monthly	Semi-annually
Cleaning supplies	Monthly	Annual
Canned foods	Monthly or bi-monthly	Annual or quarterly
Staple groceries	Monthly or bi-monthly	Annual or quarterly
Meat, poultry and eggs	Weekly or bi-monthly	Quarterly or monthly
Frozen foods	Weekly or bi-monthly	Quarterly or monthly
Fresh produce	Twice weekly or weekly	Annual*

*Formula bidding works best (see p. 152).

EVALUATION OF PRODUCT

The purchaser must check the items received to assure that the item specified and bid is being received. Failing to carry out the specifications of the bid contract is a legal matter and can mean the loss of the contract. This is usually not necessary. In a centralized system a product evaluation sheet or form is recommended to be used for reporting when the quality of the product is unsatisfactory, or to register a complaint about product, delivery, or service.

PURCHASING CANNED GOODS

Whether the purchasing is done on the open market or by formal bid, there is a need for written specifications. To write the specification some basic information is needed. When writing specifications for canned foods there are a number of different factors to specify, such as:

Grade

Canned fruits are graded according to color, uniformity of pieces, and size (Fig. 7.4). The sugar content of the liquid in which they are packed may determine the grade, with the heavier sirup the higher the grade. To reduce sugar content and cost, a fruit can be packed in a lighter syrup or even water pack. Canned vegetables are graded according to color, uniformity of size and shape, maturity or tenderness and texture. The grades for canned fruits and vegetables are:

U.S. Fancy or U.S. Grade A.—The highest quality and is almost perfect in uniform size, color, tenderness, and maturity.

U.S. Grade B (Extra Standard for Vegetables; Choice for Fruits).—A high quality product that is not as uniform in color, size, or tenderness as U.S. Grade A.

INVOICE

VENDOR NO. 797000

7209

SCHOOL NAME: _____

ADDRESS: _____

LOCATION: _____

DATE: _____

TERMS: CHARGE — NET

Cafeteria Manager: ▮

ALLOW 15 DAYS DELIVERY TIME AFTER RECEIVED BY SCHOOL LUNCH OFFICE

QUANTITY	ITEM NO.	DESCRIPTION	PRODUCT NO.	UNIT PACK	PRICE	TOTAL COST TO BE COMPLETED BY CO.
CASES	22	#332 DISPENSER NAPKIN (TALL)	675100	10 M	7.00 E	
CASES	23	#170 COMPACT NAPKIN (SHORT)	670060	15 M	12.85 E	
CASES	24	WRAPPED STRAWS 6¼"	548360	12,500	9.10 E	
	25	PORTION OR SOUFFLE CUPS				
CASES		#400 - 4 OZ.	122490	5 M	12.80 E	
CASES		#075 - ¾ OZ.	121260	5 M	6.77 E	
CASES	26	#550 LILY DISH	122750	5 M	17.50 E	
CASES	27	4 OZ. SAUCE DISH 008-0006	668390	1 M	6.56 E	
CASES	28	#419 ICE CREAM PLATE 4½ SQ.	668850	2 M	3.96 E	
CASES	29	JUICE CUP, LILY #100 W5G	153660	1200	6.50 E	
CASES	30	#P658 LID FOR JUICE CUP	104040	2500	10.10 E	
BOX	31	WAXED TISSUE (Master Savarap) 1 M Sheet	200531	1 Box	1.79 E	
CASES	32	WAXED TISSUE, PONY - 750 FEET PER ROLL	204370	6 Rolls	15.75 E	

ROLLS	33	#15 ALUMINUM FOIL - 680 FT. ROLL	229981	1 Roll	7.15 E
ROLLS	34	12 x 12 EM3 ROLL-O-WRAP (1600 Sheets)	395910	1 Roll	4.60 E
ROLLS	35	PLASTIC WRAP (11 x 2000)	380470	1 Roll	4.40 E
BOX	36	SANDWICH BAGS 6 x ¾ x 6¾	049861	1M Bags	2.05 E
BOX	37	BAG—FRENCH FRY	033241	1 M	2.00 E
TUBE	38	BUTTER CHIPS PAPER	508151	1M Tube	.39 E
TUBE	39	BAKING CUPS 4½" 500 PER TUBE	161161	1 Tube	.44 E
BOX	40	SCOTCH BRITE PADS Rubbermaid No. 6297 10 Pads	501331	1 Box	1.89 E
ONLY	41	#H 1485 A NAPKIN DISPENSER	554871	1	7.25 E
PKG.	42	PAN LINERS 25 #	339031	1 M	9.50 E
BOX	43	HAND GUARDS ELL	534491	100	1.65 E
CASES	44	#983 CHIX WET WIPES	537360	1 M	30.70 E
ONLY	45	#25 W INSULATED CHEST	357190	1	29.50 E
CASES	46C	GARBAGE CAN LINERS CP 40LD	062030	250	6.39 E
					Total Cost

Contract No. 57-72E-1153

PLEASE PRESS HARD   YOU ARE WRITING SIX COPIES

FIG. 7.3. THIS IS AN EXAMPLE OF AN ORDER FORM THAT CORRELATES THE COMPANY AND SCHOOL SYSTEM'S AC-COUNTING DEPARTMENT'S NEEDS INTO ONE FORM
Six copies of the order form are made and used as follows: Two blue copies ("Invoice"); one gold copy ("Delivery and Receipt"); one white copy ("Warehouse Copy"); one pink copy ("Manager's copy"); and one yellow copy ("Company Bookkeeping Copy").

CANNED PEACHES
Typical Samples

U.S GRADE A

Halves: Good yellow-orange color and texture typical of proper ripeness.

U.S. GRADE B

Halves: Some variation in color. Slight defects, such as a partial piece.

U.S. GRADE C

Mixed Pieces: Good average quality. Variation in color and ripeness. Some blemished pieces.

FROZEN STRAWBERRIES
Typical Samples

U.S. GRADE A

Whole: Color very good—red to pinkish red. Uniform color and size.

U.S. GRADE B

Whole: Some variation in color and size.

U.S. GRADE C

Sliced: Slight variation in color and some mushiness, characteristic of sliced style.

Courtesy of U.S. Dept. Agr.

FIG. 7.4. EXAMPLES OF DIFFERENCES IN GRADES

U.S. Standard or U.S. Grade C.—A good quality but less uniform in size, slightly less tender, and color may not be as good as for Grade B; however, this item may be used in mixed dishes. Grade B fruits may be used in pies and cobblers and the vegetables in soups and stews.

Substandard or U.S. Grade D.—This product may be broken-up and off-color, irregular in shape, and less desirable in color.

Style Pack.—The style pack means many different things, according to what the food product is. For example, it can mean:

Green Beans.—Cut, such as french style cut, kitchen style, long, whole.

Pineapple.—Sliced, tidbits, broken pieces, crushed.

Carrots.—Diced, sliced, julienne, whole.

Peaches.—Whole, halves, sliced, pieces.
Corn.—Whole kernel, creamed style.

Variety.—This may include not only the variety of fruits or vegetables but also the area of the country in which it was grown. For example: Blue Lake Green Beans, Concord or Catawba Grapes, Freestone, or Cling Peaches.

Packing Liquid.—The packing liquid may mean water, juice, sirup, butter, or vacuum packed. Sirup density for packing fruits is designated by grades. The heavier the sirup the higher the grade—"Extra Heavy," "Heavy," "Light," "Slightly Sweetened Water," and "Water."

Size.—The sieve and count are two ways of determining size. "Tender," "Small," and "Young" are other terms used to designate size. The number or count in the can may be extremely important in institutional foods where cost-per-serving is a definite consideration. If the No. 10 can of pear halves has only 25 pear halves and the food cost was figured on 30 or 35 halves to the can the cost-per-serving will be approximately 20% more than planned.

Yield or Drained Weight.—As in the case of count, the drained weight and yield of the product is an important consideration in comparing prices.

Size of Container.—See Table 7.2 for common can sizes.

Labeling

Under the Food, Drug and Cosmetic Act there are minimum requirements that the packers and distributors must abide by in labeling. The law requires, for example, for canned fruits to be labeled with the following information:

(1) The common or usual name of the fruit.
(2) The form (or style) of fruit, such as whole, slices, or halves.
(3) For some fruits, the variety or color.
(4) Sirups, sugars, or liquid in which a fruit is packed must be listed near the name of the product.
(5) The total contents (net weight) must be stated in ounces for containers holding 1 lb or less. From 1 lb to 4 lb weight must be given in both total ounces and pounds and ounces (or pounds and fractions of a pound).
(6) Any special type of treatment.
(7) Ingredients, such as spices, flavoring, coloring, special sweeteners, if used.
(8) The packer's or distributor's name and place of business.

TABLE 7.2. COMMON CAN SIZES

Can Size Industry Terms	Approx. Net Weight or Fluid Measure Per Can (Oz)	Approx. Cups	Cans Per Case	Principal Products
8 oz	8	1	48 or 72	Ready-to-serve soups, fruits, vegetables
Picnic	10½–12	1¼	48	Mainly condensed soups, some fruits, vegetables
12 oz (vac.)	12	1½	24	Principally for family size corn
No. 300	14–16	1¾	24	Family size—pork and beans, cranberry sauce, meat products
No. 303	16–17	2	24 or 36	Family size—fruits and vegetables, some meat products
No. 2	20 oz or 18 (fl)	2½	24	Family size—juices, ready-to-serve soups, some fruits
No. 2½	27–29	3½	24	Family size—fruits, some vegetables
Institutional Sizes				
No. 3 Cyl. or 46 fl oz	51 46	5¾ 5¾	12 12	Condensed soups, some vegetables, and some meats Fruit and vegetables Juices
No. 10	6 lb to 7 lb 5 oz	12–13	6	Fruits, vegetables and some other foods

Source: Adapted from *Food Buying Guide for School Food Service,* U.S. Dept. Agr. 1980.

The labeling laws will require labeling to become more complete, concise, and informative with the legislation passed in 1973. Nutrition labeling should aid school foodservices in determining the nutritional quality of the food. For most foods nutritional labeling is voluntary. If a product is fortified, the label must give the nutrients in the product. Foods such as fortified fruit juices and enriched bread or flour, will follow the format for "Nutrition Labeling," as follows:

(1) serving size,
(2) servings per container,
(3) caloric content,
(4) protein content,
(5) carbohydrate content,
(6) fat content,
(7) percentage of U.S. recommended daily allowances of protein, vitamins, and minerals.

In addition, labels may give the quality, grade, size, and/or maturity of the product. Cooking directions, recipes, and ideas for serving are sometimes found on labels.

Can Cuttings

One of the best ways of comparing brands and qualities of canned foods is to evaluate the products through a can cutting. Can cuttings may be done by a committee made up of high school students, principals, along with foodservice people. Several brands of an item can be evaluated and the *best product* for the purpose with the *most yield* and *best price* be decided upon.

An evaluation form, such as the one shown in Fig. 7.5, can be used for each person to use in evaluating the products. Labels should be removed from the cans and use codes to identify the products and price can be given to evaluator. When evaluating a product, the following factors should be considered: net weight, drained weight, texture, defects, flavor, uniformity of product, color, juice or liquid, cost per case, cost per serving, and number of servings per can. Buy the product best suited for the use is the objective. Therefore, this should be kept in mind in evaluating a product. If peaches are to be used in pies and cobblers, the fancy peach halves are unnecessary. Slices or pieces, either U.S. Grade B or U.S. Grade C, should be considered. If the sirup of the canned fruit is not going to be used, a lighter sirup decreases sugar in menu and is a good buy at a lower cost.

Date_____   Evaluator_____

Instructions: Fill in each column. Circle the item number that you find is the product recommended.

Item	Brand or Code	Weight on Can	Drained Weight	Presence of Defects	Condition of Liquid	Uniformity of Pieces	Price
Cut Green Beans							
Cut Green Beans							
Cut Green Beans							
Whole Grain Corn							
Whole Grain Corn							
Whole Grain Corn							

Factors to consider:

Presence of Defects—strings, tough, husks, bruises, dark spots.

Condition of Liquid—clear, cloudy, milky.

Uniformity of Pieces--sieve, broken pieces, size of pieces.

Maturity of product—tough, tender, starchy, ends tough, some too mature.

Color of product—color is what is expected for product, dark, pale.

FIG. 7.5. SAMPLE CAN–CUTTING EVALUATION FORM

PURCHASING STAPLES

When writing specifications for staple groceries much knowledge is needed about a great variety of products. There will be no attempt here to go into the factors to be considered in writing specifications for these products. Kotschevar (1975) goes into the characteristics of many of these products.

One of the most common staples to specify is flour. The quality and various types of wheats that flours are made from have many different characteristics. All-purpose, general-purpose flour is usually a blend which has lower protein content than bread flours, and contains enough protein to make good yeast bread but not too much for quick breads. The blends are prepared to conform to the baking demands of the different areas of the country. For example, a softer blend of flour is marketed in the south where quick breads are popular, whereas a harder blend is marketed in the north for making yeast rolls and breads.

Bread flours, hard-wheat flours, are milled from blends of hard spring and/or winter wheats. These wheats are fairly high in protein and are slightly more granular to the touch. Bread flours are milled chiefly for bakers and institutional use and may be bleached or unbleached. Cake flours are milled from soft wheat. The protein content is lower and the flour is ground fine and more uniform. It feels soft and satiny to the touch and is used primarily for cakes.

Self-rising flour is a flour to which leavening ingredients and salt have been added in proper proportion and is used primarily for household baking. Enriched flour is flour to which vitamins and minerals have been added. The milling process takes many of the vitamins and minerals out of the wheat, and enrichment puts them back in. Table 7.3 contains the minimum and maximum amounts of nutrients added per pound of flour. Either whole grain or enriched grains should be purchased.

TABLE 7.3. NUTRIENTS ADDED PER POUND OF FLOUR

Nutrient	Min (Mg)	Max (Mg)
Thiamin	1.1	1.8
Riboflavin	0.7	1.6
Niacin	10.0	15.0
Iron	8.0	12.5

It is not always a savings to buy the larger size or larger quantity if the product will inconvenience the user or if the product loses its quality before used. This is particularly true of spices—no more than a three-month supply should be purchased at a time. When the prices of different sizes are compared, the larger size may be savings over the smaller size as is the case in the foods shown in Table 7.4.

TABLE 7.4. PRICE COMPARISON OF DIFFERENT UNIT PACKS

Item	Size	Price[1] ($)	Price Comparison	Savings ($)
Flour	25-lb bag	3.95	15.80 (for 4 25-lb bags)	
	100-lb bag	11.50	11.50	4.30
Salt	24 1-lb boxes/case	7.20	0.30	0.22/lb
	25-lb bag	2.00	0.08	
Sugar, brown	24 1-lb boxes/case	13.20	0.55	
	25-lb bag	6.85	0.274	0.276/lb
Sugar, granulated	25-lb bag	14.90	57.60 (for 4 bags)	
	100-lb bag	40.82	40.82	16.78
Vanilla flavoring, imit.	qt	1.95	7.80 (4 qt)	
	gal.	3.95	3.95	3.85

[1]Prices are sample prices.

PURCHASING MEAT AND POULTRY

The largest percentage of the food dollar is spent for meats, thus specifications should assure the purchaser of getting what he wants. Meats are graded on three factors: quality, finish, and comformation. The quality is determined by the fineness of texture, deepness of color, and firmness of flesh. The distribution and firmness of the fat and the amount of fat determines the finish. Federal inspection and grading of meat is not compulsory. Meats shipped outside the State are federally inspected for wholesomeness (Fig. 7.6). Federally inspected meat was produced from animals free from disease at the time of slaughter and was packed under sanitary conditions.

Writing specifications for meat and being sure one is getting the quality specified can be a battle, depending on the reputation of the meat-packing company. Specifiying U.S. Good with 25% fat in the ground beef does not guarantee that it is delivered. One way for large-quantity meat buyers to be more assured that what is received is what was specified and paid for is by using the Meat Acceptance Service of the USDA.

IMPS

The standards used by the Meat Acceptance Service are based on USDA-approved Institutional Meat Purchase Specifications, referred to as IMPS. When meat and meat products are inspected by the Meat Acceptance Service, a USDA official must be present at all times while the meat is being ground, processed, and packaged (Fig. 7.7). This service is provided for a fee, which the supplier usually pays but will in turn pass on in the price to the purchaser. This service may increase the price of the meat as much as 6 to 10¢/lb. The question becomes whether it is needed and whether it is worth that much to the buyer.

IMPS are specifications based on extensive testing done by the Livestock Division of USDA's Consumer and Marketing Service. They may be useful in writing meat specifications even without the Meat Acceptance Service. The specifications are available in a series at little cost from the U.S. Govt. Printing Office, Washington, D.C. (See Table 7.5)

When the Meat Acceptance Service has been required by the purchaser, the Federal grader will have a copy of the specifications of what the purchaser has asked for and received prices on. The meat grader is responsible for accepting the product and certifying that it is in compliance with those specifications. The Federal grader's stamp ("USDA Accepted as Specified") will appear on each item of meat or on the sealed carton in which it is packed. Information pertaining to the Meat Acceptance Service can be obtained by writing the Meat Grading Branch, Livestock Division, Consumer and Marketing Service, U.S. Dept. of Agr., U.S. Govt. Printing Office, Washington, D.C. 20250.

FIG. 7.6. INSPECTION STAMP FOR MEAT

FIG. 7.7. USDA ACCEPTANCE SERVICE STAMP

Beef

Beef becomes less tender as the animal grows older. The grades of beef are shown in Fig. 7.8

U.S. Prime.—From steers or heifers no more than 3 yr old, it is well marbled with fat, flavorful, and very tender. This grade is used primarily by the best restaurants and hotels.

U.S. Choice.—From steers, heifers, and cows no more than 3½ yr old, it is very similar to Prime but contains less fat and may not be as tender.

U.S. Standard.—From cattle no more than 4 yr old, it has little fat, lacks the flavor of the better grades. However, this grade of beef with the addition of fat can be ground and make a very flavorful hamburger patty.

U.S. Commercial.—From cattle more than 4 yr old, this grade requires long, slow, moist cooking in order to become tender enough to eat.

U.S. Utility, Cutter, and Canner.—This grade is used in canned meat products primarily or in sausage making.

TABLE. 7.5. USDA MEAT SPECIFICATIONS

Type of Product	Series
Beef, fresh	100
Lamb and mutton, fresh	200
Veal and calf, fresh	300
Pork, fresh	400
Pork, products, cured and smoked	500
Beef products, cured	600
Edible by-products, cured	700
Sausage products	800
Canned meat products	900
Portion control products	1000

The grade of the beef does not reflect on wholesomeness of the meat. U.S. Standard beef is as wholesome and sanitary to eat as U.S. Prime. The grade does affect the nutritional value slightly in that Prime is higher in fat content then the other grades. As a matter of fact, the lower grades have less caloric value per pound and more protein, minerals, and vitamins then Prime.

But not all beef is Federally graded. Many meat companies have their own grading standards. However, if the terms U.S. Prime, U.S. Choice, etc., are used, the meat must meet the specifications set by the USDA for those grades. *The Meat Handbook* (Levie 1970) has an excellent chapter on meat specifications.

Poultry

Poultry, particularly chicken and turkey, is popular on the school menus. Chicken is classified as: fryer or broiler, roaster, capon, hen or stewing chicken, and rooster. Turkeys are classified according to age and sex as fryer or roaster, young hen or young tom, and hen or tom.

Courtesy of U.S. Dept. Agr.

FIG. 7.8. MEAT GRADES ARE INDICATED WITH A SHIELD-SHAPED GRADEMARK AND THE APPROPRIATE GRADE NAME

The poultry Inspection Act of 1959 assures the purchaser and consumer that all poultry shipped interstate has been Federally inspected for wholesomeness. Poultry is graded as U.S. grades A, B, and C. Since the grades are determined by the general condition, conformation, fat covering, disjointed, broken bones, missing parts, and flesh, Grade A is recommended for frying. Grades B and C may be good buys for stewing or roasting chicken. Chicken and turkey may be purchased whole or cut into pieces—breasts, drumsticks, thighs, wings, and backs. Due to labor cost, lack of equipment, and the waste involved, purchasing of chicken pieces of the desired cuts is usually the custom.

Chicken for frying can be purchased in all degrees of convenience—pre-cut, pre-coated, pre-browned, and fully-cooked. The fully-cooked chicken requires heating to reconstitute and is a very satisfactory product for schools. Bid chicken for frying or fully-cooked "by-the-piece" not "by-the-pound."

TEXTURED VEGETABLE PROTEIN

Textured vegetable protein products are one of the cheapest sources of protein. There has been an increased use of textured vegetable protein in school foodservices after USDA approved their use in 1971 for meeting a part of the protein requirements. FNS Notice 219 (USDA) specifies that a ratio up to 30 parts hydrated vegetable protein can be used with 70 parts uncooked meat, poultry, or fish on basis of weight. Hydrated means that moisture has been put back into the product. For example: 12 lb dry textured vegetable protein and 18 lb of water will produce 30 lb of hydrated product to which 70 lb of meat, poultry, or fish can be added. The soy product is most frequently and more successfully added to ground beef. The maximum ratio works better when it is a mixed dish with seasoning such as tacos, pizza sauce, or spaghetti sauce. Some school foodservice directors prefer using 15 to 20% hydrated to the products.

To determine ratio and brand to buy, the purchaser should experiment and test different products. Many companies are on the approved list of USDA as meeting the chemical and biological value as specified by FNS (Food and Nutrition Service) for use in the child nutrition programs. All textured vegetable proteins on the "accepted" list will have no less than 1.8 PER (Protein Efficiency Ratio) value. The higher the PER the higher the biological value of the protein.

Textured vegetable protein comes in many forms, flavors, sizes, and prices. It comes frozen and concentrated, spun or extruded. *Extrusion* is a process where high temperatures and high-pressure is used in processing the soy products. *Spinning* or "spun" soy fibers refers to soy being coagulated into filaments or fibers by machine and stretched by a series of rolls. Some of the factors to consider when purchasing the textured vegetable protein are:

(1) Should the meat processor mix the soy product with the meat, or the cook mix the soy product with the meat? Specifications can be written for the meat processing plant to put the designated percentage of soy product, water, and meat desired. A container of beef patties that has soy products added should be labeled stating the percentage of meat, percentage of water, and percentage of dry textured vegetable protein. The label may read: "The meat/meat alternate portion contains (no less than 70%) percent beef, (no more than 18%) percent water, and (no more than 12%) percent dry textured vegetable protein than is acceptable for use in FNS Child Nutrition Programs."

(2) Plain or flavored? Flavors available include chicken, ham, bacon, and beef. Also, mixes containing seasoning and textured vegetable protein are available for meat loaf, chili, tacos, pizza sauce, etc. The meat and liquids are to be added. The unflavored product is satisfactory when added to ground beef and does not require as many recipe adjustments. Custom flavoring is available from some processors.

(3) Frozen or dehydrated? Spun fibers or extruded?

(4) Size granules—minced, diced, crumbles?

(5) Colored or uncolored? Usually a caramel color is added to beef products.

(6) Package size? Frozen comes in 5-lb packages packed 3 or 6 per case. The extruded and spun are packaged in 5-, 15-, 25-, and 50-lb sizes and in pouches to be added to 10 lb of ground beef. Special recipes are available from the processing companies.

EGGS

Eggs can be purchased in many forms—liquid, frozen, dried, and fresh. Care must be taken with storing eggs of any form. Frozen eggs should be kept at 0°F or colder. After being thawed the bacteria growth starts, thus the eggs should be used withing two days, to be safe. Frozen eggs come in containers sizes up to 30 lb. The 30-lb size may seem like a bargain but very often this is too large for one to use within two days.

Dried eggs are liked by bakers and cooks who have learned to use them properly. This product can save time and assure more uniformity of product. Dried eggs may be weighed with the dry ingredients, and the water for reconstituting added with the other liquids. Dried eggs should be stored in the refrigerator after the cans are opened. *Salmonella* bacteria have been found in dried eggs, so it is recommended that dried eggs be used only in foods that are to be cooked thoroughly.

Fresh eggs are graded: U.S. Grade AA or Fresh Fancy, Grade A, and Grade B. Grade A is not necessary for all uses. However, Grade A eggs are recommended for fried, scrambled, hard-cooked eggs, and omelets. In general, baking Grade B will mean quite a saving. The grades have no effect on the nutritive value or the wholesomeness of the egg, neither does the color of an egg's shell. Eggs which are officially graded under Federal or Federal-State supervision bear a grade mark in the form of a shield which states the grade (or quality) and the size (based on weight per dozen).

Grading is voluntary and not required. However, nearly 75% of all egg products were processed under the USDA voluntary egg inspection program in 1972. It is a service that is available when the processor requests it and pays the fee.

Eggs are also classified according to size, and the U.S. weight classes for consumer's grades for shell eggs are based on net minimum weights which are expressed in ounces per dozen (Table 7.6).

TABLE 7.6. U.S. WEIGHT CLASSES FOR CONSUMER GRADES OF SHELL EGGS

Size or Class	Min. Weight Per Doz (Oz)	Min. Weight Per 30-Doz Case (Lb)
Jumbo	30	56
Extra large	27	50+
Large	24	45
Medium	21	39+
Small	18	34
Peewees	15	28+

Source: Based on information from Home and Garden Bull. *1*, U.S. Dept. Agr.

FRESH PRODUCE

Fresh produce should be purchased in the quantity needed within the keeping period of the produce. It is frequently purchased on an informal bid basis. Fresh produce is such a changing market of highly perishable products that it is a huge gamble for a vendor to quote a sealed bid price on the products for 6 to 9 months in advance. Formula bidding works well and allows for the fluctuation of prices or it may be purchased on short term fixed price bids.

Grades are of little assurance or help in buying produce unless the company they are purchased from has a good reputation. The product may be U.S. No. 1 at the time of grading but at the time of delivery it may not be usable. Whereas Fancy means top grade for canned foods, this is not always true from one fresh product to another. Grades are just now being standardized. The cost of fresh produce fluctuates with the seasons, demands, quantity of the crops, and the part of the country the product comes from. Comparative shopping can mean significant savings. Tomatoes may range in price over a year from 29¢/lb to 99¢/lb. Tomatoes differ in quality and the best quality may be the time of year when they sell for 29¢/lb. That is the season of the year tomatoes should be on the menus. Red cabbage, radishes, shredded carrots, or unpeeled cucumber slices can add color and variety to a tossed salad at a fraction of the cost of tomatoes when not in season. Canned, frozen, or dehydrated green peppers and onions may be better buys than fresh. Canned celery has been used very satisfactorily and at a savings over fresh celery when not in season.

The quantity will also affect the price. Cellophane bags of carrots in 2-lb sizes are much more expensive than 25-, 50-, or 100-lb bags. However, if only a few pounds are needed it would be wiser to pay more per pound and purchase the quantity needed. A case of lettuce is less expensive than buying by the head, but if six heads of lettuce are all that is needed within a week to eight days, buying the quantity needed would be more economical. Pre-cut lettuce is the best buy.

When writing specifications for fresh fruits and fresh vegetables the variety, size, degree of maturity, color, and texture are a few of the factors to consider. The following are examples of specifications for some fruits.

FRESH FRUITS

Apples

Eating (Counter).—U.S. Fancy or U.S. No. 1 Grade. Minimum 2½ in. diam. Varieties: Red Delicious, Golden Delicious, McIntosh, Stayman, Jonathan, Winesap, and Wagoner. Order by box or bushel and by count per box or bushel.

Cooking.—U.S. No. 2 or unclassified (depending on use). Tart or slightly acid varieties: Gravenstein, Grimes Golden, Jonathan, and Newtown. Firmer-fleshed varieties: Rome Beauty, Northern Spy, Rhode Island Greening, Wealthy, and Winesap.

Bananas

No Federal grade required. Size of 5 to 6-in. long suggested. Order by pound or by count boxes (150). Order hard ripe (takes 5 to 6 days to ripen), turning ripe (takes 3 days to ripen), or full ripe (use within 24 hr). Available the year round. Ripen at 60 to 70°F.

Cantaloupes (Muskmelons)

U.S. No. 1 Grade.—Comes in hampers, boxes, and sacks. Size No. 45 recommended for serving halves or quarters. Generally available May through September. Usually not ripe when delivered. Hold 2 to 4 days at room temperature for ripening.

Oranges

U.S. Grade No. 1.—Order by crate or dozen and by count size. Small—approx. 2½-in. diam (226 to 324 count per 1⅗ bu). Medium—approx. 3-in. diam (144−176 to 200 count per 1⅗ bu). Large—approx. 3½-in. diam (96 to 126 per 1⅗ bu). 150's or 176's are recommended size for hand eating.

Varieties.—Navel (winter), Valencia (summer), Temple, and Pineapple (lots of seeds). Strict State regulations require they be well matured before harvested when shipped out of State. When artificial color has been added it must be labeled "color added."

FRESH VEGETABLES

Since grading of fresh vegetables is not required, it is possible to get excellent quality of ungraded vegetables. If the vegetables have been graded, the container in which they are packed will bear the official USDA grade shield or the statement "Packed Under Continuous Inspection of the U.S. Dept. of Agriculture," or "USDA Inspected" (Fig. 7.9). Examples of factors to be considered in purchasing vegetables follow.

U. S. GRADE

NO. 1

FIG. 7.9. FRESH FRUITS AND VEGETABLES
GRADE SHIELD

Courtesy
of U.S. Dept. Agr.

Cabbage

U.S. No. 1.—Three major types: smooth-leaved green cabbage, crinkly-leaved savoy cabbage, and red cabbage. Heads should be firm, outer leaves green or red depending on type. Sold by pound, 40-lb bushel and mesh sack of 50 lb.

Lettuce

U.S. No. 1.—Varieties include: Iceberg lettuce (heads large, round, solid, medium-green outer leaves), Butter-head lettuce (bib or Boston, loose head, flat on top, light to dark green), Romaine lettuce (tall, cylindrical with crisp, dark-green leaves), Leaf lettuce (includes many locally grown varieties). Sold by head or crate or bushel hamper. May through July peak season, but available all year round. Pre-cut lettuce is available, packaged 10 pound.

Potatoes

U.S. No. 1 (Most Common).—Three groups: new, general purpose, and baking potatoes. "New" potatoes are newly dug before fully mature, waxy and require moist cooking—not good for mashed or French fried. General-purpose potatoes are round or oval in shape. Baking potatoes are high in starch content. Russet Burbank, White Rose, and Maine Katahdin are the most widely used baking potatoes. Sold in boxes by count indicating size (50 to 125 per box). New potatoes and all-purpose potatoes are sold in 25, 50, and 100-lb. mesh bags.

FROZEN FRUITS AND VEGETABLES

The grades of frozen foods are similar to those for canned foods. However, there are usually not as many grades to choose from in a particular food. The grades are: U.S. Grade A (Fancy), U.S. Grade B (Choice or Extra Standard), and U.S. Grade C (Standard), and Substandard. The grades are based on maturity, color, cut, absence of defects, and flavor as they are for canned.

Fruit

Frozen fruits are packaged in size ranging from 10 oz to 30-lb tins. The grades are A, B, and C, but not all grades are available in each fruit. Factors to be specified are: style (sliced, halves, whole, broken pieces, pitted, etc.), type (yellow cling, yellow freestone, light Royal Anne, dark

Bing cherries, etc.), sugar-fruit ratio, and package size. An example of strawberries specifications is:

Strawberries.—Sliced, Marshall Variety. Sugar-fruit ratio of 1.4. Medium size berries. U.S. Grade A. Packaged 30-lb containers.

Vegetables

The most common size package of frozen vegetables for institutional use are 2-, 2½-, 3- and 3½-lb packages; however, some vegetables are packaged in 20- to 30-lb bulk containers. Once vegetables are thawed they should be used. The quality deteriorates rapidly. Deliveries should be checked to assure that the food is still frozen at the time of delivery.

THAWING GUIDE

While the amount of time, equipment, and work situation will control to a degree the method of defrosting, the following guide (COOP. EXTENSION SERV. 1970) provides thawing recommendations for various food groups.

Frozen Vegetables.—Need not be thawed, except for corn-on-the-cob.

Frozen Fruits.—Thaw in the refrigerator or in running water.

Frozen Juices.—Need not be thawed.

Frozen Meats.—*Large Cuts.*—Thaw in refrigerator or in cold water.

Small Cuts.—Thaw in refrigerator or in cold water.

Frozen Poultry.—*Large Birds.*—Thaw in refrigerator.

Small Birds or Parts.—Can be cooked from the frozen state. If the parts are to be breaded or batter-dipped, they must be thawed. Thaw in refrigerator or in cold running water.

Frozen Fish.—Fillets or steaks may be cooked either frozen or thawed. If thawed, the thawing should be done in the refrigerator.

Frozen Prepared Foods.—Thaw or cook in the frozen state according to the manufacturer's directions.

DAIRY PRODUCTS

The milk to be used in the Federal milk program or as part of the meal, may be a whole milk, lowfat or skim milk, buttermilk, or chocolate milk. *Pasteurized* milk has been subjected to temperatures no lower than

145°F for not less than 30 min or 161°F for no less than 15 sec and then promptly cooled to 40°F or lower. *Homogenized* milk is pasteurized milk that has been mechanically treated to reduce the size of the milk fat globules. This stabilizes the emulsion and the fat does not rise to the top. *Vitamin D* milk is whole or skimmed milk in which the vitamin D content has been increased by a minumum of 400 USP units per quart. An example of a bid specification for milk is in Appendix IV.

Chocolate milk is a term used to indicate that whole milk has been used and sugar and chocolate is added. If cocoa is substituted for chocolate, the milk is designated as *chocolate-flavored*. *Chocolate drink* is made from skim milk or milk that contains less than 3.25% milk fat. If cocoa is used in place of chocolate it is designated as *chocolate-flavored drink*.

Butter and Margarine

Butter is not required to be graded. However, most of the butter on the market is graded by either a State or Federal grader. The grades are: U.S. Grade AA, U.S. Grade A, U.S. Grade B, and U.S. Grade C. Butter should be frozen if to be stored for more than two weeks. Margarine is a good substitute for butter in school feeding if vitamin A enriched at least 15,000 units per pound.

STEPS IN PURCHASING

Five giant steps to quality purchasing that should be remembered.

(1) Determine the items needed that best fit the use according to menus, recipes, nutritional value, equipment, personnel, and storage.
(2) Study the market and know what is available. Compare cost, quality, and yields.
(3) Develop written specifications for the items needed which enables better communication with the vendors.
(4) Write out the orders according to the specifications in a clearly written form.
(5) Check and inspect all foods received to see that what has been ordered and specified has been delivered and that the invoice is correct.

Purchase only those specials that you can use, regardless of how "big a bargain" it is. One hundred cases of canned tuna is not a bargain unless it can be utilized and the storage facilities are adequate. The largest size is not always the best buy.

Purchasing should be done on an objective basis by a designated person who has an understanding of purchasing and of food. As much as 10 to 15% can be saved on many items if purchased through a jobber and large quantities are delivered to one location. "Family style" marketing and small-lot purchasing have no place in the school operation. The manager that neglects to follow the business-like methods of purchasing is asking for financial problems. The following is a self-test for the buyer.

TEST FOR BUYERS

Do You Buy? Or Are You Sold?

Listed below are 10 questions that will help determine. Every "Yes" answer is equal 10 points. Perfect score is 100.

(1) Do you know what you want before the salesman comes or calls?___
(2) Are your menus planned in advance?___
(3) Are purchases made according to specific needs of the menu?___
(4) Do you refuse to accept personal gifts, premiums, stamps, etc.?___
(5) Are specifications written describing the food (quality, grade, etc.) best suited for your needs?___
(6) Are orders checked and inspected at time of delivery to see if they meet specifications?___
(7) Are you up-to-date on foods, packaging, new products?___
(8) Do you try new products in small quantities before buying a large supply?___
(9) Do you refuse to buy "bargains" unless they can be utilized on the menus?___
(10) Do you buy the products because they meet your needs rather than brands?___

No answers indicate that practices need re-evaluating and perhaps changed in order to be a wise buyer.

DETERMINING QUANTITY TO ORDER

New managers usually have more difficulty with purchasing of food in the correct quantities than any other phase of managing. Determining quantities needed is extremely hard to teach. The quantities purchased should be the quantities needed for the menus. Buying by the menus is the recommended procedure. Recipes will be very helpful in determining the purchasing list and quantities needed. If a recipe is not used for the items, such as for buttered spinach, then the *Food Buying Guide for School Food Service* (U.S. Dept. Agr. 1980) is an excellent guide or *Food for Fifty* (West *et al.* 1978).

Since market orders are usually placed 1 to 2 weeks before the food is to be used, sometimes a month ahead, it is necessary to keep in mind what, of the current inventory, will be used and how much more will be needed to meet the needs of the menus. Dry storage items, such as canned foods, staples, etc., usually do not require the close planning that frozen foods and perishables do. Cycle menus can be accompanied by cycle food needed from which the market order can be prepared.

The following practical exercise will be helpful to someone learning to use the *Food Buying Guide for School Food Service*.

PRACTICAL EXERCISE NO.—
DETERMINING QUANTITY OF FRUITS AND VEGETABLES
NEEDED USING FOOD BUYING GUIDE
FOR SCHOOL FOOD SERVICE

The purchase units given for 100 servings in column 5 in the *Food Buying Guide* are to be used to determine the amount needed to prepare for 100. To determine the quantity needed for a specific number to be served, move the decimal in column 5 two places to the left and multiply this number by the number of servings needed.

For Example: Green Beans, Canned—need 4.50 cans to serve 100 ½ cup servings.

To serve 225: 0.045 × 225 = 10.12 (or 11) cans

(1) Food as Purchased	(2) Purchase Unit	(3) Servings Size (Cup)	(4) Purchase Units for 100 Servings	(5) Number to be Served	Amount of food needed
Green beans, canned	No. 10 can	½	4.50	225	9.93 or 10 cans
Broccoli, frozen spears	lb	½	20.80	285	59.28 lb
Cranberries, fresh	lb	¼ cooked	9.00	335	30.15 lb
Grapes, fresh seedless	lb	¼		190	
Lettuce, head fresh	lb	½		480	
Pineapple, crushed	No. 10 can	¼		215	
Potatoes, frozen crinkle French fries	5-lb pkg.	½		375	
Orange juice, frozen con-centrated	32 fl oz can	½		425	

RECEIVING

Good purchasing practices can be of little value if the food is not checked when received to make sure that what has been purchased is the same as what is being delivered. Signing an invoice without checking what has been delivered is a very poor management practice. Managers use the excuse that checking the food is an indication to the deliveryman that he is not trusted. Trustworthy or not, an order should be checked before an invoice or delivery ticket is signed. Much inconvenience and hard feeling can result if later the manager discovers only four cases of green beans were left when six were ordered and charged for. Checking an order should include:

(1) Checking items delivered. Is it what was ordered; does it meet specifications?
(2) Quantity. Is the proper amount as the invoice indicates delivered? Is this the quantity ordered?
(3) Price. Is the price the quoted or on-bid price charged? Are the multiplication and addition correct?
(4) Condition of the items delivered. Is it in good condition? Are frozen foods frozen, refrigerated items cold, bread today's date, milk fresh according to date, food clean, carton, bags, and containers untorn?

The best time to correct errors in deliveries is while the deliveryman is there and a credit memo can be written, unwanted damaged merchandise can be returned, and indications made on the invoice before the manager signs. It should be the policy of the accounts payable department that no invoices are paid that are not signed. In turn, this should be stated on bid contracts. A clear understanding should exist between the purchaser and supplier if not on bid contract.

The responsibility of receiving deliveries should be assigned to a competent person. In order to make sure that what is received is what is ordered— in the right quantity, in good condition, and at the correct price—the person receiving the food needs some basic information and equipment, such as: (1) set of specifications, (2) weight charts for easy reference, (3) scales and thermometer, and (4) a table located near the service entrance for receiving the food. The receiving area ideally should be near the service entrance and before the area of storage. The larger the foodservice operation the more elaborate the equipment needed for checking will be. A set of accurate scales is essential. There are various types of scales from the automatic-indicating scales to recording scales which are expensive but easy to use. Beam-type scales are the most commonly used, and are available in floor and table models.

BIBLIOGRAPHY

ANON. 1975. Almanac of the Canning, Freezing, Preserving Industries. Edward E. Judge & Sons, Westminister, Md.

BEAU, F.N. 1970. Quantity Food Purchasing Guide. Institutions Magazine, Chicago, Ill.

FLANAGAN, THELMA. 1968. School Food Purchasing Guide. Joint publication ASFSA and ASBO, Chicago, Ill.

KELLY, HUGH J. 1970. Food Service Purchasing, Principles and Practices. Chain Store Publishing Corp., New York.

KOTSCHEVAR, L. 1975. Quantity Food Purchasing, 2nd Edition. John Wiley & Sons, New York.

LEVIE, A. 1970. The Meat Handbook, 3rd Edition. AVI Publishing Co., Westport, Conn.

MIESEL, G.E. 1972. What's in the can? School Foodservice J. *26*, No. 6, 32–35.

MOYER, WILLIAM C. 1976. The Buying Guide for Fresh Fruits, Vegetables, Herbs and Nuts. Blue Goose Inc., Fullerton, Ca.

NATL. CANNERS ASSOC. 1967. Canned Food Tables, 6th Edition. National Canners Assoc., Washington, D.C.

PEDDERSEN, RAYMOND B. 1977. Specs: The Comprehensive Foodservice Purchasing and Specification Manual. CBI Publishing Co., Boston, Mass.

U.S. DEPT. AGR. 1970. USDA's Acceptance Service for Meat and Meat Products. U.S. Govt. Printing Office, Washington, D.C.

U.S. DEPT. AGR. 1971. Institutional Meat Purchase Specifications general requirements. U.S. Govt. Printing Office, Washington, D.C.

U.S. DEPT. AGR. 1977. Food Purchasing Pointers for School Food Service. U.S. Govt. Printing Office, Washington, D.C.

U.S. DEPT. AGR. 1978. Food Price Sources for School Food Procurement. U.S. Govt. Printing Office, Washington, D.C.

U.S. DEPT. AGR. 1978. Study of School Food Procurement Practices. Vols. I and II. U.S. Govt. Printing Office, Washington, D.C.

U.S. DEPT. AGR. 1980. Food Buying Guide for School Food Service. U.S. Govt. Printing Office, Washington, D.C.

WEST, BESSIE BROOK, GRACE S. SHUGART, and MAXINE F. WILSON. 1978. Food for Fifty, 6th Edition. John Wiley & Sons, New York.

WEST, BESSIE, LEVELLE WOOD, VIRGINIA HARGER, and GRACE SHUGART. 1977. Food Service in Institutions, 6th Edition. John Wiley & Sons, New York.

8

Food Preparation

Food preparation in the true sense of the word is both an art and a science. Creativity and skill are required to make food attractive, appetizing, flavorful, and interesting. A scientific approach is required in order to conserve the nutritive value of food, to understand the principles of cooking, and to understand why certain things happen in food preparation. A knowledge of food preparation as an art and a science is required in school foodservices to meet the objectives of food preparation.

Today there are standardized recipes and controlled situations in equipment and supplies. School foodservice preparation does not require a "chef" *per se*. Years ago a good chef was one who had an extensive apprenticeship in preparing food. He knew how and what each ingredient did and how each reacted—this was a true art. Today, if a person has the ability to read, can follow directions, and has the knowledge of a few basic principles, he can turn out good food in large quantities.

With the increased amount of convenience foods now on the market less and less preparation is done in the kitchen. It is with this in mind that this chapter is written.

Objectives of Food Preparation

The objectives of food preparation are (1) to improve the digestibility of the food, (2) to conserve the nutritive value, (3) to improve the flavor and appearance of the food, and (4) to make the food safe for consumption. The manner in which each of these objectives is carried out will determine the quality of the food served. Food preparation starts with the quality of the purchased food. Only when starting with good quality food is it possible to serve a good quality product.

STANDARDIZED RECIPES

One of the most important tools of food preparation in large quantities is a standardized recipe. A recipe is a written direction for preparing an item. A standardized recipe is a recipe that has been tested for good quality and yield (Table 8.1). School food operations cannot affort to prepare food without a standardized recipe because this is part of the blueprint for building a good quality, sound operation. Using standardized recipes and standard weights and measures in following the recipe has many advantages:

(1) insures uniform quality and eliminates "trial and error,"
(2) helps to know the yield and prevents waste and running out,
(3) saves time and money,
(4) enables precosting of a menu,
(5) simplifies the job for the employee,
(6) helps one know what to order and quantities,
(7) helps assure compliance with meal requirements.

When standardized tested recipes are not used, the cost may vary every time a food is prepared. "Trial and error" is too risky for quantity foodservices. Customers who like a certain food want to be able to depend on the food being the same each time, especially school-age customers. If the spaghetti with meat sauce was good, they want it to taste the same the next time—then the comment, hopefully, will be "I like the spaghetti the way the school makes it."

To most foodservice managers, the two things most feared in their work are food poisoning and running out of food. Food poisoning is discussed in Chap. 9. A standardized recipe will assure the manager of a yield if the portions are controlled in a standardized method. Running out of food is bad for the reputation of a foodservice, and it cheats the student who is served a peanut butter and jelly sandwich because the cook did not use a standardized recipe and ran out of spaghetti with meat sauce.

Inexperienced and experienced cooks should use a recipe. There is still room for creativity, of improving on a recipe. Some good cooks, who have the ability to prepare good food without recipes, cannot understand why they should use one. If the students are content, the cost is not too high, and the yield is satisfactory, there may be little reason to urge a cook to change. However, a cook's art will be of no value to the foodservice if the cook becomes sick or decides to resign. The recipes should be put on paper and then be standardized.

Numerous published sources of standardized recipes are available. The *Quantity Recipes for Type A School Lunches* (U.S. Dept. Agr. 1971) are the most familiar to school foodservices. However, with yield data changes in 1980 for many foods, this set of recipes are obsolete and

TABLE 8.1. A STANDARDIZED RECIPE FOR BARBECUE BEEF THAT WILL YIELD 100 PORTIONS

Ingredients	100 Servings Weights Lb Oz	Measures	For Servings	Directions
Ground beef[1]	16 12			(1) Brown ground beef and drain thoroughly.
Tomato juice	23 (fl)	2¾ cups		(2) Combine tomato juice, tomato puree, water,
Tomato puree		1 No. 10 can or 3 qt		vinegar, catsup, sugar, chili powder, mustard,
Catsup		1¾ cups		salt, and Worcestershire
Water		2 cups		sauce.
Vinegar		1¼ cups		
Brown sugar	13	2½ cups		
Chili powder		2 tsp		
Mustard, dry		2 tsp		
Salt		¼ cup		
Worcestershire sauce		2 Tbsp		
Butter	6	¾ cup		(3) Saute onions and celery in butter until
Onions, chopped	7½	1½ cups		transparent.
Celery, chopped	6	1½ cups		(4) Add tomato mixture and cook 1½ hr. Stir often.
				(5) Add sauce to cooked meat. Heat thoroughly.
				(6) Serve on heated bun, using No. 12 scoop (approximately ⅓ cup servings).

[1]Ground pork, canned chicken, roast beef, or pork can be substituted in this recipe.

should be revised soon. These recipes are basic ones that should be the ground work for a creative cook or baker to improve on, to adjust to the taste of the locale, and to adjust to the equipment available. The adjustments should be standardized by putting into definite time, weights, and measures. Cooks and bakers should be encouraged to standardize their own recipes. The following is a guide to writing standardized recipes adapted from the *Guides for Writing and Evaluating Quantity Recipes for Type A School Lunches* (U.S. Dept. Agr. 1969). With emphasis on reducing the quantity of fat, sugar, and salt, recipes should be evaluated to determine acceptable levels of decreasing these ingredients.

QUANTITY RECIPE FORM[1]

Name of the Recipe

Use chief food in recipe or a name readily understood, descriptive terms, but simple, such as "Chicken Pot Pies," "Apple Pie," "Chocolate Cake."

[1]Use a 5 × 8 inch card.

Ingredients

List, in order used in preparing recipe, descriptive terms to indicate type product to be purchased and used. Descriptive term *before* ingredient to indicate type or style to be purchased or cooking or heating needed before used in recipe, such as "canned tomatoes," "rolled oats," "cooked rice," "hot milk." Descriptive *after* the ingredient indicating preparation needed, such as "cooked turkey, diced"; "onion, chopped"; "apples, pared, sliced."

Weights and Measures

Give weights and measures when practical, weight alone when the item is not easily measured. Use measure alone for liquids such as water, broth, and milk and for small quantities too small to weigh accurately. The booklet, *Average Weight of a Measured Cup of Various Foods* (U.S. Dept. Agr. 1977) is useful.

Directions

Should be simply written and easy to understand and follow. Number and size pans should be indicated. Baking temperature and time required to cook should be given. Many steps can be eliminated or combined to reduce time required to prepare the recipe.

Yield

Size portions in common measure or weight should be given with the total number servings the recipe will yield.

Additional Information

(1) Contribution to the meal patterns requirements is desirable information (Fig. 8.1).
(2) Cost per portion space.
(3) Variations that can be obtained by changing or replacing an ingredient, by changing the method of cooking, by method of combining ingredients, etc.

When the portions on the recipes are not the size desired, then the changes should be made. For example, if the spaghetti with meat sauce recipe will yield 100 ⅔-cup portions and the portion size desired for secondary high school students is 1 cup, the recipe will have to be increased by ⅓. Recipes are most frequently in 50 or 100 portions.

(1) SCHOOL NAME_____
(2) Date _____
(3) Day (Circle) M T W T F
(4) Meal (Check) Breakfast
                  Snack AM/PM
                  Lunch

A SAMPLE FOOD PRODUCTION RECORD

(5) MENU	Recipe Source (6)	Portion Size (7)	Number Portions Planned (8)	(9) FOOD PREPARED		(12) PORTIONS SERVED					
				Foods Used to Meet Requirement* (10)	Quantity Food Used (11)	Students (13)	Adults (14)	A la carte (15)	Other (16)	Left over (17)	Total Portions (18)
(19) MEAT/ ALTERNATES List all menu items in appropriate food category	Give source and number (e.g., USDA: D-14)	Express as weight, measure, scoop or ladle size, or size of piece or portion	Record number of portions prepared	Record name of each food used to meet meal requirement in the appropriate food category (e.g., If beef pie is the *menu item*, beef would be in the meat/alternate section; potatoes and carrots in pie would be listed in vegetable/fruit section; pie crust in the bread/ alternate section)	Use weight, measures, or numbers	Actual number	Actual number (include staff)	Do not include foods sold à la carte only	Can use this column to record portion sent out from base kitchen or rec'd by a satellite school	Measure and weigh leftovers and convert to number of portions	Total number of portions served for each menu item
(20) VEGETABLES/ FRUITS											
(21) BREAD/ ALTERNATES											
(22) MILK AS BEVERAGE											
(23) OTHER FOODS											

*Indicate if raw or precooked

(24) Sign to verify correct information

_____
Manager

Courtesy of: Chiquita Brands, Inc., United Brands Company.

FIG. 8.1. THE PRODUCTION RECORD SHOWS CONTRIBUTION TO MEAL PATTERN

Ordinarily it will be necessary to adjust recipes to serve different numbers. Adjusting recipes should be done carefully with a second person checking the mathematics. Failures are frequently caused by mathematical errors in adjusting recipes. Weights and measures should be expressed in the simplest terms (Table 8.2).

It is possible to use a home recipe and blow it up, but this is not advisable except when testing is possible. When a home recipe for 10 is increased to serve 300, the yield will be slightly more than 300 portions if multiplied by 30. The percentage of loss to the pan, in measuring, etc., which is figured into the recipe has decreased. For example, it has been shown that when a recipe for 50 is adjusted to serve 900 portions the

TABLE 8.2. ADJUSTING RECIPES

Brownie C-8

(Name and File Number of Recipe)

	100 Portions			For 400		400 Portions		
	Weights		Measures	× Factor =		Weights		Measures
Ingredients	Lb	Oz				Lb	Oz	
All-purpose flour	1	8		×4	= 6			
Sugar	3	8		×4	= 14			
Nonfat dry milk		1		×4	=		4	
Baking powder		½		×4	=		2	
Salt			3½ tsp	×4	=			¼ cup + 2 tsp
Nuts, chopped		12		×4	= 3			
Bitter chocolate	1			×4	= 4			
Shortening	1	2		×4	= 4		8	
Eggs	1	12½		×4	= 7		2	
Water			1 cup	×4	=			1 qt
Vanilla			2 tsp	×4	=			2 Tbsp + 2 tsp

recipe should be increased 18 times, but then decreased by as much as 10%. Also to be considered in adjusting a recipe, is the equipment available. If a 30-qt mixer is available, it is useless to increase a cake recipe to 400 portions when the mixer will not hold that quantity.

FOLLOWING A RECIPE

The terminology used in recipes must be understood by the person following the recipe, such as abbreviations, equivalents, and cooking terms.

Abbreviations Most Commonly Used

Teaspoon	tsp
Tablespoon	Tbsp
Ounce	oz
Pound	lb
Quart	qt
Gallon	gal.

"Cup" is not abbreviated

Oven Temperatures and Descriptive Terms

121 to 135°C—250 to 275°F	very slow oven
149 to 163°C—300 to 325°F	slow oven
177 to 191°C—350 to 375°F	moderate oven
204 to 218°C—400 to 425°F	hot oven
232 to 246°C—450 to 475°F	very hot oven
260 to 274°C—500 to 525°F	extremely hot oven

There are thousands of terms used in food preparation; however, some of the most basic terms are defined here.

Cooking Terms

Baking.—To cook covered or uncovered by dry heat, usually in an oven. This process is called roasting when applied to meats in uncovered containers.

Basting.—To moisten food with liquid or fat while cooking to add flavor and to prevent drying of the surface.

Beating.—To use a brisk regular motion to stir a mixture introducing air or making the mixture smooth.

Blanching.—To cook in boiling water or steam to inactivate enzymes and to loosen skin of some fruits and vegetables.

Blending.—To thoroughly mix together two or more ingredients.

Boiling.—To cook in water or a liquid in which the bubbles are breaking on the surface (212°F at sea level).

Braising.—To cook slowly in a covered pan in a small amount of liquid.

Breading.—To coat a food with flour, crumbs, etc., before cooking.

Broiling.—To cook by direct heat.

Candying.—To cook in heavy sirup or sugar and liquid.

Caramelizing.—To heat sugar over how heat until brown in color.

Chopping.—To cut food into small pieces with a knife or other sharp tool.

Creaming.—To mix one or more foods until soft and creamy.

Crisping.—To cause to become crisp in the case of crackers, by removing moisture, and in the case of vegetables, by adding cold water.

Cutting in.—To combine solid fat with a dry ingredient by a cutting motion. This term is used to describe the combining of fat with dry ingredients in making pastry and biscuits when the dry ingredients are made to coat the fat particles.

Dicing.—To cut food into small cubes.

Dredging.—To coat by sprinkling a food with flour or other fine mixture.

Folding.—To combine ingredients by cutting vertically through the mixture and turning over.

Fricasseeing.—To cook by browning in a small amount of fat, then covering with liquid or steaming.

Frying.—To cook in hot fat. When cooking in a small amount of fat it is also referred to as sautéing or pan frying and when cooking in a deep layer of fat it is referred to as deep-fat frying.

Glacéing.—To coat food with a thin sugar-sirup mixture.

Grilling.—To cook by direct heat.

Grinding.—To cut food into small particles.

Kneading.—To work dough with a pressing motion accompanied by folding and stretching.

Marinating.—To cover a food with liquid and let stand for a period of time to add flavor or tenderize.

Melting.—To heat to cause a food to become liquid.

Mincing.—To cut or chop a food into very small pieces, finer than if chopped but not as fine as when ground.

Mixing.—To combine two or more ingredients to blend.

Pan-broiling.—To cook uncovered on a hot surface.

Pan-frying.—To cook uncovered in a small amount of fat.

Parboiling.—To partially cook a food by boiling.

Parching.—To brown by the application of dry heat.

Paring.—To cut off the outer covering, usually with a knife.

Peeling.—To remove the outer layer.

Pot-roasting.—To cook large cuts of meat by braising.

Roasting.—To cook usually in the oven uncovered.

Sautéing.—To cook in a small amount of fat.

Scalding.—To heat a liquid or dip food into a liquid heated to a point just below boiling.

Scalloping.—To bake food with a liquid or sauce and crumbs. Sometimes layers of different ingredients are baked, as in a casserole.

Scoring.—To make shallow slits on the surface of meat.

Simmering.—To cook in a liquid at a low temperature below the boiling point.

Steaming.—To cook in steam with or without pressure.

Steeping.—To cover an ingredient with hot water and allow to stand in order to extract flavor, color, or other qualities.

Stewing.—To cook at low temperature in a small amount of liquid.

Stirring.—To mix ingredients with a circular motion in order to blend or to make of a uniform consistency.

Toasting.—To brown with direct heat.

Whipping.—To beat rapidly to increase volume by the incorporating of air.

BASIC TOOLS

The basic tools needed in preparing a standardized recipe are a set of standardized graduated measuring cups and measuring spoons, standard size pans, and table model scales for weighing small and large quantities of ingredients. Certainly it is most important to have good quality ingredients as required in the recipe. Sometimes it is necessary or desirable to make substitutions because of an emergency or shortage to save time, to utilize leftovers, to utilize USDA-donated foods, to increase nutritive value, or to reduce cost. Using substitutions requires skill and knowledge. The quality of the finished product may or may not be altered.

When preparing a recipe one should start by reading the recipe carefully. Then the utensils, tools, and ingredients needed should all be assembled before starting. The ingredients should be weighed or measured carefully. Weighing of ingredients is the most accurate method and saves time over measuring. It assures a more standardized product. Liquids may be weighed or measured. In baked products, eggs should be weighed. USDA recipes are based on "large" eggs. There are many times during the year when "medium" eggs may be the best buy. However, when the "medium" egg is used in the same number in the recipe, this can affect the outcome of the product, particularly the volume of baked products. Table 8.3 is a guide to substituting size eggs.

The directions for combining the ingredients and cooking the product— size pans, number pans, temperature, and time, should be followed carefully. The yield of the recipe cannot be depended on unless the correct size and number of pans are used and are uniformly filled.

CONTROLLING QUALITY

Quality in prepared food is determined in degrees of good or bad according to the standards of person judging the quality. The quality of

TABLE 8.3. GUIDE FOR USING WHOLE EGGS OF VARIOUS SIZES IN RECIPES

Number of Large Eggs	In Recipe Use Equivalent to:			Approximate Volume
	Extra Large Eggs	Medium Eggs	Small Eggs	
1	1	1	1	3 Tbsp
2	2	2	3	¼ cup + 2 Tbsp
3	3	4	4	½ cup + 2 Tbsp
4	3	5	6	¾ cup
5	4	6	7	1 cup
6	5	7	8	1 cup + 2 Tbsp
8	6	10	11	1½ cups
10	8	12	14	2 cups
12	10	14	17	2½ cups

food is judged on aroma, appearance, flavor, texture, consistency, and temperature. The objective for a manager of a school foodservice is to prepare and serve the quality of food considered good by the majority of the customers. Rare roast beef may not be considered good by most elementary children, though it will be by many adults. Spaghetti considered good by the student in the northeastern United States may be bland to the student in Texas. But some basic standards can be applied almost universally in quality judging. What is a good quality hamburger? The standard definition would be: a juicy, tender, flavorful piece of meat served on a fresh warmed bun with the desired condiments. The quality requires:

(1) a good quality ground beef patty,
(2) cooked at the right temperature for the right amount of time,
(3) seasoned to accentuate the flavor,
(4) served hot, as soon after cooking as possible, on a fresh warmed bun with the desired condiments.

To control quality in preparation, (1) management must know the quality desired, how to judge and obtain this quality, must set quality standards, and must check constantly on quality; (2) employees must be trained to use the basic tools for controlling quality.

Quality food preparation requires well-planned menus, standardized recipes, standardized procedures, precise purchasing specifications to guarantee the right ingredient and quality ingredient needed, good receiving and storing procedures, and well-trained personnel with good supervision. The basic tools for controlling quality are standardized recipes, thermometers, portion scales, standard measuring utensils, clocks and timers. Timing is one of the crucial factors. Scheduling preparation, so that food is ready for serving at its peak, has a definite effect on the quality. Holding food, particularly fresh produce items and protein-rich foods at warming temperatures, decreases quality rapidly. Those final touches—accentuating and improving flavors according to the likes and dislikes of the customers—can make the difference between food being considered just average or really good. One of the biggest complaints children have about preplated frozen dinners packed by national companies is the lack of flavor, either desired flavor or flavor characteristic to the locale.

Management can judge food quality and acceptability by evaluating the amount of sales, customer reaction, and plate waste. Plate waste should be checked daily. If food is coming back on the plate, the manager and employees should evaluate the food, get student opinions, and then decide what the problem is—quality, seasonings, temperature, or is it the food itself? Quality, seasoning, and temperature can and should be improved according to customer standards. If the food itself is disliked, management should plan ways of making it acceptable, should make it a choice item, or should remove it from the menu completely.

An understanding of the basic characteristics of food is needed for controlling the quality of food. If the yeast rolls fail to rise, it is important to know what could have caused this failure. Some of the basic characteristics of foods and procedures for obtaining the desired qualities which the foodservice cooks and bakers should know are discussed in the following paragraphs.

PREPARATION OF MEAT/MEAT ALTERNATES

Meat

Tenderness, flavor, and yield of meat will be determined to a great extent by the quality and grade of meat purchased. This quality may also determine the method of cooking and the length of time. The reasons for cooking meats are to destroy the pathogenic microorganisms that might be harmful and thus make the meat safe for human consumption, to make the meat tender by softening the white connective tissue, to develop the flavor and color, and to make it easier to digest. Nutritive value of protein rich foods is affected very little by ordinary cooking. However, vitamin losses increase with prolonged cooking and high temperatures.

The methods of cooking meat usually used are: (1) dry heat method— air or fat is used as the medium of heat transfer (examples: baking, roasting, and frying). (2) Moist heat method—water or other liquids are used as the medium of heat transfer (examples: braising, stewing, simmering, and steaming).

The cut, age, and quality will determine how pieces of meat should be cooked. The meat charts identify the cuts of beef, pork, veal, and lamb and indicate which method of cooking should be used (Figs. 8.2, 8.3, 8.4, 8.5). The time and temperature at which meats are cooked can, if correct, result in maximum flavor, juiciness, nutritive value retention and tenderness, and minimum shrinkage.

When baking or roasting meats, the loss due to shrinkage is of great concern. As much as 25% of the food dollar goes to the meat/meat alternate so that undue shrinkage can be costly waste. For example, a 30-lb beef roast @ $2.20 per lb costs $66.00. Under desired cooking time and temperature the roast can be expected to shrink as much as 24%, but at high temperatures the shrinkage may be as high as 45% (Table 8.4). The cost per pound and per portion is increased considerably.

TABLE 8.4. COST OF 30-LB BEEF ROAST ACCORDING TO COOKING TEMPERATURE

| Initial Cost@ $2.20/lb | Cooking Temp (°F) | Shrinkage (%) | Yield | | | Final Cost Per Serving |
			Lb Lost	Lb	No. of 2-Oz Portions	
$66.00	300–325	24	7.2	22.8	180	$0.367
$66.00	400–450	45	13.5	16.5	130	$0.508

Cooking time will be determined by (1) size cut and amount of surface area, (2) quality or grade of meat and age, (3) doneness desired, (4) cooking temperature, (5) amount in oven. A meat thermometer should be used, particularly when roasting large pieces of meat. By inserting the meat thermometer in each piece of meat the guesswork is taken out of cooking and the meat is less likely to be overcooked. It is generally agreed that salting a large piece of meat does not affect the loss of juices nor does the salt penetrate more than 1 in. Meats cooked by the dry methods, such as broiling and frying, are cooked at high temperatures and for short periods of time. This method is suggested for tender cuts of meat. Timing is also a prime factor with this method since the quality decreases with holding after it is done.

Poultry

The most important objective in cooking poultry is to cook it and handle in such a way that it is safe for human consumption. Poultry is very perishable and if contaminated with bacteria it affords a favorable environment for bacteria to multiply and possibly cause food poisoning. Points to be remembered in handling poultry are discussed in Chap. 9. However, it should be pointed out here that since poultry is very perish-

BEEF CHART

RETAIL CUTS OF BEEF — WHERE THEY COME FROM AND HOW TO COOK THEM

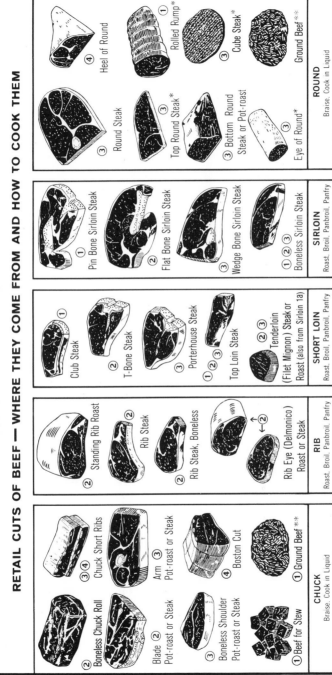

CHUCK
Braise. Cook in Liquid

② Boneless Chuck Roll

③④ Chuck Short Ribs

Blade ②
Pot-roast or Steak

Arm ③
Pot-roast or Steak

③ Boneless Shoulder
Pot-roast or Steak

④ Boston Cut

① Beef for Stew

① Ground Beef **

RIB
Roast. Broil. Panbroil. Panfry

② Standing Rib Roast

② Rib Steak

② Rib Steak, Boneless

Rib Eye (Delmonico)
Roast or Steak

SHORT LOIN
Roast. Broil. Panbroil. Panfry

① Club Steak

② T-Bone Steak

③ Porterhouse Steak

①②③ Top Loin Steak

②③ Tenderloin
(Filet Mignon) Steak or
Roast (also from Sirloin 1a)

SIRLOIN
Roast. Broil. Panbroil. Panfry

① Pin Bone Sirloin Steak

② Flat Bone Sirloin Steak

③ Wedge Bone Sirloin Steak

①②③ Boneless Sirloin Steak

ROUND
Braise. Cook in Liquid

④ Heel of Round

③ Round Steak

③ Top Round Steak *

③ Bottom Round
Steak or Pot-roast

① Rolled Rump*

③ Cube Steak *

③ Eye of Round*

Ground Beef **

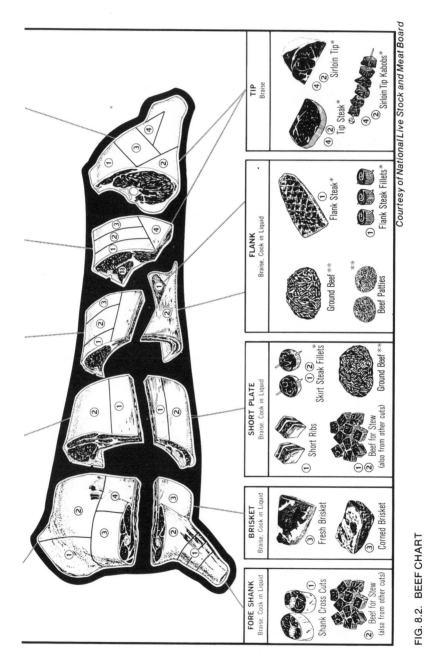

FIG. 8.2. BEEF CHART

*May be roasted, broiled or panbroiled, or panfried from high quality beef.
**May be roasted, (baked), broiled, panbroiled, or panfried.

Courtesy of National Live Stock and Meat Board

PORK CHART

RETAIL CUTS OF PORK—WHERE THEY COME FROM AND HOW TO COOK THEM

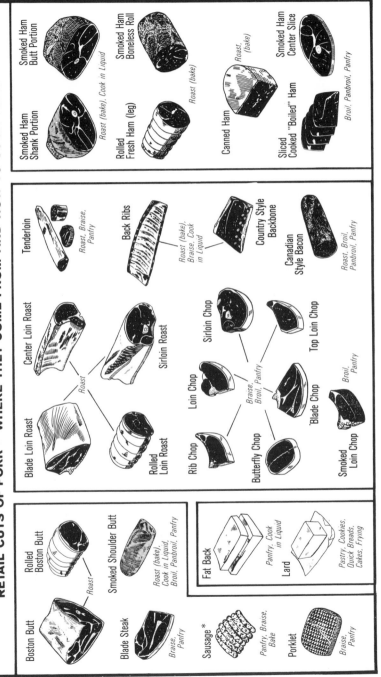

Smoked Ham Shank Portion

Smoked Ham Butt Portion

Roast (bake), Cook in Liquid

Rolled Fresh Ham (leg)

Smoked Ham Boneless Roll

Roast (bake)

Canned Ham

Roast, (bake)

Smoked Ham Center Slice

Sliced Cooked "Boiled" Ham

Broil, Panbroil, Panfry

Blade Loin Roast

Center Loin Roast

Tenderloin

Roast, Braise, Panfry

Back Ribs

Roast (bake), Braise, Cook in Liquid

Country Style Backbone

Canadian Style Bacon

Roast, Broil, Panbroil, Panfry

Sirloin Roast

Roast

Rolled Loin Roast

Sirloin Chop

Top Loin Chop

Loin Chop

Braise, Broil, Panfry

Blade Chop

Broil, Panfry

Rib Chop

Butterfly Chop

Smoked Loin Chop

Boston Butt

Rolled Boston Butt

Roast

Smoked Shoulder Butt

Roast (bake), Cook in Liquid, Broil, Panbroil, Panfry

Blade Steak

Braise, Panfry

Sausage *

Panfry, Braise, Bake

Porklet

Braise, Panfry

Fat Back

Panfry, Cook in Liquid

Lard

Pastry, Cookies, Quick Breads, Cakes, Frying

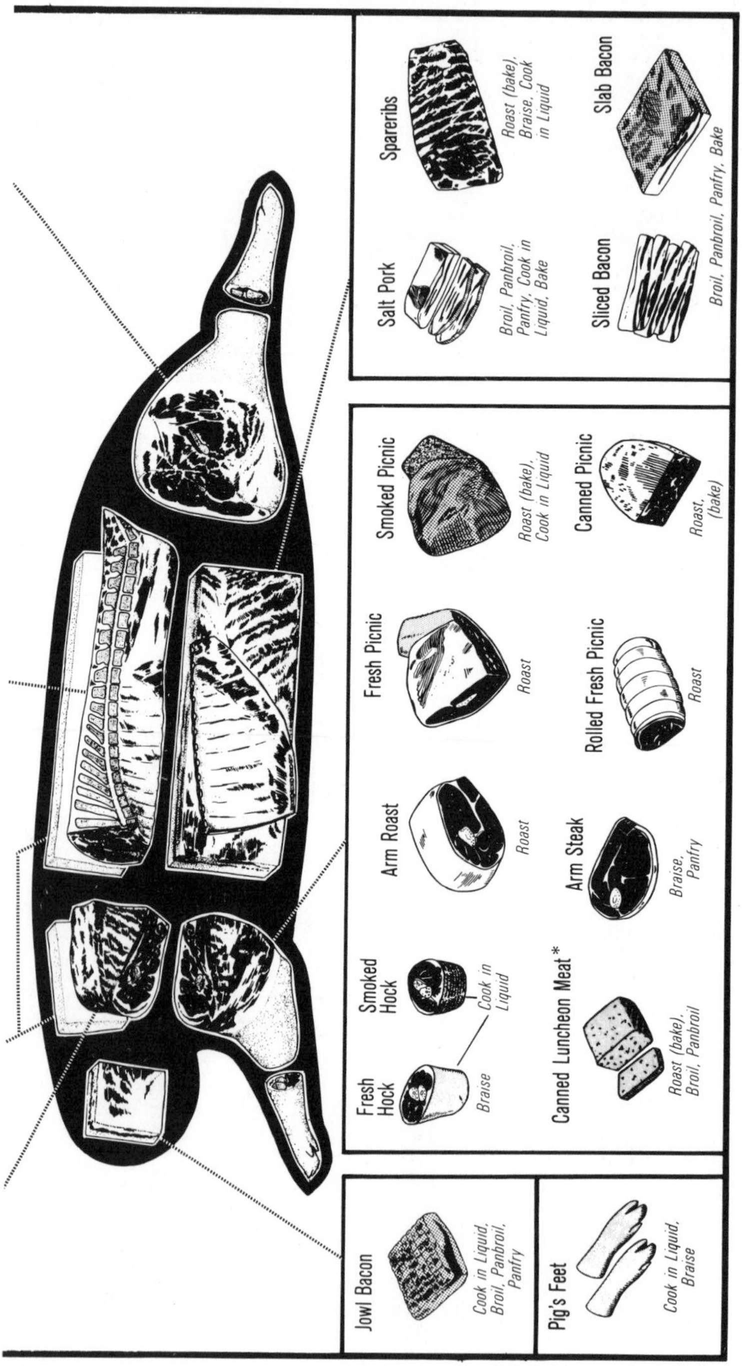

Courtesy of National Live Stock and Meat Board

Spareribs — Roast (bake), Braise, Cook in Liquid

Slab Bacon — Broil, Panbroil, Pantry, Bake

Salt Pork — Broil, Panbroil, Pantry, Cook in Liquid, Bake

Sliced Bacon

Smoked Picnic — Roast (bake), Cook in Liquid

Canned Picnic — Roast, (bake)

Fresh Picnic — Roast

Rolled Fresh Picnic — Roast

Arm Roast — Roast

Arm Steak — Braise, Panfry

Smoked Hock — Cook in Liquid

Fresh Hock — Braise

Canned Luncheon Meat* — Roast (bake), Broil, Panbroil

Jowl Bacon — Cook in Liquid, Broil, Panbroil, Panfry

Pig's Feet — Cook in Liquid, Braise

FIG. 8.3. PORK CHART

VEAL CHART

RETAIL CUTS OF VEAL — WHERE THEY COME FROM AND HOW TO COOK THEM

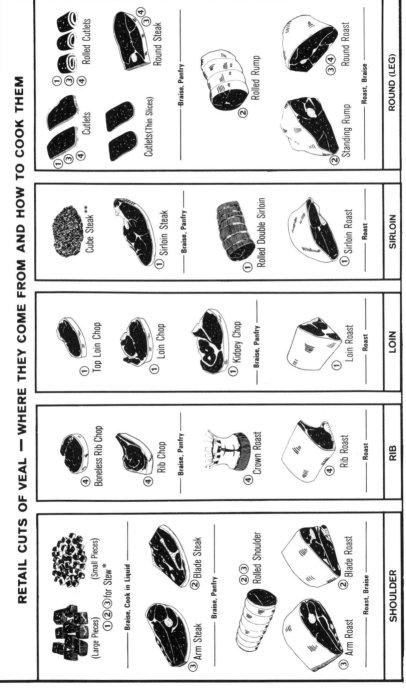

SHOULDER

(Large Pieces) (Small Pieces)
① ② ③ for Stew*

───── Braise, Cook in Liquid ─────

③ Arm Steak   ② Blade Steak

───── Braise, Panfry ─────

② ③ Rolled Shoulder

③ Arm Roast   ② Blade Roast

───── Roast, Braise ─────

RIB

④ Boneless Rib Chop

④ Rib Chop

───── Braise, Panfry ─────

④ Crown Roast

④ Rib Roast

───── Roast ─────

LOIN

① Top Loin Chop

① Loin Chop

① Kidney Chop

───── Braise, Panfry ─────

① Loin Roast

───── Roast ─────

SIRLOIN

Cube Steak**

① Sirloin Steak

───── Braise, Panfry ─────

① Rolled Double Sirloin

① Sirloin Roast

───── Roast ─────

ROUND (LEG)

① ③ ④ Rolled Cutlets

① ③ ④ Round Steak

① ③ ④ Cutlets

Cutlets (Thin Slices)

───── Braise, Panfry ─────

② Rolled Rump

② Standing Rump

③ ④ Round Roast

───── Roast, Braise ─────

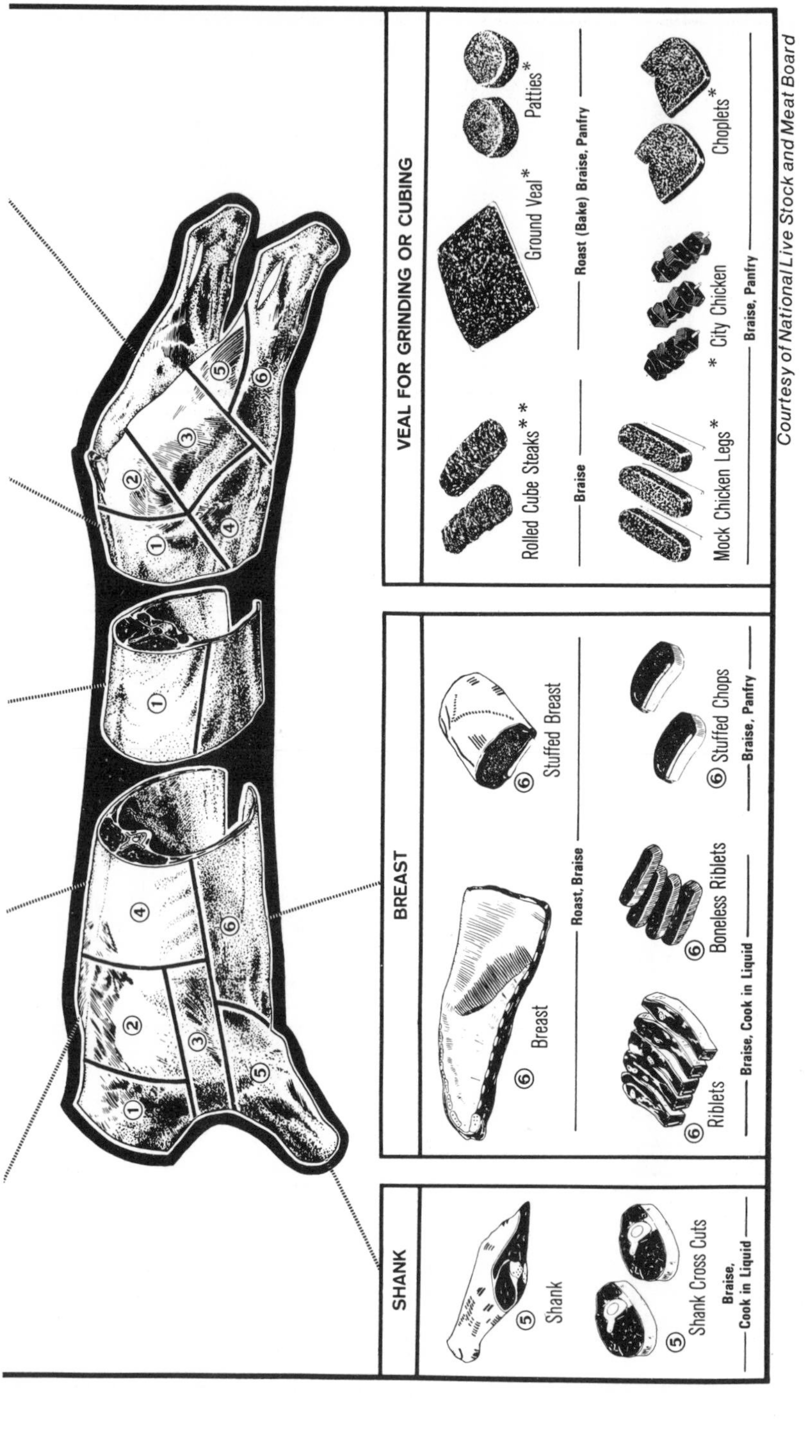

VEAL FOR GRINDING OR CUBING

Patties*

Ground Veal*
—— Roast (Bake) Braise, Panfry ——

Choplets*

City Chicken
—— Braise, Panfry ——

Rolled Cube Steaks**
—— Braise ——

Mock Chicken Legs*

Courtesy of National Live Stock and Meat Board

BREAST

Stuffed Breast
—— Roast, Braise ——

Stuffed Chops
—— Braise, Panfry ——

Breast

Boneless Riblets

Riblets
—— Braise, Cook in Liquid ——

SHANK

Shank

Shank Cross Cuts
—— Braise, Cook in Liquid ——

FIG. 8.4.   VEAL CHART

LAMB CHART

RETAIL CUTS OF LAMB — WHERE THEY COME FROM AND HOW TO COOK THEM

SHOULDER

② ③ Square Shoulder
— Roast —

② ③ Cushion Shoulder

② ③ Rolled Shoulder

② Blade Chop

③ Arm Chop
— Broil, Panbroil, Panfry —

② Saratoga Chops

Cubes for Kabobs***
— Broil —

NECK

① Neck Slices
— Braise —

RIB

① Frenched Rib Chops

① Rib Chops
— Broil, Panbroil, Panfry —

① Crown Roast
— Roast —

① Rib Roast
— Roast —

LOIN

① Loin Chops

① English Chop
— Broil, Panbroil, Panfry —

① Rolled Double Loin

① Loin Roast
— Roast —

SIRLOIN

② ③ Leg Chop (Steak)
— Broil, Panbroil, Panfry —

① Sirloin Chop
— Broil, Panbroil, Panfry —

① Rolled Double Sirloin

① Sirloin Roast
— Roast —

LEG

① ② ③ ④ Combination Leg

② Center Leg

① ② ③ ④ Rolled Leg

② ③ ④ American Leg

① ② Sirloin Half of Leg

③ ④ Shank Half of Leg

① ② ③ ④ Leg, Sirloin on

② ③ ④ Leg, Sirloin off
— Roast —

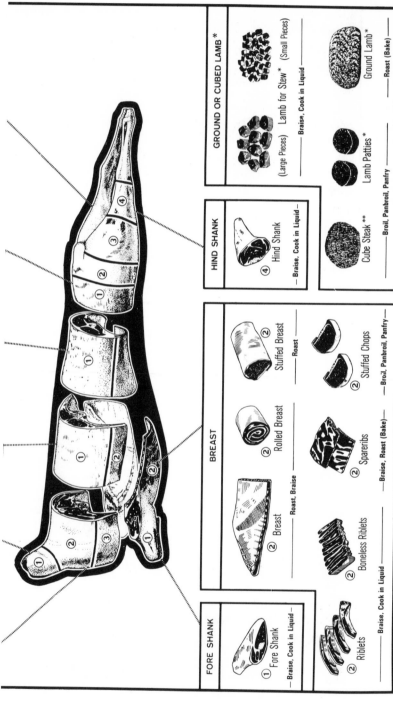

Courtesy of National Live Stock and Meat Board

FIG. 8.5.   LAMB CHART

able, defrosting of the frozen poultry should be done in the refrigerator at approximately 40°F and *not* at room temperature. Defrosting in the refrigerator may require 2 to 3 days. Poultry should be thoroughly cooked and not allowed to be held at room temperature—but rather hot (150°F or hotter) or cold (50°F or colder) until served.

Poultry has a tendency to dry out and this is a common complaint. Factors that cause the drying-out are overcooking, allowing air to dry it out, holding at warm temperatures, and cooking too far ahead. Deep-fat frying of chicken is almost out of the question for most school foodservices due to lack of deep fat fryers or to large quantities to be prepared. Oven frying can be done satisfactorily in the schools.

The age and size of poultry, like meat, will determine the tenderness and the cooking method.

Fish

Fish cookery should enhance flavor, improve appearance, and aid in digestibility. The most common problem with quality of fish is caused by overcooking. Fish has a very limited holding time from the fresh state to the cooking point and from the cooking to the serving. Fish should always be thawed under refrigeration. Smell is a good indicator of good fresh fish. Fish requires little cooking time since there is no such thing as "tough" fish. Fish is done when it flakes easily and is yet moist. Overcooking results in dry, pulp-like flesh.

Eggs

Eggs should be cooked at a low temperature for a short period of time, until just done. Temperatures too high will result in toughness and discoloration in hard-boiled eggs. Overcooking will cause a green color around the yolk. For best results in hard boiling eggs, the following pointers are given:

(1) Steam eggs in shell in a perforated pan for 15 min at 5-lb pressure; or cover eggs in shell with cold water, heat to boiling point, and turn down heat to *simmer, cook 20 min* (possibly longer, depending on the number of eggs in pot).

(2) Remove from heat and cool quickly under cold running water until cool enough to handle. Putting under cold water immediately will aid in peeling because the egg will shrink away from the shell slightly.

(3) Refrigerate immediately after peeling until time of serving or using.

For ease in peeling hard-boiled eggs use eggs a few days old (very fresh eggs are hard to shell). After cooling, start peeling at the big end of the egg where the air pocket is. When hard-cooking eggs for salads and other mixed dishes, the simplest and most satisfactory method of preparing the eggs is to place shelled eggs (fresh, frozen, or reconstituted dry eggs) in a greased baking pan (12 × 12 × 2 in. steamtable size pan will hold 25 eggs per pan), cover and bake at 350°F for 20 to 30 min or until eggs are firm. This eliminates the peeling of eggs. Dry eggs can be used for many purposes (Table 8.5), but should be restricted to dishes that are thoroughly cooked, since *Salmonella* bacteria may be present in dry eggs.

Eggs have many uses in addition to main dishes, such as:

(1) thickening custards, puddings and sauces,
(2) leavening for cakes, breads and cookies,
(3) adding flavor to dishes,
(4) adding color to dishes,
(5) binding ingredients together in such dishes as croquettes,
(6) clarifying coffee and broths,
(7) emulsifying oil and other ingredients in salad dressing,
(8) garnishing foods,
(9) holding coating of bread crumbs, flour, etc., on meats, fish and other foods.

For meringues and in baking, eggs should be at room temperature for greater volume. Removing eggs from the refrigerator a few hours before using will be sufficient. When egg whites are whipped for meringues, a small amount of salt or cream of tartar is usually used to stabilize the foam. Fat or grease on the equipment will reduce the volume. Even a drop of egg yolk can reduce volume by ½ or more. Sugar added into egg whites will decrease the volume slightly but will increase the stability. Thus, sugar should be added in small amounts near the end of the whipping to avoid reducing volume greatly. Eggs should be stored in the refrigerator, and no more than a two-week supply should be purchased at one time. When stored at room temperature, eggs lose more quality in a day than in a week in the refrigerator.

TABLE 8.5. DRIED WHOLE EGG EQUIVALENTS

Dry Egg (Oz)	+	Water	=	Shell Egg Equivalent
½ (2½ Tbsp sifted)		2½ Tbsp		1
3 (1 cup sifted)		1 cup		6
6 (2 cups sifted)		2 cups		12

Cheese

Cheese, because it is high in protein, will solidify when exposed to high temperatures. Melting takes place at warm temperatures (low), whereas at high temperature it will merely change shape, and become tough and stringy. The quality of cheese will depend on choosing the right cheese for the use and melting at a temperature no higher than 350°F. Cheese should not be served directly from the refrigerator but should be allowed to sit at room temperature for a short time. Cheese at room temperature is richer in flavor and aroma.

CONSERVING NUTRITIVE VALUE OF FRUITS AND VEGETABLES IN PREPARATION

Vegetables and fruits are our primary sources of vitamin C and contribute many other vitamins and minerals. Vitamin C and some of the B complex vitamins are very unstable and can be destroyed in preparation. Vegetables and fruits may lose much of their nutritive value if not prepared correctly.

Vegetables should be cooked *quickly* in *small* quantities of water. Water-soluble vitamins could be poured off in the water or liquid. Steam cooking has the best retention of vitamins and minerals of any method of cooking. To retain the nutritive value, cook vegetables in small amount of liquid, until *just* done, in small batches staggering the cooking time so the vegetables do not overcook and are not held for long periods of time before serving.

Chopped, shredded, or cut vegetables and fruits, and fruit juices should not be exposed to air for long periods of time uncovered. Covering will prevent the escape of vitamins into the air. Cooked fruits and vegetables do not hold up well under holding temperatures—green vegetables often turn olive green; the structure breaks down and becomes mush. Since vegetables are the most unpopular food group with school-age children, it is a challenge to prepare them to be as appetizing and appealing as possible, with proper seasoning and adequate, but not too much, cooking.

When preparing canned vegetables, some of the liquid in which the vegetable is packed may need to be drained from the vegetable. For example, when preparing canned green peas, drain and retain 1 cup of the liquid from a No. 10 can, boil the liquid and season. Pour the hot liquid over the peas which have been put into the steamtable pan from which it will be served. Heat thoroughly. Canned vegetables are already cooked; therefore, heating makes it more flavorful and safe from botulism toxin. Baking soda should *never* be added to preserve the color of vegetables. Though baking soda will make vegetables look greener, it will destroy vitamins. Vegetables can be more flavorful and attractive with the addition of one or more of the following:

(1) salt, spices,
(2) sugar, which brings out the flavor,
(3) butter, margarine, or other fat,
(4) beef, ham, or chicken base,
(5) minced onions, red and/or green peppers, pimiento,
(6) mushrooms, tiny onions, water chestnuts, or toasted almonds.

Accentuating the flavors with good seasoning and serving vegetables thoroughly heated can add much to the quality of the vegetables.

Facts to remember when cooking fresh and frozen vegetables can be summed up as:

(1) Cook for as short a time as possible, until just done.
(2) Cook in small amount of water.
(3) Avoid pouring off liquid in which vegetables were cooked.
(4) Do not add baking soda to vegetables.
(5) Cook in small batches. Avoid holding temperatures for long periods of time, but cook as needed.
(6) Do not leave chopped, shredded, or cut vegetables to stand uncovered.
(7) Use steam cooker when applicable.

The main objectives in cooking fruits and vegetables are to soften the cellulose, change the texture, and make them more digestible by changing the starch and make them more appetizing. The desired results are to have good flavor, natural color, tender yet crisp, and conserve the nutritive value.

Fresh Fruits and Vegetables

Fresh fruits and vegetables should add texture and crispness to the menu. The freshness of the vegetable will determine its quality. Crispness can be obtained with water and cold temperatures.

Some fruits, such as bananas, apples, pears, and peaches darken when pared. Preparing as near serving time as possible and dipping in citric juices (such as lemon or pineapple juice), ascorbic acid, or sugar solution quickly after paring will prevent the darkening. Vegetables that discolor can be put into salted water. Antioxidant is used satisfactorily with peeled white potatoes. Cooking or blanching fruits and vegetables will destroy the enzymes which cause discoloration.

STARCHES

Cereals and breads made from whole grain, enriched, or fortified products are classified as carbohydrate foods; however, they contribute minerals, protein, and vitamins. Cooking of cereal products is largely starch cookery, a type cooking that many cooks have trouble with. Cooking of cereals increases palatability, increases digestibility, and improves appearance. Heat and moisture are needed to soften the cellulose and start the starch granules to swell and gelatinize. Starches are used for thickening products. The thickening power is compared below.

Comparison of Thickening Qualities

To make 1 qt of medium sauce one of the following thickening agents can be used for each 1 qt liquid: 1⅓ oz cornstarch; 1½ oz fine bread crumbs; 2 oz flour; 2⅔ oz tapioca; 7 whole eggs; or 14 egg yolks.

Some of the characteristics of starch mixtures are:

(1) The finer the granules of the starch, the quicker it will dissolve and gelatinize. Lumping will result if the granules are not separated before adding to hot liquid.
(2) Starch needs to be mixed with fat, sugar, or cold liquid to separate the granules before adding to hot liquid.
(3) When large quantity of sugar is used, such as in puddings or pies, more starch is needed to obtain the same thickening.
(4) Acid will weaken the gelatinization. It is usually suggested that the acid product be added when the cooking is almost completed.
(5) Overheating with high temperatures will weaken the gel.
(6) Larger batches may require more starch in proportion.
(7) Refrigeration causes a starch-thickened product to become stiffer.
(8) Freezing will break down the gel.

So many dishes start with a white sauce or end with a gravy or sauce poured over it. Foods look larger in quantity and many foods look more attractive when the juice or liquid is thickened slightly. For example, strawberries for shortcake will go almost twice as far and make a more attractive product it thickened (Table 8.6). Sweet potatoes with orange juice added to the sauce and then thickened will go farther and look more attractive. Yellow corn, white potatoes, and green peas are frequently served in the South in a thickened liquid.

Gravies and sauces give many cooks problems. The gravy is too thin, too thick, lumpy, or a crust forms on top, are common complaints.

If gravy is too thin, add additional flour or cornstarch to cold water to make a paste and add to the gravy or sauce. Cook until thickened and starch has cooked.

TABLE 8.6. RECIPE USING CORNSTARCH TO THICKEN STRAWBERRIES FOR SHORTCAKE

| Ingredients | 100 Portions | | For ___ |
	Weights Lb Oz	Measures	Portions
Strawberries, frozen	15		
Water		1 qt	
Cornstarch	8	1¾ cups	
Sugar	8		
Red food coloring		1 Tbsp	

Directions

(1) Thaw strawberries and drain. Add 2 cups of water to liquid. Heat on medium heat.
(2) Mix cornstarch with 2 cups water (cold). Stir until mixure is smooth.
(3) Add sugar to strawberries liquid; add cornstarch mixture and cook for 10 min (until clear and very thick).
(4) Add food coloring until the desired red color is obtained.
(5) Cool mixture; add strawberries. Use ¼ cup (or No. 16 scoop) portion.

If the gravy is too thick, add more stock, milk, or water and dilute slightly until the thickness desired is reached.

If the gravy is lumpy, beat vigorously with wire whisk or in mixer, or strain through colander or cheesecloth. The next time separate the starch more carefully with fat, cold liquid, or by mixing with other dry ingredients before adding to hot liquids, and add to hot liquids slowly, stirring briskly.

If a crust forms on gravy, skim it off. Prevent this from happening by keeping a cover on the gravy or lightly covering the top of the sauce with a thin coat of fat.

Cornstarch is a good thickening agent because it is practically free of flavor and cooks to a clear, almost transparent paste in water or other clear liquid. However, it lumps more readily than flour.

METHODS OF COMBINING INGREDIENTS

Breads, cakes, and cookies are ways of adding nutrients and energy foods that add variety and taste appeal. Much skill is required in this category of cooking for a good product to be produced. The greatest skill needed is in following a recipe, accurately measuring and weighing ingredients, and in correctly mixing the ingredients as the product requires. Failure to do any of these are most obvious in baking. Methods of combining ingredients can often be the cause of the open grain, failure to rise, and coarseness. There are three main methods of combining ingredients:

Muffin Method.—Quickly mix all ingredients together. Avoid overmixing. Use for muffins, waffles, and some cakes.

Biscuit Method (Pastry Method).—Fat is cut into the dry ingredients and liquid is distributed carefully over the mixture and mixed quickly. Used for biscuits and pastry. Biscuits need kneading 10 to 15 times, whereas pastry should be handled as little as possible.

Cake Method.—Cream fat and sugar thoroughly and then add the eggs, beating thoroughly after each addition. Dry ingredients are added alternately with the liquid. Greater volume can be gained by longer mixing of the sugar and shortening and after adding the eggs, before the addition of dry ingredients containing leavening agent.

Pastry

Good pastry should be tender, flaky, delicately flavored, crisp, and light golden brown. Plain pastry includes only four ingredients: flour, fat, salt, and water. General purpose flour is recommended. Cake flour gives a crust that crumbles readily and is not as flaky. Hydrogenated shortening and lard make the best pastry. Butter makes a browner crust, flaky, but usually less tender crust. Though oil gives a tender crust, it tends to be crumbly rather than flaky. Salt is added for flavor only. Water is added to bind the ingredients together and furnishes steam in the baking which will result in a flaky crust. To obtain a good pastry follow the basic rules. If the pie crust is unsatisfactory, check Table 8.7 for possible causes of the problem.

(1) Use a standardized recipe (usually four parts flour to three parts shortening by weights).
(2) Weigh flour and shortening or fat and measure liquid carefully.
(3) Have fat chilled and broken into pieces (about ¼ lb size pieces).
(4) Cut fat into flour (avoid beating it in). The pastry blender attachment for the mixer does a cutting action; however, if not available use batter beater attachment—*do not overmix*. Work quickly and lightly. Mix until fat is just broken into small pieces. If overmixed the mixture will not take up the water which is required for a flaky pastry that will stay together.
(5) Add *cold* water, pouring over the surface of the mixture. Mix on low speed just long enough for the pastry to leave the sides of the bowl. *Do not overmix.*
(6) Chill dough slightly if sticky. *Avoid overhandling.*
(7) Roll from center out lightly, avoid stretching dough. If the pastry is stretched during rolling it will shrink back when baked.
(8) Prick the shells (pie crust) if not to be filled. Do not prick those to be cooked with pie filling it it. Make slashes on the top crust over fillings to allow steam to escape and juice to bubble up.

TABLE 8.7. SOME REASONS FOR PIE CRUST PROBLEMS

Problem	Possible Causes
Too tender, falls apart	Too much fat for flour
	Overmixing the shortening into flour
	Flour too low in gluten, soft wheat
	Not enough water added
Tough	Not enough fat
	Overmixing after water has been added
	Undermixing the shortening with flour
	Rolling and handling too much

Many school foodservices bake cobbler-type pies rather than the 9-in. pies due to the lack of oven space, time, and other equipment. The quality of fruit pies (cobbler) is thought to be better by some and to require less time when the crust is baked on a sheet pan completely separate from the filling. In this case, the crust can be cut more easily into portions before baking. The fruit filling can be prepared in a steam-jacketed kettle or pot on the range by thickening the liquid and adding the sugar and spices to the fruit. The pie filling is ready for portioning and is then topped with the golden-brown pastry squares.

Cakes

Cakes require high quality ingredients carefully weighed and mixed. Most recipes for cakes were developed in cities of low altitude; therefore, in higher altitudes the baking powder and sugar will generally need reducing and the liquid increased. Greater volume can be obtained when eggs and other ingredients are at room temperature.

For uniformity in the size of cake scaling is recommended. Scaling means to portion batter or dough into pans according to weight. For scaling cakes, use quantities in Table 8.8 as a guide.

TABLE 8.8. CAKE SCALING

Size Cake Pan (In.)	Amt Batter	
	Lb	Oz
8 round	1	8
10 round	2	—
18 × 26	7–8	—

Yeast Breads

The basic ingredients in yeast bread are flour, fat, liquid, yeast, and salt with some of the richer doughs having eggs, sugar, and spices. The flour used should be either general purpose or hard wheat bread flour since the stronger gluten is desirable. Since yeast is a live one-cell plant it is important to know under what conditions the plant will grow. Yeast needs food, moisture, and warmth. The food is obtained from the flour and sugar. Salt will retard the development of yeast as well as add flavor and aid in strengthening the gluten. Sugar can increase not only the growth, but adds flavor and aids in the browning. Temperatures are crucial to the growth of yeast. Temperatures between 78 and 90°F are ideal. The growth will slow down with lower temperature and can be destroyed with temperatures over 140°F. Yeast bread is unlike the quick breads in that thorough mixing is desirable and is needed to develop the gluten. The dough will feel springy and elastic when kneaded sufficiently, yet soft. When failures have occurred in making yeast breads it is usually due to improper timing, temperatures, or measuring (see Table 8.9).

TABLE 8.9. SOME REASONS FOR YEAST BREAD PROBLEMS

Problem	Possible Cause
Lack of volume	Improper mixing
	Too much salt
	Insufficient yeast
	Dough underproofed
	Oven temperature too high
	Dough overproofed and fallen
	Dough chilled
	Yeast killed
Too much volume	Insufficient salt
	Too much dough for pan
	Dough proofed too much
	Oven temperature too low
Crust color too pale	Insufficient sugar
	Oven temperature too low
	Dough proofed too long
Poor texture, crumbly	Dough proofed too long
	Proofed too high temperature
	Oven temperature too low
	Dough not proofed long enough
	Dough proofed too long
Gray crumb	Dough not proofed long enough
	Dough temperatures too hot
	Proofing temperatures too hot
Coarse grain	Improper mixing
	Dough proofed too long
	Dough temperatures too low
	Dough too old or too young
Poor taste and flavor (soured)	Insufficient salt
	Dough temperatures too hot
	Dough too old
	Dough overproofed

Rice

Light, tender, fluffy rice is often difficult to obtain in large quantities. Ordinarily rice is cooked in too large a batch or quantity which will most often result in an overcooked, sticky, starchy product. The two most successful methods of cooking rice are in the compartment steamer and in the oven. The oven method is very satisfactory when a compartment steamer is not available. Rice should be cooked in the correct amount of water, in small batches (approximately 50 servings per pan), and cooked until just done. Since rice continues to cook after being taken from the oven or steamer, and particularly when held on steamtable, care should be taken not to overcook. Oil added in the ratio of 2 Tbsp per lb of rice helps to separate the grains in cooking and prevents it from foaming. The rice should be covered when cooked in the oven to allow steam to make the grains tender and fluffy. Since rice is enriched it should not be washed before or after cooking unless the rice is purchased in burlap bags. In that case, the rice should be rinsed quickly before cooking. Washing before cooking may mean a loss of up to 25% of the thiamin. Rinsing after cooking will also cause loss of nutrients.

DEEP FAT FRYING

Deep fat frying is one of the most popular ways of preparing potatoes, chicken, and seafood. When deep fat frying, one should know some of the controlling factors that affect the quality of fried food. The function of the fat in deep fat frying is to surround the food being cooked with enough fat to keep it in a uniform and controlled temperature, providing an even browning and imparting flavor to the food. The kind of fat used is most important, since the flavor and aroma are affected by its temperature breaking point. Fat "breakdown" is to be avoided because when it smokes it gives off the "greasy spoon" odor and an unsatisfactory flavor. Hydrogenated vegetable oils will not reach a breaking point when heated to 400°F and have other desirable characteristics as well. Other factors, in addition to temperature being too high, can cause the breaking down of fats. Detergents remaining in the container after washing, adding salt to the food or batter in which the food is dipped, and using copper or brass utensils or tools can all cause fat breakdown. The absorption of fat in the food is usually considered undesirable and may be caused by frying at too low a temperature.

MERCHANDISING

Merchandising can be defined as selling the product. It means more—it means serving good food that looks good, at a price that the customer considers fair, in a courteous manner, and in a pleasant atmosphere. One of the greatest downfalls of school foodservice has been the lack of merchandising. This may be due to the lack of competition. It has been noted that in school systems where the manager's pay is based on the volume of sales, the manager has shown more interest in merchandising.

Students are more likely to eat what looks and tastes good than eat something "because it is good for you." People eat with their eyes to a great extent. Commercial cafeterias capitalize on this fact. Foods should be attractively displayed on the serving counter. The finishing touches can be a sprig of parsley, dash of paprika, whipped topping, piece of maraschino cherry, accentuating colors with the addition of food coloring, and adding variety with interesting shapes. For example, a delicious gingerbread looks unappetizing with white, thick lemon sauce. However, the same lemon sauce becomes appetizing with the addition of yellow food coloring to make it look the expected color. With additional liquid the lemon sauce can be the desired consistency.

Before the serving lines are opened to the customer, a good rule to remember is to take a look at the food as the customer sees it. How does the food look? How does it smell? One cannot cover poor quality food with food coloring, parsley, and other techniques of merchandising. But there is a definite correlation between good food looking good and customer satisfaction.

Another way of merchandising is to use catchy names when describing foods on the menu. ARA Food Company has used popular singing groups to name their sandwiches. "Mouth watering" descriptions can be used on the menu, such as: hot homemade rolls, tiny green peas, juicy hamburgers, and fresh green salad.

Promoting the foodservice and keeping up interest in eating at the same place each day all the school year should present a challenge to the foodservice manager. Looking at the commercial industry will give ideas on methods of promotion. Have a contest to name the dining room and pick a theme for different seasons of the year. Sell a book of lunch tickets for 10 meals at a *slight* savings. Capitalize on holidays and special school events with decorations and menus that create interest. Send favorite school recipes (in family size) home at Christmas time or during National School Lunch Week. Celebrate birthdays of the month with specially decorated cupcakes. These efforts will result not only in higher participation, but more satisfied customers.

The atmosphere can make the food more desirable or less desirable. A pleasant atmosphere with soft lighting, friendly seating, faster serving lines, soft music, longer lunch periods, and choices of food can make mealtime a social learning experience. Friendly seating, particularly in high school, with round tables or tables seating 4 to 6 students will result in fewer discipline problems. The walls of the dining room can be made interesting without great expense by using interesting shades of paint, art displays, or large posters.

Many factors determine how food is evaluated—from its quality and preparation to the atmosphere in which it is served—and they all center around satisfying the customer.

BIBLIOGRAPHY

AM. HOME ECONOMICS ASSOC. 1975. Handbook of Food Preparation, 7th Edition. AM. Home Economics Assoc., Washington, D.C.

AMENDOLA, J., and J.M. BERRINI. 1971. Practical Cooking and Baking for Schools and Institutions. Ahrens Publishing Co., New York.

ANON. 1963. Conserving the Nutritive Value of Foods. Bull. 90, U.S. Govt. Printing Office, Washington, D.C.

ANON. 1979. Nutrient Loss in Foods, Food Technology, Vol. 34, No. 2, February. Institute of Food Technologists, Chicago, Ill.

BORGSTROM, G. 1968. Principles of Food Science, Vol. II. Macmillian, New York.

CASOLA, M. 1969. Successful Mass Cookery and Volume Feeding. Ahrens Publishing Co., New York.

FOLSOM, L.A. 1974. The Professional Chef, 4th Edition. Cahners Books, Boston, Mass.

GENERAL MILLS. 1975. Baking Handbook for the School Food Service Program. General Mills, Minneapolis, Minn.

GREGG, J.B. 1967. Cooking for Food Managers. Wm. C. Brown Co., Dubuque, Iowa.

KNIGHT, JOHN and LENDAL H. KOTSCHEVAR. 1979. Quantity Food Production, Planning and Management. CBI, Boston, Mass.

KOTSCHEVAR, L. 1974. Standards, Principles, and Techniques in Quantity Food Production, 3rd Edition. CBI, Boston, Mass.

MARIO, THOMAS. 1978. Quantity Cooking. AVI Publishing Co., Westport, Conn.

SMITH, E. EVELYN, and VERA C. CRUSIUS. 1970. A Handbook on Quantity Food Management, 2nd Edition. Burgess Publishing Co., Minneapolis, Minn.

SULTAN, WILLIAM. 1976. Practical Baking, 3rd Edition. AVI Publishing Co., Westport, Conn.

TERRELL, MARGARET E. 1979. Professional Food Preparation. John Wiley & Sons, New York.

U.S. DEPT. AGR. 1969. Guides for Writing and Evaluating Quantity Recipes for Type A School Lunches. U.S. Govt. Printing Office, Washington, D.C.

U.S. DEPT. AGR. 1971. Quantity Recipes for Type A School Lunches. U.S. Govt. Printing Office, Washington, D.C.

U.S. DEPT. AGR. 1977. Average Weight of a Measured Cup of Various Foods. U.S. Govt. Printing Office, Washington, D.C.

U.S. DEPT. AGR. 1980. Menu Planning Guide for School Food Service. U.S. Govt. Printing Office, Washington, D.C.

WEST, BESSIE BROOKS, GRACE S. SHUGART, and MAXINE F. WILSON. 1978. Food for Fifty, 6th Edition. John Wiley & Sons, New York.

9

Sanitation

Good food is safe food. Safe food is free of microorganisms, chemicals, and foreign substances, such as broken glass. To be safe food it must be purchased clean and kept wholesome and free from spoilage. It must be kept safe by proper storing under sanitary conditions. Safe food must be prepared by people who have sanitary habits and who are free from communicable diseases. To be served safe, the food must be held at a safe temperature and served by people with sanitary habits and free from communicable diseases.

The primary objective in school foodservices is to serve safe, nutritious food. The responsibility of serving safe food depends on many people—from the grower of the food to the server of the prepared food. Illness from contaiminated food is most unpleasant and can even be fatal. There are more than 2 mil cases of food poisoning yearly. So many mild cases of foodborne illnesses are not reported each year that it is difficult to know how prevalent they are. The food-borne illnesses are caused by careless workers, unsanitary conditions, and lack of caution. The human element is the area where the most emphasis should be placed. Ignorance and negligence are the two greatest problems. At least 25 diseases can enter the human body through improper food handling. Such diseases as ty-phoid fever, tuberculosis, diphtheria, undulant fever, dysentery, and. gastric upsets can be traced back to contaminated foods and water.

For a foodservice to serve food that causes an outbreak is obviously very damaging to the reputation of the foodservice. The commercial foodservice would lose business. School foodservices should be particu-larly careful because it serves a captive audience. Also, food poison usu-ally affects the very young and the old the most. However, food poisoning can be prevented. Becoming familiar with the problem and wiping out ignorance on the part of all employees who come in contact with the food are the beginning.

BACTERIA-CAUSED FOOD POISONING

Bacteria are all around us, but are so small they cannot be seen with the naked eye. Some bacteria are desirable; for example, bacteria are essential to the making of buttermilk, cheese, and apple cider. However, many types of bacteria are dangerous and will cause disease if allowed to multiply and be transmitted to humans. Most bacteria grow very rapidly if the conditions are favorable—warm, moist, with food, and enough time. It should be emphasized that food contaminated with bacteria that are capable of making a person sick may have *no off-smell, no off-taste,* and *no difference in appearance.* Therefore, it may not be suspected as being contaminated. Three of the most common types of bacteria causing food poisoning are *Salmonella, Clostridium perfringens,* and *Streptococcus*; however, there are others more dreaded. Some of these bacteria and how they are transmitted, the foods most frequently associated with the infection, symptom of the food poisoning, and the time that it takes for the bacteria to make the person sick are given below.

Salmonella

Salmonella bacteria may be transmitted by careless food handlers, through animal feeds to the product such as in eggs, through contaminated shellfish, and by rodents. The foods in which the bacteria are most frequently found are poultry, eggs, salads, soups, gravies, meats, shellfish, and dairy products. The bacteria cause typhoid fever and salmonellosis, which have a variety of symptoms—abdominal pains, diarrhea, fever, vomiting, and chills. Someone who has contracted *Salmonella* will usually shown symptoms within 12 to 24 hr, except in the case of typhoid fever where it may be 3 weeks before it appears. *Salmonella* outbreaks tend to be seasonal, when the weather is very warm.

Streptococcus

Streptococcus bacteria are usually transmitted by careless food handlers with poor personal hygiene. The bacteria are carried in the discharges from the nose and throat, ears, and abscesses. When the discharges come into contact with the food, it is contaminated. Milk is one of the most favorable foods for growth of streptococci. *Streptococcus* causes scarlet fever and septic sore throat. It may not show its symptoms for 24 to 36 hr.

Clostridium perfringens

Clostridium perfringens organism is frequently associated with outbreaks of food poisoning. Since *Clostridium perfringens* is in the human intestinal tract, it is usually transmitted to food by a careless food handler who did not wash his hands after using the toilet or is transmitted by flies. The organisms are difficult to kill even with heat. The foods most favorable to the growth of this bacteria are foods that are made from leftovers, foods that are reheated after being cooked earlier. The symptoms are acute abdominal pains and diarrhea. They usually occur 8 to 22 hr after eating the contaminated food.

Shigella

The *Shigella* organism causes bacillary dysentery. It is transmitted from feces by a careless food handler or by flies and is most frequently associated with moist foods such as egg salad, ham salad, and milk products. The symptoms are diarrhea, cramps, fever, and vomiting. The symptoms occur 2 to 3 days after eating the contaminated product.

Staphylococcus

When the *Staphylococcus* bacteria have been transmitted to food and is allowed to grow it produces a toxin that causes illness. Staphylococci are on our skin, particularly in skin infections, cuts, boils, and burns in the nose. It is transmitted by the careless food handler. The foods most commonly infected are poultry, meat, salads, gravies, potato salad, cream-filled pies; and cooked ham. The toxin produced by *Staphylococcus* is extremely difficult to destroy. The symptoms are nausea, vomiting, abdominal pains, and diarrhea. The illness occurs 1 to 12 hr after eating the food containing the *Staphylococcus* toxin.

Botulism

Botulism is probably the most widely known of the food poisonings because it is usually fatal. In 1980 a pregnant woman in Everett, Washington was totally paralyzed from eating a spoonful of home canned spinach. However, she and the fetus recovered. The organism *Clostridium botulinum*, if allowed to grow, produces a toxin. It is most frequently associated with inadequately processed canned and sealed foods low in acid, such as green beans, corn, meats, fish, and spinach. However, it has been found to grow even in pickles. Ironically *Clostridium botulinum* may produce no obvious taste, smell, or visual evidence. Repugnant food spoilage, which may not even cause food poisoning, will usually produce an acid, cause coagulation of the food, and a sour odor. The smallest bite of *Clostridium botulinum* can be deadly. However, the toxin is easily destroyed by heat, but has been known to multiply at temperatures below 40°F. Canned foods, particularly home canned foods, should be heated at 212°F for 10 min before serving or even tasting. Symptoms of botulinal intoxication are dizziness, double vision, difficulty in swallowing, speaking, and breathing, and muscular weakness. The illness usually starts 12 to 36 hr after eating food.

Tuberculosis

Tuberculosis is a food-borne infectious disease that can be transmitted through food to man, particularly from tuberculous cattle through raw milk. However, with pasteurization of milk and better controls and inspection of cattle, it is rarely transmitted in this way today. It is more commonly transmitted from one infectious person to another and readily through food handling or the handling of utensils used by others to eat from. Tuberculin tests or X-rays should be required of every foodservice employee and every person who comes in contact with the food preparation and serving for others.

Infectious Hepatitis

Infectious hepatitis is a food-borne virus which may be transmitted through contaminated shellfish or water and by any foods that have been contaminated by a carrier of the disease.

Trichinosis

Trichinosis is a parasitic infection caused by a tiny worm sometimes found in pork. The tiny worm (*Trichina spiralis*) usually attacks hogs in the muscles or bones; therefore government inspection may not catch it. Trichinae are usually transmitted to the hog in the food they eat, particularly food garbage that has not been properly treated before feeding to hogs. Some foodservices sell their food garbage to farmers to feed their hogs. It is not a safe practice unless an agreement is signed that assures the farmer is abiding by health department regulations in treating the garbage. The local health department should be contacted before such practice is started. Trichinae are killed by heat. Pork should never be eaten raw or partially cooked, because it may cause an illness that is very difficult to cure. The person may recover but may never be free of this parasite. Heating fresh pork to 137°F destroys trichinae. Federal standards require that processed cured pork product that might be eaten without further cooking be subjected to an internal temperature of 160°F.

BACTERIAL GROWTH

For bacteria that cause food-borne illnesses to grow, *food,* favorable *temperature, moisture,* and enough *time* are needed. Since bacteria are all around us, it is of the utmost importance that employees know the conditions under which bacteria grow so they can control these conditions.

Food

Food for bacterial growth can be any food man eats. Botulism, the most deadly of the food poisonings, has been found in pickles, though it is usually associated with low-acid canned foods. Protein-rich foods and creamed dishes are most frequently associated with outbreaks of food poisoning. Protein-rich foods, such as poultry and ham that require a lot of handling and where time is involved in the preparation, are perfect conditions for bacterial growth. A creamed dish high in egg content and dairy products has many of the properties needed for bacterial growth— it is moist, it contains protein, and it cools slowly.

Moisture

Moisture content of food needs to be relatively high for bacteria to grow. Dehydrated foods usually do not have bacterial growth taking place until moisture has been added. Much care should be taken when using dried eggs and dried milk—once mixed with liquids they should be treated as fresh. In quantity food preparation a precautionary measure is advisable to restrict the use of dried eggs and dried milk to foods that are to be cooked. Heat will destroy the organism and make the food safe to eat.

Temperature

The temperature range at which bacteria grow best is between 60 and 120°F. However, some types of bacteria grow at temperatures as low as 0°F and as high as 140°F. Usually bacterial growth is slowed down at temperatures of 45°F and below. The most ideal temperatures for bacteria to grow are body temperature (98°F) and room temperature (78°F). When temperatures are 120°F or hotter, the growth of bacteria is slowed down, and most bacteria will not survive temperatures over 170°F. Hot foods should be kept hot, at 150°F or hotter. Cold foods should be kept cold at 45°F or colder. Freezing does not kill bacteria, but slows down the growth. If frozen food contains bacteria, the bacteria growth will start when the food is thawed. For this reason, as well as for quality reasons, it is not a good idea to refreeze thawed food—particularly those high in protein and moisture content.

The temperature at which food is held is crucial. The thermometer in Fig. 9.1 points out the temperatures that are important for foodservice employees to be conscious of.

Time

Time is needed for bacteria to grow. If the discharge, pus, from an infected cuticle were to come in contact with cooked turkey, thousands of tiny *Staphylococcus* bacteria could contaminate the food. If the turkey

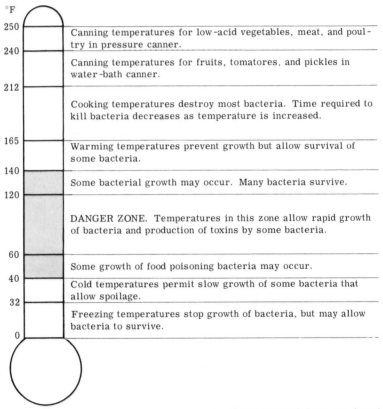

°F

250 — Canning temperatures for low-acid vegetables, meat, and poultry in pressure canner.

240 — Canning temperatures for fruits, tomatores, and pickles in water-bath canner.

212 — Cooking temperatures destroy most bacteria. Time required to kill bacteria decreases as temperature is increased.

165 — Warming temperatures prevent growth but allow survival of some bacteria.

140 — Some bacterial growth may occur. Many bacteria survive.

120 — DANGER ZONE. Temperatures in this zone allow rapid growth of bacteria and production of toxins by some bacteria.

60 — Some growth of food poisoning bacteria may occur.

40 — Cold temperatures permit slow growth of some bacteria that allow spoilage.

32 — Freezing temperatures stop growth of bacteria, but may allow bacteria to survive.

0

Courtesy of U.S. Dept. Agr. (1975)

FIG. 9.1. TEMPERATURE OF FOOD FOR CONTROL OF BACTERIA

is allowed to sit for 1 hr at room temperature, the dividing of bacteria cells could produce 8 times as many bacteria as started with (Fig. 9.2). Potentially hazardous foods should not be allowed to sit at room temperature for long periods of time. In some States, meat salads are almost something of the past in institutional food operations. The health departments have enforced a law in some parts of the country that requires protein salads be kept at 50°F or colder at all times. This means all ingredients and utensils used in the preparation have to be refrigerated in order to keep the salad from going over 50°F during the mixing process.

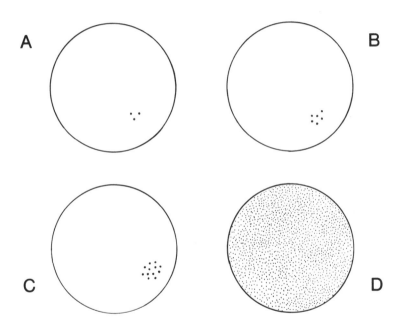

FIG. 9.2. BACTERIA MULTIPLY VERY RAPIDLY WHEN CONDITIONS ARE WARM AND MOIST AND FOOD IS AVAILABLE
A—Only 3 bacteria. B—After 20 min, 6 bacteria. C—After 40 min, 128 bacteria. D—After 3 hr, 1500 bacteria.

PREVENTING FOOD-BORNE ILLNESSES

In looking at the ways bacteria are transmitted, it is evident that in order to be sure one is serving safe, sanitary food, the food must be safe when purchased, kept safe during the storage, prepared and served in a sanitary manner by employees who are not carriers of communicable diseases and who have good personal hygiene. To be sure food is not contaminated before preparation, it is necessary to buy from reliable companies that meet sanitation standards. Canned foods should not be used if there is a swelling at the tops or bottoms of the cans, if the cans are dented along the side seams, if there is an off-odor, and if foamy.

Meat should be examined for off-odors, slimy surfaces, and for delivery in broken containers. Only pasteurized milk, commercially processed canned foods, shellfish that has been inspected, meat and poultry that have been inspected for wholesomeness should be purchased. Much care and precaution should be taken in the handling of high protein foods, particularly those such as poultry that require lengthy preparation and much handling. Some useful rules for handling turkeys are below.

Rules for Keeping Safe Turkeys Sanitary During Handling

(1) Store frozen turkeys at 0°F or below.

(2) Always defrost frozen turkeys in the wrapper in the *refrigerator* at 45°F or slightly below. It may take 3 to 4 days for defrosting.

(3) Roast turkey at an internal temperature of 165°F. A 25-lb turkey takes 4 to 6 hr to roast to 165°F. Cutting the turkey into parts can cut the roasting time in half.

(4) Do not partially cook a turkey one day and finish cooking the next day—the internal area may be perfect temperature for bacterial growth. Do not roast whole turkeys overnight in a slow oven.

(5) After the turkey has cooked, refrigerate at 45°F or below. The broth and turkey should be refrigerated separately within ½ hr after removing from oven. Store turkey in a shallow pan (2½ to 4 in deep pan) and pull turkey apart to aid the cooling. Store broth in no larger than 4-gal. quantities.

(6) Dressing should be cooked in a separate pan from the turkey and, if desired, the turkey can be stuffed after cooking.

(7) A 2-day refrigeration period for cooked turkey parts and broth is maximum recommended storage time.

(8) Employees who have colds, diarrhea, boils, or infected fingers on hands should not work with turkey or any other food.

(9) Turkeys should never stand for longer than 3 hr (total) at temperatures between 50 and 120°F; this includes cooling, boning, cutting, etc.

(10) Use clean, sanitized equipment in preparation and serving. Wooden cutting boards may be the source of transmitting *Staphylococcus* and *Salmonella*.

Laws Protecting the Public

There are 10 main laws or jurisdictional bodies important in regulating the food market and protecting the public against contaminated foods.

(1) The Pure Food, Drug and Cosmetic Act of 1938 prohibits the movement of adulterated and misbranded foods from one State to another.

(2) The Meat Inspection Act of 1906 provides for government inspection to assure that all meats sold in interstate commerce are from animals free of disease and that they are slaughtered under sanitary condition. The stamp "U.S. Government Inspected" will appear on such meat.

(3) The Poultry Products Inspection Act provides for inspection of all poultry products sold across State borders.

(4) The Agricultural Marketing Act provides for inspection and grading of fresh and processed foods other than meat. There are a number of different inspection agencies under this act. Ordinarily the agencies are located at shipping points or destination markets. Processed foods are checked for quality, identity, and fill.

(5) The Perishable Agricultural Commodities Act is administered by the USDA. It regulates the trade practices of fresh fruit and vegetables in interstate and foreign commerce.

(6) The Tea Inspection Act is administered by the Food and Drug Administration and regulates the import of tea.

(7) The Bureau of Standards in the Department of Commerce has the responsibility for controlling weights and measures.

(8) The Federal Trade Commission Act of 1915 controls the advertising to avoid misrepresenting an item.

(9) The Bureau of Public Health in the Department of Health, Education and Welfare has the greatest responsibility for protecting public health on the local level.

(10) The Bureau of Internal Revenue in the Treasury Department has regulatory powers over some foods, either through administrative practices or by law.

Choking Victim

Four thousand or more healthy individuals die yearly from choking on food or other objects. Food choking is the 6th leading cause of accidental death in our country. A person choking will die in 4 min. Over 2000 lives have been saved by someone performing the Heimlich Maneuver®. Many states require that foodservice establishments post a diagram that illustrates this procedure. The Heimlich Maneuver was originated and developed by Dr. Henry Heimlich, a world famous chest surgeon in Cincinnati, Ohio. The technique is simple. The Red Cross will often provide someone to demonstrate the technique at a workshop. Posters, kits and a slide presentation are available.

Chemical Poisoning

When purchasing food, it is also necessary for the foodservice director to check ingredients. The number of chemicals listed on the label may be staggering; however, the Delaney Law of 1958, does protect the public from harmful additives. The law states that the government is to stop production of foods containing an additive if the chemical has been demonstrated to cause cancer in animals or humans. Under this law the FDA has compiled a list of food additives ranging from salt and pepper to saccharin that is proposed to be classified legally as "generally regarded as safe" (GRAS). However, some children may be sensitive to some chemicals that are on the GRAS list. Much controversy abounds and much more research is needed. Several school districts have eliminated certain chemicals from the foods they serve.

Food poisoning from chemicals is usually accidental and is caused most frequently when chemicals are added to food by mistake. Such cases usually occur when an employee mistakes a toxic substance for salt, sugar, dry milk, or flour and puts it into food being prepared. Insecticides, pesticides, and any type poisonous chemicals, as well as detergents and cleaning supplies, should be stored in an area completely separate from where food is stored. All products should be distinctly labeled. Washing all fruits and vegetables thoroughly will remove most of the insecticides and chemical residues present.

Storage of Food

Storage of food at the proper temperature within the proper amount of time is extremely important. Refrigerated storage should be at 45°F or below. A thermometer should be placed in each refrigerated unit to keep a check on the temperature. Food needs air circulation when under refrigeration; therefore, it is recommended that it be packed loosely. Cooked foods high in protein should be refrigerated in shallow pans (no deeper than 4 in.) so they can cool through and through quickly. Foods should be covered when refrigerated to prevent foreign matter from getting into the food, to keep moisture in the food, and to prevent off-odors and off-flavors from being absorbed.

Frozen foods should be stored at 0°F or below. Once food is thawed it should be treated as highly perishable fresh food. The bacterial growth starts once the food thaws, so care should be taken in maintaining a 0°F temperature.

Some foods can be refrozen safely; however, when foods are thawed bacterial growth starts. Refreezing should be done with great care. Some foods will keep their quality when frozen for years. Table 9.1 is based on 0°F, however −10°F is better.

TABLE 9.1. APPROXIMATE STORAGE LIFE AT 0°F FOR VARIOUS FOODS

Item	No. Months
Apricots and peaches	12
Strawberries	12
Beans, snap	8–12
Beans, lima	12
Broccoli	12
Cauliflower	12
Corn, cut	12
Carrots	12
Peas	12
Spinach	12
Ground beef	3–6
Cubed beef	6–12
Veal cutlets, cubes	4–8
Bacon	1
Ham	1–2
Pork chops	4
Poultry	6–12
Bread, quick	2–4
Bread, yeast	6–12
Rolls	2–4
Cake	4–6
Cookies	4–6
Combination dishes	4–8
Fruit pies	12
Potatoes, French fries	4–8
Soups	4–6
Sandwiches	2

Hot foods to be refrigerated should be cooled slightly before refrigerating. Hot foods placed directly in the refrigerator will not sour as some think. The time required to cool will depend on the quantity. According to West et al. (1977) it takes 9 hr to cool a 4-in. deep 50-portion quantity of chicken salad from an internal temperature of 64 to 48°F in a walk-in refrigerator maintained at 35°F.

The hazard of storage is in holding the foods for any length of time at temperature above refrigerator temperature and below serving temperature of hot food (140°F).

The storage of food in the dry storeroom should be protected from rodents and insects, and from high temperature (50 to 70°F desirable), and from dirty conditions. The food should be used on a first-in, first-out basis.

Handling Leftovers

Leftovers should be handled with much caution. Food that has been held on the serving counter at 150°F (or higher) or at 45° (or lower) may be used again. Leftovers should be refrigerated as soon as possible, and no later than ½ hr after the preliminary preparation has been concluded or after the removal from the steamtable. Warm food should be pre-cooled quickly and placed in shallow pans to allow for quick cooling. Cooked foods should not be stored in a refrigerator where uncooked food items are kept. All food should be covered. Use leftovers the next day or within 36 hr. Do not plan to use the leftover a third time. Throw out leftovers that are over 36 hr old.

The Food Handler

The primary causes of food-borne illnesses are carelessness on the part of food handlers and poor personal hygiene. The health of the food handler is also important. Each employee should have a regular physical examination and a current health certificate should be required to be on file at the school foodservice. The certificate should at a minimun certify that the employee does not have tuberculosis. The discharges from the human body are chief sources of contaminating food with unwanted bacteria that can cause illness. Personal hygiene is a way of life—a habit. Many employees need on-the-job training to promote high standards of cleanliness and build new good hygiene habits. Probably the one most important rule for the employees is: WASH HANDS FREQUENTLY.

Hands should be thoroughly washed with hot water and soap *before* beginning work; serving food; handling clean dishes and utensils; per-forming any job where the hands come into direct contact with food—and *after* each visit to the toilet; handling money, tickets, or any soiled items; coughing, sneezing, and fingering face or hair. Use utensils, not hands, when possible. The mixing of salads should be done with a spoon or other utensil rather than the naked hands. When it is necessary to bring the hand in contact with food, the hands should be thoroughly washed, and when practical a plastic disposable type glove is suggested.

Employees should stay home when sick. Cuts, burns, and sores on an employee should be carefully protected so there is no possibility of a dis-charge from the infections getting on utensils or food. Dirty finger nails and broken cuticles can be food hazards. Smoking should be confined to an area where food is not being prepared or served.

Good grooming practices are a must in foodservice. Not only for sanita-tion reasons, but for public relations, the employees should be well groomed, clean, and neat. Clean, washable outer garments should be worn when preparing and serving food. Hairnets or caps are required by most health departments to confine the hair. Nobody likes to find hair in their food, and furthermore hair often has bacteria on it that can con-taminate the food. School foodservice employees often point to commercial foodservices where the persons preparing the food are not wearing hair nets or caps. For the most part, school foodservices are the cleanest, most sanitary of all foodservices and should take pride in this.

Clean Equipment

Utensils and equipment can carry many organisms that transmit sickness from one person to another. Sterilizing eating utensils is essential to prevent the spreading of viruses, particularly the common cold, as well as many more dangerous communicable diseases.

Manually.—Dishwashing, washing of pots, pans, and utensils when done manually should be done in a three-compartment sink. In the first compartment the scraped dishes or utensils should be washed in a detergent solution with water at 110 to 125°F. The second compartment is for rinsing the soap off the dishes and utensils. The third compartment is for sterilizing. There are two methods for sanitizing that are accepted: the hot water method and the chemical method. The hot water method requires water at least 170°F for not less than 30 sec and in some States the health department specifies 2 min. Since the water temperature is so essential, it should be controlled by thermostat and be constant. A booster heater will probably be necessary to maintain water at 170°F. Since the water is too hot for a person's hands, a dishbasket or rack will be necessary for immersing the utensils and dishes.

The chemical method requires immersing for a minimum of 1 min in water to which has been added a germicide or sanitizer. For a product to be called a germicide or sanitizer it must be registered with the USDA as such. Germicide is a chemical that kills or deactivates the bacteria on the surface of dishes, utensils, walls, floors, etc. It is very important that the correct amount of the product be used. The directions should be followed carefully. Chlorine may be used at 50 parts per million (ppm) or iodine at 12.5 ppm.

All utensils and dishes, regardless of whether washed by hand or in a mechanical dishwasher, should *air dry* and no towel should be used for drying. Those immersed in the hot water will dry very quickly.

Mechanically.—A mechanical dishwasher is a very important piece of equipment. It should be utilized for cleaning and sanitizing any utensil that will fit into the machine and that does not have electrical parts. The wash water must be maintained at a temperature of 140 to 160°F. If higher then 160°F it is inclined to cook food on the dishes. The first rinse should be at 170°F and the final rinse must be at 180 to 190°F. A booster heater will probably be needed to keep the water from the hot water supply at 180°F.

Detergents are needed for cleaning dishes. Manual dispensing of detergent is unsatisfactory, often unreliable, and most frequently more expensive than an automatic dispenser. Detergent requirements vary from one part of the country to another. The representative of a detergent manufacturer can recommend the right detergent and amount.

One of the greatest problems with dishwashing is the contaminating of cleaned dishes. So frequently the person handling the soiled dishes will unrack and stack the clean dishes without washing his hands. Ideally one person should rack the dirty dishes and another person should unrack the clean dishes.

Disposables.—Single-service (disposables) eating utensils are often used where dishwashing facilities are not available. An emergency supply of disposables should be kept on hand even where dishes are washed by mechanical dishwashers. If the temperature cannot be maintained at 180°F, disposables should be used until the problem is corrected.

Local Health Department

The local health department sanitarian has two important responsibilities: promote good standards of sanitation throughout the community and enforce regulations and laws. They should be consulted when in doubt, when problems with wholesomeness of food or if a case of food poisoning exists. The sanitarian also is helpful regarding the selection of equipment and planning of a facility. The sanitarian will inspect the foodservice operation and grade it in some way.

PEST CONTROL

Rats, mice, flies, roaches, and other insects are unwanted pests that may sometimes be found in any foodservice. However, when present all the time, it is a sign of poor sanitation standards. These insects and rodents can spread disease organisms and filth. The habits, dangers, life cycle, and ways of controlling three of the most common pests are shown in Table 9.2.

Controlling pests can be aided by the exterminator but basically it requires good housekeeping.

Control of Roaches, Insects, and Mites

(1) Inspect food supplies before storing or using.
(2) Keep stocks of food as fresh as possible. Rotate stock—use older food first.
(3) Store foods in containers with tight fitting lids.

TABLE 9.2. THREE COMMON PESTS: HABITS, LIFE CYCLE, AND WAYS OF CONTROLLING

Pest	Habits	Diseases and How Transmitted	Life Cycle	Control
Housefly	Carries disease bacteria on its body; lives and breeds in filth. "Fly Specks" are vomited bacteria from fly used to soften foods	Transmit more than 30 diseases, such as salmonellosis, dysentery, typhoid fever, tuberculosis, cholera, pin worms	Lays as many as 3,000 eggs in lifetime. Takes 10 to 14 days in warm weather to hatch	Remove breeding places. Screen doors and windows, fly-fans. Kill with sprays, etc. Protect food
Cock-roaches	Carry bacteria. Feed on human waste. Odor of roaches caused by oily liquid given off by the scent glands	Transmit many diseases	Eggs (25 to 30) hatch in 1 to 2 months; eats much food; grown in one year	
Rats	Eat much food, damage buildings and property with gnawing done to keep the teeth worn down. Each rat eats as much as $15.00 of food a year, and does $120.00 or more damage a year to property	Carry many diseases such as salmonellosis, leptospirosis, plague, and typhus fever	Born in litters. May have 3 to 5 litters a year—7 to 8 per litter. Average life is 2 to 3 yr	

(4) Store foods in a dry place.

(5) Do not store food or containers directly on floor.

(6) Remove and destroy infested food. Cleanup all spillage immediately.

(7) Clean shelves before adding new stock. Do not use shelf paper.

(8) Clean empty bins and containers before refilling.

Control of Flies

(1) All windows, doors, and outer openings should be screened.

(2) All doors should be self-closing and open outward.

(3) Keep all foods covered.

(4) Place all garbage promptly into nonabsorbent, easily washed garbage cans with tight-fitting lids.

(5) Clean up any spillage of garbage immediately.

(6) Have garbage and other wastes removed daily.

(7) Scald and air garbage cans daily. Use liners in containers.

Control of Rats and Mice

(1) Cleanup all piles of rubbish, boxes, rags, etc.

(2) Block all possible rodent entrances into the building.

(3) Seal all openings around pipes.

(4) Prevent access to food.

(5) Protect food supplies in safe storage areas.

(6) Do a thorough cleanup job at the end of each day.

(7) Keep garbage in tightly sealed containers.

(8) Use traps when necessary for temporary protection.

(9) Use poisons only under direction of the health department.

Four basic rules for protecting food from spreading diseases are:

(1) Buy safe food.

(2) Keep food safe.

(3) Keep food cold or keep food hot.

(4) When in doubt throw it out.

To achieve and maintain high sanitary standards requires training of all employees. A training program should be conducted frequently with refresher courses for employees to create an awareness on the part of the employees of the health aspects, the importance of their job in serving safe food, and the dangers involved. All the employees should be aware of the fundamental sanitary practices considered acceptable by the local health authorities. New employees should be given an understanding for the concepts of sanitation as a part of their orientation. The standards should be set high in school foodservices and enforced by good on-the-job supervision.

BIBLIOGRAPHY

ANON. 1966. North Carolina School Food Service Sanitation Manual. N.C. State Board of Health and School Food Service, N.C.

ANON. 1969. Sanitary Food Service. U.S. Dept. Health, Educ. and Welfare, Cincinnati, Ohio.

BLAKER, G., and E. RAMSEY. Holding temperatures and food quality. J. Am. Dietet. Assoc. 38, No. 5, 450–454.

COOP. EXTENSION SERV. 1965. Care and Handling of Prepared Frozen Foods in Food Service Establishments, Good Management Leaflet 9. Univ. of Mass., Amherst.

COOP. EXTENSION SERV. 1969. Bacterial Food Poisoning. Univ. of Mass., Amherst.

COOP. EXTENSION SERV. 1970. Frozen Foods in Food Service Establishments. Good Management Leaflet 9. Univ. of Mass., Amherst.

FOSTER, E.M. 1968. Microbial problems in today's foods. J. Am. Dietet. Assoc. 52, 485.

GRAHAM, HORACE D. 1980. The Safety of Foods, 2nd Edition. AVI Publishing Co., Westport, Conn.

GUTHRIE, RUFUS K. 1972. Food Sanitation. AVI Publishing Co., Westport, Conn.

LONGRÉE, KARLA. 1972. Quantity Food Sanitation, 2nd Edition. John Wiley & Sons, New York.

LONGRÉE, KARLA, and GERTRUDE G. BLAKER. 1971. Sanitary Techniques in Food Service. John Wiley & Sons, New York.

NATIONAL RESTAURANT ASSOCIATION. 1973. A Self Inspection Program for Foodservice Operators. National Restaurant Assoc., Chicago.

RICHARDSON, T.M. 1974. Sanitation for Food Service Workers, 2nd Edition. Cahners Books, Boston, Mass.

U.S. DEPT. AGR. 1969A. Food Storage Guide for Schools and Institutions. U.S. Govt. Printing Office, Washington, D.C.

U.S. DEPT. AGR. 1969B. Keeping Food Safe to Eat. U.S. Govt. Printing Office, Washington, D.C.

U.S. DEPT. HEALTH, EDUC. AND WELFARE. 1969. Food Labeling. Federal Register, U.S. Govt. Printing Office, Washington, D.C.

WHITE, J.C. 1966. Bacteriological Control in Sanitation. The Cornell Hotel and Restaurant Admin. Quart. 7. Statler Hall, Ithaca, N.Y.

WEST, BESSIE, LEVELLE WOOD, VIRGINIA HARGER and GRACE SHUGART. 1977. Food Service in Institutions, 6th Edition. John Wiley & Sons. New York.

10

Cost Management and Accountability

School foodservice should operate on a sound financial basis. It should not be a hit-or-miss situation. Accountability is the theme in education today, and this includes foodservice. Federal audits by the Office of the Inspector General and the Government Accounting Office during the seventies brought this need to the attention of Congress, as well as private citizens with headlines in leading newspapers.

In the early 1980s came the first threat of auditing for meal requirement compliance and sanction of funds. This threat sparked much concern among the school foodservice directors and companies selling to them. Meeting the meal requirements exactly became the challenge for the eighties. This all resulted in an increased demand for sound business practices and good cost controls. Some school districts believe that school feeding should be self-supporting, and others supplement the income of the feeding program in order to keep the price-to-the-child within the range that the people in the community can afford to pay. In many cases it is not possible to operate the type program desired on a self-supporting basis. Regardless of where the income is from, the expenditures should not be greater than the income. The most frequent reason for turning a school's foodservice over to a food management company is a financial deficit in the operation.

Good money management practices are essential in foodservice, whether commercial and profit oriented, or public and non-profit, small or large, centralized or decentralized. Effective controls are necessary to operate under a tight budget and provide good food at a low cost to the students. When the expenditures are greater than the income, too frequently the first impulse of the administration is to increase the cost to the student, decrease portion size, or decrease quality. A good look at management practices might provide other solutions to the problem.

The first step in operating a financially successful operation is for foodservice management to know the financial objectives and goals of the school board for the foodservice. Is it to be self-supporting? Who will pay utilities, fringe benefits, telephone bills, etc.? Is it to be on a profit-making or break-even basis? Who will pay for equipment replacement? The National School Lunch Act stipulates that schools participating in the federal child nutrition programs shall operate on a nonprofit basis. However, this has been interpreted to mean accumulating no more than what it would cost to operate for 1 to 2 months, depending on the state's regulations. This accumulation can be larger for a justifiable reason, such as when planning to purchase large pieces of equipment.

The next step toward operating on a sound financial basis is to know what the possible income and expenses will be. That perhaps sounds very elementary, but the lack of this knowledge of finances is a common problem among school districts. Answers to the following questions are needed: How much money is available per meal (income)? How much does each meal cost to produce and serve? It is essential for management to know what the income is and what the expenses are and to compare the two. It may not be possible to operate under the standards set for the foodservice on the income available. Management should be able to project this—and not be surprised when the deficit occurs. On the other hand, management should also be able to project profits. Management should be controlling the financial situation—profit or loss.

An elaborate accounting system is not necessary in cost control. It should be simple enough for the manager of the school foodservice to understand and be a part of. Ultimately, the entire staff should be aware of the objectives and some of the costs of operating.

COST BASED ACCOUNTING

Congress mandated with Public Law 94-105 a full cost accounting system, often called cost based accounting, because of their concern that reimbursement rates may be higher than costs of producing meals. Each state agency was responsible for the format and instructions to be used within the state with an effective date of 1978. State agencies use this cost data to assign variable reimbursement rates to school food authorities. This, in some cases, is rewarding poor management by giving higher reimbursement rates to the foodservice with the highest cost; however, this was not the intent of the law.

Allowable costs in a cost based accounting system can include: (1) cost of food used, (2) other supplies and expendable (small) equipment, (3) repairs, equipment rental and other services, (4) indirect cost or overhead, and (5) labor cost. These costs are to be distributed over all the various programs and services provided by a school food service in an equitable manner.

Additionally this mandate has encouraged other good management practices, such as keeping records with support documents, keeping records that adequately identify the source and use of all funds, having an effective control over all funds to assure use solely for authorized purposes, and have an effective audit system.

BUDGET

The school district may or may not require a budget for the foodservice. Many question the value of a budget when there are so many variables and estimations to be made. A budget in school foodservice is a plan for estimating the income and projecting the expenditures. A budget is important because through management projecting cost and income one can have a better idea of the financial picture. Budgets are usually planned on the basis of past records and on future plans. It sets controls and goals for the spending, but should be used only as an adjustable guide. Whether the school administration requires a budget or not, budgeting is another tool in controlling the financial situation and is valuable in planning expenditures.

The income and expenditures will be a combination of some fixed, but mostly projected, estimated incomes and expenditures. Fixed costs are those set costs that won't vary greatly with volume of business, such as much of the administration cost, telephone service, and management's salary. The variable costs are those directly in proportion to the number of meals served and the volume of business—such as labor cost and food cost.

Income

Projections or estimates of income are usually based on the prior operational data, prices to be charged, proposed changes in economic conditions of the community, changes in regulations and objectives, anticipated volume of sales, and student participation. The source of possible income for the school foodservice usually will come from the following:

(1) income from sale of food, based on prices to students and adults,
(2) federal reimbursement,
(3) value of USDA donated foods,
(4) state and local funds,
(5) donations.

An example of the projected income for one day may be as follows:

Elementary School
Day's Projected Income[1]

Cash Income from Children and Adult Payments:
Number 200 Paid Children Lunches @ $0.60 per lunch = $120.00
Number 25 Reduced-Price Children Lunches @ $0.20 =   5.00
Number 150 Special Milks @ $0.15 per milk =   22.50
Number 10 Adult Lunches @ $1.25 per lunch =   12.50
Federal, State, and Local Reimbursement[2] on Children Meals and
Milk:
Number of Paid Children Lunches   200
Number of Free Children Lunches   50
Number Reduced-Price Lunches   25
                                   ———
                                   275
Number 275 Children Lunches @ $0.19 =
Federal Reimbursement, Section 6   52.25
Number Free Children Lunches 50 × $0.85 =   42.50
Federal Reimbursement in addition to Section 6
Number Reduced-Price Children Lunches 25 × $0.65 =   16.25
Federal Reimbursement in addition to Section 6
Number Lunches to Children 275 × $0.09 =   24.75
Local and State Reimbursement
Number Special Milks 150 × $0.08 =   12.00
Federal Reimbursement   ———————
Projected Income $307.75

Projecting the income for a year's budget would be done similarly as the
following example shows.

Elementary School
Year's Projected Income[1]

Cash Income from Students and Adult Payments:
Average Paid Student Lunches per Day 500 × 180
Serving Days
90,000 Lunches @ $0.55 = $49,500.00
Average Reduced-Price Student Lunches
Per Day 50 × 180 Serving Days
9,000 Reduced-Price Student Lunches @ $0.20 =   1,800.00

---

[1]These are examples of income, not actual.
[2]These are examples of reimbursement rates, not actual.

Average Special Milks per Day 200 × 180
Serving Days
36,000 Milks @ $0.15 per Carton = $5,400.00
Average 8 Adult Lunches Paid Daily × 180
Serving Days
1,440 Lunches @ $1.25 per Lunch =   1,800.00

Federal, State, and Local Reimbursement[1]:
(90,000 Paid Student Lunches + 16,200 Free Student Lunches +
9,000 Reduced-Price Student Lunches)
115,200 Student Lunches × $0.20 Federal
   Reimbursement, Section 6 = $23,040.00
16,200 Free Student Lunches × $0.85 Federal
   Reimbursement, in addition to Section 6 =   13,770.00
9,000 Reduced-Price Student Lunches × $0.65
   Federal Reimbursement, in addition to Section 6 =   5,850.00
115,200 Student Lunches × $0.08 State Reimbursement =   9,216.00
36,000 Special Milks × $0.09 Federal Reimbursement =   3,240.00
115,200 Student Lunches × $0.02 Local Reimbursement =   2,304.00

Total Estimated Yearly Income $115,920.00

Projecting Cost

The menu is the most controlling factor in cost. It determines not only
the food to be purchased, but the amount of labor necessary for preparation and serving. In budgeting how the income will be used, the
estimates should be based on the proposed menus, previous year's expenses, cost of living increases, and future plans. As a guide, the percentages in Table 10.1 are suggested for on-site preparation of lunch or dinner with some use of convenience foods, such as preportioned hamburger
patties, instant potatoes, some bakery rolls, etc. Based on the income
projected, the budget of expenditures would have the following main
headings:

Elementary School
Year's Projected Expenditures

Projected Income of $115,920.00

Food Cost 52%[2] $ 60,278.40
  (Approx. $6,675.36 monthly)
Labor Cost 38%   44,049.60

---

[1]These are examples of reimbursement rates, not actual.
[2]USDA-donated Foods are not included.

Cleaning and Paper Supplies 4%	$ 4,636.80
Replacement of Equipment 1%	1,159.20
Indirect Cost 5%	5,796.00
Total Projected Expenditures	$115,920.00

Breakfast menus have less preparation than other meals and the percentages spent for food and labor would be different in most cases, as suggested below.

	% of Income
Food Cost	60–63
Labor Cost in School	28–31
Other Expenses	9

If the income for breakfast is $0.70 per breakfast, the expenditures may be kept within the following bounds:

Food Cost 60% (of $0.70)	$0.42
Labor Cost 35% (of $0.70)	0.245
Other Expenses 5% (of $0.70)	0.035
	$0.70

A comparison of the budget should be made with the actual income and expenditures (Profit and Loss Statement) at the end of each year. This will help in preparing a more accurate budget the following year. Budgeting should encourage precosting and daily costing and use of other tools of controlling cost.

TABLE 10.1. PROJECTING COST FOR ON-SITE PREPARATION OF LUNCH OR DINNER

Expenditures	Income (%)
Food cost	50–60
Labor cost in school	30–40
Cleaning and paper supplies	4
Replacement of equipment	1
Indirect cost	4–5
Total	97–100

PLANNING THE COST

Planning the cost and setting up the standards, projecting the income and expense are all done with the hopes of a balanced outcome. In the planning of cost, the following tools will aid in projecting a more accurate cost: food cost (costing recipes and menus) and labor cost (staffing formula and salary scale).

Costing

Costing usually starts with precosting of recipes and then precosting the menus. In order to cost, one must know the cost per unit of raw food products and other supplies. This information is not only needed in costing, but in computing inventories (Table 10.2). Costing recipes and menus is a time-consuming process, but it gives essential information for planning the expenditures within the budget. To cost a recipe involves totaling the cost of each ingredient to arrive at the total food cost. The food cost is then divided by number of servings the recipe will yield to arrive at *cost-per-serving*. Recipe costing is needed to set the a la carte prices to be charged as well as menu costing. It enables management to determine if it is financially possible to serve a menu within the budgeted amounts. The income per lunch may be, for example:

Student Payment in High School	$ 0.75
Federal Reimbursement, Section 6	0.20
Local or State Reimbursement	0.12
USDA-donated foods, Valued at	0.17
	$1.24

TABLE 10.2. SAMPLE OF BREAKING DOWN COST PER UNIT OF RAW FOOD PROD-UCTS TO BE USED IN COSTING

Item	Purchased Size	Price ($)	Unit	Unit Price ($)
Flour, all-purpose	100 lb	12.00	Lb	0.12
Macaroni	20 lb	5.99	Lb	0.30
Sugar	100 lb	15.15	Lb	0.16
Applesauce ($6/_{10}$)	cs	11.45	Can	1.91
Apricots, halves ($6/_{10}$)	cs	21.85	Can	3.65
Peaches,				
Halves ($6/_{10}$)	cs	16.05	Can	2.68
Slices ($6/_{10}$)	cs	16.05	Can	2.68
Beans				
Green ($6/_{10}$)	cs	10.75	Can	1.80
Red kidney ($6/_{10}$)	cs	9.50	Can	1.59
Corn ($6/_{10}$)	cs	10.90	Can	1.82
Peas ($6/_{10}$)	cs	10.95	Can	1.83
Cocoa	6/5	93.50	Lb	3.12
Coconut	10 lb	8.15	Lb	0.82
Cornstarch ($24/_1$)	cs	7.25	Lb	0.31
Pickle Relish (4/gal)	cs	12.05	Gal.	3.02
Potatoes, F.F. (30 lbs)	cs	14.10	Lb	0.47
Strawberries, frozen	30 lb	18.00	Lb	0.60
Beef, ground	10 lb	13.30	Lb	1.33
Cheese	5 lb	8.25	Lb	1.65

If the income per lunch is $1.24, and 55% is to be used for food cost, then 68.2¢ is available for food. When the recipes have been costed as shown in Fig. 10.1, it is easier to put together a menu that does not exceed the amount available. Table 10.3 is an example of one week of menus food costed.

If a menu exceeds the budgeted amount, then other menus within the week should cost less so that the week balances, as in the above example. Purchased price of foods often change within the school year and re-costing recipes and menus may be necessary.

In a survey conducted in March 1972 by the American School Food Service Assoc. across the nation the average cost of the school lunch varied from a low of 49¢ to a high of 91¢ per lunch (Table 10.4).

Recipe Chili Con Carne with Beans D-24   Date October 1980

Source ____ USDA ____   Size Portion ½ cup

                                          Yield ____ 100 ____

Ingredients	Weight	Measure	Unit Cost	Total Cost
Ground beef	9 lb		1.33/lb	$11.97
Onions, chopped	1 lb		0.40/lb	0.40
Tomato puree		1 gal	1.30/#10 can	2.60
Bean liquid and water		2 qt		
All-purpose flour	4 oz		0.12/lb	0.03
Water		1 cup		
Cooked kidney beans, canned	10 lb 6 oz		0.98/#10 can	1.96
Salt	2 oz		0.22/lb	0.028
Chili powder		⅓ cup	2.45/lb	0.20
				$17.188

Cost per Serving (100) 0.172

FIG. 10.1. SAMPLE COSTED RECIPE

Determining Labor Cost

The cost of labor-per-meal ranged from a low of 23¢ in 1979 to a high of 44¢ in the northeast according to a survey of 17 large districts (Table 10.4). To cost the labor, it would be most logical to start with the previous year's payroll cost, then add the projected raises for years of service and/or cost of living. Chapter 3 discusses staffing formulas and

TABLE 10.3. MENU COSTING FOR ONE WEEK

Item Name	Amount	Item Cost ($)
Barbecued beef	⅓ cup	0.28
Bun	1	0.058
French fries	½ cup	0.082
Catsup	1 Tbsp	0.03
Milk choice	½ pt	0.12
Fruit cup	½ cup	0.16
		0.73
Fishburger	3.6 oz	0.289
Bun	1	0.058
Tartar sauce or catsup	1 Tbsp	0.03
Orange juice	½ cup	0.067
Baby lima beans	½ cup	0.095
Milk choice	½ pt	0.12
Fruit bar	2 × 2½ in.	0.10
		0.759
Choice of: Cheese pizza and cheese/sausage pizza	5 oz	0.38
Tossed green salad	½ cup	0.11
Banana pudding	½ cup	0.10
Milk choice	½ pt	0.12
		0.71
Grilled ham and cheese sandwich	3 oz	0.35
	2 breads	0.05
Tomato soup	¾ cup	0.10
Crackers	2	0.03
Apple crisp	½ cup	0.15
Milk choice	½ pt	0.12
		0.80
Fried chicken	2 oz meat	0.34
Buttered green peas	⅓ cup	0.09
Rice and gravy	½ cup	0.08
Hot rolls	2 breads	0.045
Sliced peaches	½ cup	0.13
Milk choice	½ pt	0.12
		0.805
Average daily food cost		$0.761

salary scales. If the income per lunch is, for example, $1.08 and the labor cost is figured at 33%, approximately 36¢ is available for labor-per-meal. When management knows this, it is then important to compute the labor cost in actuality, based on staffing formula and salary scale to determine what labor-per-meal is costing. For example:

Staffed: 14 meals per labor hour
Salary: Average $4.80 per hr
Labor Cost per Meal: $4.80 ÷ 14 = $0.35

TABLE 10.4a. AVERAGE COST OF LUNCHES, MARCH 1972

Region	Food[1]	Commodities[2]	Labor[3]	Other Expenses[4]	Total[5]
Northeast	$0.3391	$0.0607	$0.2262	$0.0424	$0.6010
Southeast	$0.2856	$0.0973	$0.1608	$0.0461	$0.5864
Midwest	$0.2750	$0.0835	$0.1954	$0.0543	$0.5943
Southwest	$0.2428	$0.1075	$0.1903	$0.0607	$0.5828
Western	$0.2917	$0.0851	$0.2156	$0.1074	$0.6755
Averages for the entire U.S.	$0.2862 (based on 38 states)	$0.0832 (based on 37 states)	$0.1979 (based on 37 states)	$0.0613 (based on 36 states)	$0.6286 (based on 41 states)

[1] Actual cost of food (cash outlay) per lunch.
[2] Value of commodities or USDA-donated foods per lunch.
[3] Actual labor cost per lunch.
[4] Other expenses per lunch.
[5] Total cost to produce a lunch.
Source: With permission of *School Foodservice Journal*, copyrighted July/Aug. 1972.

TABLE 10.4b. AVERAGE COST OF LUNCHES AS REPORTED BY 17 LARGE DISTRICTS IN JUNE 1979

Food Cost, including commodities	45c–68c
Labor Cost	23c–44c
Other Expenses	7c–61c
Average cost	$1.2623

A number of factors will affect the labor cost. In foodservices with employees high on the salary scale, the labor cost may run higher on the same staffing formula and salary scale than the average. Hopefully, the number of meals produced per labor hour will be greater with the more experienced employees.

CONTROLLING COST

Precosting is an essential step toward estimating expenditures, setting standards and guides, and sound budgeting. However, the actual income and expenditures are what is important. In a centralized system with centralized menu-planning, purchasing on bid, staffing formulas and salary scales, much is pre-set, but the variance that can exist within a centralized system (within a county or city system) is surprising. The precosting may be done by the central administration but the actual daily cost should be done by the individual units in order to keep those who control the variances informed and because they are really the only ones who can do the actual daily cost. A profit and loss statement of the month's business should be furnished the manager by the 10th or 12th of the following month, showing the actual income and expenditures.

Following the menu, purchasing is probably the next most controlling force over the cost. Quantity, quality, and price are all interrelated. What quantity is needed is determined by the number to be served, the size portion, and the recipe to be used. High prices and quality do not have to be synonymous in food. However, poor quality and waste are expensive. The quality needed is the quality appropriate for the recipe and economically feasible for the foodservice to use. The original cost of foods as purchased, per pound, is not the determining factor in most cases; instead, it is how many edible portions are produced and served. The number of portions the raw food product will yield can be surprisingly lower than one might expect and in turn increase the food cost. Cooking at high temperatures may reduce the yield considerably, too.

The following will aid in controlling food cost:

(1) Proper storage and storeroom controls.
(2) Using standardized recipes.
(3) Using good preparation procedures and techniques.
(4) Serving quality food and utilizing leftovers.
(5) Using standardized portion control.
(6) Keeping daily records.
(7) Using the monthly profit and loss statement.

Daily Food Cost

The costing may be of little value in itself if the controls are not carried out in preparation and serving. Precosting sets a standard by which the actual cost can be checked. Food costing should be done daily and has to be done by the individual food preparation unit of what was actually used, sold, and left over. It may be too late to find out at the end of the following month that the foodservice has operated at a deficit. If known on a daily basis, some measures can be taken to curtail the problem. Daily food costing can be a quick, almost instant picture, and it can be done in a simple manner such as illustrated in Fig. 10.2 The cost can be compared with the actual income. This gives the manager and staff a daily picture of the finances. The accounting office cannot control the cost alone, nor can management control the cost. All the employees must be aware of the goals and be a part of controlling the cost. Unless employees are made aware of the cost, it is easy for an employee to look at a storeroom full, and which is continually replenished, and think the food and supplies are free. When using a No. 10 can of walnuts, the baker, who has no idea that those walnuts cost $2.08 per pound, may be generous in its usage. But if the baker is aware of the cost, he may be more conservative and perhaps, if the daily cost cannot afford it, decide the brownies could be made without nuts.

Breakfast Worksheet.—Another example of compiling daily cost is given in Table 10.5. The food cost in this example was $13.19, with miscellaneous cost $4.49 and labor cost $12.37, making the total cost for producing 50 breakfasts $30.05. The average cost per meal is ($30.05 ÷ 50) $0.601. According to a study funded by the Comptroller General of the United States during 1978, the average cost of breakfast was $0.588.

PORTION CONTROL

The first time you look up from serving and see another 25 students coming through the door and you have only 10 more servings of meat loaf, you will know what portion control isn't.

Portion control means giving a definite quantity of food for a definite price, and it means getting the number of servings planned from a given recipe or product. An employee who opens 6 No. 10 cans of green beans may figure that each No. 10 can will yield 22 ½-cup servings, and 6 cans will serve 132 ½-cup servings. But after serving only 125 students he has run out. The employee did the first part of portion control by figuring how many cans he needed to serve 132 ½-cup servings and how many servings in a No. 10 can. However, in order to assure the person who serves gets that many servings, the size of the serving must be exactly

Date: Sept. 20			Menu Cycle No. 222
Item	Quantity Used	Unit Cost	Total Cost
Hamburger patties	500	$0.19	$95.00
Hamburger buns	42 doz	0.67	28.14
French fries	69 lb	0.44	30.36
Orange juice (32 oz) frozen	16 cans	1.80	28.80
Brownie (recipe)	500	7.25/100	36.25
Catsup	4 cans	2.25	9.00
½ pt milk (milk bill)	800	0.15	120.00
			.60
Paper supplies: Straws and Napkins			1.50
Juice cups			4.00
Cleaning supplies			4.00
Administrative cost (Indirect cost)			45.00
Other expenses (Telephone, utilities, etc.)			24.90
Labor cost			190.00
TOTAL EXPENDITURES FOR DAY			617.55

INCOME: Total income from receipts (bank deposit) $338.00
Federal Reimbursement:

$$\frac{490}{\text{No. Student Lunches}} \times \frac{0.185}{\text{Rate of Reim.}} = \frac{90.65}{}$$

$$\frac{50}{\text{No. Free Lunches}} \times \frac{0.82}{\text{Rate of Reim.}} = \frac{41.00}{}$$

$$\frac{10}{\text{No. Reduced Price}} \times \frac{0.62}{\text{Rate of Reim.}} = \frac{6.20}{}$$

$$\frac{300}{\text{No. Special Milks}} \times \frac{0.06}{\text{Rate of Reim.}} = \frac{18.00}{}$$

Other Income:

$$\frac{50}{\text{No. Free Lunches}} \times \frac{0.12}{\substack{\text{Local \& State} \\ \text{Reimbursement}}} = \frac{6.00}{}$$

Value of USDA-donated foods used = 100.00

TOTAL INCOME FOR DAY $599.85
Less (Minus) Expenditures 617.55
PROFIT (+) OR LOSS (−) −17.70

FIG. 10.2. SAMPLE FORM FOR DAILY COST

TABLE 10.5 SAMPLE DAILY COST SHEET FOR BREAKFAST
Week of: Sept. 6–10

| No. Served | Menu | Size Portion | USDA-donated Foods | | Purchased Foods Used | | | | Misc. Cost ($) | Labor (Hr) |
			Food	Quantity	Food	Quantity	Unit Cost ($)	Total Cost ($)		
50	Orange Juice	½ cup			Orange juice	1½ cans	1.30	1.95	Straws 0.19	1½ @4.75/hr
	Scrambled eggs	1	Butter	½ lb	Eggs	50	0.075	3.75	Napkins 0.50	1 @5.25/hr
	Cinnamon toast	1 slice			Bread	2 loaves	0.65	1.30	Detergents 0.45	
	Milk	½ pt			Sugar and cinnamon	1 cup		0.27	Cups	
					cinnamon	2 Tbsp		0.02		
					Milk	50	0.118	5.90	0.85	
									Indirect Cost 2.50	
						Totals		$13.19	$4.49	$12.37

½-cup, not heaping ½-cup servings (which could easily account for coming up 7 servings short).

The number of portions to be obtained from a given dish should be predetermined by the manager. Standardized recipes will give the total yield in number and size of servings. It is extremely important to control portion sizes in order to control cost, prevent waste, and also create good will—make the customers happy. It is important to a student, as well as a teacher, that his piece of cake is as large as the person's in front of him. If, when preparing roast beef, the manager planned the cost on 2-oz servings at a cost of 40¢ per portion, but when the beef is sliced the portions run 3 to 4 oz—not only will there be a shortage of servings, but the cost per serving will go up to 80¢, or double. Those who chose to eat lunch for the roast beef will be unhappy when bologna sandwiches are served them after the roast beef runs out. In elementary schools, a lunch count may be given, so that the manager has some idea as to how many will be served. In secondary schools it is usually not that easy and may be a guessing game. In that case, it takes good planning to use leftovers. There is no excuse for the "habit of running out." It is poor management, particularly if a count is given. However, it is not wise to cook so much that it isn't possible to run out, because the cost is prohibitive. Waste has to be controlled. Leftovers crowd the refrigerator and are sanitation hazards.

The success of many of the leading chain fast foods is due to keeping the prices reasonable. This is possible primarily because of portion control. Each hamburger pattie is the same size, and so is the quantity of sauce inside the bun.

Portion control starts with the recipe. In order for the yield of the recipe to be standard, the foods used in preparing must be measured and handled correctly. The product must be cooked in the size containers called for in the recipe. For example, if the cake recipe reads: "two 18 × 26 × 2½ in. pans," and instead two 12 × 20 × 2½ in. pans are used, the yield will be different. If smaller or larger pans are used, the yield may be different. The baker prepares a recipe that yields 25 pie crusts. How can she be sure the dough will yield 25 pie crusts? Weigh the dough and then divide by 25. It is called scaling of the dough when the dough is weighed for each pan, so that the correct amount is used. All 25 pie crusts will be equal, no more or no less. These 25 pies should yield 200 servings (8 equal parts). In this case portioning may be done with a pie marker, or if not available, "by eye." The eye can divide in halves more accurately than by thirds or fourths, so it is more uniform to cut in half and then each half in halves, etc. (Fig. 10.3), as when cutting a sheet cake.

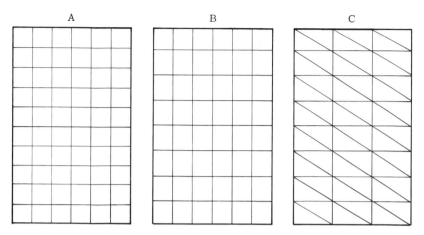

FIG. 10.3. PORTION CONTROL—CUTTING A SHEET CAKE
A—18 × 26 in. sheet pan cut 6 × 10; yield: 60 servings.
B—18 × 26 in. sheet pan cut 6 × 8; yield: 48 servings.
C—18 × 26 in. sheet pan cut 3 × 8 and then diagonally; yield: 48 servings.

Seconds

Children may ask for seconds or for larger portions. This requires that a policy be set that will determine if seconds will be given and if other than standard portions can be given. If seconds are to be given, it is wise to decide what food can be given as seconds or in larger portions and prepare for the quantities. It should usually be a less expensive item on the menu. For example, on the day when the menu is Salisbury steaks, mashed potatoes and gravy, green beans, roll, butter, milk, and cookies, mashed potatoes would probably be the food to give seconds on. The full meal has met the student's nutritional requirements; therefore, a filler is what may be needed. In the above menu, potatoes would be quick to prepare if more were needed, using the instant granules.

Portion Tools

There are many portion control tools available. The serving scoops are some of the most familiar. The steamtable capacity chart below can be very helpful in determining the yield that can be expected from a steam-table pan full of food (Table 10.6). To establish standardized service and avoid running out of food, employees need to know size and yield of all pans, scoop ladles, and other small equipment used in the serving. Charts should be posted at convenient places for easy reference indicating the size of scoops and yields.

TABLE 10.6.

PAN CAPACITY-PORTION CHART

Food Service Pans: Use for Cooking and Serving

SIZE PAN (INCHES)	DEPTH (INCHES)	CAPACITY		SIZE PORTION		NO. PORTIONS YIELD*
		QUARTS	CUPS	CUP	SCOOP	
FULL SIZE	2¼	7½	30	¼	16	120
				⅓	12	90
				⅜	10	80
12 × 20				½	8	60
FULL SIZE	4	13	52	¼	16	208
				⅓	12	156
				⅜	10	138
12 × 20				½	8	104
FULL SIZE	6	19½	78	¼	16	312
				⅓	12	234
				⅜	10	208
12 × 20				½	8	156
				1	8 oz. Ladle	78
HALF SIZE	2½	3¾	15	¼	16	60
				⅓	12	45
				⅜	10	40
12 × 10				½	8	30
HALF SIZE	4	6½	26	¼	16	104
				⅓	12	78
				⅜	10	69
12 × 10				½	8	52
HALF SIZE	6	9¾	39	¼	16	156
				⅓	12	117
				⅜	10	104
12 × 10				½	8	78
				1	8 oz. Ladle	39
THIRD SIZE	2½	2⅖	9⅗	⅛	2 TBSP	76
				¼	16	38
				⅓	12	28
12 × 6⅞				⅜	10	25
THIRD SIZE	4	3⅞	15½	⅛	2 TBSP	124
				¼	16	62
				⅓	12	46
12 × 6⅞				⅜	10	41

*ROUNDED OFF TO LOWER FULL PORTION

It is far more accurate to use the level measure of ½ cup (No. 8 scoop) than to use a heaping ⅓ cup (No. 12 scoop) to obtain the ½ cup. The scoop number can be remembered easily by remembering how many of the scoops it takes to equal 1 qt. For example, No. 8 scoop equals ½ cup; there are 8 ½-cups in a quart. See Tables 10.7 and 10.8 for scoop and ladle sizes.

TABLE 10.7. SCOOP SIZES

Scoop Number	Measure	Equivalent Weight (Oz)
6	⅔ cup (10 Tbsp +)	6
8	½ cup (8 Tbsp)	4−5
10	⅜ cup (6 Tbsp)	3−4
12	⅓ cup (5 Tbsp +)	2½−3
16	¼ cup (4 Tbsp)	2−2¼
20	3⅕ Tbsp	1¾−2
24	2⅔ Tbsp	1½−1¾
30	2⅕ Tbsp	1−1½
40	1⅗ Tbsp	¾−1

TABLE 10.8. LADLE SIZES

Ladles (Oz)	Approximate Measure (Cup)
2	¼
4	½
6	¾
8	1

Portion control is the final determining factor in food cost control. It is impossible to have effective food cost control without accurate portion control. Many commercial cafeterias employ line supervisors whose main duty is keeping uniformity in the servings.

Of course, portion sizes will vary according to the type of food being served, its relationship in the meal, and meeting the nutritional requirements. The number of items on the menu, size or age of the person, cost of the food, and the appearance of the portion will affect the decision of the size portion to be given. One-dish meals, such as spaghetti, require larger portions than would be served if a meat and potato menu is being used. The richness and lightness of the food may determine the size of the portion. The lunch pattern sets many of the limitations on portion sizes in school feeding.

There will not be many worse moments for a manager than when he runs out of food. Heavy-handed servers can do the damage, cause running out of food and high food cost. Production records should be kept: including quantity prepared, yield, and leftovers. If the yield is different from the recipe, this indicates that the yield is incorrect or that the servings were not controlled. Some suggestions for portion control are:

(1) Indicate on menus during planning the size portion to be given.
(2) Prepare for the size portions and be sure the person serving knows the portion size.
(3) Furnish portion control tools, such as scales for weighing meats, scoops, ladles, portion cups, etc.
(4) Set up example plates with correct portions on it for server.
(5) Check quantity in steamtable pans or number items to know if the quantity prepared will serve the estimated number.

Leftovers are costly and should be avoided as much as possible. If 200 hamburgers are prepared and only 125 sold, the waste would increase the food cost over 50%. Even if the ground beef can be used in spaghetti sauce or chili, the pattie probably costs more than ground beef in bulk, and the labor involved becomes a waste.

REASONS FOR EXCESSIVE FOOD COST AND WAYS OF REDUCING FOOD COST

Perhaps the first problem is deciding if the food cost is really higher than it should be. What is the norm? If the recipes and menus have been precosted, this should help set the norm. Also, in a centralized school system, the cost of similar operations can be compared. When data processing is available, the detailed information can be readily available and extremely valuable if used. The actual cost norm may be slightly more or less than the precosted and still be in line.

If food cost runs much less than precosted, one may question if the portions are large enough, if the entire meal was served, or was a different quality of raw materials used in preparation of the food. Why is the food cost too high? Frequently it is not obvious but an accumulation of several various factors. It may be a matter of pennies added up to dollars when waste loss is involved. Following are some reasons that can be responsible for excessive food cost with suggested ways of reducing food cost.

Failure to Follow Well-planned Menus

Changing menus or planning the menus at the last minute often results in expensive menus. Menus should be planned and precosted before the purchasing is done. Menus should be planned within the financial limits.

Failure to Purchase on Bid or from Wholesale Vendors

Food purchased off-bid is usually considerably higher in price. Buying at the local grocery store should be forbidden. "Family-size" pack may be costing 4 to 5 times more than institutional-size packs. Buying on bid and by written specification can mean lower prices.

Poor Purchasing Practices

Purchasing bargains that cannot be used to the best advantage is not a savings. Purchasing ready-made food that can be made by employees will increase cost. Increasing the use of convenience without decreasing labor cost can result in an unbalanced budget. Failure to purchase the grade, quality, or type pack food best suited for its use is a poor purchasing practice. For example, fancy peach halves are more expensive than pie peaches. Pie peaches would be the best suited for a cobbler. Purchasing food out of season can be too costly. For example, green peppers at 79¢ each out of season is a poor choice.

Purchased Food is Not Yielding Planned Quantity

For example: if precosting has been done on ten frankfurters per pound but eight frankfurters per pound are being delivered, the food cost per serving will be greater and perhaps more than can be afforded. If lettuce is of a poor quality the yield may be less than planned. Product evaluation should be done continuously on purchased items—not only on quality but quantity yield.

Failure to Check Deliveries

Shortage in deliveries, substitutions in items, and overcharging may occur. Checking deliveries can assure what was ordered is delivered and in good condition.

Lack of Accountability of Food Purchased and Prepared

Is food disappearing out of the storeroom? Keep the storeroom locked except for the time needed for filling the needs for the day. Do employees carry leftovers home? This is a practice that should be discontinued. No food should go home with *any employee*. (Leftovers should be utilized the next day or destroyed.) Are too many meals being served free to adults? Unless a person is paying social security tax on the meal, he should not be receiving a meal free. Are uncollected charges mounting? "Charge it" can become a habit with students. A policy of no charges may have to be enforced.

Failure to Follow Standardized Recipes

One of the greatest disadvantages is not knowing how much is being prepared and how many servings it will yield. Recipe failures are expensive. What quantity is being prepared? Most recipes are in 50 or 100 portions. When 325 portions are needed, but 400 portions are prepared, this is far too many—wasteful and costly.

Failure to Use Portion Controls

Is the correct number of servings obtained from the recipe? The heavy-handed server can cause food cost to mount. Are seconds being given? Can they be afforded? Are correct tools of portion control being used? Standardization of serving size is fair.

Excessive Leftovers

Failure to utilize leftovers is costly. Careful planning may be necessary to utilize leftovers in a way that students will not object to. In schools where precount is obtained and/or where the number served is fairly predictable, leftovers should be at a minimum.

Excessive Waste in Preparation

Overcooking and cooking at high temperatures cause shrinkage which is expensive. Broken cookies, burned cakes, and product failures are expensive. Careless trimming of produce, cutting off the outer leaves of lettuce and cabbage, and tops of celery and not utilizing them is wasteful.

Failure to Utilize USDA-Donated Foods

The USDA-donated foods distributed in 1980 were valued at 15¾¢ per meal. If the donated foods are not used or utilized in the same way as purchased food, the value of the foods will not be realized. It requires careful planning and ingenuity to utilize some foods effectively. The attitude toward USDA-donated foods may be an important factor—if thought of as free food, given in addition to other food the value of the commodity is not realized. It should be utilized in the same manner as purchased foods.

Poor Storage Practices

How many foods are thrown out due to spoilage? This is waste. Is it due to improper storage practices? Foods should be purchased according to shelf-life or keeping qualities. A three-week supply of lettuce and tomatoes will probably not keep under any conditions. The temperatures of storeroom, the refrigerator, and the freezer should be carefully checked.

Economizing is a way of life that some employees are not accustomed to. Putting prices on cases of food in the storeroom will make the employees more cost conscious and also will be an aid at inventory time. Substituting a less expensive food that will not reduce the quality of the product substantially, can be a step toward cutting cost. For example, when fresh tomatoes are out of season and higher in price, red cabbage, radishes, and carrots will make variety and color in a tossed salad at a fraction of the cost. Textured vegetable proteins have been used to reduce the cost of the protein-rich food in the menu (Table 10.9).

TABLE 10.9. COMPARISON OF MEAT COST WITH MEAT–TEXTURE VEGETABLE PROTEIN COST

	Formula A		Formula B	
Composition	100 lb ground beef @$1.60/lb =	$160.00	85 lb ground beef @$1.60/lb =	$136.00
			6 lb textured vegetable protein @$0.60 =	3.60
			9 lb water	0.00
Total cost		$160.00		$139.60
Cost per lb		1.60		1.40
Cost per serving (5.8 per lb)		0.276		0.241
Cost per yr[1]	30,000 × 0.276 =	$8280.00	30,000 × 0.241 =	$7,230.00
Approximate savings per yr				$1,050.00

[1]50 times on the menu × average number served (600) = 30,000 servings.

REDUCING LABOR COST

Reducing labor cost may be harder than reducing food cost. The first question that should be asked "Is the operation over-staffed?" One of the staffing formulas in Chap. 3 may be used as a norm or guide in determining if over-staffing exists. If the majority of the employees are high on the pay scale due to years of service, this can cause a high labor cost. Are substitutes being used frequently? Why? Is the employee's time being used efficiently? Can the business volume be increased rather than reducing the labor force?

Small operations serving less than 300 to 350 lunches will find it difficult to keep the productivity high and the labor cost within the desired bounds. It may be impossible for an operation of that size or smaller to be self-supporting. Other systems may be considered to replace on-site preparation, which is discussed in Chap. 12.

Cost of labor is taking increasingly more of the school foodservice dollar and thus puts more need for it to be well planned and utilized. A foodservice that had a starting salary of $1.80 an hour in 1972 may be paying 2 to 3 times that today. If the labor cost is excessive, it may be due to several factors. The following should be considered as ways of reducing labor cost:

(1) Increasing productivity through training.
(2) Increasing productivity through using work simplification principles.
(3) Rearranging kitchen and service areas to save steps and motions.
(4) Using work schedules and making wise distribution of labor hours over the day. If an employee is not really needed until 10 a.m., do not have her come in at 9 a.m.
(5) Planning menus that require less preparation.
(6) Rescheduling serving periods.
(7) Using vending machines for dispensing some items.
(8) Looking at time-consuming jobs and finding more efficient ways.
(9) Comparing cost of using more prepared foods and reducing labor cost.
(10) Comparing cost of using disposables versus dishwashing.
(11) Using more labor-saving equipment.

RECORDS

Costing recipes and menus and daily costing are only a part of the records. Each State has records required of the individual operations as to number served, income, and expenditures. Much of the accounting is required by the States to furnish the information needed for Federal reimbursement claim form. From the initiation of the pilot breakfast program, the records required for Federal reimbursement have been detailed. Many school systems using data processing have found themselves back to a hand process. However, the records required are records that any well-managed operation would normally do in one form or another in order to know their daily income and expenditures. The records required include the following information:

Breakfast Served

Daily Number Students Served Free Breakfast
Daily Number Students Served Reduced-Price Breakfast
Daily Number Students Served Paid Breakfast
Daily Number Adults Served Paid Breakfast
Daily Number Adults Served Free Breakfast

Income

Income from Student Payment
Income from Adult Payment
Income from Other Sales
Income from Federal, State, and Local Reimbursement

Expenditure

Amount of Purchased Food Used and Cost
Amount of USDA-donated Foods Used and Value
Cost of Procuring USDA-donated Food (Transporting, Storing, etc.)
Labor Cost
Other Cost Directly Related to Breakfast

Menu Served

Menu Items and Size Serving

The *Profit and Loss Statement* is a summary of all the records and should tell the actual total financial situation. The inventory value is an important factor in arriving at the total cost for the month and should be shown on the profit and loss statement.

Inventory

The value of the food on hand at the end of an accounting period (usually a month) is the *physical inventory*. It entails actually counting all goods on hand and placing a value to them. The *opening inventory* is the value of food and supplies on hand at the beginning of the month. The value of the food on hand at the end of the month is the *closing inventory*. The profit and loss will show the opening inventory value plus purchases, less the closing inventory value, as the cost of the food and supplies used for the month. For example:

Opening Inventory (beginning of month)	$2,800.00
Total Purchases	4,800.00
Less Closing Inventory (end of month)	1,805.00
Month's Total Food and Supplies	$5,795.00

Two people can take inventory very efficiently, with one counting and the other tabulating. Prices put on the cases will be helpful. The storeroom and inventory sheet should be organized in the same sequence. If the storeroom is organized in categories and alphabetically arranged and the inventory sheet is set up in the same order, the inventory taking will not only be easier but probably more accurate (Table 10.10).

In a single unit small operation, the workers may each take what is needed from the storeroom without anyone to check what is being taken. This may work satisfactorily. The larger the operation the more important it is that one or more persons be responsible for controlling what is taken from the storeroom and keeping a record. The storeroom requisition will then be necessary. A *requisition* is a request for something, and in this case it will show the items, quantity wanted, and perhaps the price. The requisition can become a part of the perpetual inventory system. A *perpetual inventory* is a running record, up-to-date, of each item on hand in the storeroom. It provides ready information for a manager in making her orders. In small operations it may not be feasible to keep a perpetual inventory. However, with a form such as in Table 10.11 placed on the door of the walk-in refrigerator or just inside the storeroom, a perpetual inventory could be kept rather easily. This also gives a double check on the physical inventory.

Evaluating Records

Evaluating the records of an operation month-to-month an give valuable insight into the operation. The participation records will show the trend of sales. Are sales up or down? Why? Is the staffing adequate for the number being served? Does over-staffing exist? What percentage of the income is spent on food, labor, and miscellaneous? If a deficit (minus balance) exists, an analysis of the profit and loss statement should tell why.

In a centralized system, norms can be arrived at through comparison of operations. The food cost can be broken down to percentage going to meats, produce, canned foods, frozen, etc., and when compared with several other operations of similar size, tell where the cost is too high. Perhaps high food cost can be traced to over-usage, waste, and can be corrected.

Data Processing

Data Processing is relieving personnel from many time-consuming, clerical type duties and with greater efficiency than manual calculations. It is being used in calculating nutritional values, planning menus, ordering, and inventory. Memphis City Schools (Tenn.) is using the computer for paying invoices, commodity inventory, bi-weekly time reports, free lunch

TABLE 10.10. SAMPLE MONTHLY PHYSICAL INVENTORY FORM

Page 1

| PURCHASED | | | | | PURCHASED | | | | |
ITEM	PACK	No. on Hand	Cost per Pack	TOTAL VALUE	ITEM	PACK	No. on Hand	Cost per Pack	TOTAL VALUE
CANNED: FRUIT					Pears, diced	6/10		$21.75	
Apples, sliced	6/10		$17.75			Can		3.63	
	Can		2.96		Pears, halves	6/10		21.75	
Applesacue	6/10		12.10			Can		3.63	
	Can		2.02		Pineapple, cubes	6/10		20.30	
Apricots	6/10		24.60			Can		3.38	
	Can		4.10		Plums	6/10		15.10	
Cherries, Maraschino	Gal		8.60			Can		2.52	
Fruit Cocktail	6/10		20.50		Raisins	30lb		42.95	
	Can		3.42			lb		1.43	
Peaches, diced	6/10		19.70						
	Can		3.28						
Peaches, halves	6/10		20.40						
	Can		.40						

Total this page $_____

Source: Fairfax County Schools (VA), Food Services Office.

TABLE 10.11. SAMPLE WEEKLY RECORD OF FOODS ON HAND AND USED

Item (a)	Quantity on Hand (b) (Date)	Quantity Used					Quantity Used (h)	Quantity Left (i)	Quantity Received (j)	Quantity Hand (k) (Date)
		Mon. (c)	Tues. (d)	Wed. (e)	Thurs. (f)	Fri. (g)				

application approval, school lunch program analysis, State statistical and financial reports, profit and loss statements, monthly and year-to-date balance sheets, small equipment inventory, allocation of commodities, expense by item by schools, report of equipment repairs, and accounts payable. There are unlimited possibilities with the use of data processing's speed and accuracy to obtain more detailed money management controls and information. If the problem can be pinpointed, the correcting is usually a relatively simple solution. In order to obtain this information, however, norms must be set with controls built into the programmed data processing. If the meal patterns are replaced with nutritive value of the foods, data processing will be more valuable to the school foodservice.

BIBLIOGRAPHY

ANON. 1972. State directors cost out school meals. School Foodservice J. *26*, No. 7, 20–23.

ASFSA and ASBO. 1970. A Guide for Financing School Food and Nutrition Services. Research Corporation of Association of School Business Officials and American School Food Service Association, Denver, Colo.

COMPTROLLER GENERAL OF THE UNITED STATES. 1978. Major Factors Inhibit Expansion of the School Breakfast Program. U.S. Govt. Printing Office, Washington, D.C.

KAHRL, WILLIAM L. 1974. Foodservice on a Budget for Schools, Senior Citizens, Nursing Homes, Hospitals, Industrial and Correctional Institutions. Cahners Publishing Co., Boston, Mass.

KEISER J. and E. KALLIO. 1974. Controlling and Analyzing Costs in Food Service Operations. John Wiley & Sons, New York.

KOTSCHEVAR, L. 1966. Standards, Principles, and Techniques in Quantity Food Production. McCutchan, Berkeley, Calif.

MILLER, E. 1966. Profitable Cafeteria Operation. Ahrens and Co., New York.

STOKES, J.W. 1973. How to Manage a Restaurant or Institutional Food Service. W.C. Brown Co., Dubuque, Iowa.

U.S. DEPT. AGR. 1973. School Food Service Financial Management Handbook for Uniform Accounting. U.S. Govt. Printing Office, Washington, D.C.

U.S. DEPT. AGR. 1975. Financial Management—Cost-Based Accountability. U.S. Govt. Printing Office, Washington, D.C.

U.S. DEPT. AGR. 1979. A Guide for Precosting Food for School Food Service. U.S. Govt. Printing Office, Washington, D.C.

WEST, BESSIE, LEVELLE WOOD, VIRGINIA HARGER and GRACE SHUGART. 1977. Food Service in Institutions. 6th Edition. John Wiley & Sons, Inc., New York.

11

The Foodservice Management Company

When foodservice management companies first entered school feeding more than 25 yr ago, they did not have the benefits of Federal funds, cash reimbursements, or USDA-donated foods. A few schools then, and today over 6 percent of all school foodservice programs, are operated by food management companies. In 1970 the Child Nutrition Act was amended, at the encouragement of the White House Council on Nutrition to read as follows:

(d) Any School Food Authority may employ a food service management company in the conduct of its feeding operations, in one or more schools. A School Food Authority that employs a food service management company shall remain responsible for seeing that the feeding operation is in conformance with its agreement with the State Agency or the FNS Regional Office. The contract between the School Food Authority and the foodservice management company shall expressly provide that:

(1) The food service management company shall maintain such records (supported by invoices, receipts, or other evidence) as the School Food Authority will need to meet its responsibilities under this part, and shall report thereon to the School Food Authority promptly at the end of each month;

(2) Any Federally donated commodities received by the School Food Authority and made available to the food service management company shall enure only to the benefit of the School Food Authority's feeding operation and be utilized therein; and

(3) The books and records of the food service management company pertaining to the School Food Authority's feeding operation shall be available, for a period of 3 yr from the close of the Federal fiscal year to which they pertain, for inspection and audit by representatives of the State Agency, of the Department, and of the General Accounting Office at any reasonable time and place.

In 1979 some guidance on contracting with foodservice management companies was released by USDA. Section 210.8 of the regulations authorized a school food authority to employ a foodservice management company to provide and operate its foodservice program. However, the responsibility for assuring that all the provisions of the regulations are followed is still that of the school authority. The state agency does not have the power of prohibiting a school from contracting with any reputable company that agrees to provide nutritious meals which will meet the program's requirements. Contracts, however, must be reviewed by the state agency.

With these rulings, foodservice management companies can enter into a contract with a school or a school district and, though profit oriented, may still receive Federal funds and USDA-donated foods. Many school foodservice leaders have feared that the relaxed laws would put and end to school lunch as it has been known. The American School Food Service Association's house of delegates voted in 1978 to disallow management company employees membership in the Association. Some of the fears expressed by some were that:

(1) Industry will take over, and there will be no place left for school foodservice people.
(2) The nutritional aspect will be ignored and profit will be the chief motive for having a foodservice.
(3) The prices will be higher than the students can afford to pay; therefore the diet at school will be junk foods.

Management companies have said that these fears are unfounded. They point out the advantages of having a food management company with their business experience and management ability.

Free and Reduced-Price Lunches

The school food authority is responsible for handling free and reduced-price lunches, applications and approval, and for claiming the Federal and State reimbursement funds.

Experience

Foodservice management companies have slowly entered the school feeding world for many reasons—such as Federal regulations and low profits.

The quality of foodservice companies' management varies as with any management. They have used as main selling-points their professionalism, efficiency, and expertise, pointing out that the educator should not have to worry with running a restaurant, but should leave that to the experts. The competition that school foodservice management has had as a result of relaxing the law and the addition of business-oriented companies has been for the most part good for school feeding.

Nutrition and Meal Requirements

The ARA Company has developed the Rainbow System a la carte or choice menu type lunches (Fig.i11.1). This approach to selecting nutritious foods uses four colors to stand for the requirements of the lunch pattern: red for protein, bread and butter; green for fruits and vegetables rich in vitamin A; yellow for fruits and vegetables rich in vitamin C; and blue for milk. With choices of foods in the first three groups, the students are guided to choose one food from each color group, thus fulfilling the lunch requirements. Federal audits in 1978–79 pointed up the need to assure that the food being served by management companies meet meal requirements. The responsibility for meeting Federal requirements is the school food authority, however, penalties can be written into the contract for failing to meet certain requirements.

WHEN A FOOD MANAGEMENT COMPANY IS NEEDED

There is a place and a need for food management companies in school feeding. The leading food management companies have trained their people and are business oriented. Indeed, a shortage of qualified school foodservice people for supervisory positions exists in some parts of the country. When is a food management company needed?

(1) When a trained school foodservice supervisor is not available.
(2) When the current management has failed.
(3) When the district or school is too small to afford the salary of a trained school foodservice supervisor.
(4) When student demands require changes that cannot be brought about by the present operation.

Too frequently management is considered to have failed, but the standards by which they are judged were set at the time of judging. When can a foodservice be considered a failure? To a business manager or a board of education, the standards for judging may be three-fold: that the foodservice is financially sound, that students are satisfied with the food and service, and that it is a smooth operation in concord with the administration.

Courtesy of ARA Services

FIG. 11.1. THE RAINBOW LUNCH IS TEACHING NUTRITION THROUGH GUIDING STUDENTS TO CHOOSE A NUTRITIONALLY BALANCED MEAL

Entering Into Contract

Contracting must adhere to procurement standards and the invitation to bid must be advertised. Checking with the state agency is advisable. When a school or school district enters into contract with a foodservice management company, both should be fair to each other and have a clear understanding of what the profits or management fee will be. A school administration should not fool itself that the management company will be giving all the service without receiving enough to cover the cost of labor and food and to provide a profit for the company. In some cases the school or school district will come out with a more efficient service with better food at no greater cost to the student with a management company, regardless of the profits figured into the contract. A very clear understanding and a detailed contract between the administration and management company are essential for both parties to avoid the problems that could arrive later. Additionally the specifications should require that records to support reimbursement claims be provided the school food authority on a timely bases and that all such records be kept for three years; health certification for facilities outside school where foods is prepared be current; and that no payment will be made for meals spoiled or unwholesome at time of delivery or do not meet specification; and that the contracting company is responsible for directing those who will serve the food and provide sufficient quantities to meet the Federal meal requirements.

Foodservice management companies supply food, management expertise, service—separately or all together, depending on what is needed or wanted. Federal regulations prohibit contracts that permit all receipts and expenses to accrue to management company to figure their income or profits based on "cost-plus-a-percentage-of-cost" or "cost-plus-a-percentage-of-income." Management fees established on a per meal basis serve as an incentive to the contractor to serve more meals and has worked best for most. A fixed fee does not motivate the company to provide the best meal. Profits based on performance is much healthier.

The three main ways management companies are involved in school foodservice are: as a consultant, providing food, and providing food and service.

Management Company as the Consultant.—If the school foodservice has good leadership but has problems financially, with low-productivity of labor, inability to supply quantity needed, low participation, low sanitation standards, or labor problems, the expertise of a foodservice management company as a consultant may be extremely beneficial. Most frequently what the school foodservice needs is business advice and direction which a consultant may be able to furnish. This seems to be the area where the foodservice management companies could work most effectively.

Management Company Furnishing the Food.—Where facilities are not available or inadequate for on-site preparation, the management company may be equipped to furnish good food at a price per lunch that can be afforded. Many large city systems have turned large kitchens into central kitchens preparing thousands of lunches to go out to many different schools daily. Other districts do not feel they want to make the large capital outlay, nor do they want to enter the food industry. Food companies may be the answer in such cases.

Management Company Furnishing Food and Service.—The food may be prepared in commissary or on-site for serving by the company. Some administrators want this complete service rather than getting involved in feeding children, or because need exists and this seems to be the best solution.

What Does the Company Offer?

School administrations, in deciding what is needed, should ask the following questions:

(1) What are the objectives or standards for the school foodservice? Administrative? Student? Community?
(2) Can the school's own foodservice meet these objectives? If not, why? What is needed?
(3) What can the food management company offer? At what cost? Can the administration afford it? Students?

As long as the school administration furnishes the customers (with closed campus, a captive customer), the equipment, and housing for a foodservice they are involved. A food management company cannot relieve the school administration of all involvement.

The school administration and foodservice management company should have an understanding (written agreement) about the following aspects of the operation:

Is the foodservice to be operated under the Federal regulations and receive Federal reimbursement and USDA-donated foods? If so, who does the claim forms for the State agency? Who takes care of the transportation and storage of the USDA-donated foods?

(1) What quality and quantity of food will be served? Will textured protein be used? Enriched products?
(2) What menus will be served? Are they acceptable menus with variety? Will a la carte be sold? Will choices be given in the menu?
(3) What type service will be used? Will speed lines, vending machines and/or made-to-order service be offered?
(4) Where will the food be prepared? Will it be prepared at a commissary, on-site, and when?
(5) What are the nutritious standards of the food to be served? Will they be presented in such a way to encourage acceptance?

(6) What are the costs to be borne by each party?
  (a) Labor cost, payroll, personnel records, fringe benefits.
  (b) Trash and garbage collection and disposal.
  (c) Free and reduced-price lunches.
  (d) Accounting system for Federal and State claim forms.
  (e) Payment of bills, payroll.
  (f) Insurance—liability, workmen's compensation, fire insurance, and theft.
  (g) Maintenance and replacement of equipment.
  (h) Utilities—electricity, water, gas, etc.
  (i) Extermination service.
  (j) Cleaning of the dining room, kitchen, tables and chairs in dining area, floors, walls, and waxing of floors.
  (k) Sales tax.
  (l) Telephone.
  (m) Leftovers, over-ordering, school dismissal due to emergency and students not eating at school that day.
(7) Who is responsible for:
  (a) Setting lunch hours.
  (b) Purchasing food.
  (c) Ordering quantities, counts, etc.
  (d) Cashiering, bank deposits, records, and reports.
  (e) Sanitation standards, outbreak of food poisoning.
  (f) Labor negotiations.
  (g) Price charged to students.
  (h) Hearing student, parent, faculty, and community complaints.
  (i) Sale of lunch tickets or means used to maintain anonymity of the student receiving his lunch free.
  (j) Training new employees.

School administrators and foodservice management company administrators may need to decide if there are financial advantages in being under the Federal school lunch program or if more flexibility is desired. The cost to the student can be reduced under the Federal program because of the cash subsidy (18¾¢ per lunch in 1980) and USDA-donated foods (valued by USDA as about 15¢ per lunch in 1980). The regulations set by Congress and enforced by USDA can help protect the student and school administration.

Profits

Foodservice management companies are realizing that the amount of profits to be obtained from serving school-age customers nutritious food is only in quantity since the percentage of markup is low. For a company to have a future in school feeding it must keep the quality high, prices low, sanitation standards high, customers happy, and give good service. A good working relationship between the company, students, and administration of the school can be very valuable to the success of the program. A committee made up of teachers, students, parents, school administration, and the company management working together on menus, grievances, and plans can be effective.

In order to qualify for the Federal subsidy and USDA-donated foods, the foodservice management company must comply with the regulations as set forth in the National School Lunch Act (Appendix I) and the Child Nutrition Act of 1966, As Amended (Appendix II). The guides for menu planning and organization and management are basically the same for a management company as for the school's own management of the foodservices.

Competitive Bids

When the school districts were required to competitively bid the services of management companies, many administrations have found that problems start. It is difficult to write quality into specifications. To assure profits for the company after bidding "too close" the quality may have to be cut; they may have less labor, therefore less service, and smaller portions. A 60-day cancellation clause is required to be written into the contract to protect the school and the company.

A 21-day cycle menu should be included in the specifications or, with state approval, it can be requested that the proposal from the bidding companies contain menus. The company winning the contract must adhere to that cycle the first 21 days (and why 21 days?) and thereafter may make changes, with the school system's approval. Additionally an advisory board at the school is required and it is to be composed of parents, teachers, and students with the purpose of planning menus and evaluating the services.

Some of the questions asked by administrators are: "What happens to my present employees if a management company comes in? Are they given jobs? Will the large boys get enough food to fill them up within a cost they can afford? How is the value of USDA-donated foods figured into the income or cost? What happens if the USDA-donated foods are not furnished in the quantity expected or planned on?"

VENDING MACHINES IN SCHOOL FEEDING

Vending machines are most frequently connected with commercially operated, profit-making machines dispensing candy, carbonated beverages, gum, and cigarettes. However, there are some few vending machines operated by profit-making foodservices dispensing milk, ice cream, apples, cans of soup, sandwiches, and even full lunches (Fig. 11.2).

Commercially operated vending machines in schools on the National School Lunch Program or Special Milk Program operated illegally prior to September 1972, and for sometime after that their legality was questionable.

The vending machines have been used in schools where no foodservice facilities are available, where there is an over-crowded situation, where time is a huge factor, and where there are split shifts. The vending machine has been one solution for offering "something" in the way of a snack to students.

Nutritious Foods

Vending machines are a part of the fast-food generation of the seventies. They can be used in a truly beneficial way and have a definite place in school feeding. Dispensing good, nutritious food can be a means

Courtesy of The Macke Company, Washington, D.C.

FIG. 11.2. FOOD VENDING MACHINES ATTRACTIVELY INSTALLED IN SQUARE COLUMNS ENABLE YORKTOWN HIGH SCHOOL (ARLINGTON, VA.) STUDENTS TO EASILY SELECT DESIRED ITEMS

of teaching nutrition education and making nutritious foods appealing. If children regularly see good, nutritious foods with eye appeal in the vending machine and have a choice of nutritious foods such as an apple or orange, a ham or a peanut-butter and jelly sandwich, real or enriched orange and grape juice over ice or in a zip top can, they may start expecting that quality of good food all the time.

Many nutritionists and school foodservice-oriented people are afraid, and rightfully so, of what can result in school feeding if the commercial vending companies have free range in schools, with the student government organizations seeing the rebate dangling before their eyes.

Local authorities have the authority to determine what and, if any, competitive foods can be sold in their schools, even if the Federal laws are relaxed. According to the USDA, the American diet has increased considerably in the proportion of sugar and other sweeteners consumed in the last two generations. The White House Conference on Food, Nutrition, and Health in 1969, expressed concern over the eating habits of the American people and their lack of nutrition knowledge. It was pointed out in the report of this conference that:

Significant changes in our eating patterns are taking place, including the consumption of more snack foods between meals, more eating away from home, and greater use of convenience foods . . . .
Every child has a right to the nutritional resources he needs to achieve optimal health. The school is unequaled as the institution by which this right can be fulfilled, and with enormous impact on the nutritional status of the people as a whole.

Outstanding nutritionists at this conference expressed their concerns then about snacks, fads, empty calories, and foods high in carbohydrates becoming the most serious nutritional problem facing this country. The competitive food regulations of 1979 restricts slightly what can be sold.

Labor-saving Advantages

Vending machines dispensing nutritious food can speed up the service, require little labor, save on space, make it possible to spread foodservice out, and make food available at any time during the day. The problems sometimes experienced are with mechanical breakdowns, the use of slugs, and impersonal atmosphere.

Vending Companies

Vending companies may or may not share the receipts with the school. The percentage of profit to the schools has been known to range from none to as high as 20% when vending companies operate the service. As with any other type of contracted food company, keeping the quality high, and the prices down are the greatest problems. The freshness of the food being sold should be checked carefully as well as the sanitary conditions. Sometimes students, particularly boys, find they are spending almost twice as much money to "get full" when there are only vending foods. The reputation of the company for freshness, quality, and for good sanitary practices is what one has to rely on. Sometimes the prices are low to begin with and slowly rise. Many school systems find they have to go out on bid for this service, with the lowest bidder receiving the business. Specifications are difficult to write in order to keep quality and sanitation high.

As discussed previously, the school administrator should know what he is getting and how much it is costing him before signing a contract. Vending machines with microwave ovens along side them can use a considerable amount of electricity. Payments for utilities and cleanup are usually the school's responsibility. Also, attendants are needed to continually load the machines and make change. Who will furnish the attendant—the school or the vending company? Maintenance of the machines may prove to be quite a problem if trained mechanics are not readily available.

BIBLIOGRAPHY

ANON. 1970A. Federal Register, *35*, No. 41, 3900.

ANON. 1970B. School food service: new laws can help you provide it. Nation's Schools *86*, No. 5, 61–63.

ANON. 1972A. Contract Foodservice—pros and cons. School Foodservice J. *26*, No. 9, 45–46.

ANON. 1972B. Teaching nutrition with rainbows. Food Management 7, No. 1, 72–75.

ANON. 1972C. Wait and see is watchword on section 7. School Foodservice J. *26*, No. 10, 29–30.

BARD. B. 1968. The School Lunchroom: Time of Trial. John Wiley & Sons, New York.

CRIMMINS, MARY BETH. 1978. We Belong in School Foodservice. Food Management 13, No. 1, 31–32.

ELLER, J. 1972. FTU: before and after fee-management. School Foodservice J. *26*, No. 4, 19–20.

FARLEY, T.J. 1970. Expanding the conventional school food service program. *In* Proc. Northeast School Food Service Seminar, Univ. Mass., 86–104.

GARDNER, JERRY G. 1973. Contract Foodservice/Vending. Cahner's Publishing Co., Boston, Mass.

HOLGATE, MARJORIE. 1970. Utilizing outside contractors to expand school food service operations. *In* Proc. Northeast School Food Service Seminar, Univ. Mass., 179—189.

LICHTENFELT, R.J. 1971. Let's tell it like it is. School Lunch J. *26*, No. 2, 47—48.

PAGE, D. 1970. Food management in school foodservice. *In* Proc. Southwestern Regional Seminar for School Food Service Administrators, Oklahoma State University, Stillwater, 105—122.

PAYNE, N.E., A.L. DUNGAN, and D.L. CALL. 1973. The Economics of Alternative School Feeding Systems. College of Agriculture and Life Sciences, Cornell University, New York.

PERRYMAN, JOHN. 1968. Food management companies threaten. School Lunch J. *21*, No. 10, 70—72.

U.S. DEPT. AGR. 1977. Evaluation of the Child Nutrition Programs. U.S. Govt. Printing Office, Washington, D.C.

U.S. PUBLIC LAW 91-248, 91ST CONGRESS. 1970. 84 Stat. 207 (May 14).

WHITE HOUSE CONF. ON FOOD, NUTR. AND HEALTH. 1970. Final Report, U.S. Govt. Printing Office, Washington, D.C.

12

Food Systems

This book has been geared primarily to on-site preparation which is still the most common system used in feeding children at school. However, in the last 15 yr, new systems and some of the old, began to flourish and now produce 20% of the meals. This has happened due to many reasons, but the main ones have been: (1) decreasing enrollment; (2) high labor cost and rising operating costs; (3) Federal funds made available for free and reduced-price lunches increasing the number to be served; and (4) Federal funds made available for purchasing equipment. Inner-city schools, such as in Philadelphia, Baltimore, St. Louis, and Cleveland, that were built without kitchen facilities, have had the most rapid growth. Systems have been developed out of necessity by those charged with the responsibility, and by manufacturing companies who had products to sell along with their particular system. Most agree that on-site preparation is preferred for most situations, but impossible or impractical for others. Central kitchens and commissary-type preparation that resemble a factory have come from the need to prepare food in one location for transporting to another for serving. *Central kitchen* is defined as any centrally located kitchen where preparation of food is done for serving in other locations. The central kitchen may be referred to as the *feeder school*. The school receiving the food prepared at the central kitchen is referred to as a *satellite* or *receiving school*.

Commercial frozen food companies have entered school foodservice by preparing frozen entrees, resembling a TV dinner or modified in-flight meal for reheating in the school before serving. Also available are multiportion frozen foods in throw away steamtable inserts.

Some school districts have manufacturing kitchens preparing parts or all the lunch, particularly baked products for the entire district or city. Los Angeles and Corpus Christi are preparing food in manufacturing kitchens for serving in many of their schools. Most school districts, however, are not large enough or do not have the capital outlay to get into the manufacturing business.

The food systems are classified here as follows:

On-site Preparation System.—Self-contained unit prepares and serves the food for customers housed on-site.

Bulk Transporting System.—Food is prepared at one location and carried in bulk to another location to be portioned into individual servings. This may be in a frozen, hot, or chilled state, or a combination.

Hot-and-Cold Pack Transport System.—Food is transported ready to serve. The food is prepared, portioned, and transported in insulated containers in the hot state or cold state, to be served at another location.

Cold-pack System (Vit-A-Lunch, Astro Pak, Super Sack, etc.).—A complete cold lunch is packaged in a paper bag or on a tray covered with plastic film in one location to be served at another location.

Preplated Hot and Cold Pack System (TV Dinner, In-Flight System, Ecko, Lincoln, etc.).—Lunch is made up of two parts; one, the hot portion, is packaged in ovenware or aluminum foil trays for reheating; and the other portion, the cold portion, is packaged in trays covered with plastic film. These hot and cold trays may be prepared by the local school foodservice or purchased ready prepared (Fig. 12.1).

School districts that have gone into satellite feeding usually have done so out of necessity—increased number of lunches to served, inadequate facilities, or to reduce cost. Some of the different systems are discussed below, giving their pros and cons and describing how they work.

Meal Acceptability and Nutrition

A recently completed study by Colorado State University of sixteen systems showed that the management of the program rather than system types had the greatest impact on nutritive value and microbiological safety of the meal. The delivery systems tested were: (1) on-site, (2) base or central bulk transport, (3) base or central hot-and-cold pack transport, and (4) commercially purchased preportioned frozen.

Meals served in bulk form were more acceptable to students than those served in preportioned form. However, within each delivery system, some schools had higher acceptability than did others.

CENTRAL KITCHEN

School administrators sometimes go into one of the satelliting systems with false hopes of becoming a profitable or self-supporting program. The central kitchen does not solve the problem of a poorly functioning foodservice. As a matter of fact, it takes good management in centralized

FIG.   12.1. PREPLATED
HOT PORTION OF THE
LUNCH IS BEING PRE-
PARED BY THE SCHOOL
FOODSERVICE

Courtesy of Keyes Fibre Company

preparation where large quantities are being prepared and large numbers of employees are to be supervised. For a central kitchen to be productive and efficient, well-trained employees are required. Time and motion economy are of utmost importance. Layout faults are more noticeable and become more of a problem. Work scheduling and time scheduling are absolutes for high productivity. Production-line type work that is required may be a morale problem for employees. Some other arguments against central kitchen, when compared with on-site preparation, are (1) high transportation cost, (2) delivery equipment cost, (3) limited menus, (4) loss of nutritional value, (5) loss of quality, (6) lack of personal service to the student at the satellite school, (7) waste from leftovers, (8) cost of warehousing, and (9) expense of equipping the central kitchen.

Some of the advantages of central kitchen versus a kitchen for every location have been found to be:

(1) Fewer supervisory and trained personnel required.
(2) Greater productivity and lower labor cost.
(3) Capital outlay savings—two kitchens would cost ⅓ more than one large kitchen large enough to serve the two. Savings increase with the number of satellites.
(4) Standardization of quality and quality control.
(5) Centralizing of purchasing for better prices.
(6) Uniformity of portions and portion control.

How many central kitchens and where should they be located are questions asked by administrators. In a large area, such as Washington, D.C., with traffic problems, a number of central kitchens would be recommended over one huge one. New York City has seen the problems of serving over 600 locations from one kitchen. Points to be considered are (1) length of haul to receiving schools, (2) breakdown problems, (3) expansion, and (4) ethnic groups and menu modifications. The central kitchen should be located where it is accessible to the primary traffic routes into the area where receiving schools are located. Noise and traffic from the delivery trucks may be distracting unless the central kitchen is located separate from the school proper.

Some central kitchens take the form of a junior or senior high school kitchen which has been enlarged or built for the purpose of preparing for surrounding schools. Actually, many kitchens can prepare another 200 to 400 lunches without additional equipment. Using the large kitchen of a junior or senior high has worked particularly well when the other schools, usually elementary schools, are within a short distance. Columbia City, (Md.) was able to build their schools with this plan in mind, and did realize the capital outlay savings. Yorktown Senior High (Va.) for example had its kitchen turned into a preparation kitchen for 11 elementary schools. The rising cost and lack of skilled labor, teamed with low productivity, particularly in small elementary schools serving less than 200 to 250, have been the main factors for satelliting food in many areas. Along with the advantages of satelliting come the disadvantages, which include (1) food sometimes cold, (2) menus limited, (3) high cost of warehousing, (4) difficulty in finding drivers for transporting food, and (5) lack of personal pride in food preparation since not served by the same people.

COLD PACKAGED LUNCH SYSTEM

The Cold-Pack Lunch System may be known as the Super Sack lunch, Vit-A-Lunch, Vita Pak, Astro-Pak, and other names. The brown bag lunch is the most familiar way for a student to get a lunch by the cold-packaged method. However, it is more familiar as one brought from home. When the cold packaged method is used institutionally to provide lunches for students, the sanitation aspects will limit what can go into the lunch, how long it can be held, and at what temperature it must be held. When these lunches are to be prepared under the Federal program for reimbursement, then it must provide the Meal Pattern nutritional requirements (Fig. 12.2).

Courtesy of ITT Continental Baking Company

FIG. 12.2. THE BOX LUNCH IS DESIGNED FOR SCHOOLS WITHOUT HEATING EQUIPMENT, FOR FIELD TRIPS, AND FOR SUMMER PROGRAMS AT PLAYGROUNDS

Bag Lunch

The bag lunch program can be initiated at less cost and more quickly than any other method. The District of Columbia had at one time the largest bag lunch program in the country, producing thousands daily to be distributed to schools without facilities.

Good communications between the preparation kitchen and the receiving school are always essential in satelliting food to avoid waste. In large production, the projected counts are needed far as a week ahead with adjusting the count on the morning of distribution.

A typical menu for a bag lunch is sliced ham sandwich, cole slaw, mustard (individual pack), apple, and ½ pt of milk. Preparation for this menu may be scheduled as follows:

Afternoon Before

(1) Slice meat.
(2) Wash lettuce and break up.
(3) Wash and clean cabbage and other vegetables for slaw.
(4) Wash apples.
(5) Whip butter to go on sandwiches.

Morning

(1) Prepare cole slaw. Portion into 4-oz cups with tight-fitting lids.
(2) Prepare sandwiches in assembly line. Cut and wrap.
(3) Fill the paper bags in an assembly line fashion—dessert, salad, sandwich and unit pack (napkin, straw, fork), and mustard pack.
(4) Place bags in tote container, same number in each container or as otherwise indicated.
(5) Refrigerate until time of pickup.

Careful coordination is necessary to get the food to the children without it reaching temperature above 50°F. The trucks, or whatever means of transportation, can deliver the lunches to the school and pick up the tote boxes from the day before. By having two sets of tote boxes, it will save a trip to the school to pick them up after lunch is served. The receiving school will need someone to serve the lunches and collect the money. It is desirable to have refrigeration at the receiving school for storing the milk and keeping the bags cold until serving time.

Prince George's County (Md.) took the bag lunch concept a step further by making it available as a choice, as convenient to those on the go, and for those who think of lunch as a sandwich-type lunch. Fairfax County (Va.) merchandised the bag lunch by putting it in a decorative bag and calling it a "Super Sack." The popularity of the bag lunch in these counties prove the importance of merchandising.

Vit-A-Lunch

The Vit-A-Lunch or Vita Pak is a Type A, cold-packed lunch, packed on a disposable tray covered with clear cellophane. It is a method used to assemble lunches at one location for another location where no kitchen facilities are available. St. Louis (Mo.) Public School Food Service developed the Vit-A-Lunch in 1967, though the lunches were at first packed in a paper bag. The program was developed when their foodservice expanded suddenly from feeding 55 elementary schools to feeding 158 elementary schools. The name Vit-A-Lunch is a descriptive name that combines "Vit" for nutritionally sound, "A" for Type A, and "Lunch."

Menus.—The most satisfactory menus used in the cold-packaged lunches consist of a meat, cheese or peanut butter and jelly sandwich, or sliced bread and fried chicken, a salad or raw vegetable, fruit and cookies or dessert, and milk (Table 12.1). More variety can be obtained in the Vit-A-Lunch or tray-covered lunch than in the bag. Baltimore City Public Schools have found that the cold vegetable and salads were often not eaten by the children. They then tried 2 fruits for meeting the ¾ cup fruit and/or vegetable requirement. This was better accepted. Salad-type sandwiches do not hold up well because the bread becomes soaked and requires much care in refrigeration to avoid bacterial count increases which might result in food poisoning.

Assembly.—The tray-covered packaged lunches lend themselves more to an assembly on a conveyor belt than do the paper bag lunches. An assembly line with the conveyor belt to promote the speed with 8 to 10 people can assemble the entire lunch on the conveyor except for portioning out the canned fruits or combination salads and gelatin which are usually done as a separate operation, perhaps on the conveyor. Philadelphia has found they average 21 Vita-Pak lunches a minute in their centralized assembly on the conveyor line. A disposable tray (approximately 6 X 10 in.) similar to the meat tray used in grocery stores or with higher sides are used for the Vit-A-Lunch. On the assembly line the unit pak containing a straw, napkin and "spork" or spoon, is packed on the bottom of the tray. The sandwich can be assembled on the tray as the conveyor belt moves with one person putting on each part of the sandwich, bottom slice of bread, then meat or cheese, lettuce, and then top slice of bread. The relish, mayonnaise, and mustard in individual packages can be made available at the receiving school or put in the packaged lunch. The amount of preparation, the length of the conveyor belt, number of people on the assembly, and speed of the belt will affect the number of meals per man-hour produced; however, 20 to 25 meals per man-hour is average. The cellophane or polyethylene shrink film can be put on by hand or by automation. A shrink tunnel machine on the conveyor belt will increase the production. The shrink tunnel machines are made by several equipment companies (Fig. 12.3). These seal the film over the tray in an air-tight fashion. The completed lunches are often packaged the day before they are to be served, refrigerated overnight,

TABLE 12.1. VIT-A-LUNCH MENUS

As Served in St. Louis City (Mo.) Public Schools in 1973

Tuesday, Feb. 24	Wednesday, Feb. 25	Thursday, Feb. 26	Friday, Feb. 27
Bologna sandwich (2 oz)	Salami sandwich (2 oz)	Braunschweiger sandwich (2 oz)	Turkey sandwich (2 oz)
Pickled green beans (½ cup)	Potato salad (½ cup)	Cole slaw (½ cup)	Carrot sticks (½ cup)
Blue plums (½ cup)	Orange	Banana	Raisins (½ cup)
Mustard cup	Mustard cup	Mustard cup	Mustard cup
Crackers, jelly and butter	Crackers, butter and peanut butter	Crackers and butter	½ pt milk
½ pt milk	½ pt milk	½ pt milk	Ice cream novelties
Ice cream novelties	Ice cream novelties	Ice cream novelties	

Tuesday, March 3	Wednesday, March 4	Thursday, March 5	Friday, March 6
Cheese sandwich w/ dill pickle slices (2 oz)	Salami and bologna (1 oz each)	Minced ham sandwich (2 oz)	Meat loaf sandwich (2 oz)
Salad dressing cup	Catsup cup	Mustard cup	Celery sticks (½ cup)
Tossed salad (½ cup)	Baked beans (½ cup)	Cole slaw (½ cup)	Pineapple chunks (½ cup)
Apple	Molded fruit cocktail (½ cup)	Banana	Crackers, butter, and jelly
Crackers and butter	Crackers, butter, and peanut butter	Crackers and butter	½ pt milk
½ pt milk	½ pt milk	½ pt milk	Ice cream novelties
Ice cream novelties	Ice cream novelties	Ice cream novelties	

and then transported by refrigerated truck the day it is to be served to the receiving school. The cold packaged lunches can be transported in corrugated cartons (30 to 36 per carton) or in wire baskets made for that purpose that will accommodate from 9 to 15 tray-covered lunches (Fig. 12.4). The wire baskets are stackable and fit onto a dolly that facilitates ease in loading and unloading. The space between each basket is sufficient for good air circulation and prevents the lunch from getting mashed.

Courtesy of Servpak Packaging Machinery Systems and Service

FIG. 12.3. THIS SEALING MACHINE AUTOMATICALLY SEALS, CUTS FILM AND DISCHARGES TRAY FROM THE MACHINE

Transporting.—The method of transporting the lunches differs according to weather conditions, temperatures, health regulations and what is in the lunches, and what type transportation is available. The refrigerated special vehicles for this purpose are more convenient for loading and unloading and also allow for more variety in the menu. However, school buses, station wagons, and trucks have and are being used.

FIG. 12.4. WIRE BASKETS USED FOR TRANSPORTING COLD OR HOT PACK MEALS

Courtesy of Keyes Fibre Company

Advantages.—The cold-packaged lunch system is an interim solution. It is a way of getting a nutritious lunch to children where there are no facilities. With this method it is possible to serve the lunch in the classroom or at any other location without any equipment. It is desirable to have a milk-cooler, otherwise the milk delivery will have to be carefully timed or be sent with the lunches on the refrigerated truck. The "kitchen" where the assembly of the lunch is done, may not resemble a kitchen at all. Actually the essentials are the assemblying space (preferably with a conveyor belt), refrigeration, and dry storage. No cooking is necessary, but it does add some variety. Sandwich meats and cheese can be purchased pre-sliced and delivered frequently to assure freshness; therefore, a slicer and freezer are unnecessary. Bakery bread and cookies, butter or margarine, canned fruits, fresh fruits and vegetables or juices, with ½ pt of milk can complete the menu.

One assembly line with shrink tunnel can pack, with 10 people, from 6000 to 9000 cold lunches daily on a 6-hr work shift. The containers containing the cold pack lunch can be delivered directly to the classroom with the milk, or the children can come to a dispensing area to pick up the lunch. When the costs of different systems are compared, the cold-pack system is the least expensive to produce.

Disadvantages.—Disadvantages are obvious, such as: limited variety in menus, lack of hot food, the factory approach removing the atmosphere of the social aspect of eating, finding drivers of the transporting vehicle, cost of transportation, and breakdowns of conveyor belt or shrink tunnel requiring trained mechanics immediately. Timing is a huge factor and speed is essential. The food cost may run higher than for on-site preparation of the hot lunch, but the labor will be considerably less. USDA commodities do not lend themselves to much utilization in this method. Contracting a bakery to take such items as flour, nonfat dry milk, shortening, butter, and peanut butter and using them in reducing the cost of bakery breads and labor have helped in the utilization of USDA commodities without reducing the convenience aspect of this system of feeding children.

This system is used usually until a better system can be instituted. This was the case in Washington, D.C., and St. Louis (Mo.) where the Vit-A-Lunch was originated, which has become Vit-A-Lunch Plus with the addition of hot food into the menus.

Few problems have arisen in school districts using this system that influence the quality, safety, and nutritive value of the food. Acceptability varies from one part of the country to another.

BULK TRANSPORTING

Transporting food in bulk is one of the oldest methods and most successful used for moving prepared food from the point of preparation to the point of serving. The food is transported in insulated containers, heated food carriers and cold food carriers, to the receiving school where the food is portioned and served. This system allows for service most resembling on-site preparation. Many school districts are using this system very effectively such as Baltimore Co. (Md.) Public Schools. Frequently, the students and parents are not aware that the food was not prepared in their own schools' kitchens.

Some of the reasons that this system of satelliting might be chosen are:

(1) Kitchen facilities are available but participation is too low to afford the labor to prepare the food. The school has a deficit. (Schools serving less than 250 lunches have difficulty being self-supporting with on-site preparation.)

(2) Kitchen facilities are inadequate for the number to be served. Space and/or money for enlarging the facilities are not available.

(3) Facilities and staff at a large kitchen nearby are capable of greater productivity.

(4) Trained management and labor are not available.

(5) Food quality is poor at the school.

(6) Satelliting is planned to save money in the building and equipping of new schools.

Equipment

Food carriers are available that are well insulated and electrically heated. These usually require pre-heating for 45 to 60 min and then will maintain the temperature at which the food was put into the carriers for up to 3 hr. The carriers are available that will hold five 12 × 20 × 2½ in. pans and three 12 × 20 × 4 in. pans. Utility carriers, used with euclectic plates for keeping food cold, are available that hold 12 × 20 in. or 18 × 26 in. pans. In addition to euclectic plates, insulated containers and dry ice are used to keep the food cold (Fig. 12.5). The carriers can be obtained with wheels or fitted with dollies for ease in handling. Food is prepared and transported in steamtable pans or sheet pans from which the food can be served. The advantages of the module design of equipment are exemplified in this method of satelliting food. The carriers are designed to accommodate the 12 × 20 in. pan which also fits into the compartment steamers, ovens and steamtable, or serving counter openings. This eliminates unnecessary handling of the food and means less pot and pan washing.

Courtesy of Polyfoam Packers Corp.

FIG. 12.5. BULK FOOD TRANSPORTER INSULATED TO KEEP FOOD HOT OR COLD

Bulk satelliting requires more equipment at the receiving school than the prepacked methods. It is desirable that the receiving school have (1) serving counter (perhaps portable), (2) refrigerator, (3) milk cooler, (4) three-compartment sink, and (5) work table. Optional equipment includes (6) dishwashing facilities and (7) oven.

Serving

Students may be served from a serving line, cafeteria-style, picking up their tray, milk, silverware, and napkin. The receiving school may need from 1 to 3 employees at serving time, depending on the size of operation and whether disposables are used.

An emergency backup supply of food is recommended for the receiving (satellite) school in case of truck breakdown, spillage, or an unexpected high lunch count. An emergency shelf might contain such items as canned beef or pork, canned tuna, canned spaghetti and meatballs, peanut butter, canned fruits and vegetables, canned juices, canned soups, and crackers.

There must be good communication between the feeder school and the satellite schools. The feeder (central) kitchen may need projected figures as much as two weeks ahead for ordering and preparing food. This count of meals will need to be accurately given on the day the food is being sent. This is necessary in order to eliminate the waste of leftovers from sending too much or the running out from not sending enough. The waste that results from "guessing" may be too costly for this system to work without accurate counts from the satellite schools. The quantities sent must be measured carefully and the portioning of the food at serving time must be exact to prevent overage or shortage. The steamtable charts in Chap. 10 are excellent guides to capacity of the steamtable pans and the size portions to be used for a specific number of servings. Good communication is necessary between the employee preparing the quantities to go to the satellite school and the employee serving the food at the satellite school. Each food container should be labeled with number and size portions. If this system is conscientiously used and an accurate count is obtained from the satellite school, a smooth operation can result without costly leftovers.

Advantages

The greatest advantage to this system is that it maintains the personal atmosphere in the serving of food characteristic of on-site preparation and serving. Also, portions can be adjusted to the size of the student, appetites, and personal likes and dislikes. Quality and nutritive value of the food will be affected very little by this method if extreme care is taken in limiting holding time and temperatures. There are few limitations to the menu necessary with this system. Disposables may be used in the serving of the food, or re-usable dishes and silverware used when dishwashing facilities are available.

To maintain the quality, nutritive value, and safety of the food, the food should be held at temperatures of 150°F or hotter and 45°F or colder. Food should not be held at the hot temperature more than 3 hr. Extreme care should be taken to keep food from being held at temperatures of 60° to 120°F, since bacterial growth is most rapid at that temperature. Local and State health departments have regulations concerning the handling and serving of transported foods. Their advice and regulations should be carried out.

Disadvantages

The most frequent complaint against this system is running out of food. This problem can be eliminated with more careful planning and better communication. Transporting of the food may present problems. The food containers may be heavy and require lifting. A loading dock at the feeder kitchen and the satellite school needs to be level with the transporting vehicle. A truck, bus, or large station wagon is needed. The serving time at the satellite school may require more labor hours than is economically practical.

Procedures

To exemplify this method of feeding, a hypothetical example is used. Rogers Senior High School serves 700 lunches and a la carte to its student body and prepares 300 lunches for bulk satelliting to two nearby elementary schools.

Rogers' kitchen is staffed with a manager and nine employees for a total of 60 hr. Each of the elementary schools have a cashier and server, two 3-hr employees, who arrive 45 min before serving time.

One person is in charge at each of the elementary schools. The duties of the central kitchen manager and the person-in-charge at the satellite school are well defined. (An explanation of these duties follows.)

Preparation is always begun at Rogers the day before, in order to assure that the food will be ready the next morning. The food for the satellite school will be prepared in much the same way as it would for serving the students at Rogers, in some instances as a part of the same mixing and preparation. The food must be ready and in the carriers for transporting to the elementary schools by 10:30, where lunch is served at 11:15 at one of the schools, and 11:30 at the other.

The temperature of the food is recorded (Fig. 12.6), quantities are recorded, and a final check made by the manager to assure that all parts and correct quantities of the menu are loaded in the carriers for transporting. The carriers and clean pans are returned to the central kitchen later in the day. The two employees at each of the satellite schools have their duties detailed on work schedules prepared by the manager of the central kitchen. Milk is delivered directly to the satellite schools daily. When the food leaves Rogers' central kitchen for the satellite schools, the employees start setting up for the 700 lunches to be served and the a la carte at their own school.

Duties of Central Kitchen Manager for Satellites

The responsibilities of the central kitchen manager at the satellite kitchen may be as follows:

(1) General supervision for preparation of good food.
(2) Verification of the quantity food being transported.
(3) Checking all hot foods to see that temperatures are 150°F or hotter, and cold food temperatures are 45°F or colder.
(4) Labeling food carriers as to contents and quantity, indicating size portion (scoop or ladle number, etc.) to be given.
(5) Completing central kitchen's part of Satellite Record (Fig. 12.6).
(6) Responsible for accurate records being kept of what is sent to satellite.
(7) Responsible for records (information needed and required for reimbursement) being kept at satellite.
(8) Responsible for daily bank deposit being made.
(9) Making work schedules for each employee at satellite school.
(10) Training new employees.
(11) Visiting and evaluating the program at the satellite school. Keeping in contact with the principal for comments, complaints, and suggestions.
(12) Responsible for time sheet and payroll reports at satellite school.
(13) Responsible for obtaining substitute workers when needed.
(14) Planning salad menus for teachers and sending copy to satellite school for posting.

Duties of Person-in-charge at Satellite School

The responsibilities of satellite kitchen person-in-charge may be as follows:

DAILY TALLY OF REQUESTED MEALS AND SALADS FOR RECEIVING SCHOOLS

SCHOOL _____   DATE _____

TEACHER A LA CARTE   FOOD ITEM
Name

_____	_____	**MEAL COUNT TELEPHONED IN BY**
_____	_____	**RECEIVING SCHOOL:**
_____	_____	Student Lunch
_____	_____	Hot Lunches: _____
_____	_____	Salad Lunches: _____
_____	_____	Super Sack Lunches: _____
_____	_____	Adult Lunch
_____	_____	Hot Lunches: _____
_____	_____	Salad Lunches: _____
_____	_____	Super Sack Lunches: _____
_____	_____	A la Carte _____

TOTAL: _____

Components of Meal	Serving Size	PRODUCTION KITCHEN Completes Columns 1 and 2		RECEIVING KITCHEN Completes Columns 3, 4, and 5		
		Column 1 No. of Servings Transported	Column 2 Departing Temp	Column 3 Receiving Temp.	Column 4 No. Served	Column 5 No. of Servings Left Over
Entree: _____						
Vegetables/ fruit						
Bread or Rolls:						
Dessert: _____						
Other: _____						
		Initial _____		Initial _____		

Complete 2 copies: Return 1 copy to the production kitchen at the end of the day and retain 1 copy in the receiving kitchen.

Fig. 12.6. SAMPLE SATELLITE SCHOOL RECORD

(1) Follow work schedules and see that other employees understand and carry out their jobs.
(2) Check quantity of food on arrival at school to see that all parts of the menu have been delivered.
(3) Check label on carriers for portion size and utensils to use.
(4) Check information on Satellite Record (Fig. 12.6) and record temperature of food upon arrival at school.
(5) Refrigerate all cold foods upon arrival. Use proper procedures for maintaining the hot temperatures.
(6) Order milk and ice cream for the following day. Order napkins, straws, etc., from central kitchen.
(7) Check milk and ice cream deliveries and sign invoices.
(8) Inform central kitchen immediately if additional meals are needed.
(9) Complete all necessary reports and keep information needed by central kitchen.
(10) Collect money for meals and deposit in bank daily.
(11) Check and record temperature of last pan of food served.
(12) Complete satellite's portion of the Satellite Record.
(13) Inform central kitchen manager of any problems, complaints, and suggestions.
(14) Work with principal and teachers in making the program a part of the education program.

HINGED-TRAY SYSTEM

The simplest of the preplated hot and cold portion lunches is the hinged-tray system. A hinged styrofoam tray is used to hold the hot portion of the meal, and is capable of keeping the food hot up to 3 hr when kept in insulated tote boxes, but it is recommended that it be served within 2 hr. The food is fully cooked, ready for eating when portioned into the trays and other dishes. Casseroles and foods in liquid hold hot temperature best, whereas hamburgers and fishburger-type menus may not hold as well. The fully cooked food is portioned by one kitchen for delivery to another school. This system may be used when hot lunches are desired and the distance between the feeder school and the satellite school is short. This system is most frequently used when less than 100 are to be served. It would seldom be recommended for over 200 lunches. The most important factor to be considered in this system is time—how long from the time the food is portioned until it is served. The trays should be filled just before time to be transported and placed into insulated tote boxes.

Assembly

The trays should be filled in an assembly line fashion with hot foods. The food can be portioned into the trays from the regular serving line. The filled trays are covered with a styrofoam lid and placed into an insulated tote box which holds approximately 26 to 36 trays (Figs. 12.7A and 12.7B). The cold portion of the lunch may be put into a tray or into lidded bowls. Bread can usually be put with the hot portion. The students will pick up the tray, milk, and napkin-straw-silverware pack. Juice and soups are usually transported best in bulk in thermos jugs and portioned at the school. However, cups with tight-fitting lids are available for preportioning the juice and soup to be transported.

A

B

Courtesy of Polyfoam Packers Corp.

FIG. 12.7A. STYROFOAM TRAYS CONTAINING THE HOT OR COLD PORTION OF THE MEAL ARE PACKED INTO AN INSULATED TOTE BOX TO MAINTAIN THE TEMPERATURE UNTIL SERVING TIME

FIG. 12.7B. THE TOTE BOXES ARE LIGHT IN WEIGHT

Advantages

Some of the advantages of using this system are:

(1) There is speed in serving.
(2) Utilizes the labor at another school for preparing.
(3) Requires little or no labor at the receiving (satellite) school.
(4) Requires no additional equipment.
(5) Containers of food are light in weight.

(6) Tote boxes for transporting the food trays are inexpensive.

(7) Children can be served directly from the tote box anywhere desired.

(8) Tote boxes are light in weight (Fig. 12.7B).

Disadvantages

This method is limited by the time factor. When used for over 200 lunches, it is usually a temporary solution. Some foods transport better than others, and the menu may be slightly affected and limited. Caution must be taken with sanitation in preparing, portioning, transporting, and serving food. The food must be *very hot* or *very cold* when portioned in order to hold the temperature below 45°F or above 150°F until served for eating. Foods that are leftovers should be destroyed and not reheated.

The biggest complain against this system is food is sometimes cold. Disposing of the trays and other paper may be a problem.

HOT AND COLD PREPLATED SCHOOL MEALS IN-FLIGHT SYSTEM

The hot and cold preplated school meals can be prepared in a central kitchen or commissary or in one school's kitchen for another, or may be purchased commercially already preplated. The hot portion resembles a "TV Dinner" entree. Either prepared by the schools or commercially, the meal can meet the Federal regulations and qualify for Federal cash subsidy and commodities. This system uses disposables that eliminate the need for dishwashing equipment and labor. The preplated lunches (hot and cold) are being used widely over the country and some of the reasons given may be:

(1) It enables schools with limited kitchen facilities to serve hot lunches.

(2) Saves space and equipment capital investment in building of new schools.

(3) Cuts the operating cost, greater productivity, less labor.

(4) Quality control.

(5) Portion control.

(6) Faster service.

Who Preplates the Meal.—Some school districts started preplating their own lunches before commercial companies were allowed under Federal regulations to qualify for the Federal aid. Some of the school districts prefer preplating their own, both hot and cold. They feel they can give better quality, meet the likes and dislikes of the children, and have a better program. Other school districts prefer not being in the business of preplating, saying it requires far more expertise than they have or that they cannot produce the lunches as economically as the commercial operations. Some school districts preplated only the cold portion (which is the easier of the two) and purchase the hot portion from a commercial company. Other school districts purchase both the hot and cold portions and reconstitute them before serving. There are many names for the system, some bearing the manufacturer of the equipment, disposables, or the frozen food company packaging the food used, such as Ecko, Lincoln, Mighty Mort system.

The hot portion of the lunch is usually a main dish and one vegetable or a combination dish that includes a vegetable in the preparation with the cold portion containing the bread and butter, one other fruit or vegetables, and a dessert and unit pack containing the napkin-straw-silverware. The hot portion is packaged in disposable aluminum foil or ovenware container (approximately 4 × 6 in.) and capped with an ovenware cover. The cold pack is packaged on a plastic tray or paper, or styrofoam tray and covered with a plastic film. The food may or may not be fully cooked. It may or may not be frozen. It may or may not require reheating (Fig. 12.8).

Courtesy of Continental Baking Company

FIG. 12.8. PREPLATED MEALS HAVE A HOT PACK WHICH IS REHEATED BEFORE SERVING AND A COLD PACK WHICH IS TO BE KEPT COLD UNTIL SERVING TIME

School Preplated Meals.—The school foodservice may choose to pre-plate the hot and/or cold portion of their lunch with the hot portion to be reheated at the receiving school before serving. One or more central kitchen or commissary may prepare the food, portion and distribute the preplated lunches in a refrigerated or frozen state. Bremerton (Wash.) was one of the first school systems to use this system. Hundreds of school districts have used this method totally or partially to get food to children.

The hot portion of the lunch may be flash frozen or refrigerated and reheated for use within 36 hr. The regulations governing the handling of food for transporting differ from one state to another. The local health department should be contacted for regulations. The freezing of food for reconstituting at a later time requires strict controls, temperatures at −40°F or below, and technical knowledge for maintaining the quality and low bacterial count of the food. The characteristics of foods under freezing conditions differ. Since many school districts do not have the equipment and/or technical knowledge, they have relied primarily on preparing the food, refrigerating, and reheating within the designated time.

Assembly.—For efficiency, the food is portioned into the hot and cold trays on a conveyor belt. An aluminum or oven film cover is placed on the hot portion by hand or with an automatic hooding machine. The same conveyor can be used for the cold pack with a plastic film applied either by hand or automatically and sealed by a shrink tunnel where heat is applied.

The sealed trays are placed into wire baskets which allow for good air circulation. Equipment is available that is made for this system and can make for greater efficiency. Wire baskets are made that hold the trays and that fit on a dolly where the baskets are stackable. The loaded wire baskets fit into the ovens and refrigerators (Fig. 12.9A−12.9F). Insulated blankets may be used to cover the loaded wire racks for transporting to maintain the temperatures.

A complete lunch consists of a hot package, a cold package, and a ½ pt of milk. The menus in Table 12.2 show a typical hot and cold packaged lunch. The hot pack usually contains one to two items placed on a flat or compartment tray. The food is often prepared the day before it is to be served, then cooled and packaged into portions and refrigerated at below 40°F until time for reheating. The cold portion usually contains the bread, butter, a vegetable or fruit and dessert, and unit pack containing napkin, straw and plastic ware. This is held at 40°F until time for serving. The food is transported at temperatures of 40°F to the receiving school where the food is refrigerated until just before serving. The hot portion is heated for 15 to 30 min or until the internal temperature is 155 to 160°F.

FIG. 12.9A. TRAYS ARE DEPOSITED ONTO A TRAVELING CONVEYOR BELT

FIG. 12.9B. ENTREE ITEMS ARE PUT ON THE TRAYS AS THEY MOVE ON THE CONVEYOR BELT

FIG. 12.9C. EACH PERSON ON THE ASSEMBLY ADDS A PART OF THE MEAL

FIG. 12.9D. SPEED HAS TO BE KEPT UP AS THE TRAYS MOVE TOWARD THE SEALING MACHINE

FIG. 12.9E. SEALING UNIT CUTS AND SEALS A HEAT-RESISTANT FILM OVER THE CONTAINERS

FIG. 12.9F. MEALS ARE PACKED INTO WIRE BASKETS ON A DOLLY FOR MOVING TO REFRIGERATION UNTIL TRANSPORTING TO SATELLITE SCHOOL FOR REHEATING

TABLE 12.2. ELEMENTARY MENUS FOR PREPLATED HOT AND COLD PACKED MEALS

Monday, Feb. 1	Tuesday, Feb. 2	Wednesday, Feb. 3	Thursday, Feb. 4	Friday, Feb. 5
Hot: Hot dog—roll Baked beans	Hot: Spaghetti w/meat sauce	Hot: Hamburger—roll Bu. corn	Hot: Turkey Mashed potatoes	Hot: Fishwich—roll Tator tots
Cold: Jellied salad Peaches Milk	Cold: Shredded lettuce French bread Fruit crisp Milk	Cold: Tossed salad Ice cream Milk	Cold: Jellied fruit salad Roll—Butter Baked dessert Milk	Cold: Pepper cole slaw Ice cream Milk

Monday, Feb. 8	Tuesday, Feb. 9	Wednesday, Feb. 10	Thursday, Feb. 11	Friday, Feb. 12
Hot: Cheeseburger —roll Tator tots Bu. mixed vegetables	Hot: Meatloaf—gravy Mashed potatoes Green beans	Hot: Chicken Green peas	Hot: Pizza	Hot: Salisbury steak Mashed potatoes Bu. broccoli
Cold: Lincoln logs Milk	Cold: Roll—Butter Fruit Milk	Cold: Sweetheart salad Roll—Butter Valentine cake Milk	Cold: Green salad Potato chips Fruit jello Milk	Cold: Roll—Butter Pineapple tidbits Milk

Monday, Feb. 15	Tuesday, Feb. 16	Wednesday, Feb. 17	Thursday, Feb. 18	Friday, Feb. 19
Hot: Hot dog—roll Baked beans	Hot: Spaghetti w/meat sauce	Hot: Meat loaf—gravy Mashed potatoes Green beans	Hot: Chili con carne	Hot: Fishwich—roll Tator tots
Cold: Jellied salad Peaches Milk	Cold: Shredded lettuce French bread Fruit crisp Milk	Cold: Roll—Butter Baked dessert Milk	Cold: Tossed salad French bread Fruit Milk	Cold: Pepper cole slaw Ice cream Milk

Source: Arlington Public Schools (Va.), Food Services.

Equipment

The central kitchen will need equipment adequate for the preparation of the food and adequate refrigeration. Large amounts of refrigeration—both freezing and refrigerating temperatures—will be needed. Greater efficiency can be achieved with conveyor belt, packaging closure equipment, wire baskets made for the packing material, and mobile dollies on which the baskets are stacked for greated mobility. Ovens and refrigeration are made to accommodate the wire baskets and this reduces the handling necessary. It is possible for a small operation to package 25 to 50 meals per min. The speed of the conveyor belt can be regulated according to the number of employees on the assembly line and their speed. Additional equipment recommended for packaging up to 1000 hot and cold pack lunches are (1) 10-ft long conveyor, (2) automatic sealing machine, and (3) shrink tunnel.

The satellite or receiving school will need the following equipment as a minimum (1) oven for heating the hot portion and (2) milk cooler. Optional items are (1) refrigeration-refrigerator and freezer, (2) 3-compartment sink, and (3) worktable.

If refrigeration is available at the receiving school, the scheduling of delivery of the food is more flexible and desirable. A double set of baskets is suggested so the driver of the truck can deliver the number of meals needed for the day's lunch and pick up the baskets from the previous day.

Using Commercially Preplated Frozen Meals

Commercial frozen food companies did not enter school feeding with much enthusiasm until 1970, after the Federal regulations were changed. Money for free lunches was made available and there was an increased need for serving more students in areas where equipment and facilities were not adequate. The frozen food companies contributed toward meeting this need. Many of the leading manufacturing companies of home "TV" dinners have come up with hot and cold packs that, with ½ pt milk, will meet the nutritional requirements set by the meal pattern and qualify for Federal subsidy. There is limited use of USDA-donated foods in the preparation of the meals. The companies have been more successful in elementary school feeding than in secondary school feeding. Some of the companies offer the product and the equipment on a purchased or leased plan.

Many school districts have chosen to pack their own cold pack and utilize more commodities in this portion of the lunch and use the commercially prepared and packaged hot portion. The hot portion and cold portion of the meal are delivered in the frozen state ready for reconstituting. It requires storing at frozen temperatures until day before use. Storage and distribution of the dinners are possibly the greatest problems facing school districts. Central warehouses are usually necessary to obtain the meals at quantity prices. Some school districts have found it more economical or feasible for them to purchase through a local distributor and have scheduled deliveries once or twice a week.

Purchasing on competitive bid basis can mean better prices, but very detailed, explicit specifications are needed to assure quality and quantity desired. Controlling the quality and quantity (portion control) is a problem that even some of the commercial companies have.

A receiving school will need from 1 to 3 employees for heating and serving the food and collecting the money or tickets. The labor recommended for a school serving 300 to 500 is one 4-hr worker and one 3-hr cashier.

Procedures.—A typical day in a school where frozen dinners are used may go as follows:

(1) Cold portion of the lunch, put into the refrigerator the day before, will be taken out to serve just before serving time.
(2) 1 hr before serving time, the frozen entrees are placed on wire racks to be reconstituted.
(3) 35 min before serving time the entrees are put into a preheated oven for up to 25 min.
(4) Serving time the students move through the line picking up the cold pack, then the hot pack, unit pack (containing the napkin-straw- and plasticware), and ½ pt milk.

The coverings on both the hot and cold pack are removed by the students. The varieties available in the entree and cold pack vary from one company to another. An example of a week's menu using the commercially prepared hot and cold pack is shown in Table 12.3.

When school districts are starting such a progarm at the building stage, many of the companies have professional advise and offer recommendations as to the equipment needs and space requirements for most efficiency.

Advantages of using the preplated dinners:

(1) Less labor is required. The industry packing the preplated dinners insists that one employee can serve 800 lunches using the preplated hot and cold pack. The timing would have to be perfect with much cooperation and organization of the students to accomplish that, but certainly two people could serve this number, which is considerably less labor than required if serving on the conventional line.

(2) Less training or less experienced employees can carry out the job.

(3) Less equipment and space is needed.

(4) Quality is controlled.

(5) Sanitation may be more controlled.

(6) Conservation of nutrients may be better than if untrained employees with poor preparation techniques have been preparing the meals.

(7) Quantity is controlled with more uniform servings.

Disadvantages that have been noted:

(1) Lack of pride on the part of the employees in their work because of the feeling that anybody could do this.

(2) Lack of the personal preference of seasonings.

(3) Limited variety.

(4) Increased possibility of plate waste because of all portions being the same, since a first grader may not want or need the quantity that a sixth grader needs or wants.

TABLE 12.3. WEEK OF MENUS USING COMMERCIALLY PREPARED HOT AND COLD PACK

Monday	Hot:	Sicilian meat loaf
		Golden corn niblets
	Cold:	Georgia peaches in jel
		Golden twin roll
Tuesday	Hot:	Sliced roast turkey with savory dressing and gravy
		Sweet taters
	Cold:	California strawberries in jel
		Golden twin roll
Wednesday	Hot:	Milano pizza topped w/beef 'n cheese
	Cold:	Creamy cole slaw
		Fruit medley in jel
Thursday	Hot:	Southern deep fried chicken
		Sweet and tender corn
	Cold:	Potomac cherries in jel
		Golden twin roll
Friday	Hot:	Fish 'n cheese burger
		Mixed-up vegetables
	Cold:	Puerto Rican pineapple in jel
		Burger bun

Source: ITT Continental Baking Company.

INTRODUCING NEW SYSTEMS

Any time a new system providing food is being started in a school—particularly when replacing on-site preparation—the school administration, parents, and students have to be receptive to the system in order for the system to work well. Not all of the systems described above will work for all situations. Each fits a different need. If no foodservice at all has been available, parents and students are more receptive to any system that will make food available. Making parents aware of the plans through parent-teacher meetings and involving the students in menu planning, etc., will help with acceptability.

System of Tomorrow

Little is known about the aseptic system in school foodservice in this country, and it may well be the best of all the systems for holding cooked foods for serving later. Military feeding operations have used it as rations successfully and the space program were fore-runners in this means of preserving foods. The aseptic system uses hot air sterilization and packages the products in retort-type pouches or containers. It becomes shelf stable and has a shelf life of six months or longer, depending on the food. The retention of nutrients, color, and flavor is excellent. The system has been slow to catch on. It seems to be a case of industry not ready to leave traditional ways and expensive machinery for new machinery. The cost has discouraged school foodservice directors from taking a serious look at the products, however, with volume the costs would bring it in line with regularly canned foods in cylinder number 10 cans. It is conceivable that a production kitchen could have its own packaging machines, whereas spaghetti sauce could be prepared and packaged for serving several weeks later, and stored on the storeroom shelf until time for reheating for serving. With our concern for energy and increasing needs for freezer space, the idea is exciting.

BIBLIOGRAPHY

ANON. 1966. Which system suits your needs? School Lunch J. 20, No. 7, 13–32.

ANON. 1972. The cup-can approach. School Foodservice J. 26, No. 10, 41, 43.

ANON. 1976. Contract Feeders Survey. American School Food Service Association, Denver, Colo.

ANON. 1976. Pilot Study to Assess, Audit and Evaluate Food Delivery Systems Used in School Food Service. Colorado State University, Fort Collins, Colo.

AVERY, A.C. 1967. Work design and food service systems. J. Am. Dietet. Assoc. *51*, No. 8, 148.

BLAKER, G., and E. RAMSEY. 1961. Holding temperatures and food quality. J. Am. Dietet. Assoc. *38*, No. 5, 450–454.

FAIRFAX COUNTY (VA) FOOD SERVICE DIVISION. 1976. Food Service Manual, Fairfax County Schools, Fairfax, Va.

POLEDOR, ANDREW P. 1977. Determining the Feasibility of a Total Convenience Food System. CBI Publishing Company, Boston, Mass.

U.S. DEPT. AGR. 1965C. Establishing Central School Lunch Kitchens in Urban Areas: Problems and Costs. Econ. Report *72*, U.S. Govt. Printing Office, Washington, D.C.

U.S. DEPT. AGR. 1977. Evaluation of the Child Nutrition Programs. U.S. Printing Office, Washington, D.C.

13

Planning Foodservice Facilities

The question most frequently asked by boards of education is "Should we continue to build kitchens and equip them for the preparation of food?" For many years the kitchenless kitchen of the Kaisers Foundation Hospital (Calif.) was pointed at as the trend setter. It was predicted in 1980 by some that by 1990, each school can have its own machines for packing foods that are shelf-stable, as used by the military, which would cause much change in school feeding. There has been a continuation of central kitchens, commissaries, and satellite feeding for many years. There has been even a greater increase in the number of self-contained units being built, as school foodservice has doubled its operation in the past few years. The self-contained units are still the rule. For some situations and locations the food factory is the solution, and for others the use of frozen dinners may be the solution. With summer feeding, breakfast programs, and feeding the elderly as possibilities of the future, most planners feel it is best to be prepared with kitchens. A few areas of the country have been able to effectively plan the secondary school in the center surrounded by elementary schools. This presents the ideal situation for the secondary school to be the feeder school supplying the elementary schools with food. There is no set solution that will meet the needs of all.

PLANNING FLOOR LAYOUT

Good planning is necessary for high productivity and the greatest efficiency. When working in an old building with construction faults and poor layout, the waste of time and motion is costly, but often unavoidable. However, when a new facility is being planned and constructed, it would be expected that these faults are corrected. Too frequently the same mistakes are made or new ones are planned in. With the virtues and faults of so many school plants to use as guides, it would seem that a perfect plan could be developed.

Common Fault.—When the construction funds run low, often the kitchen becomes smaller and results in too small a facility for the number to be served. However, too large a kitchen may be almost as bad since it results in wasted time walking between work areas and results in low productivity. Plans should be made on the basis of what is needed now and with consideration for future needs.

Floor Plans

Foodservice management must insist on being a part of the proposed school's planning team. It is hard to explain so many poorly planned and poorly arranged kitchens still being built. One of the reasons, it seems, is that foodservice people are not involved in the planning. The planning team should consist of (1) representatives of the school board, (2) architects, (3) construction specialists, and (4) those who will use the facilities. The local and state health departments should be consulted through the planning stages. Since such facilities are a long-range project and a great cost, the planning should be done carefully.

Factors.—Some of the factors to be considered in planning a school foodservice are:

(1) The capacity of the school.
(2) Future expansion plans.
(3) How many meals will be served—breakfast, lunch, dinner.
(4) Menus and type service to be offered—single menu, choice menus, a la carte, vending machines, etc.
(5) Age of children.
(6) Location of building.
(7) Will the foodservice be a feeder kitchen preparing for other schools?
(8) Type of equipment needed.
(9) Utilities to be used.
(10) The uses of the school building and foodservice by the community.

Locations.—The kitchen should be located on the ground floor with a service driveway accessible for deliveries to be made. The delivery entrance should be located away from the playground and students' traffic lane. The kitchen should have an outside entrance that opens onto a loading dock. The dining room should be attached to the kitchen and convenient for students to reach. If the foodservice facilities are a separate building, a covered walkway is desirable. The noise of the kitchen should be considered in locating the facility.

Space Needed.—Since the kitchen is not easy to enlarge, it should be built to accommodate future needs. The space required in square feet depends on what equipment is needed to do the preparation and serving. So, ideally the equipment would be decided upon and arranged for the best flow of work with adequate aisle space around the equipment. Some guides are needed in the early stages of planning and should be based on standard equipment (see Table 13.1).

TABLE 13.1. GUIDE TO SPACE (IN SQUARE FEET) NEEDS FOR SCHOOL FOODSERVICE ON-SITE PREPARATION

Area	Meals			
	Up to 350	351−500	501−700	701−1000
Receiving area				
Loading platform	60	80	100	100
Receiving area inside building	48	48	60	80
Storage				
Dry Storage				
⅓−½ sq ft per meal	175	250	300	450
Nonfood storage	30	50	70	90
Office space	40−48	48	60	80
Lockers and toilet for employees	45	60	75	85
Kitchen and Serving				
Preparation including refrigeration 1.1−1.5 sq ft per meal	500	650	800	980
Serving	200	300	400	600
Dishwashing	150	150	180	210
Maintenance area				
Mop area	25	25	30	30
Garbage area	30	48	60	75
Total kitchen and serving area	1303	1709	2135	2780
Dining area (based on two seatings)				
Elementary				
10 sq ft/meal	1750	1750−2500	2500−3500	3500−5000
Secondary				
12 sq ft/meal	2100	2100−3000	3000−4200	4200−6000
Total dining, kitchen and serving area				
Elementary	3053	4209	5635	7780
Secondary	4303	4709	6335	8780

Dining Area

The dining area should be attached to the kitchen and convenient to the students from all parts of the school building. It should be constructed as attractively as possible. The cost of construction is such that it is hard to justify a room of the size of a dining room for use only 2 hr a day. Many elementary schools use the dining room as a multi-purpose room. In secondary grades, the dining room lends itself to be used as a lounge, activity room with music, games, relaxing, or as a study hall. With breakfast and dinner being added to some foodservices, the dining room may be used as a place of eating 4 or 6 hr a day. If at all possible, the furnishings should accommodate small groups in senior high schools, middle-size groups in junior high schools, and perhaps larger groups in elementary schools. Even in elementary schools, when small groups of students eat together rather than at long institution type tables, the discipline problems have been far fewer. The increased enjoyment of the lunch hour is also noticeable.

The room should be attractive, bright colored, cheerful, non-institutional in atmosphere, and interesting. The tables and chairs should be varied in size and shape and color. Since elementary schools often use the dining room as a multi-purpose room, the tables may need to be with chairs attached and that fold with rollers. The different size and shape tables that seat 4 to 12 people *can create* an entirely different atmosphere. The atmosphere should be carefully planned.

The space needed will depend on how many are to be seated at one time and the seating arrangement (small groups, long tables, etc.).

Ordinarily the seating should accommodate 30 to 40% of the projected enrollment at one time. The following is a guide to space needs per student to be seated:

10 sq ft for elementary schools
12 sq ft for secondary schools

For example, if the projected enrollment for an elementary school is 800, then:

$$\frac{800}{0.40} = 320 \text{ (per seating)}$$

$$320 \times 10 = 3200 \text{ sq ft}$$

This is with the idea that the students will be divided into 3 seatings. If only 2 seatings are the plan, then 50% of the students should be seated at one time. With continuous service the space requirement can be cut considerably.

With long rectangular tables, it is possible to cut the space requirement from 10 sq ft for elementary students to 7 to 8 sq ft per student and from 12 sq ft per person for secondary students to 8 to 10 sq ft per student. When seating capacity needs to be more than 350, two similar dining rooms should be considered.

The serving area, trash area, and dishwashing area should be closed off from the dining area. The walls lend themselves to art exhibits and other attractive displays. Draperies and carpets will help absorb the sounds. If the tables are to be used for elementary students, the tables should be 26 in. high with chairs or stools 15 in. high. A table 29 in. high is satisfactory for secondary age and can be used by all age groups. The chair will need to be a standard 17 in. seat height.

Serving Area

The serving area should be separate from the dining area and with some type of partition separating it from the prepartion area. Cafeteria type service is most commonly used in school feeding. The arrangement of the serving lines should be such as to accommodate all the foods and encourage fast service. How many serving lines are needed? In elementary schools a serving line can serve 10 to 12 children per minute. In secondary school the serving line should provide for serving 12 to 14 per minute. The number of serving lines needed will depend on the speed of service, number to be served, and turnover. One serving line can serve approximately 150 students in 13 min. Students do not like to stand in line, and discipline problems may result when it is necessary. In estimating the space needed per serving area, allow for the following:

Student lane space	30 in.
Tray slide	1 ft
Serving counter width	2 to 3 ft
Worker's space	4 ft
Counter in back of worker	2½ ft

The menu, number of choices, will determine the length of the serving counter. Ordinarily 20 ft is the minimun length, with a height that fits the student. The area must be equipped to keep the temperatures either hot or cold on perishable foods. Heated units are needed to hold hot food at 150°F or hotter, and refrigerated units are needed to hold cold foods at 45°F or colder. With this type of service the student is usually expected to pick up the tray, napkin, flatware, and milk. Self-service can be increased to include desserts, salads, bread, and other foods. The sequence of these items should be studied to avoid a bottleneck at any one point in the line. Tray and silver carts that are mobile for taking to the dishroom for refilling are recommended. Dish storage at the line has also been improved with dish storage carts that are mobile. Sneeze guards should protect all foods on display on the serving line. A left-to-right serving line lends to greater speed in serving.

Straight-line serving counters are the most common. However, some secondary schools have tried the rotary counter or the shopping-center type lines, referred to as the "island type," "scramble," "hollow square," and other names. When multiple choice menus and/or a la carte items are available, the rotary counter and shopping center approach make for much flexibility. With the shopping center service, the serving line is broken up into sections, thus the student who wants just a bowl of soup can go directly to the section and not have to wait in line behind someone who wants the whole lunch. A cashier station is located at the exit for the lines. The broken-up serving line concept has been used satisfactorily in commercial, college, in-plant, and school cafeterias. Avoiding bottlenecks in the shopping-center serving line is difficult and requires careful planning. Stations with popular items like hamburgers and French fries may need duplicating.

The rotary mechanized foodservice serving counters have successfully worked for schools, by eliminating long lines and speeding up service. The popularity of salad bars and self-service is opening up a new concept in feeding people both institutionally and commercially.

Kitchen

The flow of the work should be smooth and in a logical sequence from receiving through the stages of preparation to serving. The principles of time and motion are applicable in planning the arrangement of the equipment. The flow of the work desired can be the first step in planning the arrangement or layout. To check the flow, trace the steps of several foods from the receiving through the preparation and to serving. With the use of colored pencil and arrows one can easily trace the flow and spot any problem (Fig. 13.1). The flow should be direct in sequence with the minimum of crossing and back-tracking. The layout can be divided into work centers. The larger the operation the more specialized the work centers will be. A *work center* is the area within which one person works with perhaps an assistant. Each work center should have in it basically all the equipment needed to perform the job. Occasionally a piece of equipment is used by more than one work center. When possible this piece of equipment should be put on wheels. If the piece of equipment does not warrant duplicates, it should be stationed in the work center that uses it most.

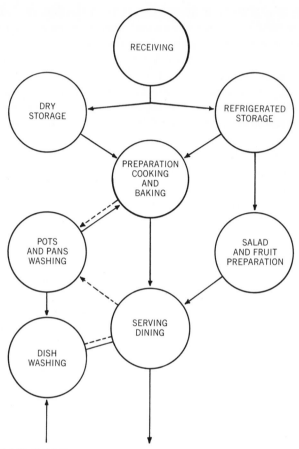

FIG. 13.1. FLOW CHART

If the equipment within these work centers is placed in sequence, then little of the working time is wasted because of layout. The work centers should be located only as far away from each other as is necessary for an adequate traffic lane. The layout should aim at maximum utilization of space and equipment. Most foodservice managers would select a kitchen slightly smaller than desired over one too large.

ARRANGEMENT OF EQUIPMENT

General Plans

The overall features to consider when planning the layout are space needed and the arrangement of the equipment in that space. It should be done in such a way that will encourage a smooth flow of work, provide adequate facilities and space for accomplishing the work in an efficient manner, aid in fast service with a pleasant atmosphere, and contribute to high sanitation standards.

The traffic in the kitchen should be planned with main traffic aisles adequate to accommodate the movement of mobile equipment. These aisles should be approximately 5 ft wide. The work centers should allow 3 to 4 ft aisle space for the employees to move freely. When doors open into the aisle, 4 ft is recommended. The centers should be planned to discourage traffic through the center. Common arrangements are straightline, parallel arrangement, U-arrangement and L-arrangement. The U-arrangement most discourages through traffic.

The kitchen is often planned around the cooking area, and perhaps this is where one might start the plans working outward. The cooking and baking equipment is often grouped back-to-back. With that grouping, one hood with ventilation can be used, and the power lines are convenient for installing as well as repairing.

The kitchen should be planned with good lighting and soft colors reducing the glare. Light intensity of 35 to 50 ft-candles is recommended with the 40 for general preparation and serving areas and 50 at the sink and cooking areas. Shadows should be avoided. Sound-absorbing materials, if meeting local health codes can be used in construction to reduce the sound of the equipment. Good circulation of air is necessary with air cooling in the warmer areas of the country. The comfort of the employees is directly connected to productivity.

When arranging and planning the layout, the most helpful tools are templets. *Equipment templets* are paper or cardboard scale models of equipment. The scale most commonly used is ¼ in. equals 1 ft. If the templets are on the same scale as the plans drawn, one can fasten the templets into place with pins and get a miniature picture of the arrangements. Many of the larger equipment companies can supply these scale models.

Receiving Area

The receiving area should be located near the outside entrance but connected to the kitchen convenient to the storage area. The doors leading in and out of this area should be wide enough to accommodate the kitchen equipment that may need to pass through the area. The receiving area should be equipped with scales for weighing foods received and a table or counter on which the invoices may be signed and small items can be put. A covered ramp at the loading and unloading area is desirable at a height that will fit the bed of the delivery trucks. The depth of this ramp should be 8 ft with the width planned according to the number of trucks expected at one time. If the school will satellite other schools, this area should be planned carefully for ease in loading and unloading the transporting vehicles, with space for two to three vehicles.

Manager's Office

Even the smallest operation needs an office for the manager. The space should be adequate for a least a desk, two chairs, and file cabinet. Larger operations will need larger offices to afford room for the cashiers counting money and for conferences. The manager's office should be located where the manager can sit at the desk and have a view of the kitchen and outside entrances. Enclosures with glass above 4 ft are most satisfactory.

Employee Facilities

Locker rooms for employees are recommended where each employee can hang his coat and store his personal belongings safely. These areas are usually connected with the toilet area. Many States have regulations forbidding the opening of a toilet directly into any food storage, serving, or preparation area.

Hand-washing sinks with towels and soap should be located conveniently throughout the kitchen, especially near the locker room and in the toilet areas. Foot controls of the faucet are recommended for the sink.

Storage Area

The dry storeroom should be located near the receiving area but convenient to the kitchen. The area should be so situated that the coming and going out of the room can be seen from the kitchen. The storeroom should be dry, well ventilated with turnover of air 6 times per hour and cool with a temperature of 50 to 70°F. However, in many parts of the country that temperature range is possible only with air conditioning. The humidity should be kept between 50 and 60%. In warm and cold climates it may require controls of the temperature and storage of canned and dry foods. The area should be free of direct sunlight and unwanted heat, such as the heat from a self-contained refrigerator or freezer. The lighting should not be as bright as in other parts of the kitchen.

Shelving in this area should be steel wire type, washable, rust proof, off the floor, with space enough underneath to clean. Most State and local health departments have definite regulations as to the height these shelves should be off the floor and away from the wall. In order to get maximum storage space from the area, the shelves should save space (Figs. 13.2 and 13.3). The width, depth of the shelves should be planned to accommodate the items to be stored there. For example, two of the most common institutional can sizes would require the following space:

Can Size	Diam	Height	No. Cans/Case	Size of Case
No. 3 (cylinder)	4¼ in.	7½ in.	12	17½ × 13½ × 7¾ in.
No. 10	6¼ in.	7½ in.	6	19× 12¾ × 7¼ in.

Good planning can triple the storage capacity of an area. The height of the shelves from the floor to the top shelf should not exceed 7½ ft. One of the best and most efficient systems is the hi-density shelving system,

FIG. 13.2. SPACE-SAVING STORAGE RACKS CAN BE BUILT-IN THROUGH A WALL BETWEEN STORAGE AREA AND KITCHEN FOR A FIRST-IN, FIRST-OUT FEED.

Courtesy of Storage Unlimited Inc.

FIG. 13.3. WIRE SHELV-
ING IS EASY TO CLEAN

Courtesy of Metropolitan Wire Goods Corp.

which increases the storage capacity by 40% or more depending upon number of units used. The shelving units are mobile, rolling on a track like an accordian, allowing space between two units when needed and closing the other units together. The units are available in many different sizes and with different weight capacities.

Salads and Fruit Preparation Center

This center is used for pre-preparation of raw foods for the cooking center. However, with the increased use of convenience foods less and less pre-preparation is being done in the kitchen. This area should contain a two-compartment sink for cleaning fruits and vegetables. A work table and cutting machines will be needed. The center should be located near a refrigerator where the finished salads and fruits can be held until serving time. A reach-through refrigerator that opens onto the serving line can be a labor-saving arrangement. Additional equipment that may be included in the center are disposals and vertical-cutter-mixer. This area lends itself to a U-shape or L-shape design that would discourage traffic.

Cooking Center

The cooking area is usually the hub of the kitchen. The space needed will depend on the amount of equipment needed for the size operation. The basic equipment needed are a range, work table, scales for weighing ingredients, and steam kettle. A sink and refrigerator should be convenient to this area. In the large operations this area should have a one-compartment sink. A water supply will be needed for the kettle usually in the form of a swivel faucet. Equipment in this area may also include compartment steamers, slicing machine, hot food storage boxes, refrigeration, mixer, and ovens. This area may need a mixer or vertical-cutter-mixer for mixing meat loaves, potatoes, etc. Does the area need its own mixer or VCM? This will depend on how frequently this piece of equipment is needed and if it can be scheduled so it does not interfere with the baker's schedule. The flow of food should be from the area to the serving line, and therefore the equipment should be arranged in a logical sequence to that point.

Storage space for pots, pans, and utensils for measuring and mixing will be needed as well as for spices frequently used. The cook's table often is equipped with a pot rack for holding the frequently used pots. Portable racks that can be moved from washing area to point of use are most convenient and are recommended. In planning the work space for this area, plan for a "landing" space for hot food from each piece of cooking equipment.

Baking Center

Baking centers are being utilized in different ways today then previously. Many schools are using mixes for their cakes and contracting their breads out. However, the center is equipped very much the same as it was 15 yr ago. This center will need a convection oven, mixer or VCM, work table, portable bins, scales for weighing ingredients, and cooling rack. Other equipment that may be included are sink, refrigeration, small kettle or range top, and proofing box. This arrangement should be in a sequence that will encourage a flow of the work to the oven and to the serving line. This area should be convenient to refrigeration, a sink and the serving line.

The baker's table has changed much from the wood-top tables with bins underneath to stainless steel tops with portable bins. Some wood-top tables are in use, but for the most part have been replaced by the more durable and sanitary stainless steel. Storage areas for items frequently used are needed and will reduce the number of steps to the storage area.

Sandwich Center

In secondary schools with sandwich lines or a la carte service, a sandwich-making center may be essential. This area will need access to refrigeration, sink, slicing machine, chopping machines, and a work table with cutting boards.

Cleaning Center

The dishwashing area has an important part in the sanitation of the operation. This area should be located near the serving line for returning the clean dishes and attached to the dining room for students to return the soiled dishes. A frequent mistake in planning is the locating of the serving line near the traffic of the dishroom, resulting in criss-crossing.

The facilities needed in this area are soiled dish tables (100 ft minimum), pre-rinse sink and disposal, dishwasher adequate for the size operation, booster heater, clean dish table (minimum 100 ft). The pre-rinse sink should be approximately 24 in. sq with rails that will guide the dish racks over the sink. A disposal located in the pre-rinse sink works very satisfactorily. The water temperature must be at 140 to 160°F for wash, and the final rinse must be 180 to 200°F. The area will need ventilation to remove the steam buildup.

A three-compartment sink for pot washing may be located in this area near to the cooking area. If the pot sink is located in the dish machine area, the pots and pans can be washed and sterilized in the dish machine. If the dish machine is not used for washing and sterilizing, the pot washing area will need rinse water at 180°F (or chemicals could be used for sterilizing). Drainboards are needed on the sink for air drying. A portable rack for the pots and pans is convenient.

Consultant

This chapter has not attempted to go into the details of layouts and planning and construction. The purpose has been to give an overall feel for the arrangement of the layout and flow of work, relationship of work centers, and need for careful planning around actual needs. The size and amount of equipment to go into the construction and arrangement should be determined through the foodservice management working closely with architect. A knowledgeable consultant can save not only headaches but money.

BIBLIOGRAPHY

BARNES, R.M. 1968. Motion and Time Study: Design and Measurement of Work, 6th Edition. John Wiley & Sons, New York.

BUCHANAN, ROBERT D. *et al.* 1975. The Anatomy of Foodservice, Design 1. Cahners Books, Boston, Mass.

KAZARIAN, EDWARD A. 1975. Food Service Facilities Planning. AVI Publishing Co., Westport, Conn.

KAZARIAN, EDWARD A. 1979. Work Analysis & Design for Hotels, Restaurants, and Institutions. AVI Publishing Co., Westport, Conn.

KOTSCHEVAR L.H., and MARGARET E. TERRELL, 2nd Edition. 1977. Foodservice Planning Layout and Equipment. John Wiley & Sons, New York.

McGUFFEY, C.W., and D.J. HARRISON. 1970. What is the best seating for lunchrooms? School Lunch J. *25*, No. 9, 59—68.

MILLER, E. 1966. Profitable Cafeteria Operation. Ahrens Book Co., New York.

MYERS, JAMES R. 1979. Commercial Kitchens, 6th Edition. American Gas Association, Arlington, Va.

U.S. DEPT. AGR. 1974. Equipment Guide for On-Site School Kitchens. U.S. Govt. Printing Office, Washington, D.C.

U.S. DEPT. AGR. 1975. Food Storage Guide for Schools and Institutions. PA. 403. U.S. Govt. Printing Office, Washington, D.C.

U.S. DEPT. AGR. 1980. Food Service Equipment Guide for Child Care Institutions. U.S. Govt. Printing Office, Washington, D.C.

WEST, BESSIE, LEVELLE WOOD, VIRGINIA HARGER and GRACE SHUGART. 1977. Food Service in Institutions, 6th Edition. John Wiley & Sons, New York.

14

Equipment

Today there are so many equipment companies in business that the challenge is becoming greater for the foodservice administrator to specify and purchase a good piece of equipment that will do the job. The range in quality is almost as great as that for home equipment, but harder for the buyer to judge without the aid of consumer studies. The answers to the following questions will help determine what specific piece of equipment should be purchased:

(1) How much money is available?
(2) How large an operation is the equipment for?
(3) What is the expected growth in the next 10 yr?
(4) What is the cost of labor? Is labor available? Is equipment needed that will take the place of labor?
(5) What is the menu, the variety to be prepared? What will the equipment be used for? How frequently?
(6) What form will the food be purchased in—fresh, frozen, prepared, etc.?
(7) What is the floor plan? How much space is available?

Not only the initial price of the equipment is to be considered, but the cost of installation, repairs, and operating. Also to be considered are the years of service that can be expected from the piece of equipment and the value of the equipment to the operation. Individual pieces of equipment should be judged on their design, durability, cleanability, construction, safety, and the materials used in relation to the job to be performed.

Equipment for institutional foods was made 30 yr ago to last a lifetime, and it was expensive in those years. Some of those pieces of equipment are still in use today; however, for the most part foodservices have outgrown them, have found a need for a more efficient piece of equipment, or the parts for repairing the equipment are not available today.

With the advances made yearly, the foodservice administration should not necessarily be buying equipment to last a lifetime or even 30 yr.

Equipment should be purchased for one or more of the following reasons: to improve sanitation, to reduce labor cost, to improve the nutritional value of food at serving, to lower food cost, to add appeal and variety to the menu, or to make the work easier. Equipment should be purchased to meet the particular need of that foodservice purchasing it. A 60-qt mixer may be a white elephant in the kitchen of one school but a practical necessity in another.

The amount of equipment needed for a foodservice should not be determined by a chart in a book, but rather by the operation's needs. However, as a basic guide, Table 14.1 may be helpful.

Construction of Equipment

The materials from which equipment is being manufactured are constantly changing. Many man-made materials have proved very satisfactory and in some cases do the job better and less expensively than their counterparts. An all-stainless-steel kitchen was once thought to be the ultimate. Other materials have been used very satisfactorily, sometimes adding color, reducing the price, and making for a lighter weight piece of equipment that is more flexible and moveable. The National Sanitation Foundation has established minimum requirements for materials that can be used by purchasers in writing specifications.

Gage refers to the thickness of the metal or the weight of the metal. Gages are designated by numbers, 10 to 22 gage being most common in foodservice equipment. The larger the number, the thinner and lighter in weight the metal (Fig. 14.1).

The *finish* of metals may be polished or dull. The more polished the metal the easier it is scratched.

Equipment should be constructed to do the job in a sanitary and safe way. The National Sanitation Foundation has done much to improve construction standards.

National Sanitation Foundation

National Sanitation Foundation was started in 1948 by public health authorities, industrialists, and businessmen who saw a need for research to be done in the field of environment, need for uniform equipment standards to be set, need for laboratory testing of equipment and materials by an independent testing laboratory, some means of identifying equipment that did meet the standard (Seal of Approval), and a need for relating the research and test-findings to the industry, public health people,

TABLE 14.1. EQUIPMENT RECOMMENDATIONS FOR ON-SITE PREPARATION KITCHENS

Equipment	Number of Lunches Prepared Per Day				
	Up to 250	251–400	401–600	601–800	801–1000
Ovens					
Convection oven	1	1	2	2	3
Range					
Range with oven to hold 2 pans	1 section	1	2	2	2
Steam					
Compartment steamer (optional) or			2	2	3
Jacketed kettle	20 gal.	30 gal.	40 gal.	40 gal. and 30 gal.	(2) 40 gal.
Mixer					
Mixer with attachments and	30 qt	60 qt	60 qt and 20 qt	60 qt and 30 qt	60 qt and 30 qt
Food cutter (optional) or				1 large	1 large
Vertical cutter mixer			40 qt	40 qt	60 qt
Slicer	1 electric	1 electric	1 automatic (angle feed)	1 automatic (angle feed)	1 automatic (angle feed)
Deep fat fryer (optional)	15-lb capacity	26-lb capacity	35-lb capacity	45-lb capacity	(2) 35-lb capacity
Refrigeration					
Reach-in refrigerator	71-cu ft capacity	71-cu ft capacity		47-cu ft capacity	71-cu ft capacity
Pass-through refrigerator		25-cu ft capacity	(2) 25-cu ft capacity	(2) 25-cu ft capacity	(3) 25-cu ft capacity
Walk-in refrigerator			7 × 10 ft	9 × 11 ft	9 × 11 ft
Reach-in freezer	47-cu ft capacity	47-cu ft capacity	71-cu ft capacity		
Walk-in freezer				9 × 6 ft	9 × 8 ft
Milk Cooler	(1) 10-cu ft	(1) 10-cu ft	(2) 10-cu ft	(3) 10-cu ft	(3) 10-cu ft
Work tables					
Cook's table with pan rack	(1) 6 ft × 30 in. × 34 in. high	(1) 6 ft × 30 in. × 34 in. high	(1) 8 ft × 30 in. × 34 in. high	(2) 6 ft × 30 in. × 34 in. high	(2) 8 ft × 42 in. × 34 in. high

Baker's table with portable storage bins	(1) 6 ft × 30 in. × 34 in. high	(1) 6 ft × 30 in. × 34 in. high	(1) 8 ft × 30 in. × 34 in. high	(1) 8 ft × 30 in. × 34 in. high	(1) 8 ft × 30 in. × 34 in. high
Preparation table		(1) 6 ft × 30 in.	(1) 6 ft × 30 in.	(1) 8 ft × 42 in.	(2) 8 ft × 42 in.
Portable table		(1) 5 ft × 30 in. × 34 in. high	(1) 5 ft × 30 in. × 34 in. high	(1) 5 ft × 30 in. × 34 in. high	(1) 5 ft x 30 in. × 34 in. high
Dish machine					
Single tank (door)	1				
Single tank (conveyor)		1	1		
Double tank (conveyor)				1	1
Soiled-dish table with disposal	9 ft	9 ft	10 ft	11 ft	12 ft
Clean-dish table	8 ft	9 ft	10 ft	11 ft	12 ft
Dishwashing racks (plastic)	3 (plate) 1 (flat)	5 (plate) 2 (flat)	6 (plate) 2 (flat)	8 (plate) 3 (flat)	8 (plate) 4 (flat)
Disposal unit (optional)	¾ HP	1 HP	1 HP	1 HP	(2) 1 hp (2 dish windows)
Sinks					
Pot sink (3 compartment)	1	1	1	1	1
Vegetable sink (2 compartment)	1	1	1	1	1
Cook sink (1 compartment)				1	1
Utility carts	2	2	3	3	3–4
Cooling racks	1	1	2	3	3
Scales					
Portion 5 lb × ⅛ oz	1	1	1	2	2
Baker's with scoop and weight	1	1	1	1	2
Platform with beam scale 500-lb capacity, ¼ in. graduations	1	1	1	1	1
Serving					
Counter	1 line	1 line	1–2 lines	2 lines	3 lines

THICKNESS OF STAINLESS STEEL

Gage Number	Approximate Decimal Parts of an Inch	Approximate Equivalents (mm)
10	.140625	3.57
11	.125	3.18
12	.109375	2.77
13	.09375	2.38
14	.078125	1.98
15	.0703125	1.78
16	.0625	1.59
17	.05625	1.43
18	.050	1.27
19	.04375	1.11
20	.0375	0.95
22	.031	0.81

FIG. 14.1. THE THICKNESS OF STAINLESS STEEL IS SPECIFIED BY GAGE, DECIMAL PART OF AN INCH, AND/OR BY METRIC MEASUREMENT
The use of gage to designate approximate thickness dates back to the years when sheet metal was cut on hand mills and broad tolerances were necessary. The decimal part of an inch is used to designate exact thickness and is slowly being converted to metric equivalents.

and the public. They are an authoritative liaison for business, industry, and health authorities. The headquarters are at the University of Michigan. It is a non-commercial, non-profit organization. In the purpose as stated by the National Sanitation Foundation, it is "dedicated to the prevention of illness, the promotion of health, and the enrichment of the quality of American living through preplanning of preventive programs for the improvement of the environment." The NSF booklets of standards on different pieces of equipment may be helpful in writing specifications. The insigne, NSF, on a piece of equipment indicates that it meets the requirements set in the standards booklet and that NSF checks periodically this manufacturer's methods in the factory and that the pieces of equipment design and model have been tested for performance in the laboratory and in the field. The seal of approval is no guarantee that this particular piece of equipment will be free of defect, but it must meet the minimum standards set forth by the National Sanitation Foundation.

WRITING SPECIFICATIONS

Specifications for equipment must be in writing. For the best price, bid buying should be carried out. However, federal regulations do not require advertising procurements of $10,000 or less unless required by states. Specifications in writing will prevent hard feelings and misunderstandings. They should define exactly what is desired and conditions under which the equipment is to be purchased in a precise, clear manner. Other school foodservice's specifications can be helpful in writing specifications, but the needs of one foodservice will differ from another. There are a few guides that can be turned to in writing specifications. The best aids are: experience with the equipment, comparing the printed literature, equipment manufacturers' representatives or salesmen, the United States Government bid specifications, and the National Sanitation Foundation standards. Specifications can be broad and descriptive or may be short and specify manufacturers and model. Usually when brands and models are specified, "approved equal" is indicated as being acceptable.

Specifications should include any features desired, such as metal to be used on the exterior and interior finishes, attachments or additional pieces to the equipment, and options desired. The purchaser should not take for granted that the equipment comes with certain "necessities"; these may be considered extras by the company. For example, do not take for granted that four racks come with the dishwasher or six shelves come in the refrigerator. Instead, specify how many racks are wanted. Additional racks or shelves and other extras can often be obtained at a better price when purchased with the equipment than separately at a later time. Specifications should include a demonstration of the equipment to be given following the installation, and two operational manuals be furnished—one for the equipment file and the other for use in the kitchen. Indicate in the specifications if the equipment is to be installed by the seller or buyer, date and time of delivery, method of delivery, type of warranty or guarantee expected, and method of payment the vendor can expect. Also, it is important that parts and service be available in the area. Ordinarily equipment is drop-shipped to the loading dock of the kitchen in a crate if not otherwise specified. When equipment is out on competitive bid, a better price can be obtained. Grouping of similar equipment to be purchased into an aggregate can mean an even better price. The larger the order, the better the prices may be. Vendors often cut their profits close when bidding, therefore the buyer should have every specification in detail of what he wants and must not start adding after the bid has been awarded.

Specifications should indicate the seals of approval, such as NSF, ASA, UL, and others when applicable. These seals protect the customer to some degree, and some health departments require the NSF seal on equipment. When selecting and writing specifications for equipment, some basic concepts should be kept in mind.

Modular Equipment Concept

Modular equipment concept means uniform sizing, with the common modules being 14 × 18 in., 18 × 26 in. and 12 × 20 in. Coordinating equipment is a rather new idea. Twenty years ago, oven manufacturers made their ovens with chambers all different sizes. They seemed to change the size as models and designs changed. The companies manufacturing pans went their separate way making pans in whatever size they liked. This was also true with refrigerators and dishwashers. Often a school's menu was governed by which pans fit in which oven. The results could be an oven with 28 × 34 in. chambers, the range oven with chambers 18 × 20 in., baking pans 22 × 22 in., and the pot washing sink 20 × 20 in. Nothing fit exactly, resulting in wasted space, wasted money, and exasperation. Then the manufacturers started working together. The modules are standard today with other sizes being the exceptions.

Modules make for adaptability and better utilization of space. Every piece of equipment works together, interchangeably and coordinating. Cooling racks, ovens, refrigerators, steamers, carts, pot sinks, and pans can all be purchased with the interchanging, fitting-together concept. The three sizes of pans that fit the modulars are:

18 × 26 in.—bun pans, baking sheet pans, roasting pans
14 × 20 in.—cafeteria trays
12 × 20 in.—steamtable pans (20 in. measure from outer rim; these pans will fit the 18 in. modulars)

Standard or Custom-made Equipment

Standard stock equipment means equipment produced in quantity by a standard design. It is far less expensive than is custom-designed equipment. Custom-made equipment is made according to the customer's specifications. Yet, most foodservice buyers find the job of designing a custom piece of equipment may be a headache. Standard stock equipment has the advantages of being tested and the problems being corrected. For most foodservice needs, the standard piece of equipment is the best buy.

Self-contained or Remote Control

Self-contained equipment is less expensive than the remote control units. This is particularly true with refrigerators. Self-contained means the motor and controls are a part of the construction. Remote controls means the motor and/or controls are located separately from the piece of equipment. In some cases it is advisable and desirable to pay more to have the remote control, such as with walk-in refrigeration.

Over-sizing

Over-equipping and over-designing a kitchen is a waste of materials and will hamper efficiency. Buying for the anticipated needs with reasonable compromise is more desirable than purchasing over-sized equipment anticipating the future growth many years away. Over-sized equipment can cause much wasted effort as can equipment too small for the job.

Man-made or Stainless Steel

Man-made materials have been used very satisfactorily in many pieces of equipment that previously had to be stainless steel. Stainless steel has been the ultimate in quality for many years but has also been much higher in price. An all stainless-steel kitchen was the pride of the designer, but a nightmare for those who had to remove the smudges and streaks. Today plastics, fiberglass, other man-made fabrics and new processed enamels on aluminum are being considered cautiously. There is a place for using these new materials if they lower the cost of the equipment, make for easier cleaning, are lighter in weight, or for adding color, as long as they still maintain durability and do the job. Tests have shown that plastics and fiberglass are being made that are as strong as the strongest metals.

Mobile Units

"Put it on wheels" has been the motto of leaders in their work simplification drives. Mobile or portable units are now available in most types of equipment. Mobile units, particularly tables and carts, can reduce the amount of equipment needed. When a piece of equipment is used by more than one work center, and it is possible to schedule the use of the piece of equipment to perform for the different centers, putting that piece of equipment on wheels would make it more accessible. This makes it possible to take the equipment to where the work is done, saving steps, lessening fatigue, and reducing labor. The principles of time and motion are exemplified in this concept.

Obsolete Equipment

Equipment of the past, such as vegetable peelers, meat saws, huge mixers, and meat grinders, should be removed from the kitchen if not being used. These pieces of equipment have been displaced by convenience foods, preportioned and dehydrated and frozen prepared foods. There are other pieces of equipment that are "obsolete" for some foodservices. Some of the equipment put into new schools is obsolete by the time the school opens. This is perhaps true because the plans were designed years before, and since that time the philosophy of the foodservice and the needs have changed. An example of this is an eastern university where the foodservice in one of the dormitories was equipped with $85,000.00 of preparation equipment, from a rotary oven to a combination steamer and numerous kettles. This plan was against the recommendations of the food director. Three years later the equipment had still not been used, and was in the way of the Foster Recon unit that reconstituted the frozen foods. Though that food director has since left, the university's foodservice philosophy now is—due to labor cost and supply—basically that the bakeries can bake for less, that preportioned meats are more economical, and that the frozen prepared entrees are a better solution than on-site preparation. The equipment for a foodservice with this philosophy is different from that one where on-site preparation is still being done. The equipment for an existing kitchen or for a new construction should be what the foodservice needs. Thus, those in foodservice should be a part of the planning committee that determines the equipment to be purchased.

Is This the Piece of Equipment Needed to Do the Job?

Will this piece of equipment be used daily? Weekly? Monthly? Can the job this equipment does be obtained in any other way? For example, potato peelers have continued to go into some new constructions with the argument that it is needed for parsley potatoes. How often are parsley potatoes on the menu? Weekly at the most. Frozen and canned whole potatoes are available. Will these products work satisfactorily in place of fresh, considering the cost and flavor? The decision is for the individual foodservice to make. Buy only equipment that is needed and that will be used. Tables in the kitchen can be catch-alls. So often when there is a space, a table is put there. Is it needed? Does a foodservice need more work-tables than workers?

Labor-saving Equipment

Labor-saving equipment has become more important to the food industry as the labor costs have increased. The number of employees has decreased; however, more is being expected from fewer people in less time. This is possible with the aid of labor-saving equipment, such as:

(1) Automatic instead of manual slicer.
(2) Conveyor dishwasher instead of door type dishwasher.
(3) Convection oven instead of conventional deck oven.
(4) Automatic timer shut-offs on equipment instead of watching the clock.
(5) Automatic counters on a slicer instead of employee counting the slices.
(6) Vertical-cutter-mixer cutting and mixing in seconds instead of the worker cutting and mixing by hand.
(7) Automatic defrost and condensator instead of the employee taking food out and defrosting.
(8) Pre-rinse on dishwasher instead of the employee scraping and pre-rinsing.
(9) Conveyor belts on assembly line instead of manual movements.
(10) Utility carts, portable tables, wheels on equipment to save on number of steps taken.

Energy-Saving Equipment

The concern for conserving energy has brought about tremendous changes in the equipment purchased and development of new pieces or new features. Recovering and reusing heat energy from exhaust air, laundry dryer exhaust, kitchen hot exhaust and condenser water from refrigerators has presented many challenges. The uses include preheating incoming cold water to the hot water heater, reducing the energy to raise the temperature to 140°, 160° or 180°F. Soon to come are computers in ovens and use of more aseptic processing.

Making employees aware of ways they are wasting energy can help considerably. Knowing what the usage of energy is and charting it month-by-month from year-to-year can motivate the employees to help reduce usage. Areas to be considered:

(1) preheating cooking equipment only as long as necessary at the temperature desired,
(2) adjust heat of top stove cooking to size of pan,
(3) cook at the lowest temperature needed,
(4) load to capacity, scheduling to use receding heat,

(5) use timers,

(6) turn lights off in area not being used, such as manager's office and storeroom,

(7) repair leaky faucets,

(8) determine if a low temperature washing of pots and pans and dishes is advantageous,

(9) load and unload refrigeration in the shortest time possible and open units as seldom as possible,

(10) install entry drapes on walk-in refrigeration, and

(11) establish a pre-maintenance program.

PREPARATION EQUIPMENT

The preparation of food for cooking and serving is time consuming without power equipment. The amount and type of preparation equipment needed for the foodservice will be directly related to the amount of preparation to be done. When pre-sliced meats and cheese are purchased, the need for a slicing machine may be questioned. Some of the most commonly used preparation equipment are discussed below.

Mixing Machines

Mixers come in many different sizes and are manufactured by many different companies. This is usually a trouble-free piece of equipment, if properly operated. The size mixers most frequently used in school preparation are 20 qt, 30 qt, and 60 qt. The size mixer is very important in saving time and being efficient. A mixer too large can be as much a problem for the operator as one too small. The correct size mixer can reduce the time spent in preparation by one-half. If a baker is mixing a cake for 400 servings in a 30-qt mixer, two mixings will be required. This means that ingredients have to be weighed and combined twice, and the possibility of error in weighing is triple, since the average baker becomes less cautious on the second weighing. Yet, if a 60-qt mixer is available the mixing takes half the baker's time. Economy of time and materials will result with correct size equipment. Some companies have bowl adapters for their mixers. Thus, a 30-qt bowl will fit a 60-qt mixer, and a 20-qt bowl can be used on the 30-qt mixer. Again, determining the size mixer needed depends on what is to be mixed, and how much. To compute this accurately, the menus and recipes should be consulted. The capacity of mixers given in Table 14.2 will be helpful.

The bench model mixers are usually 5 to 20 qt. Mixers 20 qt or over are attached to the floor. Features recommended are sealed-in motor, stain-

TABLE 14.2. MIXER CAPACITIES

Capacity	20-Qt Mixer	30-Qt Mixer	60-Qt Mixer
Cookies	420 (35 doz)	600 (50 doz)	1200 (100 doz)
Sheet cakes	20 lb	30 lb	60 lb
Pie dough	18 lb	27 lb	50 lb
Yeast rolls	27 lb	45 lb	80 lb

less steel bowls, timer, adequate horsepower (½ hp for 20 qt, ¾ hp for 30 qt, and 1½ hp for a 60 qt), an attachment hub, service available in area and part replacement possible. The larger mixers—60 qt and up—need the bowl dollies and an electric bowl raiser is also available. Additional extras for mixers are dough arms (particularly good for mixing yeast bread), pastry blending beater (used for cutting in fat), bowl rim extenders, and bowl covers (Figs. 14.2A and 14.2B).

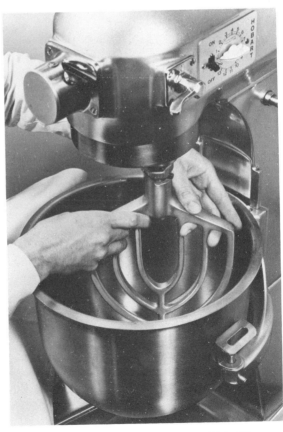

FIG. 14.2A. MIXER WITH BATTER BEATER ATTACHMENT

Courtesy of Hobart Company

FIG. 14.2B. MIXER WITH PASTRY BLENDING BEATER ATTACHMENT

Courtesy of Hobart Company

Attachment hub allows the motor of the mixer to be used for operating attachments that will slice, dice, grate, and chop. The standard equipment that comes with most mixers are a flat beater, a wire whip, and a tinned steel bowl. The attachments for slicing, dicing, grating, and chopping are purchased separately. The tinned steel bowl has a short life, thus stainless steel bowls are recommended.

Cutting Machines

Food cutters are available in two very different pieces of equipment. One is referred to as a food cutter and the other a vertical-cutter-mixer. The food cutter has a rotating bowl with two power-driven knives (Figs. 14.3A and 14.3B) ranging in size and power. Some cutters have the attachment hub with which the motor can be used for attachments that will slice, dice, grate, and chop. If the mixer and the cutter are made by

FIG. 14.3A. FOOD CUTTER AND SLICER

the same manufacturing company the attachments are interchangeable. Safety features are of utmost importance on this piece of equipment. It should be easy to clean and be heavy duty with sufficient horsepower. The cutters are available as bench type or on a pedestal. The cutter can be utilized more efficiently in most kitchens when on a mobile table.

The vertical-cutter-mixer (VCM) when first introduced to this country about 20 to 25 yr ago was called a schnellcutter, German for "fast cutting." The vertical cutter operates at very high speeds, and will cut, mix, and blend in seconds (Fig. 14.4). It has replaced both the mixer and cutter in some foodservices at a reduced cost and with increased efficiency. The VCM will not incorporate air, therefore will not whip meringues or cream. The VCM comes in 25, 40, 60, and larger sizes on special order. Since the VCM has such speed, sometimes a smaller size of the VCM is selected; however, to obtain the maximum speed and labor saving that this piece of equipment will provide, a large foodservice should purchase the size most near the size mixer for the operation. Recipes may need slight adjustments in order for cakes, breads, cookies, pastries, and dressings previously mixed in the mixer to be mixed in the VCM. A water supply and drainage are needed at the location. Special

Courtesy of U.S. Dept. Agr.

FIG. 14.3B. FOOD CUTTER

wiring may be required. The staff must be properly trained to get the full benefit from this piece of equipment. Training is imperative—and it takes more than one demonstration.

For efficient use and ease of cleaning a source of water must be available at the VCM. Three-phase electrical outlets are required. The 40-qt VCM operates at 9 hp 1750 rpm and at 12 hp 3500 rpm. A recessed floor drain enclosure is desirable; however, other types of drains can be hooked up. The bowl tilts forward for easy pouring. A mobile cart is available that puts the pans at the right height for the lip of the bowl when it is tilted for easy pouring.

Slicing machines come in a variety of sizes. The diameter of the blades determines the size pieces of foods can be sliced. The thickness desired is easily set on all models and the range in thickness is broad. The gravity feed, which is at an angle, is recommended over the vertical which requires more physical manpower to operate (Fig. 14.5). An automatic gravity feed is also available and is a labor-saving feature to be considered in larger foodservices.

Much of the exterior should be stainless steel with anodized aluminum used for economy. The knives should be of high quality stainless steel

Courtesy of Hobart Company

FIG. 14.4.   VERTICAL-CUTTER-MIXER HAS MANY USES

that will take and hold a keen edge. Sharpening devices are needed. The knives should be well-guarded with all safety features possible. The machine should be easy to take apart for cleaning with no crevices where food will get caught. Self-contained portion scales to weight portions as they are sliced, and counters that will count the portions as sliced are added features available on some brands.

COOKING EQUIPMENT

How much and what type of cooking equipment will best aid the staff in preparation and cooking? The type food to be prepared and how much is to be prepared are prime concerns in making the selections.

Oven Cooking

Ovens have changed a great deal in the last 20 yr with a greater variety available to choose from and with the standardization of chambers. Convection ovens are rapidly replacing deck ovens. The traditional

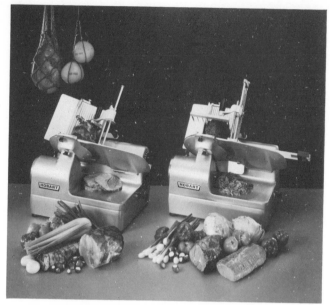

Courtesy of Hobart Company

FIG. 14.5.   SLICING MACHINE WITH GRAVITY FEED

(standard) deck ovens have been reduced in size and bulkiness but increased in capacity. The heavy-duty ovens are standardized to fit the 18-in. modular. For school foodservice the standard heavy-duty oven is recommended over the restaurant range-type ovens. Ovens are available in two main deck heights, known as bake ovens and roast ovens. Bake oven decks are 4 to 8 in. high. Roast oven decks are between 11 and 15 in. high. Frequently a roast oven and a bake oven are stacked. The height of the ovens when stacked should be considered. More than two ovens stacked may put the top deck door too high for the operator to remove pans and then it becomes a safety hazard when a stool is required for the employee to remove the food. The bottom deck, if too close to the floor presents another problem.

An oven should be easy to clean, safe to use, have good insulation, handles that are cool to the touch, doors that will hold up under weight, thermostatic controls of 150 to 550°F on each deck, signal lights to indicate when the oven is on, vented chambers, dampered with baffling, controls in front, easy-to-get-to heights that can be reached by the operator, and be made of 16 to 18 gage metal. The oven should preheat to 450°F in 20 min and have good recovery. The insulation is very important to the efficient, economical operation of the oven. If it is gas operated, the decks give best results when separately fired. When decks are stacked the heat sometimes is uneven and affected by the heat from the decks over or below. Insulation and proper venting are important, particularly when ovens are stacked.

Convection ovens are one of the answers to economy of space and time. These ovens can produce more in 30% less space than the conventional ovens. The ovens have high-speed blowers that constantly circulate the heated air around the food in the oven. The forced air motion increases the absorption of heat, decreases the time needed for cooking most foods, and the temperature at which most foods are cooked is on the average of 25 degrees lower than in the conventional ovens. The decreased time and lower temperatures needed for cooking mean an economy of fuel in operation. The oven bakes, roast/browns, reconstitutes, defrosts, and reheats food (Figs. 14.6A and 14.6B).

The outside dimensions differ from one manufacturer to another, but most standard single-stack ovens hold up to 11 × 18 × 26 in. pans.

Courtesy of U.S. Dept. Agr.

FIG. 14.6A. CONVECTION OVEN WITH FORCED CIRCULATED HEAT WILL BROWN, BAKE, RECONSTITUTE, DEFROST AND REHEAT

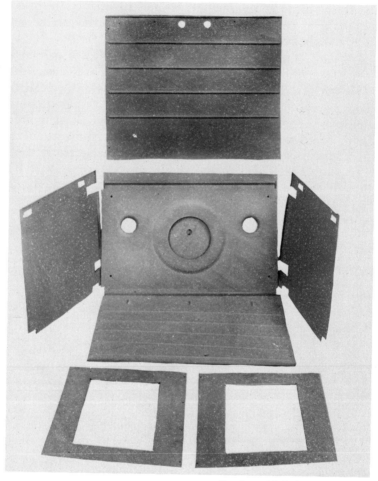

Courtesy of G. S. Blodgett Company

FIG. 14.6B. CONVECTION OVENS WITH REMOVABLE PANELS ARE EASILY
CLEANED

Double stacks can be used if there is limited space in the kitchen. The
thermostat controls are more reliable on single stacks. Some manufacturers have had problems with thermostats when units are stacked.

The oven front should be of stainless steel with either a stainless steel
or porcelainized interior. A minimum of a ¾-hp driven motor is needed on
the fan. The sides and back may be of enamel or stainless steel finishes.

Different types of doors are available, but the French doors have proved very accessible. Heavy-duty chrome-plated racks are recommended. Also, other desirable features include: controls located on front with timer; overload protection; easy-to-read dials that will keep the printed numbers after wear; and lights on the inside with see-through windows.

The capacity of one convection oven has been estimated by Wilkinson (1975) as:

Reheats 88 frozen meals to hot in 20 min.
Cooks 150 lb of beef at one time.
Cooks 120 lb of poultry at one time.
Cooks 480 orders of 2 eggs each.
Bakes six 18- by 26-in. pans of pastries.
Bakes 24 1¼-lb loaves of bread.
Bakes 36 8- to 10-in. pies.
Bakes 75 casserole dishes.
Bakes 3 bushels of 80-count Idaho potatoes.

The roll-in rack convection oven has been designed to be used with the reconstituting of frozen dinners (Fig. 14.7). The dinners can be placed into the rack to store overnight in the freezer or refrigerator then rolled into the oven for reconstitution. The same racks are rolled from the oven to the serving area to be served from. This reduces the handling and saves time. The manufacturers have designed efficiency into these pieces of equipment.

Temperature Controls

Temperature of the oven is very important and should be checked frequently for accuracy.

Microwave ovens are being used very successfully in connection with vending machines in some operations and occasionally used as a backup to the serving counter. The capacity varies from large enough to cook or heat individual entrees up to large enough to cook or heat food in bulk. Microwave ovens are used for thawing, heating, and reheat, but may not brown. The advantage of the microwave oven is the speed. It cooks in seconds. This means that a single serving can be reheated in seconds and can be operated by the students. The food is heated by electromagnetic energy. The length of time required for heating depends on:

(1) Quantity of food being heated.
(2) Temperature of the food being heated.

Courtesy of Vulcan-Hart Corp.

FIG. 14.7. CONVECTION OVEN WITH HIGH-CART DOCKING DEVICE

(3) How large the area of the food in diameter.
(4) Moisture content of the food.
(5) The density of the food.

One potato, requiring 60 min in the conventional oven and 50 min in the convection oven, will bake in 2 min and 15 sec in the microwave oven. However, it takes 3½ min to bake 2 potatoes and 5½ min to bake 4 potatoes. The microwave oven is not efficient enough in quantity cooking but is excellent as a support to quantity cooking.

Top-of-stove Cooking

Ranges (top-of-the-stove cooking) are not being used as much today with tilting skillet and steam-cooking equipment. Some kitchens are completely without top-of-the-stove cooking facilities. The ranges with the magnetic field, which is energized by a coil under the cooking surface, have brought new interest to top-of-stove cooking. The range top does not heat up the room and utilizes energy quite efficiently as the heat goes directly into the pan and stops when the pan is removed.

The heavy-duty or hotel range is designed for large-volume cooking and the wear resulting from use of heavy utensils. The tops are of three main kinds: open top (conventional), hot top (closed top), and fry top (griddle top). Open top has grates directly over the burners. The heat is instant and may be shut off instantly. It has less capacity than the hot tops. The hot tops or closed tops have continuous heat under the top and its efficiency depends on the type and location of the burners. The range can have an oven underneath or a cabinet for storage.

Griddles are being used by some schools to prepare breakfast foods, such as pancakes, bacon, etc. It is particularly good for cooking steaks. The input of Btu is very important, for example a modern gas-fired griddle would need about 30,000 Btu input per burner. It is important that specifications state the Btu input per squre inch with thermostats evenly spaced with "snap-action" thermostats. The griddle ranges in size from 18 in. to 72 in. width, with a level surface, whereas fat does not accumulate but runs off providing an ungreased surface.

Steam Equipment

Steam cooking is efficient and fast. There are three different pieces of equipment using steam to cook: the combination steamer and steam-jacketed kettle, the convection steamer and the countertop steamer (Figs. 14.8, 14.9a and 14.9b). To utilize regular steam cooking to its fullest, there are five requirements of the physical layout. However, this is not needed with the pressureless countertop units.

(1) Adequate Steam Pressure.—A minimum of 15 lb per sq. in. is needed the year round. Live steam from the boiler may produce uneven pressure in different seasons of the year. Self-contained steam-operated equipment is available. An independent boiler for just the foodservice is usually more economical and performs more satisfactorily than the self-contained units.

(2) Water Supply.—The supply of hot and cold water is needed at the point of use. A swing or swivel faucet is recommended, particularly with the steam-jacketed kettle.

Courtesy of U.S. Dept. Agr.

FIG. 14.8.   STEAM KETTLE IS OFTEN USED FOR SAUCES, SOUPS, AND GRAVIES

(3) Adequate Drainage.—Drainage at the point of use is essential for ease in cleaning. A recessed floor with adequate size drain pipes of at least 4 in. are needed. For more than two pieces of steam equipment, 6-in. pipes or 2 4-in. pipes are recommended.

(4) Ventilation.—Good ventilation is necessary. The area needs to be hooded with exhaust fans to remove the steam.

(5) Power Source Adequate.—Adequate voltage and phase are required, and if a gas unit, the supply of gas must be sufficient for efficient use of the equipment.

Steamers use the live-steam injected into the cooking area in direct contact with the food. It is a method of cooking preferred for cooking vegetables, especially because the retention of nutritional food value is greater than with most other methods of cooking. Steamers are fast, efficient, eliminate the need for heavy pots and pans, and encourage batch (as you need it) preparation which helps eliminate leftovers. The color and texture of food are preserved. There is a reduction in shrinkage of meats when cooked by steam. The food is cooked and served in the same pans, thus eliminating some pot and pan washing. Many foods can

Courtesy of Cleveland Range Co.

FIG. 14.9a. THIS COUNTERTOP NATURAL CONVECTION STEAMER HAS A SELF-CONTAINED STEAM GENERATOR. PERFECT FOR BATCH COOKING RIGHT BEHIND THE SERVING LINE, IT MAKES OFFERING CHOICES MORE POSSIBLE

Courtesy of Cleveland Range Co.

FIG. 14.9b. THIS REVOLUTIONARY STEAMER IS A PRESSURELESS FORCED CONVECTION STEAMER. THE FULLY AUTOMATIC OPERATION PROVIDES FASTER COOKING AND CAN BE OPENED SAFELY WITH THE TOUCH ON THE PANEL

be cooked efficiently by steam, in addition to vegetables, such as pasta and rice, eggs, and moist-heat cooked meats.

Further argument in favor of the steamer is that it requires little floor space, reduces the loss of heat in the kitchen while cooking, and it is possible to cook different foods in the same chamber without transfer of flavor.

Steamers should be of stainless steel interior finish with automatic safety devices that will prevent the door from being opened when the unit is on. Baked-on enamel is a satisfactory exterior finish; however, stainless steel is available. The low-pressure steamers operate at 5- to 8-lb pressure, and the high compression steamers operate at 15-lb pressure and cook considerably faster. Employees are often afraid to use steam equipment, so thorough demonstration and follow-up is recommended to be certain the steam equipment is utilized. New employees should be trained in how to operate steam equipment. A convection-steamer is the combined convection cooking and steam. The steam circulates through convection generators around food with a cooking speed compared to 15 pound pressure. Since there is no pressure in the compartment you can open the door at any point adding more food without interrupting the cooking. Each compartment has the capacity for three 12 × 20 × 2½ inch steamtable pans.

The steam-jacketed kettle is described by Jule Wilkinson in *The Complete Book of Cooking Equipment* (1975), as "two stainless steel hemispheres, or bowls, one sealed inside the other with about 2 in. of space in between for the steam." Steam-jacketed kettles come full jacketed, with steam all the way to the top, and ⅔ jacketed. The diameters vary as well as the capacity. Kettles range in size from 1 qt to 200 gal. The most common size table models are 10 to 20-qt tilting kettles, sometimes referred to as a *trunnion* kettle. The floor or wall models come in many sizes but the most commonly-used sizes in school feeding are 20, 30, 40, and 60 gal. Above 60-gal. kettles are actually too large for people to operate—too high and really unmanageable. Two 30-gal. kettles, or a 40 and a 20, would be a better choice, perhaps, than a 60-gal. kettle. A stationary large kettle is safer, less trouble, and more satisfactory for a school foodservice than the large tilting kettles.

Selecting the size kettle needed should be determined by:

(1) Number preparing for.
(2) Size portions to be prepared.
(3) Type foods to be prepared.

Table 14.3 is a good guide for determining size. If spaghetti sauce and soup are on the menu frequently, the one-cup portion will probably be used; therefore, the kettle chosen should be large enough to prepare in one batch the total amount of soup or sauce needed for serving one-cup portions. The kettle lends itself to the cooking of soups, sauces, gravies, chili con carne, stews, puddings, pie fillings, gelatins, and other such type foods that can be prepared in bulk and not in small batches.

TABLE 14.3. TOTAL USABLE CAPACITIES OF STEAM–JACKETED KETTLES[1]

| Kettle Size (Gal.) | Total Usable Capacity | | | | |
| | | Number of Individual Servings | | | |
	Gal.	Full Cup	¾ Cup	½ Cup	¼ Cup
20	16	256	341	512	1024
30	24	384	512	768	1536
40	32	512	683	1024	2048
60	48	768	1024	1536	3072

Source: *Planning School Food Service Facilities,* U.S. Dept. Agr., Washington, D.C.
[1]The above table is based on 80% usable capacity. Manufacturers generally express kettle size as total kettle capacity (level full) and the usable capacity is approximately 20% less than what is stated.

A trunnion or tilting kettle—table mounted, with a 10 to 20 qt capacity—along with a steam-jacketed kettle can replace the need for top-
of-the-stove cooking. The small kettles that tilt can be used for everything ordinarily done on the top of the stove.

The interior of the steam-jacketed kettle is 18-8 gage stainless steel,
and the exterior is stainless steel or aluminum with the former recommended. The rim should be rounded for safety. A draw-off valve is
very convenient. There should be safety features, such as a safety valve
and pressure gage that is easy to read located in a convenient place. The
stationary kettles can be mounted on legs, on a wall, or on a pedestal.
Tilting braising pan is an oversized skillet. You can do many types of
cooking in this one pan, from sauteeing to cooking with moisture. It can
be used to grill meats, scramble eggs, saute vegetables, cook soups or
cereals, fry bacon, or make a casserole. The piece of equipment can be
mobile or permanently installed. A floor drain is desirable. The pans have
thermostatically controlled temperatures and are made of stainless steel
or cast iron.

Fryers

Deep-fat fryers are more and more prevalent in school feeding today
with deep fried foods being very popular. Features to look for in a deep
fat fryer are: temperature control; fast recovery time; self-draining devices with fat filtering; sturdy, heavy duty features; ease of cleaning; and
all the safety features possible. To estimate the number of fryers needed
and the capacity of the fryers needed, calculate the quantity of food to be
fried during the meal. This can be done by multiplying the number
served per serving period by the largest item fried (in ounces), to find the
number of pounds of food to be fried. For example: with a student
participation of 300 and two seatings, with no more than 200 in any
seating; 200 × 4 oz of French fries equal 800 oz or 50 lb of French fries.

Pressure fryers cook with fat as the medium in a tightly covered "pot".
Moisture is held in and the temperature at which you cook can be
lowered. Since water is an enemy to fat, it is essential that the condensate be removed.

CLEANING EQUIPMENT

Dishwashing machines are an intricate part of sanitation, and they are
a large investment. The price difference of models often encourages unwise decisions. The size of the operation, the number of dishes, the
amount of labor, and the time within which to wash dishes are to be considered in making a selection. Will a door-type, a single- or double-tank
conveyor or a flight-type dishwasher be needed?

Dish Table

The dish table setup is as important to the efficient operation as the dishwasher. A minimum of 100 in. of clean dish table is needed for a conveyor machine. And if only one dishroom operator is available, 120 in. should be considered minimum. The 100 in. is sufficient space for four racks to dry. The soiled dish table should be a minimum of 100 in. The tables should be constructed of 14-gage polished stainless steel. The arrangement of the disposable and pre-rinse sink can make for an efficiently flowing operation or become a bottle neck. The length and arrangement of the layout can yield maximum efficiency or, if incorrect, can cut the output to 25% or less.

General Features of Dishwashers

General features desired in a dishwasher are that the interior be constructed of 16 gage stainless steel or of a material that has been proved will hold up under the heat and detergents. Galvanized metals have a life of 7 to 10 yr, whereas stainless steel can be expected to last 14 to 20 yr depending on care and use. A 14 to 16 gage stainless steel is recommended for the interior and exterior of the machine. Automatic thermostats and automatic cycles are essential for the best operation. The legs should be seated with adjustable bullet-type or sanitary-type feet. A front inspection door is recommended. Ease in cleaning the machine should be considered. The NSF and UL approval seals should be on the machine.

The 20 × 20 in. racks are standard. The all plastic racks are light in weight and hold up well. Adequate supply of water is essential. The wash water temperature must be at 140 to 160°F with the rinse water 180 to 200°F. A booster heater or electric tank heater is used to raise the temperature of the fill water from 140 to 180°F. Three dial-type hydraulic thermometers at the top of the machine should indicate the temperatures of the water in each cycle. Adequate ventilation is necessary for removing the steam and heat. Electronic or hydraulic detergent dispensers and rinse injectors are available and recommended.

With increased concerns for energy costs have come many advancements and changes in equipment. The low-temperature dishwashers reduce energy usage, have a lower initial cost, but have a lower capacity. For example, a single rack machine will wash only 28 racks of dishes per hour compared to 53 racks per hour for the hot-temperature machines. The level of sanitation with chemicals in the low-temperature dishwasher is higher than with the hot-temperature machine.

The base price of a dishwasher may be deceiving. The options that may be considered as essentials by the purchaser will change the price considerably. The standard number of racks furnished with each machine is usually not adequate. The efficiency of the machine would be hampered by lack of racks.

The capacity of a machine can be misleading. The companies' advertisements may be based on 100% capacity which is impossible to accomplish in a normal operation. Seventy percent of the actual capacity of the machine is a more realistic figure.

Door-type Machine.—The door-type single-tank machines will operate acceptably for up to 250, possibly 300 lunches. It requires opening and closing of the doors. The machine fits into a small area for a straight-through operation or a corner operation. Manually or electrically timed wash and rinse cycles are available. The electrically timed is recommended.

Single-tank Conveyor.—The single-tank conveyor is adequate for 600 to 800 lunches. The conveyor machine has curtains at either end and the racks are carried by a conveyor through the machine, from the wash to the rinse, and to the drying, and out the machine (Fig. 14.10). The clearance (height) inside the tank should be noted. The water is usually recycled, and thus helps economize on water used. The speed of the conveyor is preset under regulations of the National Sanitation Foundation.

Two-tank machines.—The two-tank machines feature power-wash and power-rinse that cuts the time, resulting in a faster operation. This size machine can accommodate dishes for 2000 satisfactorily. The quantity of water used by a particular machine should be considered. The addition of a belt conveyor leading into the machine can increase the efficiency of the operation two-fold. The belt tends to cause the employees to work rhythmically and to keep their minds on the assembling and speed of the operation.

Three-tank machine.—The three-tank machine has a prewash tank that saves considerable time. Many of the one-, two-, and three-tank machines with forced water have been able to virtually eliminate the need for pre-rinse which can slow-down an operation. The only objection is the food accumulation and the water being recycled. A high-pressured, hand-operated spray over a sink with disposal unit is efficient if employees are trained in using for pre-rinsing racked dishes.

Flight-type Machine.—The flight-type machine is a rackless operation that is available with one, two or three tanks. It has continuous action and therefore uses a lot of water and detergents. Two to four people are required for loading and unloading this machine to obtain the efficiency intended. It does accommodate all sizes and shapes of dishes and small

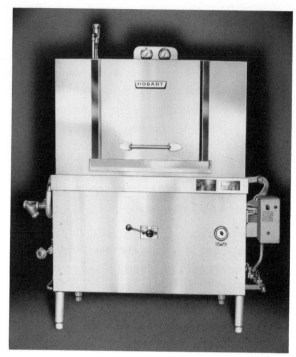

FIG. 14.10. CONVEYOR
DISHWASHER

Courtesy of Hobart Company

equipment, and there is no lifting of trays. The speed of the conveyor can
be regulated according to number on assembly and number of soiled
dishes. This is a piece of equipment that may be considered when serving
over 1000 lunches. Considerable space is required.

Using a Dishwasher

The use of a dishwasher as only a sterilizer is a complete waste of
detergent and water. The machine should be used for cleaning as well as
sterilizing. Dishwashers can and should be used to wash utensils and
equipment other than dishes. Any piece of equipment that can be immersed into 180°F water and that will fit into or on a rack with sufficient
top of machine clearance—and this should be checked carefully—can be
washed quickly, sterilized and started on its way to drying by the dishwasher, especially pots and pans. With energy conservation; however,
low temperature dishwashing, using chemicals for sanitizing, will slow the
drying process.

Sinks

Sinks are ordinarily a part of the initial layout, and sinks made of stainless steel will usually last the life of the building. However, if it is necessary to purchase a sink, only stainless steel should be considered. Galvanized is most unsatisfactory. The sinks should be constructed of stainless steel, welded seamless, with coved corners, drain boards that slope toward center for draining, bottom to slope to drain and a mixing faucet with swing spout.

Local and state health department codes will determine the minimum number of hand sinks and compartments sinks needed in a foodservice. The basic design and construction of a pot sink, vegetable sink, or cook's sink should include rounded corners, made of 14 gage 18-8 stainless steel with one-piece or seamless construction and knee-action drain stoppers. The legs are of 14 gage tubular stainless steel with adjusting bullet feet. The height of the sink bottom from the floor should be considered, as well as the dimensions of the compartments. A vegetable sink has two compartments, and the recommended size for each compartment is 20 × 20 and 14 in. deep, inside measurement. Two drainboards each 24 in. long are suggested both draining into the sink. The pot and pan sink is a three-compartment sink with drainboards at either end. The cook's sink may be only one-compartment sink, as small as 15 × 15 × 8 in. and 12 in. deep.

REFRIGERATION

Self-contained refrigerator and freezer units have far more capacity today than a few years back. The compressors are more compact and are frequently housed at the top, which means the unit can be taller, utilizing all the space and increasing capacity. Self-defrosting refrigeration can be equipped with cycle-timed clock, which automatically defrosts at specific times of the day with continuous condensate evaporation. This has eliminated the need for a plumbing connection and for manual defrosting. A one-piece constructed interior of stainless steel is recommended. The exterior may be of porcelain enamel finish, aluminum, or stainless steel. The porcelain enamel finishes have added colors to the kitchen. Mounted exterior thermometer should be visible on the front of the unit with color indicating temperature zones: for example, red markings indicating danger zone, with green indicating safe temperatures. A visual alarm system that will indicate when the temperature is above the recommended safe zone is helpful.

The doors of refrigerators and freezers come full or half, hinged, and self-closing or sliding. The quality of the hinges and tightness of the gasket fit should be closely checked. The standard number of shelves supplied with the units are usually not sufficient for most foodservices. The shelves should be of heavy-duty material that have adjustable brackets to space the shelves as wanted. If over 60 cu ft of refrigeration is needed, a walk-in unit is recommended. The shelves should be adjustable and the size to accommodate the modulars of 14 × 18 and 18 × 26 in. The self-contained units are not built to take rough treatment. The storage of heavy meats and crates will show on the unit quickly. Refrigeration units seem to be the least durable of kitchen equipment today and need considerable improvement.

Refrigerated units come in reach-ins, pass-thrus, roll-ins, counter-type refrigeration, display refrigeration, portable or mobile refrigeration, and refrigerated dispensers (Fig. 14.11). Ice makers may be needed. Salad bars have increased that need. The size refrigerator or freezer needed depends on whether a walk-in unit is available and what is going to be stored in the unit and how much. With an increase in frozen foods used,

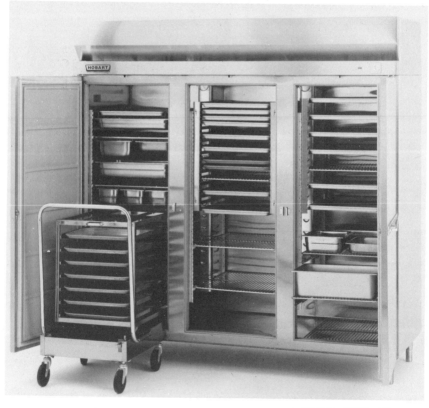

Courtesy of Hobart Company

FIG. 14.11. REFRIGERATOR WITH PAN FILES

many foodservices need more freezer space than previously allocated. In determining the number of cubic feet of space needed, it is helpful to know that one cubic foot will hold approximately 30 lb of food. Approximately 2.1 lb of food (as purchased) is used in preparing one meal. Schools serving 125 to 200 meals per day will need 17 to 20 cu ft of refrigeration. Plan for 10 cu ft more per each 100 meals (Fig. 14.12).

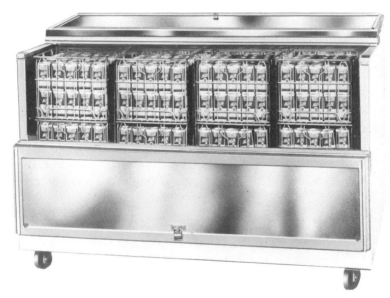

Courtesy of Beverage-Air Sales Company

FIG. 14.12. MILK COOLER WITH FRONT LOADING WILL HOLD AS MANY AS 16 CASES OF MILK

MOBILE EQUIPMENT

Mobile equipment is flexible and convenient, saving space and man-hours. Mobile equipment makes work easier and reduces the handling of foods and supplies. A lightweight cart will not hold up under heavy-duty jobs. Mobile equipment is subject to heavy impact loads and heavy stress, and the design materials, and construction have to be adequate to take this. Mobile equipment should contain few bolts and screws and be welded where possible. The wheels should be easy to roll and built to maneuver quietly and easily. The capacity of mobile units and the size wheels should be coordinated. The 3-in. wheels will hold loads up to 200 lb; 5-in. wheels will hold loads up to 400 lb; 8-in. wheels will hold up to 600 lb; and 10-in. wheels will carry loads exceeding 600 lb. Therefore, utility carts and wheel size needed will be determined by the load to be carried and the space for maneuvering the carts in.

Wheels are easier to guide when two rigid casters are at the guiding end and the swivel casters are at the front end. All-swivel casters on a piece of equipment ensure easy movement from side to side, and these are recommended for dolly equipment that is to be moved short distances. However, all-swivel casters are hard to guide in straight travel. Wheel locks that will hold when the cart is stopped are recommended. Bumpers on the equipment will protect the walls and other equipment. Rubber tread wheels with ball-bearings are recommended.

SMALL EQUIPMENT

When purchasing small equipment, check for durable, heavy-duty construction and for material that will withstand sterilizing temperatures and strong detergents. Institutional small equipment should be of a better, heavier quality than would normally be used at home. One of the most common problems with metal equipment is rusting. Stainless steel and heavy aluminum are recommended. The materials used for construction should be smooth, nontoxic, nonabsorbent, sanitary, and corrosion resistant.

Aluminum has the advantage of being lighter in weight than some other metals and a good conductor of heat. However, aluminum utensils may become discolored by alkali and acid foods.

Stainless steel wears indefinitely. It has the advantage of being easy to clean, resistant to ordinary stains and corrosion, and sanitary. Stainless steel withstands temperatures and holds up well in sudden change in temperatures.

Plastics are most frequently used for tableware in schools. The choices are limitless, and checking quality and durability is the job of the foodservice. Small equipment includes numerous items with many grades and designs to choose from. Therefore, they will not be discussed in detail here. The trade catalogs and current publications offer the most help in writing specifications and making selections. Testing small quantities before purchasing in large quantities is recommended.

RECORDS

Records should be kept on each piece of large or mechanical equipment purchased. These records should contain information as to when purchased, from whom, model, serial number, electrical information, etc. (Figs. 14.13 and 14.14). For guaranteed equipment, the warranty card has to be completed and returned to the manufacturer. The guarantee

Item_____ Trade Name___ _____

Manufacturer_____ Model No. _____

Serial No. _____ Description_____

Capacity_____ Attachments _____

Operation: _____ Gas _____ Steam _____ Hand _____ Elect _____ Voltage_____

Cycle_____ Phase_____

Dealer or Vendor_____ Address _____

_____ Person to Contact _____ Phone No. _____

Date Purchased_____ Warranty Period_____

Purchased Price_____ Life of Equipment___ _____

Remarks:

SERVICE AND REPAIRS

Date	Nature of Service	Parts, etc.	Service Co.	Cost

FIG. 14.13. SAMPLE FOOD SERVICE EQUIPMENT RECORD

period should be recorded. Repairs and problems with the piece of equipment should be recorded. This information will be very useful in the future for determining if a brand of equipment should be purchased again. This record may be kept by the individual food service or by the main office if a centralized system is to be used.

DEPRECIATION OF EQUIPMENT

Depreciation of nonexpendable equipment is required to be calculated in connection with cost based accounting if depreciation is to be used as an expense. It is usually to the advantage of the school foodservice program to use equipment depreciation to justify full reimbursement rates. Nonexpendable equipment includes all foodservice equipment with a useful life of more than one year and a purchase price of $300 or more.

BOARD OF EDUCATION OF BALTIMORE COUNTY SCHOOL LUNCH OFFICE

TOWSON, MARYLAND 21204

SCHOOL LUNCH PREVENTIVE MAINTENANCE CHECKLIST

School _____   School No. _____   Address _____

Dishwasher
- ☐ Lubricate all points
- ☐ Change oil in transmission (once a year)
- ☐ Check pump assembly for leaks
- ☐ Check pump impeller
- ☐ Check pump pressure
- ☐ Check manifolds for play
- ☐ Check spray tubes
- ☐ Check and clean rinse nozzles
- ☐ Check final rinse lever
- ☐ Check drain and overflow
- ☐ Check fill valve washers for leaks
- ☐ Check rinse rapid action valve
- ☐ Check conveyor for tension and adjustment
- ☐ Check curtains (2 complete sets)
- ☐ Check door cables and pulley
- ☐ Check thermometers
- ☐ Check scrap trays
- ☐ Clean pump intake screen

Convection Oven
- ☐ Lubricate all points
- ☐ Check chamber seal
- ☐ Check timer
- ☐ Replace defective bulbs
- ☐ Check and adjust door tension

Slicers
- ☐ Sharpen blade
- ☐ Lubricate all points

T & S Pre-Rinse
- ☐ Check base
- ☐ Check squeeze valve
- ☐ Check check valves
- ☐ Check rubber bumper
- ☐ Clean spray head
- ☐ Check bracket
- ☐ Check hose

Can Opener
- ☐ Check blades
- ☐ Check gears
- ☐ Lubricate
- ☐ Leave (1) extra blade*

Stock Kettle
- ☐ Drain, flush and refill with rush inhibitor
- ☐ Check safety valves

Refrigeration Units
- ☐ Clean condensers and unit
- ☐ Lubricate all points
- ☐ Check belts, condition, tension and alignment
- ☐ Check head and back pressure
- ☐ Check sight glass for proper charge
- ☐ Check gaskets on water cooled condensers
- ☐ Check oil in compressor body
- ☐ Check tubing brackets
- ☐ Check and eliminate tubing rub
- ☐ Check door gaskets for condition and seal

Food Chopper

- ☐ Hone blades
- ☐ Tighten and adjust knives
- ☐ Lubricate all points
- ☐ Check hydraulic system
- ☐ Check for play in shaft
- ☐ Check brushes
- ☐ Check bowl rotation
- ☐ Clean and lubricate under bowl and top of plate

Steamers

- ☐ Drain, clean, flush and refill boiler
- ☐ Check safety valves
- ☐ Check door gaskets
- ☐ Lubricate handwheel shaft
- ☐ Check thermostatic vent
- ☐ Replace hand hole gasket
- ☐ Check muffler

Knives

- ☐ Sharpen and hone all knives
  (Except Wearever(Serrated

Dippers

- ☐ Replace springs
- ☐ Leave (2) extra springs*

*Note–Dipper springs (2) and extra can opener blade will be left on school's copy of checklist–on table in kitchen.

- ☐ Check door hinges and latches
- ☐ Check door locks
- ☐ Clean all fixture drains
- ☐ Oil condenser fan motor
- ☐ Check fan blades for alignment
- ☐ Note if suction line insulation is needed

Note: Pump down all open units on the spring check; electrically disconnect all others

Mixer or VCM

- ☐ Lubricate
- ☐ Check for oil leaks
- ☐ Remove broken whip wires
- ☐ Check switch
- ☐ Check blades
- ☐ Check lid gasket

Disposal

- ☐ Lubricate all points
- ☐ Check for sharpness
- ☐ Check seals for leaks
- ☐ Check flow switch and rapid action valve

Equipment Maintenance _____ Signature of Service Man _____ Date _____ Signature of School Representative

Refrigeration Maintenance _____ Signature of Service Man _____ Date _____ Signature of School Representative

BC-32-740-72

Courtesy of Baltimore County (Md.) Board of Education, School Lunch Office

FIG. 14.14. PREVENTIVE MAINTENANCE CHECKLIST

Depreciation is based on the concept of "using up" the equipment. For example, if a piece of equipment is expected to last 12 years, one-twelfth of the equipment's usefulness is "used up" each year of service. After the 12 years it is considered fully depreciated.

A depreciation record is needed on each piece of nonexpendable equipment with basic information to include: (1) net acquisition cost, (2) date purchased, (3) Federal equipment funds used, if any, and (4) depreciable life. All non-expendable equipment is considered to have a useful life of 12 years, whereas transporting equipment, used in transporting food from one location to another, has a shorter life. The state agency will provide information on life expectancy and details for figuring the depreciation. When Federal equipment funds have contributed to the purchase, that is subtracted from acquisition cost before depreciation is figured.

TRAINING AND DEMONSTRATIONS

On-the-job training is important for employees to operate the piece of equipment correctly and to get full value of the equipment. If steps are to be followed in sequence of operation it may be numbered and written on the equipment or posted near the equipment. Giving a worker the manual to read does not accomplish what on-the-job training does by demonstration of the correct ways to use, care for, and clean. Vendors should be requested to give demonstration and instruction on use and care of the new piece of equipment. This should be written into the bid specifications. Films are available that show step-by-step direction of using and cleaning pieces of equipment. The manufacturers can furnish these films.

CARE AND MAINTENANCE

High-quality equipment, though more expensive initially, may be more economical in the long run. Handling and care of equipment by employees will determine the life of the equipment. An untrained employee operating a mixer can do considerable damage to the motor.

Preventive maintenance requires periodic checking of equipment for loose bolts, worn parts, greasing if needed, and general repairs before the equipment has broken down. The advantages, as proven by Lyle Root of Baltimore County (Md.), are longer equipment life and reduced maintenance costs (Fig. 14.14). Breakdowns of equipment during operation are inconvenient to the operator and are more costly than preventive maintenance in time and money.

A franchised factory service agency should be used when repairs are needed. Manufacturers will stand behind service and usually have servicemen better trained for the type of equipment. Specifications for purchasing equipment may include that a local service company carries parts for the equipment purchased. Many larger school systems have their own maintenance department with servicemen trained to repair the equipment in the schools.

Food Service Equipment Assistance Program

Under the Federal Food Service Assistance Program funds have been made available for several years for establishing, maintaining and expanding food services. The funds provide up to 75% of the costs where 33% of the children qualify for free and reduced-price meals.

BIBLIOGRAPHY

AVERY, ARTHUR C. 1980. A Modern Guide to Foodservice Equipment. CBI Publishing Co., Boston.

JERNIGAN, A.K. 1968. The NSF seal of approval. Hospital *12*, 98.

JERNIGAN, ANNA KATHERINE, and LYNNE NANNEN ROSS. 1974. Food Service Equipment: Selection, Arrangement, and Use. Iowa State Univ. Press, Ames, Iowa.

KAZARIAN, EDWARD A. 1975. Food Service Facilities Planning. AVI Publishing Company, Westport, Conn.

KOTSCHEVAR, L.H., and MARGARET E. TERRELL. 1977. Foodservice Planning Layout and Equipment. 2nd Edition. John Wiley & Sons, New York.

KRIMMEL, GARY. 1977. Energy and the kitchen. Food Management 12, No. 6, 43−46+.

MYERS, MAES R. 1979. Commercial Kitchens. 6th Edition. American Gas Association, Arlington, Va.

U.S. DEPT. AGR. 1974. Equipment Guide for On-Site School Kitchens. U.S. Govt. Printing Office, Washington, D.C.

U.S. DEPT. AGR. 1980. Equipment Guide for Child Care Centers. U.S. Govt. Printing Office, Washington, D.C.

U.S. DEPT. LABOR. 1970. All About OSHA. U.S. Govt Printing Office, Washington, D.C.

WEST, BESSIE B., LEVELLE WOOD, VIRGINIA HARGER, and GRACE SHUGART. 1977. Food Service in Institutions. 6th Edition. John Wiley & Sons, New York.

WILKINSON, J. 1975. The Complete Book of Cooking Equipment. Revised Edition. Cahners Publishing Co., Boston, Mass.

APPENDIX I

National School Lunch Act Public Law 396—79th Congress

ORIGINAL BILL—JUNE 4, 1946—AN ACT

To provide assistance to the States in the establishment, maintenance, operation, and expansion of school-lunch programs, and for other purposes.

Be it enacted by the Senate and House of Representatives of the United States of America in Congress assembled. That this Act may be cited as the "National School Lunch Act".

DECLARATION OF POLICY

SEC. 2. It is hereby declared to be the policy of Congress, as a measure of national security, to safeguard the health and well-being of the Nation's children and to encourage the domestic consumption of nutritious agricultural commodities and other food, by assisting the States, through grants-in-aid and other means, in providing an adequate supply of foods and other facilities for the establishment, maintenance operation, and expansion of nonprofit school-lunch programs.

APPROPRIATIONS AUTHORIZED

SEC. 3. For each fiscal year, beginning with the fiscal year ending June 30, 1947, there is hereby authorized to be appropriated, out of money in the Treasury not otherwise appropriated, such sums as may be necessary to enable the Secretary of Agriculture (hereinafter referred to as "the Secretary") to carry out the provisions of this Act.

APPORTIONMENTS TO STATES

SEC. 4. The sums appropriated for any fiscal year pursuant to the authorization contained in section 3 of this Act, excluding the sum specified in section 5, shall be available to the Secretary for supplying, during such fiscal year, agricultural commodities and other foods for the school-lunch program in accordance with the provisions of this Act. The Secretary shall apportion among the States during each fiscal year not less than 75 per centum of the aforesaid funds made available for such year for supplying agricultural commodities and other foods under the provisions of this Act, except that the total of such apportionment of funds for use in Alaska, Territory of Hawaii, Puerto Rico, and the Virgin Islands shall not exceed 3 per centum of the funds appropriated for agricultural commodities and other food for the school-lunch program. Apportionment among the States shall be made on the basis of two factors: (1) The number of school children in the State and (2) the need for assistance in the State as indicated by the relation of the per capita income in the United States to the per capita income in the State. The amount of the initial apportionment to any State shall be determined by the following method: First, determine an index for the State by multiplying factors (1) and (2); second, divide this index by the sum of the indices for all the States; and, finally, apply the figure thus obtained to the total funds to be apportioned. For the purpose of this section, the number of school children in the State shall be the number of children therein between the ages of five and seventeen, inclusive; such figures and per capita income figures shall be the latest figures certified by the Department of Commerce. For the purposes of this Act, "school" means any public or nonprofit private school of high-school grade or under and, with respect to Puerto Rico, shall also include nonprofit child-care centers certified as such by the Governor of Puerto Rico. If any State cannot utilize all funds so apportioned to it, or if additional funds are available under this Act for apportionment among the States, the Secretary shall make further apportionments to the remaining States in the same manner.

SEC. 5. Of the sums appropriated for any fiscal year pursuant to the authorization contained in section 3 of this Act, $10,000,000 shall be available to the secretary for the purpose of providing, during such fiscal year, nonfood assistance for the school-lunch program pursuant to the provisions of this Act. The Secretary shall apportion among the States during each fiscal year the aforesaid sum of $10,000,000, and such apportionment among the States shall be on the basis of the factors, and in accordance with the standards, set forth in section 4 with respect to the apportionment for agricultural commodities and other foods. The total of such funds apportioned for nonfood assistance for use in Alaska, Territory of Hawaii, Puerto Rico, and the Virgin Islands shall not exceed 3 per centum of the funds appropriated for nonfood assistance in accordance with the provisions of this Act.

DIRECT FEDERAL EXPENDITURES

SEC. 6. The funds appropriated for any fiscal year for carrying out the provisions of this Act, less not to exceed 3½ per centum thereof hereby made available to the Secretary for his administrative expenses and less the amount apportioned by him pursuant to sections 4, 5, and 10, shall be available to the Secretary during such year for direct expenditure by him for agricultural commodities and other foods to be distributed among the States and schools participating in the school-lunch program under this Act in accordance with the needs as determined by the local school authorities. The provisions of law contained in the proviso of the Act of June 28, 1937 (50 Stat. 323), facilitating operations with respect to the purchase and disposition of surplus agricultural commodities under section 32 of the Act approved August 24, 1935 (49 Stat. 774), as amended, shall, to the extent not inconsistent with the provisions of this Act, also be applicable to expenditures of funds by the Secretary under this Act.

PAYMENTS TO STATES

SEC. 7. Funds apportioned to any State pursuant to section 4 or 5 during any fiscal year shall be available for payment to such State for disbursement by the State educational agency, in accordance with such agreements not inconsistent with the provisions of this Act, as may be entered into by the Secretary and such State educational agency, for the purpose of assisting schools of that State during such fiscal year, in supplying (1) agricultural commodities and other foods for consumption by children and (2) nonfood assistance in furtherance of the school-lunch program authorized under this Act. Such payments to any State in any fiscal year during the period 1947 to 1950, inclusive, shall be made upon condition that each dollar thereof will be matched during such year by $1 from sources within the State determined by the Secretary to have been expended in connection with the school-lunch program under this Act. Such payments in any fiscal year during the period 1951 to 1955, inclusive, shall be made upon condition that each dollar thereof will be so matched by one and one-half dollars; and for any fiscal year thereafter, such payments shall be made upon condition that each dollar will be so matched by $3. In the case of any State whose per capita income is less than the per capita income of the United States, the matching required for any fiscal year shall be decreased by the percentage which the State per capita income is below the per capita income of the United States. For the purpose of determining whether the matching requirements of this section and section 10, respectively, have been met, the reasonable value of donated services, suppliers, facilities, and equipment as certified, respectively, by the State educational agency and in case of schools receiving funds pursuant to section 10, by such schools (but not the cost or value of land, of the acquisition, construction, or alteration of buildings of commodities donated by the Secretary, or of Federal contributions), may be regarded as funds from sources within the State expended in connection with the school-lunch program. The Secretary shall certify to the Secretary of the Treasury from time to time the amounts to be paid to any State under this section and the time or times such amounts are to be paid; and the Secretary of the Treasury shall pay to the State at the time or times fixed by the Secretary the amounts so certified.

STATE DISBURSEMENT TO SCHOOLS

SEC. 8. Funds paid to any State during any fiscal year pursuant to section 4 or 5 shall be disbursed by the State educational acency, in accordance with such agreements approved by the Secretary as may be entered into by such State agency and the schools in the State, to those schools in the State which the State educational agency, taking into account need and attendance, determines are eligible to participate in the school-lunch program. Such disbursement to any school shall be made only for the purpose of reimbursing it for the cost of obtaining agricultural commodities and other foods for consumption by children in the school-lunch program and nonfood assistance in connection with such program. Such food costs may include, in addition to the purchase price of agricultural commodities and other foods, the cost of processing, distributing, transporting, storing, or handling thereof. In no event shall such disbursement for food to any school for any fiscal year exceed an amount determined by multiplying the number of lunches served in the school in the school-lunch program under this Act during such year by the maximum Federal food-cost contribution rate for the State, for the type of lunch served, as prescribed by the Secretary.

NUTRITIONAL AND OTHER PROGRAM REQUIREMENTS

SEC. 9. Lunches served by schools participating in the school-lunch program under this Act shall meet minimum nutritional requirements prescribed by the Secretary on the basis of tested nutritional research.

Such meals shall be served without cost or at a reduced cost to children who are determined by local school authorities to be unable to pay the full cost of the lunch. No physical segregation of or other discrimination against any child shall be made by the school because of his inability to pay. School-lunch programs under this Act shall be operated on a non-profit basis. Each school shall, insofar as practicable, utilize in its lunch program commodities designated from time to time by the Secretary as being in abundance, either nationally or in the school area, or commodities donated by the Secretary. Commodities purchased under the authority of section 32 of the Act of August 24, 1935 (49 Stat. 774), as amended, may be donated by the Secretary to schools, in accordance with the needs as determined by local school authorities, for utilization in the school-lunch program under this Act as well as to other schools carrying out nonprofit school-lunch programs and institutions authorized to receive such commodities.

SEC. 10. If, in any State, the State educational agency is not permitted by law to disburse the funds paid to it under this Act to nonprofit private schools in the State, or is not permitted by law to match Federal funds made available for use by such nonprofit private schools, the Secretary shall withhold from the funds apportioned to any such State under sections 4 and 5 of this Act the same proportion of the funds as the number of children between the ages of five and seventeen, inclusive, attending nonprofit private schools within the State is of the total number of persons of those ages within the State attending school. The Secretary shall disburse the funds so withheld directly to the nonprofit private schools within said State for the same purposes and subject to the same conditions as are authorized or required with respect to the disbursements to schools within the State by the State educational agency, including the requirement that any such payment or payments shall be matched, in the proportion specified in section 7 for such State, by funds from sources within the State expended by nonprofit private schools within the State participating in the school-lunch program under this Act. Such funds shall not be considered a part of the funds constituting the matching funds under the terms of section 7.

MISCELLANEOUS PROVISIONS AND DEFINITIONS

SEC. 11 (a) States, State educational agencies, and schools participating in the school-lunch program under this Act shall keep such accounts and records as may be necessary to enable the Secretary to determine whether the provisions of this Act are being complied with. Such accounts and records shall at all times be available for inspection and audit by representatives of the Secretary and shall be preserved for such period of time, not in excess of five years, as the Secretary determines is necessary.

(b) The Secretary shall incorporate, in his agreements with the State educational agencies, the express requirements under this Act with respect to the operation of the school-lunch program under this Act insofar as they may be applicable and such other provisions as in his opinion are reasonably necessary or appropriate to effectuate the purposes of this Act.

(c) In carrying out the provisions of this Act, neither the Secretary nor the State shall impose any requirement with respect to teaching, personnel, curriculum, instruction, methods of instruction, and materials of instruction in any school. If a State maintains separate schools for minority and for majority races, no funds made available pursuant to this Act shall be paid or disbursed to it unless a just and equitable distribution is made within the State, for the benefit of such minority races, of funds paid to it under this Act.

(d) For the purposes of this Act—

(1) "State" includes any of the forty-eight States and the District of Columbia, Territory of Hawaii, Puerto Rico, Alaska, and the Virgin Islands.

(2) "State educational agency" means, as the State legislature may determine, (a) the chief State school officer (such as the State superintendent of public instruction, commissioner of education, or similar officer), or (b) a board of education controlling the State department of education; except that in the District of Columbia it shall mean the Board of Education, and except that for the period ending June 30, 1948, "State educational agency" may mean any agency or agencies within the State designated by the Governor to carry out the functions herein required of a State educational agency.

(3) "Nonprofit private school" means any private school exempt from income tax under section 101 (6) of the Internal Revenue Code, as amended.

(4) "Nonfood assistance" means equipment used on school premises in storing, preparing, or serving food for school children.

Approved June 4, 1946.

Chapter 281—2D Session
H. R. 3370

APPENDIX II

Child Nutrition Act of 1966, As Amended

(Provisions no longer effective as of 11-10-78 have been deleted.)

AN ACT

To strengthen and expand food service programs for children.

Be it enacted by the Senate and House of Representatives of the United States of America in Congress assembled, That this Act may be cited as the "Child Nutrition Act of 1966."

DECLARATION OF PURPOSE

SEC. 2. In recognition of the demonstrated relationship between food and good nutrition and the capacity of children to develop and learn, based on the years of cumulative successful experience under the national school lunch program with its significant contributions in the field of applied nutrition research, it is hereby declared to be the policy of Congress that these efforts shall be extended, expanded, and strengthened under the authority of the Secretary of Agriculture as a measure to safeguard the health and well-being of the Nation's children, and to encourage the domestic consumption of agricultural and other foods, by assisting States, through grants-in-aid and other means, to meet more effectively the nutritional needs of our children.

SPECIAL MILK PROGRAM AUTHORIZATION

SEC. 3. There is hereby authorized to be appropriated for the fiscal year ending June 30, 1970, and for each succeeding fiscal year, such sums as may be necessary to enable the Secretary of Agriculture, under such rules and regulations as he may deem in the public interest, to encourage consumption of fluid milk by children in the United States in (1) nonprofit schools of high school grade and under, and (2) nonprofit nursery schools, child-care centers, settlement houses, summer camps, and similar nonprofit institutions devoted to the care and training of children. For the purposes of this section 'United States' means the fifty States, Guam, the Commonwealth of Puerto Rico, the Virgin Islands, American Samoa, the Trust Territories of the Pacific Islands, and the District of Columbia. The Secretary shall administer the special milk program provided for by this section to the maximum extent practicable in the same manner as he administered the special milk program provided for by Public Law 89-642, as amended, during the fiscal year ending June 30, 1969. Any school or nonprofit child care institution shall receive the special milk program upon their request. Children who qualify for free lunches under guidelines established by the Secretary shall, at the option of the school involved (or of the local education agency involved in the case of a public school) also be eligible for free milk upon their request. For the fiscal year ending June 30, 1975, and for subsequent school years, the minimum rate of reimbursement for a half-pint of milk served in schools and other eligible institutions shall not be less than 5 cents per half-pint served to eligible children, and such minimum rate of reimbursement shall be adjusted on an annual basis each school year to reflect changes in the Producer Price Index for Fresh Processed Milk published by the Bureau of Labor Statistics of the Department of Labor. Such adjustment shall be computed to the nearest one-fourth cent. Not withstanding any other provision of this section, in no event shall the minimum rate of reimbursement exceed the cost of the school or institution of milk served to children.

SCHOOL BREAKFAST PROGRAM AUTHORIZATION

SEC. 4. (a) There is hereby authorized to be appropriated such sums as are necessary to enable the Secretary to carry out a program to assist the States and the Department of Defense through grants-in-aid and other means to initiate, maintain, or expand nonprofit breakfast programs in all schools which make application for assistance and agree to carry out a nonprofit breakfast program in accordance with this Act. Appropriations and expenditures for this Act shall be considered Health, Education, and Welfare functions for budget purposes rather than functions of Agriculture.

APPORTIONMENT TO STATES

(b) (1) Of the funds appropriated for the purposes of this section, the Secretary shall for each fiscal year ending June 30, 1973, (1) apportion $2,600,000 equally among the States other than Guam, the Virgin Islands, American Samoa, and the Trust Territory of the Pacific Islands, and $45,000 equally among Guam, the Virgin Islands, American Samoa, and the Trust Territory of the Pacific Islands, and (2) apportion the remainder among the States in accordance with the apportionment formula contained in section 4 of the National School Lunch Act, as amended. For each fiscal year beginning with the fiscal year ending June 30, 1974, the Secretary shall make breakfast assistance payments, at such times as he may determine, from the sums appropriated therefor, to each State educational agency; in a total amount equal to the result obtained by (1) multiplying the number of breakfasts (consisting of a combination of foods which meet the minimum nutritional requirements prescribed by the Secretary pursuant to subsection (e) of this section) served during such fiscal year to children in schools in such States which participate in the breakfast program under this section under agreements with such State educational agency by a national average breakfast payment prescribed by the Secretary for such fiscal year to carry out the purposes of this section; (2) multiplying the number of such breakfasts served free to children eligible for free breakfasts in such schools during such fiscal year to carry out the purposes of this section; and (3) multiplying the number of reduced price breakfasts served to children eligible for reduced price breakfasts in such schools during such fiscal year by a national average reduced price breakfast payment prescribed by the Secretary for such fiscal year to carry out the provisions of this section: *Provided,* That in any fiscal year the aggregate amount of the breakfast assistance payments made by the Secretary to each State educational agency for any fiscal year shall not be less than the amount of the payments made by the State educational agency to participating schools within the State for the fiscal year ending June 30, 1972, to carry out the purposes of this section. The national average payment established by the Secretary for all breakfasts served to eligible children shall not be less than 8 cents; an amount of not less than 15 cents shall be added for each reduced-price breakfast; and an amount of not less than 20 cents shall be added for each free breakfast.

(2)(A) The Secretary shall make additional payments for breakfasts served to children qualifying for a free or reduced-price meal at schools that are in severe need.

(B) The maximum payment for each such free breakfast shall be the higher of—

(i) the national average payment established by the Secretary for free breakfasts plus 10 cents, or

(ii) 45 cents, which shall be adjusted on a semiannual basis each July 1 and January 1 to the nearest one-fourth cent in accordance with changes in the series for food away from home of the Consumer Price Index published by the Bureau of Labor Statistics of the Department of Labor for the most recent six-month period for which such data are available, except that the initial such adjustment shall reflect the change in the series of food away from home during the period November 1, 1976, to October 31, 1977.

(C) The maximum payment for each such reduced-price breakfast shall be five cents less than the maximum payment for each free breakfast as determined under clause (B) of this paragraph.

STATE DISBURSEMENT TO SCHOOLS

(c) Funds apportioned and paid to any State for the purpose of this section shall be disbursed by the State educational agency to schools selected by the State educational agency to assist such schools in financing the costs of operating a breakfast program and for the purpose of subsection (d). Disbursement to schools shall be made at such rates per meal or on such other basis as the Secretary shall prescribe. In selecting schools for participation, the State educational agency shall, to the extent practicable, give first consideration to those schools drawing attendance from areas in which poor economic conditions exist, to those schools in which a substantial proportion of the children enrolled must travel long distances daily, and to those schools in which there is a special need for improving the nutrition and dietary practices of children of working mothers and children from low-income families. Breakfast assistance disbursements to schools under this section may be made in advance or by way of reimbursement in accordance with procedures prescribed by the Secretary.

(d) Each State education agency shall establish eligibility standards for providing additional assistance to schools in severe need, which shall include those schools in which the service of breakfasts is required pursuant to State law and those schools (having a breakfast program or desiring to initiate a breakfast program) in which, during the most recent second preceding school year for which lunches were served, 40 percent or more of the lunches served to students at the school were served free or at a reduced price and in which the rate per meal established by the Secretary is insufficient to cover the costs of the breakfast program. Such eligibility standards shall be submitted to the Secretary for approval and included in the State plan of child nutrition operations required by section 11 (e)(1) of the National School Lunch Act. Pursuant to those State eligibility standards, a school, upon the submission of appropriate documentation about the need circumstances in that school and the school's eligibility for additional assistance, shall be entitled to receive 100 percent of the operating costs of the breakfast program, including the costs of obtaining, preparing, and serving food, or the meal reimbursement rate specified in paragraph (2) of section 4(b) of this Act, whichever is less.

NUTRITIONAL AND OTHER PROGRAM REQUIREMENTS

(e) Breakfasts served by schools participating in the school breakfast program under this section shall consist of a combination of foods and shall meet minimum nutritional requirements prescribed by the Secretary on the basis of tested nutritional research. Such breakfasts shall be served free or at a reduced price to children in school under the same terms and conditions as are set forth with respect to the services of lunches free or at a reduced price in section 9 of the National School Lunch Act.[1]

ALTERNATE FOODS

The Secretary shall not limit or prohibit, during the school year 1978–79, the use of formulated grain-fruit products currently approved for use in the school breakfast program. The Secretary shall consult experts in child nutrition, industry representatives, and school food service personnel and school administrators (including personnel and administrators in school systems using such products) with respect to the continued use of formulated grain-fruit products in the school breakfast program, and shall also take into account the findings and recommendations in the report on this subject of the General Accounting Office. The Secretary shall not promulgate a final rule disapproving the use of such products in the school breakfast program beyond the 1978–79 school year until the Secretary has notified the appropriate committees of Congress, and such rule shall not take effect until sixty days after such notification.

---

[1]Although Section 6(d) of P.L. 95-627 was not made a part of the Child Nutrition Act of 1966, Section 6(d) relates to section 4(e) of that Act and therefore is set forth below.

NONPROFIT PRIVATE SCHOOLS

(f) For the fiscal year ending June 20, 1973, any withholding of funds for and disbursement to nonprofit private schools shall be effected in the manner used prior to such fiscal year. Beginning with the fiscal year ending June 30, 1974, the Secretary shall make payments from the sums appropriated for any fiscal year for the purposes of this section directly to the schools (as defined in section 15(c) of this Act which are private and nonprofit as defined in the last sentence of section 15(c) of this Act) within a State, that participate in the breakfast program under an agreement with the Secretary, for the same purposes and subject to the same conditions as are authorized or required under this section with respect to the disbursements by State educational agencies.

(g) As a national nutrition and health policy, it is the purpose and intent of the Congress that the school breakfast program be made available in all schools where it is needed to provide adequate nutrition for children in attendance. The Secretary is hereby directed, in cooperation with State educational agencies, to carry out a program of information in further-ance of this policy. Within 4 months after the enactment of this subsec-tion, the Secretary shall report to the committees of jurisdiction in the Congress his plans and those of the cooperating State agencies to bring about the needed expansion in the school breakfast program.

FOOD SERVICE EQUIPMENT ASSISTANCE

SEC. 5. (a) There is hereby authorized to be appropriated for the fiscal year ending June 30, 1975, not to exceed $40,000,000 and for each succeeding fiscal year, not to exceed $75,000,000 to enable the Secretary to formulate and carry out a program to assist the States through grants-in-aid and other means to supply schools drawing attendance from areas in which poor economic conditions exist with equipment, other than land or buildings, for the storage, preparation, transportation, and serving of food to enable such schools to establish, maintain, and expand school food service programs. In the case of a nonprofit private school, such equipment shall be for use of such school principally in con-nection with child feeding programs authorized in this Act and in the National School Lunch Act, as amended.

APPORTIONMENTS TO STATES

(b) Except for the funds reserved under subsection (e) of this section, the Secretary shall apportion the funds appropriated for the purposes of this section among the States on the basis of the ratio that the number of lunches (consisting of a combination of foods which meet the minimum nutritional requirements prescribed by the Secretary pursuant to section 9 of the National School Lunch Act, served in each State in the latest preceding school year for which the Secretary determines data are available at the time such funds are apportioned bears to the total number of such lunches served in all States in such preceding school year. If any State cannot utilize all of the funds apportioned to it under the provisions of this subsection, the Secretary shall make further apportionments to the remaining States in the manner set forth in this subsection for apportioning funds among all the States. Payments to any State of funds apportioned under the provisions of this subsection for any fiscal year shall be made upon condition that at least one-fourth of the cost of equipment financed under this subsection shall be borne by funds from sources within the State, except that such condition shall not apply with respect to funds used under this section to assist schools that are especially needy, as determined by criteria to be established by each State and approved by the Secretary. States shall apportion their share of funds under this subsection by giving priority to schools without a food service program, schools that do not serve both breakfasts and lunches but that will use food service equipment to initiate the service of breakfasts or lunches, and schools without facilities to prepare and cook hot meals at the schools (including schools having equipment that is so antiquated or impaired as to endanger the continuation of an adequate food service program or the ability to prepare and cook hot meals) or at a kitchen that serves the schools and that is operated by the local school district or by a nonprofit private school or the authority that is responsible for the administration of one or more nonprofit private schools. After making funds available to such schools, the Secretary shall make the remaining funds available to eligible schools that do not meet the priority criteria, for the purpose of purchasing needed replacement equipment.

STATE DISBURSEMENT TO SCHOOLS

(c) Funds apportioned and paid to any State for the purpose of this section shall be disbursed by the State educational agency to assist schools which draw attendance from areas in which poor economic conditions exist and which have no, or grossly inadequate, equipment to conduct a school food service program, and to acquire such equipment. In the selection of schools to receive assistance under this section, the State educational agency shall require applicant schools to provide justification of the need for such assistance and the inability of the school to finance the food service equipment needed. Disbursements to any school may be made, by advances or reimbursements, only after approval by the State educational agency of a request by the school for funds, accompanied by a detailed description of the equipment to be acquired and the plans for the use thereof in effectively meeting the nutritional needs of children in the school.

NONPROFIT PRIVATE SCHOOLS

(d) If, in any State, the State educational agency is prohibited by law from administering the program authorized by this section in nonprofit private schools within the State, the Secretary shall administer such program in such private schools. In such event, the Secretary shall withhold from the funds apportioned to any such State under the provisions of subsection (b) of this section an amount which bears the same ratio to such funds as the number of lunches (consisting of a combination of foods which meet the minimum nutritional requirements prescribed by the Secretary pursuant to section 9(a) of the National School Lunch Act), served in nonprofit private schools in such State in the latest preceding school year for which the Secretary determines data are available at the time such funds are withheld bears to the total number of such lunches served in all schools within such State in such preceding school year.

RESERVE OF FUNDS

(e) For the fiscal years ending September 30, 1978, September 30, 1979, and September 30, 1980, 40 percent of the funds appropriated for the purposes of this section shall be reserved to the Secretary to assist schools without a foodservice program and schools that do not serve breakfasts or lunches but that plan to use food service equipment to initiate a breakfast or lunch program. The Secretary shall apportion the funds so reserved among the States on the basis of the ratio of the number of children in each State enrolled in schools without a food service program and in schools moving toward the initiation of the service of breakfasts to the number of children in all States enrolled in schools without a foodservice program and in schools moving toward the initiation of the service of breakfasts. In those States in which the Secretary administers the food service equipment assistance program in nonprofit private schools, the Secretary shall withhold from the funds apportioned to any such State under this subsection an amount which bears the same ratio to such funds as the number of children enrolled in nonprofit private schools without a food service program or moving toward the initiation of the service of breakfasts in such State bears to the total number of children enrolled in all schools without a food service program or moving toward the initiation of the service of breakfasts in such State.

The funds so reserved, apportioned, and withheld shall be used by the State, or the Secretary in the case of nonprofit private schools, only to assist schools without a food service program and schools moving toward the initiation of the service of breakfasts. If any State cannot use all the funds apportioned to it under the provisions of this subsection, the Secretary shall make further apportionment to the remaining States for use only in assisting schools without a food service program and schools moving toward the initiation of the service of breakfasts. If after such further apportionment, any funds received under this subsection remain unused, the Secretary shall immediately apportion such funds among the States in accordance with the provisions of subsection (b) of this section. Payment to any State of funds under the provisions of this subsection shall be made upon the condition that at least one-fourth of the cost of the equipment financed shall be borne by funds from sources within the State, except that such condition shall not apply with respect to funds used under this subsection to assist schools that are especially needy, as determined by criteria established by each State and approved by the Secretary.

(f)(1) Funds authorized for the purposes of this section shall be used only for facilities that enable schools, or local public or private nonprofit institutions under the conditons prescribed in paragraph (2) of this subsection, to prepare and cook hot meals or receive hot meals at the school or institution unless the school can demonstrate to the satisfaction of the State (or, in the case of nonprofit private schools in States where the Secretary administers the food service equipment program in such schools, to the satisfaction of the Secretary) that an alternative method of meal preparation is necessary for the introduction or continued existence of the school lunch or breakfast program in such school or to improve the consumption of food or the participation of eligible children in the program.

(2) If a school authorized to receive funds under this section cannot establish a food service program of hot meals prepared and cooked by the school, or received by the school, and the school enters into an agreement with a public or private nonprofit institution to provide the school lunch or breakfast program for children attending the school, the funds provided under this section may be used for food service facilities to be located at such institution, if (A) the school retains legal title to such facilities and, (B) in the case of funds made available under subsection (e) of this section, the institution would otherwise be without such facilities.

PAYMENTS TO STATES

SEC. 6. The Secretary shall certify to the Secretary of the Treasury from time to time the amounts to be paid to any State under sections 3 through 7 of this Act and the time or times such amounts are to be paid and the Secretary of the Treasury shall pay to the State at the time or times fixed by the Secretary the amounts so certified.

STATE ADMINISTRATIVE EXPENSES

SEC. 7 (a)(1) Each fiscal year, the Secretary shall make available to the States for their administrative costs an amount equal to not less than 1½ percent of the Federal funds expended under sections 4, 11, and 17 of the National School Lunch Act and 3, 4, and 5 of this Act during the second preceding fiscal year. The Secretary shall allocate the funds so provided in accordance with paragraphs (2), (3), and (4) of this subsection. There are hereby authorized to be appropriated such sums as may be necessary to carry out the purposes of this section.

(2) The Secretary shall allocate to each State for administrative costs incurred in any fiscal year in connection with the programs authorized under the National School Lunch Act or under this Act, except for the programs authorized under section 13 or 17 of the National School Lunch Act or under section 17 of this Act, an amount equal to not less than 1 percent and not more than 1½ percent of the funds expended by each State under sections 4 and 11 of the National School Lunch Act and sections 3, 4, and 5 of this Act during the second preceding fiscal year. In no case shall the grant available to any State under this subsection be less than the amount such State was allocated in the fiscal year ending September 30, 1978, or $100,000, whichever is larger.

(3) The Secretary shall allocate to each State for its administrative costs incurred under the program authorized by section 17 of the National School Lunch Act in any fiscal year an amount, based upon funds expended under that program in the second preceding fiscal year, equal to (A) 20 percent of the first $50,000, (B) 10 percent of the next $100,000, (C) 5 percent of the next $250,000, and (D) 2½ percent of any remaining funds. The Secretary may adjust any State's allocation to reflect changes in the size of its program.

(4) The remaining funds appropriated under this section shall be allocated among the States by the Secretary in amounts the Secretary determines necessary for the improvements in the States of the administration of the programs authorized under the National School Lunch Act and this Act, except for section 17 of this Act, including, but not limited to, improved program integrity and the quality of meals served to children.

(5) Funds available to States under this subsection and under Section 13 (K) (1) of the National School Lunch Act shall be used for the costs of administration of the programs for which the allocations are made,

except that States may transfer up to 10 percent of any of the amounts allocated among such programs.

(6) Where the Secretary is responsible for the administration of programs under this Act or the National School Lunch Act, the amount of funds that would be allocated to the State agency under this section and under section 14(K)(1) of the National School Lunch Act shall be retained by the Secretary for the Secretary's use in the administration of such programs.

(b) The Secretary, in cooperation with the several States, shall develop State staffing standards for the administration by each State of sections 4, 11, and 17 of the National School Lunch Act, and sections 3, 4, and 5 of this Act, that will ensure sufficient staff for the planning and administration of programs covered by State administrative expenses.

(c) Funds paid to a State under subsection (a) of this section may be used to pay salaries, including employee benefits and travel expenses, for administrative and supervisory personnel; for support services; for office equipment; and for staff development.

(d) If any State agency agrees to assume responsibility for the administration of food service programs in nonprofit private schools or child care institutions that were previously administered by the Secretary, an appropriate adjustment shall be made in the administrative funds paid under this section to the state not later than the succeeding fiscal year.

(e) Notwithstanding any other provision of law, funds available to each State under this section for fiscal year 1978 that are not obligated or expended in that fiscal year shall remain available for obligation and expenditure by that State is fiscal year 1979. For fiscal year 1979, and the succeeding fiscal year, the Secretary shall establish a date by which each State shall submit to the Secretary a plan for the disbursement of funds provided under this section for each such year, and the Secretary shall reallocate any unused funds, as evidenced by such plans, to other States as the Secretary deems appropriate.

(f) The State may use a portion of the funds available under this section to assist in the administration of the commodity distribution program.

(g) Each State shall submit to the Secretary for approval by October 1 of each year an annual plan for the use of State administrative expense funds, including a staff formula for State personnel, system level supervisory and operating personnel, and school level personnel.

(h) Payments of funds under this section shall be made only to states that agree to maintain a level of funding out of State revenues, for administrative costs in connection with programs under this Act (except section 17 of this Act) and the National School Lunch Act (except section

13 of the Act), not less than the amount expended or obligated in fiscal year 1977.

(i) For the fiscal year beginning October 1, 1977, and ending September 30, 1980, there are hereby authorized to be appropriated such sums as may be necessary for the purposes of this section.

UTILIZATION OF FOODS

SEC. 8. Each school participating under section 4 of this Act shall insofar as practicable, utilize in its program foods designated from time to time by the Secretary as being in abundance either nationally or in the school area, or foods donated by the Secretary. Foods available under section 416 of the Agricultural Act of 1949 (63 Stat. 1058), as amended, or purchased under section 32 of the Act of August 24, 1935 (49 Stat. 774), as amended, or section 709 of the Food and Agriculture Act of 1965 (79 Stat. 1212), may be donated by the Secretary to schools, in accordance with the needs as determined by local school authorities, for utilization in their feeding programs under this Act.

NONPROFIT PROGRAMS

SEC. 9. The food and milk service programs in schools and nonprofit institutions receiving assistance under this Act shall be conducted on a nonprofit basis.

REGULATIONS

SEC. 10. The Secretary shall prescribe such regulations as he may deem necessary to carry out this Act and the National School Lunch Act, including regulations relating to the service of food in participating schools and service institutions in competition with the programs authorized under this Act and the National School Lunch Act. Such regulations shall not prohibit the sale of competitive foods approved by the secretary in food service facilities or areas during the time of service of food under this Act or the National School Lunch Act if the proceeds from the sales of such foods will inure to the benefit of the schools or of organizations of students approved by the schools. In such regulations the Secretary may provide for the transfer of funds by any State between the programs authorized under this Act and the National School Lunch Act on the basis of an approved State plan of operation for the use of the funds and may provide for the reserve of up to 1 per centum of the funds available for apportionment to any State to carry out special developmental projects.

PROHIBITIONS

SEC. 11. (a) In carrying out the provisions of sections 3 through 5 of this Act, neither the Secretary nor the State shall impose any requirements with respect to teaching personnel, curriculum, instruction, methods of instruction, and materials of instruction.

(b) The value of assistance to children under this Act shall not be considered to be income or resources for any purpose under any Federal or State laws including but not limited to laws relating to taxation, welfare, and public assistance programs. Expenditures of funds from State and local sources for the maintenance of food programs for children shall not be diminished as a result of funds received under this Act.

PRESCHOOL PROGRAMS

SEC. 12. The Secretary may extend the benefits of all school feeding programs conducted and supervised by the Department of Agriculture to include preschool programs operated as part of the school system.

CENTRALIZATION OF ADMINISTRATION

SEC. 13. Authority for the conduct and supervision of Federal programs to assist schools in providing food service programs for children is assigned to the Department of Agriculture. To the extent practicable, other Federal agencies administering programs under which funds are to be provided to schools for such assistance shall transfer such funds to the Department of Agriculture for distribution through the administrative channels and in accordance with the standards established under this Act and the National School Lunch Act.

SEC. 14. There is hereby authorized to be appropriated for any fiscal year such sums as may be necessary to the Secretary for his administrative expense under this Act.

MISCELLANEOUS PROVISIONS AND DEFINITIONS

SEC. 15. For the purposes of this Act—

(a) "State" means any of the fifty States, the District of Columbia, the Commonwealth of Puerto Rico, the Virgin Islands, Guam, American Samoa, or the Trust Territories of the Pacific Islands.

(b) "State educational agency" means, as the State legislature may determine, (1) the chief State school officer (such as the State superintendent of public instruction, commissioner of education, or similar officer), or (2) a board of education controlling the State department of education.

(c) "School" means (A) any public or nonprofit private school of high school grade or under, including kindergarten and preschool programs operated by such school (B) any public or licensed nonprofit private residential child care institution (including, but not limited to orphanages and homes for the mentally retarded), and (C), with respect to the Commonwealth of Puerto Rico, nonprofit child care centers certified as such by the Governor of Puerto Rico. For purposes of (A) and (B) of this subsection, the term "nonprofit", when applied to any such private school or institution, means any such school or institution which is exempt from tax under section 501 (c)(3) of the Internal Revenue Code of 1954.

(d) "Secretary" means the Secretary of Agriculture.

(e) "School year" means the annual period from July 1 through June 30.

(f) Except as used in section 17 of this Act, the terms "child" and "children" as used in this Act, shall be deemed to include persons regardless of age who are determined by the State educational agency, in accordance with regulations prescribed by the Secretary, to be mentally or physically handicapped and who are attending any nonresidential public or nonprofit private school of high school grade or under for the purpose of participating in a school program established for mentally or physically handicapped.

ACCOUNTS AND RECORDS

SEC. 16. States, State educational agencies, schools, and nonprofit institutions participating in programs under this Act shall keep such accounts and records as may be necessary to enable the Secretary to determine whether there has been compliance with this Act and the regulations hereunder. Such accounts and records shall at all times be available for inspection and audit by representatives of the Secretary and shall be preserved for such period of time, not in excess of three years, as the Secretary determines is necessary.

SPECIAL SUPPLEMENTAL FOOD PROGRAM

(not included herein as this book deals with school foodservice only)

CASH GRANTS FOR NUTRITION EDUCATION

SEC. 18. (a) The Secretary is hereby authorized and directed to make cash grants to State educational agencies for the purpose of conducting experimental or demonstration projects to teach school children the nutritional value of foods and the relationship of nutrition to human health.

(b) In order to carry out the program, provided for in subsection (a) of this section, there is hereby authorized to be appropriated not to exceed $1,000,000 annually. The Secretary shall withhold not less than 1 per centum of any funds appropriated under this section and shall expend these funds to carry out research and development projects relevant to the purpose of this section, particularly to develop materials and techniques for the innovative presentation of nutritional information.

NUTRITION EDUCATION AND TRAINING

SEC. 19. (a) Congress find that—

(1) the proper nutrition of the Nation's children is a matter of highest priority;

(2) the lack of understanding of the principles of good nutrition and their relationship to health can contribute to a child's rejection of highly nutritious foods and consequent plate waste in school food service operations;

(3) many school food service personnel have not had adequate training in food service management skills and principals, and many teachers and school food service operators have not had adequate training in the fundamentals of nutrition or how to convey this information so as to motivate children to practice sound eating habits;

(4) parents exert a significant influence on children in the development of nutritional habits and lack of nutritional knowledge on the part of parents can have detrimental effects on children's nutritional development; and

(5) there is a need to create opportunities for children to learn about the importance of the principles of good nutrition in their daily lives and how these principles are applied in the school cafeteria.

PURPOSE

(b) It is the purpose of this section to encourage effective dissemination of scientifically valid information to children participating or eligible to participate in the school lunch and related child nutrition programs by establishing a system of grants to State educational agencies for the development of comprehensive nutrition information and education programs. Such nutrition education programs shall fully use as a learning laboratory the school lunch and child nutrition programs.

DEFINITIONS

(c) For purposes of this section, the term "nutrition information and education program" means a multidisciplinary program by which scientifically valid information about foods and nutrients is imparted in a manner that individuals receiving such information will understand the principles of nutrition and seek to maximize their well-being through food consumption practices. Nutrition education programs shall include, but not be limited to, (A) instructing students with regard to the nutritional value of foods and the relationship between food and human health; (B) training school food service personnel in the principles and practices of food service management; (C) instructing teachers in sound principles of nutrition education; and (D) developing and using classroom materials and curricula.

NUTRITION INFORMATION AND TRAINING

(d)(1) The Secretary is authorized to formulate and carry out a nutrition information and education program, through a system of grants to State educational agencies, to provide for (A) the nutritional training of educational and food service personnel, (B) the food service management training of school food service personnel, and (C) the conduct of nutrition education activities in schools and child care institutions.

(2) The program is to be coordinated at the State level with other nutrition activities conducted by education, health, and State Cooperative Extension Service agencies. In formulating the program, the Secretary and the State may solicit the advice and recommendations of the National Advisory Council on Child Nutrition; State educational agencies; the Department of Health, Education, and Welfare; and other interested groups and individuals concerned with improvement of child nutrition.

(3) If a State educational agency is conducting or applying to conduct a health education program which includes a school-related nutrition education component as defined by the Secretary, and that health education program is eligible for funds under programs administered by the Department of Health, Education, and Welfare, the Secretary may make funds authorized in this section available to the Department of Health, Education, and Welfare to fund the nutrition education component of the State program without requiring an additional grant application.

(4) The Secretary, in carrying out the provisions of this subsection, shall make grants to State educational agencies who, in turn, may contract with land-grant colleges eligible to receive funds under the Act of July 2, 1862 (12 Stat. 503, as amended: 7 U.S.C. 301-305, 307, and 308), or the Act of August 30, 1980 (26 Stat. 417, as amended; 7 U.S.C. 321-326 and 328), including the Tuskegee Institute, other institutions of higher education, and nonprofit organizations and agencies, for the training of educational and school food service personnel with respect to providing nutrition education programs in schools and the training of school food

service personnel in school food service management. Such grants may be used to develop and conduct training programs for early childhood, elementary, and secondary educational personnel and food service personnel with respect to the relationship between food, nutrition, and health, educational methods and techniques, and issues relating to nutrition education and principles and skills of food service management for cafeteria personnel.

(5) The State, in carrying out the provisions of this subsection may contract with State and local educational agencies, land-grant colleges eligible to receive funds under the Act of July 2, 1862 (12 Stat. 503, as amended, 7 U.S.C. 301-305, 307 and 308), or the Act of August 30, 1890 (26 Stat. 417, as amended, 7 U.S.C. 321-326 and 328), including the Tuskegee Institute, other institutions of higher education, and other public or private nonprofit educational or research agencies, institutions, or organizations to pay the cost of pilot demonstration projects in elementary and secondary schools with respect to nutrition education. Such projects may include, but are not limited to, projects for the development, demonstration, testing, and evaluation of curricula for use in early childhood, elementary, and secondary education programs.

(6) Notwithstanding any other provision of this section, if, in any State the State educational agency is prohibited by law from administering the program authorized by this section in nonprofit private schools and institutions, the Secretary may administer the program with respect to such schools and institutions.

AGREEMENTS WITH STATE AGENCIES

(e) The Secretary is authorized to enter into agreement with State educational agencies incorporating the provisions of this section, and issue such regulations as are necessary to implement this section.

USE OF FUNDS

(f)(1) The funds made available under this section may under guidelines established by the Secretary, be used by State educational agencies for (A) employing a nutrition education specialist to coordinate the program including travel and related personnel costs, (B) undertaking an assessment of the nutrition education needs of the State; (C) developing a State plan of operation and management for nutrition education; (D) applying for and carrying out planning and assessment grants; (E) pilot projects and related purposes; (F) the planning, development, and conduct of nutrition education programs and workshops for food service and educational personnel; (G) coordinating and promoting nutrition information and education activities in local school districts (incorporating, to the maximum extent practicable, as a learning laboratory, the child nutrition programs); (H) contracting with public and private nonprofit educational institutions for the conduct of nutrition education instruction and programs relating to the purposes of this section; and (I) related nutrition education purposes, including the preparation, testing, distribution, and evaluation of visual aids and other information and educational materials.

(2) Any State desiring to receive grants authorized by this section may, from the funds appropriated to carry out this section, receive a planning and assessment grant for the purpose of carrying out the responsibilities described in clauses (A), (B), (C), and (D) of paragraph (1) of this subsection. Any State receiving a planning and assessment grant, may during the first year of participation, be advanced a portion of the funds necessary to carry out such responsibilities: *Provided*, That in order to receive additional funding, the State must carry out such responsibilities.

(3) An amount not to exceed 15 percent of each State's grant may be used for up to 50 percent of the expenditures for overall administrative and supervisory purposes in connection with the program authorized under this section.

(4) Nothing in this section shall prohibit State or local educational agencies from making available or distributing to adults nutrition education materials, resources, activities, or programs authorized under this section.

ACCOUNTS, RECORDS AND REPORTS

(g)(1) State educational agencies participating in programs under this section shall keep such accounts and records as may be necessary to enable the Secretary to determine whether there has been compliance with this section and the regulations issued hereunder. Such accounts and records shall at all times be available for inspection and audit by representatives of the Secretary and shall be preserved for such period of time, not in excess of five years, as the Secretary determines to be necessary.

(2) State educational agencies shall provide reports on expenditures of Federal funds, program participation, program costs, and related matters, in such form and at such times as the Secretary may prescribe.

STATE COORDINATORS FOR NUTRITION: STATE PLAN

(h)(1) In order to be eligible for assistance under this section, a State shall appoint a nutrition education specialist to serve as a State coordinator for school nutrition education. It shall be the responsibility of the

State coordinator to make an assessment of the nutrition education needs in the State as provided in paragraph (2) of this subsection, prepare a State plan as provided in paragraph (3) of this subsection, and coordinate programs under this Act with all other nutrition education programs provided by the State with Federal or State funds.

(2) Upon receipt of funds authorized by this section, the State coordinator shall prepare an itemized budget and assess the nutrition education needs of the State. Such assessment shall include, but not be limited to, the identification and location of all students in need of nutrition education. The assessment shall also identify State and local individual, group, and institutional resources within the State for materials, facilities, staffs, and methods related to nutrition education.

(3) Within nine months after the award of the planning and assessment grant, the State coordinator shall develop, prepare, and furnish the Secretary, for approval, a comprehensive plan for nutrition education within such State, the Secretary shall act on such plan not later than sixty days after it is received. Each such plan shall describe (A) the findings of the nutrition education needs assessments within the State; (B) provisions for coordinating the nutrition education program carried out with funds made available under this section with any related publicly support programs being carried out within the State; (C) plans for soliciting the advice and recommendations of the National Advisory Council on Child Nutrition, the State educational agency, interested teachers, food nutrition professionals and paraprofessionals, school food service personnel, administrators, representatives from consumer groups, parents, and other individuals concerned with the improvement of child nutrition; (D) plans for reaching all students in the State with instruction in the nutritional value of foods and the relationships among food, nutrition, and health, for training food service personnel in the principles and skills of food service management, and for instructing teachers in sound principles of nutrition education; and (E) plans for using on a priority basis, the resources of the land-grant colleges eligible to receive funds under the Act of July 2, 1862 (12 Stat. 503; 7 U.S.C. 301-305, 307, and 308), or the Act of August 30, 1890 (26 Stat. 417, as amended; 7 U.S.C. 321-326 and 328), including the Tuskegee Institute. To the maximum extent practicable, the State's performance under such plan shall be reviewed and evaluated by the Secretary on a regular basis, including the use of public hearings.

APPROPRIATIONS AUTHORIZED

(j)(1) For the fiscal years beginning October 1, 1977, and October 1, 1978, grants to the States for the conduct of nutrition education and information programs shall be based on a rate of 50 cents for each child enrolled in school or in intitutions within the State, except that no State shall receive an amount less than $75,000 per year.

(2) For the fiscal year beginning October 1, 1979, there is hereby authorized to be appropriated for grants to each State for the conduct of nutrition education and information programs, an amount equal to the higher of (A) 50 cents for each child enrolled in schools or in institutions within each State, or (B) $75,000 for each State. Grants to each State from such appropriations shall be based on a rate of 50 cents for each child enrolled in schools or in institutions within such State, except that no State shall receive an amount less than $75,000 for that year. If funds appropriated for such year are insufficient to pay the amount to which each State is entitled under the preceding sentence, the amount of such grant shall be ratably reduced to the extent necessary so that the total of such amounts paid does not exceed the amount of appropriated funds. If additional funds become available for making such payments, such amounts shall be increased on the same basis as they were reduced.

(3) Enrollment data used for purposes of this subsection shall be the latest available as certified by the Office of Education of the Department of Health, Education, and Welfare.

DEPARTMENT OF DEFENSE OVERSEAS DEPENDENTS' SCHOOL

SEC. 20.(a) For the purpose of obtaining Federal payment and commodities in conjunction with the provision of breakfasts to students attending Department of Defense dependents' schools which are located outside the United States, its territories or possessions, the Secretary of Agriculture shall make available to the Department of Defense from funds appropriated for such purposes, the same payments and commodities as are provided to States for schools participating in the school breakfast program in the United States.

(b) The Secretary of Defense shall administer breakfast programs authorized by this section and shall determine eligibility for free and reduced-price breakfasts under the criteria published by the Secretary of Agriculture, except that the Secretary of Defense shall prescribe regulation governing computation of income eligibility standards for families of student participating in the school breakfast program under this section.

(c) The Secretary of Defense shall be required to offer meals meeting nutritional standards prescribed by the Secretary of Agriculture; however, the Secretary of Defense may authorize deviations from Department of Agriculture prescribed meal patterns and fluid milk requirements when local conditions preclude strict compliance or when such compliance is highly impracticable.

(d) Funds are hereby authorized to be appropriated for any fiscal year in such amounts as may be necessary for the administrative expenses of the Department of Defense under this section and for payment of the difference between the value of commodities and payments received from the Secretary of Agriculture and (1) the full cost of each breakfast for each student eligible for a free breakfast, and (2) the full cost of each breakfast, less any amounts required by law or regulation to be paid by each student eligible for a reduced-price breakfast.

(e) The Secretary of Agriculture shall provide the Secretary of Defense with technical assistance in the administration of the school breakfast programs authorized by this section.

APPENDIX III

National School Lunch Act, As Amended

(Provisions no longer effective as of 11/10/78, have been deleted and are indicated by asterisks.)

AN ACT

To provide assistance to the States in the establishment, maintenance, operation, and expansion of school lunch programs, and for other purposes.

Be it enacted by the Senate and House of Representatives of the United States of America in Congress assembled, That this Act may be cited as the "National School Lunch Act."

DECLARATION OF POLICY

SEC. 2. It is hereby declared to be the policy of Congress, as a measure of national security, to safeguard the health and well-being of the Nation's children and to encourage the domestic consumption of nutritious agricultural commodities and other food, by assisting the States, through grants-in-aid and other means, in providing an adequate supply of foods and other facilities for the establishment, maintenance, operation, and expansion of nonprofit school lunch programs.

APPROPRIATONS AUTHORIZED

SEC. 3. For each fiscal year there is hereby authorized to be appropriated, out of money in the Treasury not otherwise appropriated, such sums as may be necessary to enable the Secretary of Agriculture (herein-after referred to as "the Secretary") to carry out the provisions of this Act, other than sections 13, 17, and 19. Appropriations to carry out the provisions of this Act and of the Child Nutrition Act of 1966 for any fiscal year are authorized to be made a year in advance of the beginning of the fiscal year in which the funds will become available for disburse-ment to the States. Notwithstanding any other provision of law, any funds appropriated to carry out the provisions of such Acts shall remain available for the purposes of the Act for which appropriated until ex-pended.

APPORTIONMENTS TO STATES

SEC. 4. The sums appropriated for any fiscal year pursuant to the authorizations contained in section 3 of this Act, excluding the sum specified in section 5, shall be available to the Secretary for supplying agricultural commodities and other food for the program in accordance with the provisions of this Act. For each fiscal year the Secretary shall make food assistance payments, at such times as he may determine, from the sums appropriated therefor, to each State educational agency, in a total amount equal to the result obtained by multiplying the number of lunches (consisting of a combination of foods which meet the minimum nutritional requirements prescribed by the Secretary under subsection 9(a) of this Act) served during such fiscal year to children in schools in such State, which participate in the school lunch program under this Act under agreements with such State educational agency, by a national average payment per lunch for such fiscal year determined by the Sec-retary to be necessary to carry out the purposes of this Act: *Provided*, That in any fiscal year such national average payment shall not be less than 10 cents per lunch and that the aggregate amount of the food assistance payments made by the Secretary to each State educational agency for any fiscal year shall not be less than the amount of the payments made by the State agency to participating schools within the State for the fiscal year ending June 30, 1972, to carry out the pur-pose of this section 4.

FOOD SERVICE EQUIPMENT ASSISTANCE

SEC. 5. Of the sums appropriated for any fiscal year pursuant to the authorization contained in section 3 of this Act, $10,000,000 shall be available to the Secretary for the purpose of providing, during such fiscal year, Food Service Equipment Assistance for the school lunch program pursuant to the provisions of this Act. The secretary shall apportion among the States during each fiscal year the aforesaid sum of $10,000,000, and such apportionment among the States shall be on the basis of the factors, and in accordance with the standards set forth in section 4 with respect to the apportionment for agricultural commodities and other foods.

DIRECT FEDERAL EXPENDITURES

SEC. 6.(a) The funds provided by appropriation or transfer from other accounts for any fiscal year for carrying out the provisions of this Act, and for carrying out the provisions of the Child Nutrition Act of 1966, other than section 3 thereof, less

(1) not to exceed $3\frac{1}{2}$ per centum thereof which per centum is hereby made available to the Secretary for his administrative expenses under this Act and under the Child Nutrition Act of 1966;

(2) the amount apportioned by him pursuant to sections 4 and 5 of this Act and the amount appropriated pursuant to sections 11 and 13 of this Act and sections 4, 5, and 7 of the Child Nutrition Act of 1966; and

(3) not to exceed 1 per centum of the funds provided for carrying out the programs under this Act and the programs under the Child Nutrition Act of 1966, other than section 3, which per centum is hereby made available to the Secretary to supplement the nutritional benefits of these programs through grants to States and other means for nutritional training and education for workers, cooperators, and participants in these programs for pilot projects and the cash-in-lieu of commodities study required to be carried out under section 20 of this Act, and for necessary surveys and studies of requirements for food service programs in furtherance of the purposes expressed in section 2 of this Act and section 2 of the Child Nutrition Act of 1966,

shall be available to the Secretary during such year for direct expenditure by him for agricultural commodities and other foods to be distributed among the States and schools and service institutions participating in the food service programs under this Act and under the Child Nutrition Act of 1966, in accordance with the needs as determined by the local school and service institution authorities. Any school participating in food service programs under this Act may refuse to accept delivery of not more than 20 percent of the total value of agricultural commodities and other foods tendered to it in any school year; and if a school so refuses, that school may receive, in lieu of the refused commodities, other commodities to the extent that other commodities are available to the State during that year. The provisions of law contained in the proviso of the Act of June 28, 1937 (50 Stat. 323), facilitating operations with respect to the purchase and disposition of surplus agricultural commodities under section 32 of the Act approved August 24, 1935 (49 Stat. 774), as amended, shall, to the extent not inconsistent with the provisions of this Act, also be applicable to expenditures of funds by the Secretary under this Act. In making purchases of such agricultural commodities and other foods, the Secretary shall not issue specifications which restrict participation of local producers unless such specifications will result in significant advantages to the food service programs authorized by this Act and the Child Nutrition Act of 1966.

(b) Not later than May 15 of each school year, the Secretary shall make an estimate of the value of agricultural commodities and other foods that will be delivered during that school year to States for the school lunch program. If such estimated value is less than the total level of assistance authorized under subsection (e) of this section, the Secretary shall pay to each State educational agency, not later than June 15 of that school year, an amount of funds that is equal to the difference between the value of such deliveries as then programmed for such State and the total level of assistance authorized under subsection (e) of this section. In any State in which the Secretary directly administers the school lunch program in any of the schools of the State, the Secretary shall withhold from the funds to be paid to such State under the provisions of this subsection an amount that bears the same ratio to the total of such payment as the number of lunches served in schools in which the school lunch program is directly administered by the Secretary during the school year bears to the total of such lunches served under the school lunch program in all the schools in such State in such school year. Each State educational agency, and the Secretary in the case of private schools in which the Secretary directly administers the school lunch program, shall promptly and equitably disburse such funds to the schools participating in the school lunch program, and such disbursements shall be used by such schools to purchase United States agricultural commodities and other foods for their food service program. Such foods shall be limited to the requirements for lunches and breakfasts for children as provided for in regulations issued by the Secretary.

(c) Notwithstanding any other provision of law, the Secretary until such time as a supplemental appropriation may provide additional funds for the purpose of subsection (b) of this section, shall use funds appropriated by section 32 of the Act of August 24, 1935 (7 U.S.C. 612c) to make any payments to States authorized under such subsection. Any section 32 funds utilized to make such payments shall be reimbursed out of any supplemental appropriation hereafter enacted for the purpose of carrying out subsection (b) of this section and such reimbursement shall be deposited into the fund established pursuant to section 32 of the Act of August 24, 1935, to be available for the purposes of said section 32.

(d) Any funds made available under subsection (b) or (c) of this section shall not be subject to the State matching provisions of section 7 of this Act.

(e) For the fiscal year ending June 30, 1975, and subsequent school years, the national average value of donated foods, or cash payments in lieu thereof, shall not be less than 10 cents per lunch, and that amount shall be adjusted on an annual basis each school year after June 30, 1975, to reflect changes in the Price Index for Food Used in School and Institutions. The Index shall be computed using five major food components in the Bureau of Labor Statistics' Producer Price Index (cereal and bakery products, meat, poultry and fish, dairy products, processed fruits and vegetables, and fats and oils). Each component shall be weighed using the same relative weight as determined by the Bureau of Labor Statistics. The value of food assistance for each meal shall be adjusted each July 1 by the annual percentage change in a three-month simple average value of the Price Index for Foods Used in Schools and Institutions for March, April, and May each year. Such adjustments shall be computed to the nearest one-fourth cent. Among those commodities delivered under this section, the Secretary shall give special emphasis to high protein foods, meat, and meat alternates (which may include domestic seafood commodities and their products.[1] Notwithstanding any other provision of this section, not less than 75 per centum of the assistance provided under this (e) shall be in the form of donated foods for the school lunch program.

PAYMENTS TO STATES

SEC. 7. Funds apportioned to any State pursuant to section 4 or 5 during any fiscal year shall be available for payment to such State for disbursement by the State educational agencies, in accordance with such agreements, not inconsistent with the provisions of this Act, as may be entered into by the Secretary and such State educational agencies, for the purpose of assisting schools of that State in supplying (1) agricultural commodities and other foods for consumption by children and (2) food service equipment assistance in furtherance of the school lunch program authorized under this Act. Such payments to any State in any fiscal

---

[1]Sec 12(a) of P.L. 95-627 amended section 6(e) by inserting in the second (sic) sentence "(which may include domestic seafood commodities and their products)" after "alternatives" (sic).

year*** shall be made upon condition that each dollar thereof will be matched during such year*** from sources within the State determined by the Secretary to have been expended in connection with the school lunch program under this Act.****; and for any fiscal year (after 1955)***, such payments shall be made upon condition that each dollar will be so matched by $3. In the case of any State whose per capita income is less than the per capita income of the United States, the matching required for any fiscal year shall be decreased by the percentage which the State per capita income is below the per capita income of the United States. For the purpose of determining whether the matching requirements of this section and section 10, respectively, have been met, the reasonable value of donated services, supplies, facilities, and equipment as certified, respectively, by the State educational agency and in case of schools receiving funds pursuant to section 10, by such schools (but not the cost or value of land, of the acquisition, construction, or alteration of buildings, of commodities donated by the Secretary, or of Federal contributions), may be regarded as funds from sources within the State, expended in connection with the school lunch program.

For the school year beginning 1976, State revenue (other than revenues derived from the program) appropriated or utilized specifically for program purposes (other than salaries and administrative expenses at the State, as distinguished from local level) shall constitute at least 8 percent of the matching requirement for the preceding school year, or, at the discretion of the Secretary, fiscal year, and for each school year thereafter, at least 10 percent of the matching requirement for the preceding school year.

The State revenues made available pursuant to the preceding sentence shall be disbursed to schools, to the extent the State deems practicable, in such manner that each school receives the same proportionate share of such revenues as it receives of the funds apportioned to the State for the same year under sections 4 and 11 of the National School Lunch Act and sections 4 and 5 of the Child Nutrition Act of 1966. The requirement in this section that each dollar of Federal assistance be matched by $3 from sources within the State (with adjustments for the per capita income of the State) shall not be applicable with respect to the payments made to participating schools under section 4 of this Act for free and reduced price lunches: *Provided*, That the foregoing provision shall not affect the level of State matching required by the sixth sentence of this section. The Secretary shall certify to the Secretary of the Treasury from time to time the amounts to be paid to any State under this section and the time or times such amounts are to be paid; and the Secretary of the Treasury shall pay to the State at the time or times fixed by the Secretary the amounts so certified.

STATE DISBURSEMENT TO SCHOOLS

SEC. 8. Funds paid to any State during any fiscal year pursuant to section 4 or 5 shall be disbursed by the State educational agency, in accordance with such agreements approved by the Secretary as may be entered into by such State agency and the schools in the State, to those schools in the State which the State educational agency, taking into account need and attendance, determines are eligible to participate in the school lunch program. Such disbursement to any school shall be made only for the purpose of assisting it to finance the cost of obtaining agricultural commodities and other foods for consumption by children in the school lunch program and food service equipment assistance in connection with such program. The terms 'child' and 'children' as used in this Act shall be deemed to include persons regardless of age who are determined by the State educational agency, in accordance with regulations prescribed by the Secretary, to be mentally or physically handicapped and who are attending any child care institution as defined in section 17 of this Act or any nonresidential public or nonprofit private school of high school grade or under for the purpose of participating in a school program established for mentally or physically handicapped: *Provided*, That no institution that is not otherwise eligible to participate in the program under section 17 of this Act shall be deemed so eligible because of this sentence. Such food costs may include, in addition to the purchase price of agricultural commodities and other foods, the cost of processing, distributing, transporting, storing, or handling thereof. In no event shall such disbursement for food to any school for any fiscal year exceed an amount determined by multiplying the number of lunches served in the school in the school-lunch program under this Act during such year by the maximum Federal food-cost contribution rate for the state, for the type of lunch served, as prescribed by the Secretary. In any fiscal year in which the national average payment per lunch determined under section 4 is increased above the amount prescribed in the previous fiscal year, the maximum Federal food-cost contribution rate, for the type of lunch served, shall be increased by a like amount. Lunch assistance disbursements to schools under this section and under section 11 of this Act may be made in advance or by way of reimbursement in accordance with procedures prescribed by the Secretary.

NUTRITIONAL AND OTHER PROGRAM REQUIREMENTS

SEC. 9. (a) Lunches served by the schools participating in the school lunch program under this Act shall meet minimum nutritional requirements prescribed by the Secretary on the basis of tested nutritional research, except that such minimum nutritional requirements shall not be construed to prohibit the substitution of foods to accommodate the medical or other special dietary need of individual students. The Secretary shall establish, in cooperation with State educational agencies, administrative procedures, which shall include local educational agency and student participation, designed to diminish waste of foods which are served by schools participating in the school lunch program under this Act without endangering the nutritional integrity of the lunches served by such schools. Students in senior high schools that participate in the school lunch program under this Act (and, when approved by the local school district or nonprofit private schools, students in any other grade level in any junior high school or middle school) shall not be required to accept offered foods they do not intend to consume, and any such failure to accept offered foods shall not affect the full charge to the student for a lunch meeting the requirements of this subsection or the amount of payments made under this Act to any such school for such lunch.

(b)(1) No later than June 1 of each fiscal year the Secretary shall issue revised income poverty guideline, for use during the subsequent 12-month period from July through June. The income poverty guidelines shall be the nonfarm income poverty guidelines prescribed by the Office of Management and Budget adjusted annually under section 625 of the Economic Opportunity Act of 1964, as amended (42 U.S.C. 2971d): *Provided*, That the income poverty guidelines for the period commencing July 1, 1978, shall be made as up to date as possible by multiplying the nonfarm income poverty guidelines based on the average 1977 Consumer Price Index, by the change between the average 1977 Consumer Price Index and the Consumer Price Index of March 1978, using the most current procedures of the Office of Management and Budget. The income poverty guidelines for future periods shall be similarly adjusted. Any child who is a member of a household which has an annual income not above the applicable family-size income level set forth in the income poverty guidelines prescribed by the Secretary shall be served a free lunch. Following the announcement by the Secretary of the income poverty guidelines for each 12-month period, each State educational agency shall prescribe the income poverty guidelines, by family size, to be used by schools in the State during such 12 month period in making determinations of those eligible for a free lunch as prescribed in this section. The income guidelines for free lunches shall be prescribed at 25 percent above the applicable family size income levels in the income poverty guidelines prescribed by the Secretary. Each fiscal year, each State educational agency shall also prescribe income guidelines, by family size, to be used by schools in the State during the 12-month period from July through June in making determinations of those children eligible for a lunch at a reduced price, not to exceed 20 cents. Such income guidelines for reduced-price lunches shall be prescribed at 95 per centum above the applicable family size income levels in the income poverty guidelines prescribed by the Secretary. Any child who is a member of a household, if that household has an annual income which falls between (A) the applicable family size income level of the income guidelines for free lunches prescribed by the State educational agency and (B) 95 per centum above the applicable family size income levels in the income poverty guidelines prescribed by the Secretary, shall be served a reduced price lunch at a price not to exceed 20 cents. Local school authorities shall publicly announce such income guidelines on or at the opening of school each fiscal year, and shall make determinations with respect to the annual incomes of any household solely on the basis of a statement executed in such form as the Secretary may prescribe by an adult member of such household: *Provided*, That such local school authorities may for cause seek verification of the data in such application. No physical segregation of or other discrimination against any child eligible for a free lunch or a reduced price lunch shall be made by the school nor shall there be any overt identification of any child by special tokens or tickets, announced or published lists of names, or by other means. For purposes of this subsection, "Consumer Price Index" means the Consumer Price Index published each month by the Bureau of Labor Statistics of the Department of Labor.

(2) Any child who has a parent or guardian who (A) is responsible for the principal support of such child and (B) is unemployed shall be served a free or reduced price lunch, respectively, during any period (i) in which such child's parent or guardian continues to be unemployed and (ii) the income of the child's parents or guardians during such period of unemployment falls within the income eligibility criteria for free lunches or reduced price lunches, respectively, based on the current rate of income of such parents or guardians. Local school authorities shall publicly announce that such children are eligible for a free or reduced price lunch, and shall make determinations with respect to the status of any parent or guardian of any child under clauses (A) and (B) of the preceding sentence solely on the basis of a statement executed in such form as the Secretary may prescribe by such parent or guardian. No physical segregation of, or other discrimination against, any child eligible for a free or reduced price lunch under this paragraph shall be made by the school nor shall there be any overt identification of any such child by special tokens or tickets, announced or published lists of names, or by any other means.

(c) School lunch programs under this Act shall be operated on a nonprofit basis. Each school shall, insofar as practicable, utilize in its lunch program commodities designated from time to time by the Secretary as being in abundance, either nationally or in the school area, or commodities donated by the Secretary. Commodities purchased under the authority of section 32 of the Act of August 24, 1935 (49 Stat. 774), as amended, may be donated by the Secretary to schools, in accordance with the needs as determined by local school authorities, for utilization in the school lunch program under this Act as well as to other schools carrying out nonprofit school lunch programs and institutions authorized to receive such commodities. The Secretary is authorized to prescribe terms and conditions respecting the use of commodities donated under such section 32, under section 416 of the Agricultural Act of 1949, as amended, and under section 709 of the Food and Agriculture Act of 1965, as amended, as will maximize the nutritional and financial contributions of such donated commodities in such schools and institutions. The requirements of this section relating to the service of meals without cost or at a reduced cost shall apply to the lunch program of any school utilizing commodities donated under any of the provisions of law referred to in the preceding sentence. None of the requirements of this section in respect to the amount for 'reduced cost' meals and to eligibility for meals without cost shall apply to schools (as defined in section 12(d)(6) of this Act which are private and nonprofit as defined in the last sentence of section 12(d)(6) of this Act) which participate in the school lunch program under this Act until such time as the State educational agency, or in the case of such schools which participate under the provisions of section 10 of this Act the Secretary certifies that sufficient funds from sources other than children's payments are available to enable such schools to meet these requirements.

DISBURSEMENT TO SCHOOLS BY THE SECRETARY

SEC. 10. If, in any State, the State educational agency is not permitted by law to disburse the funds paid to it under this Act to any of the schools in the State, or is not permitted by law to match Federal funds made available for use by such schools, the Secretary shall disburse the funds directly to such schools within the State for the same purposes and subject to the same conditions as are authorized or required with respect to the disbursements to schools within the State by the State educational agency, including the requirement that any such payment or payments shall be matched, in the proportion specified in section 7 for such State, by funds from sources within the State expended by such schools within the State participating in the school lunch program under this Act. Such funds shall not be considered a part of the funds constituting the matching funds under the terms of section 7.

SPECIAL ASSISTANCE

SEC. 11.(a) Except as provided in section 10 of this Act, in each fiscal year each State educational agency shall receive special-assistance payments in an amount equal to the sum of the product obtained by multiplying the number of lunches (consisting of a combination of foods which meet the minimum nutritional requirements prescribed by the Secretary pursuant to subsection 9 (a) of this Act) served free to children eligible for such lunches in schools within that State during such fiscal year by the special-assistance factor for free lunches prescribed by the Secretary for such fiscal year and the product obtained by multiplying the number of lunches served at a reduced price to children eligible for such reduced-price lunches in schools within that State during such fiscal year by the special-assistance factor for reduced-price lunches prescribed by the Secretary for such fiscal year. In the case of any school which determines that at least 80 percent of the children in attendance during a school year (herein after in this sentence referred to as the 'first school year') are eligible for free lunches or reduced-price lunches, special-assistance payments shall be paid to the State educational agency with respect to that school, if that school so requests for the school year following the first school year, on the basis of the number of free lunches or reduced-price lunches, as the case may be, that are served by that school during the school year for which the request is made, to those children who were determined to be so eligible in the first school year and the number of free lunches and reduced-price lunches served during that year to other children determined for that year to be eligible for such lunches. In the case of any school that (1) elects to serve all children in that school free lunches under the school lunch program during any period of three successive school years and (2) pays, from sources other than Federal funds, for the costs of serving such lunches which are in excess of the value of assistance received under this Act with respect to the number of lunches served during that period, special-assistance payments shall be paid to the state educational agency with respect to that school during that period on the basis of the number of lunches determined under the succeeding sentence. For purposes of making special-assistance payments in accordance with the preceding sentence, the number of lunches served by a school to children eligible for free lunches and reduced-price lunches during each school year of the three-school-year period shall be deemed to be the number of lunches served by that school to children eligible for free lunches and reduced-price lunches during the first school year of such period, unless that school elects, for purposes of computing the amount of such payments, to determine on a more frequent basis the number of children eligible for free and reduced-price lunches who are served lunches during such period.

For the fiscal year beginning July 1, 1973, the Secretary shall prescribe a special-assistance factor for free lunches of not less than 45 cents and a special-assistance factor for reduced-price lunches which shall be 20 cents less than the special-assistance factor for free lunches: *Provided*, That if in any State all schools charge students a uniform price for reduced-price lunches, and such price is less than 20 cents, the special assistance factor prescribed for reduced-price lunches in such State shall be equal to the special assistance factor for free lunches reduced by either 10 cents or the price charged for reduced-price lunches in such State, whichever is greater. The Secretary shall prescribe on July 1 of each fiscal year, and on January 1, of each fiscal year, semiannual adjustments in the national average rates for lunches served under section 4 of the National School Lunch Act and the special-assistance factor for the lunches served under section 11 of the National School Lunch Act, and the national average rates for breakfasts served under section 4 of the Child Nutrition Act of 1966, as amended, that shall reflect changes in the cost of operating a school lunch and breakfast program under these Acts, as indicated by the change in the series for food away from home of the Consumer Price Index for all Urban Consumers published by the Bureau of Labor Statistics of the Department of Labor: *Provided*, That the initial such adjustment shall reflect the change in the series for food away from home during the period September 1973, through November 1973: *Provided further*, That such adjustments shall reflect the changes in the series for food away from home for the most recent six-month period for which such data are available: *Provided further*, That such adjustments shall be computed to the nearest one-fourth cent. Notwithstanding the foregoing two sentences, (1) for the fiscal year beginning July 1, 1973, no assistance factor under this section 11 shall, for any State, be less than the average reimbursement paid for each free lunch (in the case of the special assistance factor for free lunches), or for each reduced price lunch (in the case of the special assistance factor for reduced price lunches), in such State under this section in the fiscal year beginning July 1, 1972; and (2) adjustments required by the sentence immediately preceding this sentence shall be based on the special assistance factors for the fiscal year beginning July 1, 1973, as determined without regard to any increase required by the application of this sentence.

(b) Except as provided in section 10 of the Child Nutrition Act of 1966, the special-assistance payments made to each State agency during each fiscal year under the provisions of this section shall be used by such State agency to assist schools of that State in financing the cost of providing free and reduced-price lunches served to children pursuant to subsection 9(b) of this Act. The amount of such special assistance funds that a school shall from time to time receive, within a maximum per lunch amount established by the Secretary for all States, shall be based on the need of the school for such special assistance. Such maximum per lunch amount established by the Secretary shall not be less than 60 cents.

(c) Special assistance payments to any State under this section shall be made as provided in the last sentence of section 7 of this Act.

(d) In carrying out this section, the terms and conditions governing the operation of the school lunch program set forth in other sections of this Act, including those applicable to funds apportioned or paid pursuant to section 4 or 5 but excluding the provisions of section 7 relating to matching, shall be applicable to the extent they are not inconsistent with the express requirements of this section.

(e)(1) Each year by not later than a date specified by the Secretary each State educational agency shall submit to the Secretary, for approval by him as a prerequisite to receipt of Federal funds or any commodities donated by the Secretary for use in programs under this Act and the Child Nutrition Act of 1966, a State plan of child nutrition operations for the following fiscal year, which shall include, as a minimum, a description of the manner in which the State educational agency proposes (A) to use the funds provided under this Act and funds from sources within the State to furnish a free or reduced-price lunch to every needy child in accordance with the provisions of section 9; (B) to extend the school lunch program under this Act to every school within the State, and (C) to use the funds provided under section 13 of this Act and section 4 of the Child Nutrition Act of 1966 and funds from sources within the State to the maximum extent practicable to reach needy children.

(2) Each school participating in the school lunch program under this Act shall report each month to its State educational agency the average number of children in the school who received free lunches and the average number of children who received reduced-price lunches during the immediately preceding month. Each participating school shall provide an estimate, as of October 1 and March 1 of each year, of the number of children who are eligible for a free or reduced-price lunch.

(3) The State educational agency of each State shall report to the Secretary each month the average number of children in the State who received free lunches and the average number of children in the State who received reduced price lunches during the immediately preceding month. Each State educational agency shall provide an estimate as of October 1 and March 1 of each year, of the number of children who are eligible for a free or reduced-price lunch.

MISCELLANEOUS PROVISIONS AND DEFINITIONS

SEC. 12.(a) States, State educational agencies, and schools participating in the school lunch program under this Act shall keep such accounts and records as may be necessary to enable the Secretary to determine whether the provisions of this Act are being complied with. Such accounts and records shall at all times be available for inspection and audit by representatives of the Secretary and shall be preserved for such period of time, not in excess of five years, as the Secretary determines is necessary.

(b) The Secretary shall incorporate, in his agreements with the State educational agencies, the express requirements under this Act with respect to the operation of the school lunch program under this Act insofar as they may be applicable and such other provisions as in his opinion are reasonably necessary or appropriate to effectuate the purposes of this Act.

(c) In carrying out the provisions of this Act, neither the Secretary nor the State shall impose any requirement with respect to teaching personnel, curriculum, instruction, methods of instruction and materials of instruction in any school.

(d) For the purposes of this Act—

(1) 'State' means any of the fifty States, the District of Columbia, the Commonwealth of Puerto Rico, the Virgin Islands, Guam, American Samoa, or the Trust Territory of the Pacific Islands.

(2) 'State educational agency' means, as the State legislature may determine, (A) the chief State school officer (such as the state superintendent of public instruction, commissioner of education, or similar officer), or (B) a board of education controlling the State department of education.

(3) "Food Service Equipment Assistance" means equipment used by schools in storing, preparing, or serving food for school children.

(4) 'Participation rate' for a State means a number equal to the number of lunches, consisting of a combination of foods and meeting the minimum requirements prescribed by the Secretary pursuant to section 9, served in the fiscal year beginning two years immediately prior to the fiscal year for which the Federal funds are appropriated by schools participating in the program under this Act in the State, as determined by the Secretary.

(5) 'Assistance need rate' (A) in the case of any State having an average annual per capita income equal to or greater than the average annual per capita income for all the States, shall be 5; and (B) in the case of any State having an average annual per capita income less than the average annual per capita income for all the States, shall be the product of 5 and the quotient obtained by dividing the average annual per capita income for all the States by the average annual per capita income for such State, except that such product may not exceed 9 for any such State. For the purposes of this paragraph, the average annual per capita income for any State and for all the States shall be determined by the Secretary on the

basis of the average annual per capita income for each State and for all the States for the three most recent years for which such data are available and certified to the Secretary by the Department of Commerce.***

(6) 'School' means (A) any public or nonprofit private school of high school grade or under (B) any public or licensed nonprofit private residential child care institution (including, but not limited to, orphanages and homes for the mentally retarded), and (C) with respect to the Commonwealth of Puerto Rico, nonprofit child care centers certified as such by the Governor of Puerto Rico. For purposes of clauses (A) and (B) of this paragraph, the term 'nonprofit' when applied to any such private school or institution, means any such school or institution, which is exempt from tax under section 501(c)(3) of the Internal Revenue Code of 1954.

(7) "School year" means the annual period from July 1 through June 30.

(e) The value of assistance to children under this Act shall not be considered to be income or resources for any purposes under any Federal or State laws, including laws relating to taxation and welfare and public assistance programs.

(f) In providing assistance for school breakfasts and lunches served in Alaska, Hawaii, Guam, American Samoa, Puerto Rico, the Virgin Islands of the United States, the Trust Territory of the Pacific Islands, and the Commonwealth of the Northern Mariana Islands, the Secretary may establish appropriate adjustments for each such State to the national average payment rates prescribed under sections 4 and 11 of this Act and section 4 of the Child Nutrition Act of 1966, to reflect the differences between the costs of providing lunches and breakfasts in those States and the costs of providing lunches and breakfasts in all other States.

(g) Whoever embezzles, willfully misapplies, steals, or obtains by fraud any funds, assets, or property that are the subject of a grant or other form of assistance under this Act or the Child Nutrition Act of 1966, whether received directly or indirectly from the United States Department of Agriculture, or whoever receives, conceals, or retains such funds, assets, or property to his use or gain, knowing such funds, assets, or property have been embezzled, willfully misapplied, stolen or obtained by fraud shall, if such funds, assets, or property are of the value of $100 or more, be fined not more than $10,000 or imprisoned not more than five years, or both, or, if such funds, assets, or property are of a value of less than $100, shall be fined not more than $1,000 or imprisoned for not more than one year, or both.

(h) No provision of this Act or of the Child Nutrition Act of 1966 shall require any school receiving funds under this Act and the Child Nutrition Act of 1966 to account separately for the cost incurred in the school lunch and school breakfast programs. In no event, however, shall reimbursement to school food authorities exceed the net cost of operating both the lunch and breakfast programs, taking into account the total costs and total incomes of both programs.

SUMMER FOOD SERVICE PROGRAM FOR CHILDREN

is not included since this book deals with school food service.

COMMODITY DISTRIBUTION PROGRAM

SEC. 14.(a) Notwithstanding any other provision of law, the Secretary, during the period of beginning July 1, 1974, and ending September 30, 1982 shall—

(1) use funds available to carry out the provisions of section 32 of the Act of August 24, 1935 (7 U.S.C. 612c) which are not expended or needed to carry out such provisions to purchase (without regard to the provisions of existing law governing the expenditure of public funds) agricultural commodities and their products of the types customarily purchased under such section, (which may include domestic seafood commodities and their products) for donation to maintain the annually programmed level of assistance for programs carried on under this Act, the Child Nutrition Act of 1966, and title VII of the Older Americans Act of 1965; and

(2) if stocks of the Commodity Credit Corporation are not available, use the funds of such Corporation to purchase agricultural commodities and their products of the types customarily available under section 416 of the Agricultural Act of 1949 (7 U.S.C. 1431), for such donation.

(b) Among the products to be included in the food donations to the school lunch program shall be cereal and shortening and oil products.

(c) The Secretary may use funds appropriated from the general fund of the Treasury to purchase agricultural commodities and their products of the types customarily purchased for donation under section 311 (a)(4) of the Older Americans Act of 1965, as amended, (42 U.S.C. 3045f(a)(4)) or for cash payments in lieu of such donations under section 311 (c)(1) of such Act (42 U.S.C. 3045f(d)(1)). There are hereby authorized to be appropriated such sums as are necessary to carry out the purposes of this subsection.

(d) In providing assistance under this Act and the Child Nutrition Act of 1966 for school lunch and breakfast programs, the Secretary shall establish procedures which will—

(1) ensure that the views of local school districts and private nonprofit schools with respect to the type of commodity assistance needed in schools are fully and accurately reflected in reports to the Secretary by

the State with respect to State commodity preferences and that such views are considered by the Secretary in the purchase and distribution of commodities and by the States in the allocation of such commodities among schools within the States;

(2) solicit the views of States with respect to the acceptability of commodities;

(3) ensure that the timing of commodity deliveries to States is consistent with State school year calendars and that such deliveries occur with sufficient advance notice;

(4) provide for systematic review of the cost and benefits of providing commodities of the kind and quantity that are suitable to the needs of local school districts and private nonprofit schools;

(5) make available technical assistance on the use of commodities available under this Act and the Child Nutrition Act of 1966.

Within eighteen months after the date of the enactment of this subsection, the Secretary shall report to Congress on the impact of procedures established under this subsection, including the nutritional, economic, and administrative benefits of such procedures. In purchasing commodities for programs carried out under this Act and the Child Nutrition Act of 1966, the Secretary shall establish procedures to ensure that contracts for the purchase of such commodities shall not be entered into unless the previous history and current patterns of the contracting party with respect to compliance with applicable meat inspection laws and with other appropriate standards relating the the wholesomeness of food for human consumption are taken into account.

(e) Each State educational agency that receives food assistance payment under this section for any school year shall establish for such year an advisory council, which shall be composed of representatives of schools in the State that participate in the school lunch program. The Council shall advise such State agency with respect to the needs of such schools relating to the manner of selection and distribution of commodity assistance for such program.

NATIONAL ADVISORY COUNCIL

SEC. 15.(a) There is hereby established a council to be know as the National Advisory Council on Child Nutrition (hereinafter in this section referred to as the 'Council') which shall be composed of nineteen members appointed by the Secretary. One member shall be a school administrator, one member shall be a person engaged in child welfare work, one member shall be a person engaged in vocational education work, one member shall be a nutrition expert, one member shall be a school food service management expert, one member shall be a State superintendent of schools (or the equivalent thereof), one member shall be a supervisor of a school lunch program in a school system in an urban area (or the equivalent thereof), one member shall be a supervisor of a school lunch program in a school system in a rural area, one member shall be a State school lunch director (or the equivalent thereof), one member shall be a person serving on a school board, one member shall be a classroom teacher, two members shall be parents of children in schools that participate in the school lunch program under this Act, two members shall be senior high school students who participate in the school lunch program under this Act, and four members shall be officers of employees of the Department of Agriculture specially qualified to serve on the Council because of their education, training, experience, and knowledge in matters relating to child food programs.

(b) The fifteen members of the Council appointed from outside the Department of Agriculture shall be appointed for terms of two years, except that the appointments for 1978 shall be made as follows: Two replacements, one parent, and one senior high school student shall be appointed for terms of two years and two replacements, one parent, and one senior high school student shall be appointed for terms of one year. Thereafter, all appointments shall be for a term of two years, except that a person appointed to fill an unexpired term shall serve only for the remainder of such term. Parents and senior high school students appointed to the Council shall be members of State or school district child nutrition councils or committees actively engaged in providing program advice and guidance to school officials administering the school lunch program. Such appointments shall be made in a manner to balance rural and urban representation between parents and students. Members appointed from the Department of Agriculture shall serve at the pleasure of the Secretary.

(c) The secretary shall designate one of the members to serve as Chairman and one to serve as Vice Chairman of the Council.

(d) The Council shall meet at the call of the Chairman but shall meet at least once a year.

(e) Eight members shall constitute a quorum and a vacancy on the Council shall not affect its powers.

(f) It shall be the function of the Council to make a continuing study of the operation of programs carried out under the National School Lunch Act, the Child Nutrition Act of 1966, and any related Act under which meals are provided for children, with a view to determining how such programs may be improved. The Council shall submit to the President and to the Congress annually a written report of the results of its study together with such recommendations for administrative and legislative changes as it deems appropriate.

(g) The Secretary shall provide the Council with such technical and other assistance, including secretarial and clerical assistance, as may be required to carry out its functions under this Act.

(h) Members of the Council shall serve without compensation but shall receive reimbursement for necessary travel and subsistence expenses incurred by them in the performance of the duties of the Council: *Provided*, That members serving as parents, in addition to reimbursement for necessary travel and subsistence, shall, at the discretion of the Secretary, be compensated for other personal expenses related to participation on the Council, such as child care expenses and lost wages during scheduled Council meetings.

ELECTION TO RECEIVE CASH PAYMENTS

SEC.16(a) Notwithstanding any other provision of law, where a State phased out its commodity distribution facilities prior to June 30, 1974, such State may, for purposes of the programs authorized by this Act and the Child Nutrition Act of 1966, elect to receive cash payments in lieu of donated foods. Where such an election is made, the Secretary shall make cash payments to such State in an amount equivalent in value to the donated foods that the State would otherwise have received if it had retained its commodity distribution facilities. The amount of cash payments in the case of lunches shall be governed by section 6 (e) of this Act.

(b) When such payments are made, the State educational agency shall promptly and equitably disburse any cash it receives in lieu of commodities to eligible schools and institutions, and such disbursements shall be used by such schools and institutions to purchase United States agricultural commodities and other foods for their food service programs.

CHILD CARE FOOD PROGRAM

is not included since this book deals with school foodservice only.

NUTRITION PROGRAM STAFF STUDY APPROPRIATIONS FOR THE TRUST TERRITORY OF THE PACIFIC ISLANDS PILOT PROJECTS

are not included since these are temporary.

REDUCTION OF PAPERWORK

SEC. 21. In carrying out functions under this Act and the Child Nutrition Act of 1966, the Secretary shall reduce, to the maximum extent possible, the paperwork required of State and local educational agencies, schools, and other agencies participating in child nutrition programs under such Acts. The Secretary shall report to Congress not later than one year after the date of enactment of this section on the extent to which a reduction in such paperwork has occurred.

DEPARTMENT OF DEFENSE OVERSEAS DEPENDENTS' SCHOOLS

SEC. 22.(a) For the purpose of obtaining Federal payments and commodities in conjunction with the provision of lunches to students attending Department of Defense dependents' school which are located outside the United States, its territories or possessions, the Secretary of Agriculture shall make available to the Department of Defense, from funds appropriated for such purpose, the same payments and commodities as are provided to States for schools participating in the National School Lunch Program in the United States.

(b) The Secretary of Defense shall administer lunch programs authorized by this section and shall determine eligibility for free and reduced-price lunches under the criteria published by the Secretary of Agriculture, except that the Secretary of Defense shall prescribe regulations governing computation of income eligibility standards for families of students participating in the National School Lunch Program under this section.

(c) The Secretary of Defense shall be required to offer meals meeting nutritional standards prescribed by the Secretary of Agriculture; however, the Secretary of Defense may authorize deviations from Department of Agriculture prescribed meal patterns and fluid milk requirements when local conditions preclude strict compliance or when such compliance is impracticable.

(d) Funds are hereby authorized to be appropriated for any fiscal year in such amounts as may be necessary for the administrative expenses of the Department of Defense under this section and for payment of the difference between the value of commodities and payments received from the Secretary of Agriculture and (1) the full cost of each lunch for each student eligible for a free lunch, and (2) the full cost of each lunch, less any amounts required by law or regulation to be paid by each student eligible for a reduced-price lunch.

(e) The Secretary of Agriculture shall provide the Secretary of Defense with technical assistance in the Administration of the school lunch programs authorized by this section."

STUDY OF MENU CHOICE

SEC. 22. As a means of diminishing waste of foods without endangering nutritional integrity of meals served, the Secretary shall conduct a study to determine the cost and feasibility of requiring schools to offer a choice of menu items within the required meal patterns. This study shall, as a minimum, include different needs and capabilities of elementary and secondary schools for such a requirement. The Secretary shall develop regulations designed to diminish such waste based on the results of this study.

APPENDIX IV

Milk Bid Sample

This milk bid form is an excellent example of how to write specifications.[1]

IV. MILK BID (Sample)

A. Sealed bids will be received by the Director of Food Service of the _____ Independent School District # _____ of the Administration Building or School Office until 9:00 a.m. on _____.

B. All bids shall be submitted on this prepared proposal blank. Bidder should retain a copy and return the original and one copy as his bid.

C. The Board of Education reserves the right to reject any or all bids and to terminate the contract at any time if the bidder fails, neglects, or refuses to comply with the terms of the bid.

D. Standards and specifications for milk to be delivered to the_____ School cafeteria(s) in quantities "more or less" as set forth herein for the period _____ through _____ .

E. All milk products must be produced, handled, and pasteurized in conformity and in accordance with the provisions of the Standard Milk Ordinance and Code, 1953 revision, recommended by the United States Public Health Service and in accordance with any future upward revisions and of the above recommended ordinance and code. In addition to compliance with the Standard Milk Ordinance and Code, all milk and chocolate milk must comply with the following specifications:

---

[1] Adapted from the Oklahoma State Department of Education form and Fairfax County (VA) Schools bid specifications.

1. MILK—GRADE A
   (a) All milk products shall be date coded according to milk code regulation 1003.18. The milk shall have at least seven (7) days remaining on date code when delivered.
   (b) Shall show a bacterial count of not more than 30,000 per cc at any time of delivery or coliform count exceeding 10 per milliliter in any of 3 or 4 samples examined.
   (c) Shall contain no added water, preservatives, oils, coloring matter, or any foreign matter.
   (d) Shall be pasteurized at not less than 143°F. for not less than 30 minutes or at not less than 161°F. for not less than 15 seconds.

2. PRICE ADJUSTMENT
   (a) Price adjustment allowances based on "Milk Only" will be considered. Upward and downward adjustments in the delivered price of milk products will be considered, according to the provisions of Article 21, as amended by Chapter 383 of the Laws of 1937 of the Agricultural Marketing Agreement Act, and/or the Washington, D.C. Milk Marketing Order. Adjustments in the price paid for Class I Milk may be made when the price is increased or decreased by twenty cents ($.20) or more per hundred weight, and published by the Federal Milk Market Administrator in the Market Administrator Bulletin, Federal Order No. 1.
   (b) Price change will not be automatic. Any request for price adjustment must be initiated by the contractor in writing and supported by Applicable Milk Market Administrator Bulletin.
   (c) Price adjustment(s) will only be authorized by contract amendment approved by the contracting authority and the effective date of the change will be the date of the amendment.

3. DELIVERY
   (a) Deliveries are to be made daily, Monday through Friday, to the school sites listed below.
   (b) Times of delivery shall be between 7:30 a.m. and 2:30 p.m.
   (c) It is to be understood by each bidder that deliveries will be discontinued during regular school vacation periods as shown by a school calendar which will be provided to the successful bidder. In cases of variation from this calendar, ample notice shall be given the supplier.
   (d) Milk is to be delivered in refrigerated trucks and placed in the

refrigerated box provided by the school district. At the time of each delivery, all milk in the box is to be on top of the milk delivered that day.

(e) The dairy agrees to be responsible for damage to the milk boxes that are a direct result of carelessness of the delivery man.

DESCRIPTION (QUOTE LOWEST NET PRICES INCLUDING ALL DELIVERY CHARGES)	INSERT UNIT PRICE AND EXTENSION AGAINST EACH ITEM FOR WHICH YOU ARE BIDDING			
	Quantity	Unit	Unit Price	Extension
PRICING SCHEDULE	8/25/80			
1. *Milk*, Low fat, Class 1, Pasteurized, 8 ounce containers, 2.0% milk fat. Homogenized, Vitamin A and Vitamin D fortified. Milk shall not be fortified with additional milk solids.		8 oz.	$_____	$_____
Number of Containers per case: _____				
Net Weight per case: _____				
Maximum elapsed time between Production Date and Delivery Date: _____				
2. *Milk*, Class I, Pasteurized, 3.25% milk fat. Homogenized, Vitamin D fortified. 8 oz. Container, packaged for vending machines in standard gable top Pure-Pak cartons.		8 oz.	$_____	$_____
Number of Containers per case: _____				

Net Weight per case: _____

Maximum elapsed time between Production Date and Delivery Date: _____

3. *Chocolate Flavored Milk*, Low Fat, Class 1, Pasteurized, 8 ounce containers, Homogenized. Chocolate shall not exceed 1% of the total solids. Product must be non-setting and non-creaming. Artificial flavorings or additives are unacceptable. Milk shall not be fortified with additional milk solids.

8 oz.	$ _____		$ _____

Number of Containers per case: _____

Net Weight per case: _____

Maximum elapsed time between Production Date and Delivery Date: _____

4. *Chocolate Flavored Milk*, 3.25% milk fat, Grade A pasteurized. 8 ounce container, packaged for vending machine in standard gable top Pure-Pak cartons.

8 oz.	$ _____		$ _____

Number of Containers per case: _____

Net Weight per case: _____

Maximum elapsed time between Production Date and Delivery Date: _____

SCHOOL SITES TO WHICH DELIVERIES ARE TO BE MADE

Schools   Addresses

_____   _____
_____   _____
_____   _____
_____   _____

The aggregate amount of milk to be delivered each day will be approximately _____ half pints. The contractor will also deliver other commonly marketed dairy products not included under this contract at regular wholesale prices as needed by the individual schools.

In the event of failure of the contractor to make deliveries of the milk products in such quantities as may be required in accordance with the specifications herein set forth, the authorized agent of the Board of Education, _____ School District, reserves the right to cancel this contract to purchase milk in the open market or to make new contracts with other bidders. Any excessive costs resulting from purchases under this provision will be charged to the supplier under this contract.

BOND: The successful bidder will be required to furnish a $5,000 performance bond.

CONTRACT SECTION

The undersigned firm agrees to furnish dairy products according to the preceding specifications in approximate quantities as stated, at the price shown, and for the period as stated in this proposal. Bids may be made on the entire quantity of milk to be delivered to the schools listed.

Name of Firm _____

Signed By _____ Title _____

Date _____

The above bid proposal is hereby accepted and becomes a contract according to specifications and conditions stated herein.
Food Service Director _____ Date _____

INDEX

Other AVI Books

MICROWAVE HEATING
   2nd Edition   *Copson*
MODERN PASTRY CHEF
   Vols. 1 and 2   *Sultan*
PRACTICAL BAKING
   3rd Edition   *Sultan*
PRACTICAL BAKING MANUAL
   Sultan
PROGRESS IN HUMAN NUTRITION
   Vol. 1   *Margen*
   Vol. 2   *Margen and Ogar*
QUANTITY COOKING
   Mario